CCIE™ 350-001: Routing and Switching Prep Kit

BaerWolf, Inc.

Contents
at a Glance

Introduction   1

I Topic Overview   7
1 General Network Overview   9
2 General Topic Overview   25

II The LAN   55
3 Ethernet   57
4 Token-Ring and FDDI   71
5 LANE—LAN Emulation   85

III Switching and Bridging   103
6 LAN Switching   105
7 Other Bridging Technologies   123

IV Routing TCP/IP   149
8 TCP/IP   151
9 Routing Concept Overview   179
10 RIP   195
11 IGRP and EIGRP   209
12 OSPF   227
13 BGP   245
14 Managing Routing   261

V Other Network Protocols   287
15 IPX: Internet Packet Exchange   289
16 AppleTalk   307
17 Other LAN Protocols   325

VI The WAN   337
18 ISDN and DDR   339
19 X.25   365
20 Frame Relay   393
21 ATM: Asynchronous Transfer Mode   413

VII Appendixes   429
A Objectives Index   431
B Glossary   443
C CCIE Certification Process and Testing Tips   475
D Alternative Resources   481
E Using the CD-ROM   483
F Lab Exercises   485

Index   493

A Division of Macmillan Computer Publishing, USA
201 W. 103rd Street
Indianapolis, Indiana 46290

C0-AMI-633

CCIE™ 350-001: Routing and Switching Prep Kit

Copyright© 2000 by Que® Corporation.

International Standard Book Number: 0-7897-2359-x

Library of Congress Catalog Card Number: 00-100682

Printed in the United States of America

First Printing: June, 2000

02   01   00   4   3   2   1

Trademarks

Warning and Disclaimer

Credits

Associate Publisher
Greg Wiegand

Acquisitions Editor
Tracy Williams

Development Editors
Rick Kughen
Hugh Vandivier

Managing Editor
Thomas Hayes

Project Editor
Tonya Simpson

Copy Editor
Michael Dietsch

Indexer
Kevin Kent

Proofreader
Maribeth Echard

Technical Editor
Matthew Luallen

Team Coordinator
Vicki Harding

Media Developer
Jay Payne

Interior Designer
Anne Jones

Cover Designers
Anne Jones
Kevin Spear

Copywriter
Eric Borgert

Production
Darin Crone

Composed in ***AGaramond*** and ***Futura*** by Que Corporation.

Acknowledgments

I would like to thank the engineers and consultants of Lucent NetworkCare (listed below) for their collective expertise and effort that was invested in this book. Most of you wrote your contributions in addition to serving your clients on a full-time basis. I thank you on behalf of myself, BaerWolf, Inc., Macmillan Publishing (Que), and the readers.

I would also like to thank BaerWolf, Inc. for entrusting me with this project. I have endeavored to coordinate this effort with your best interest in mind and contribute my technical expertise wherever needed.

Finally, I must thank my wife. Over the last five months you have unconditionally encouraged me—despite the very long hours, lack of time off, and the mental energy that I have spent on this project instead of on you and our beautiful four-month-old son. I am forever in your debt for your faith, strength, friendship, and love.

—*Tom Knobel-Piehl, Coordinating Author*

About the Authors

BaerWolf, Inc. delivers targeted training solutions for businesses that specifically address their unique training needs. The most popular BaerWolf services for the IT and skills development markets include programming, networking, IT management, and the development of programming and networking course content like you see in this Cisco Certified Internetwork Expert (CCIE) book.

BaerWolf works with you to develop a training program uniquely suited to your situation and circumstances. With BaerWolf, training is delivered to you when you need it, where you need it, and in a format that best matches your desired learning style. Our customized approach to training solutions includes helping you assess your training goals, determining the existing skills of those who need training, and delivering the training to you in the method you want, including in a classroom, mentoring, in a lab/workshop, online, as self-study materials, or a combination of these methods.

BaerWolf's long list of satisfied clients include Andersen Consulting, Boeing, Born Information Services Group, Gateway 2000, Lutheran Brotherhood, Macmillan USA, Mayo Medical Center, MCC Behavioral Care, and US West Communications, Inc. We look forward to adding your company to this list. Contact us today at `http://www.baerwolf.com`.

Lucent Technologies NetworkCare is a global provider of network consulting and software solutions for the full lifecycle of a network, including planning and design, implementation, and operations. Lucent NetworkCare maintains expertise in the most complex network technologies and multivendor environments plus offers industry-leading software solutions for managing and optimizing application-ready networks.

An approach to helping customers stay ahead of network problems is at the heart of Lucent NetworkCare's Network Engagement Methodology (NEM). This collaborative knowledge management tool helps assure quality, consistency, and best practices in every Lucent NetworkCare network consulting engagement.

At the root of NEM is Lucent NetworkCare's Network Lifecycle Methodology (NLM), the basis for providing quality solutions to NetworkCare's clients. NLM provides the consultants with a framework for applying their technology expertise during the various stages of the network lifecycle to assure maximum client benefits from our services.

This book was written through a collaborative effort with BaerWolf, Inc. and more than a dozen Lucent NetworkCare engineers and consultants who are subject-matter experts averaging more than 10 years' networking experience, and most of whom are Cisco Certified Internetwork Experts (CCIE), Cisco Certified Network Professionals (CCNP), Cisco Certified Networking Associates (CCNA), and/or Cisco Certified Design Associates (CCDA).

Lucent NetworkCare: Solving your most challenging network problems with the best minds in the business. Visit us at http://www.networkcare.com.

Contributing Authors

John Hein

Jim Stewart

Russ Campbell

Sean Boulter

Clair LaBrie

Mike Balistreri

Mike Speed

John Markatos

Rajvir Wadhwa

Dan Overland

Jon Grubbs

Dennis Olds

Sean Snyder

Glenn Boyle

Dave McMillan

Tell Us What You Think!

As the reader of this book, *you* are our most important critic and commentator. We value your opinion and want to know what we're doing right, what we could do better, what areas you'd like to see us publish in, and any other words of wisdom you're willing to pass our way.

As an associate publisher for Que, I welcome your comments. You can fax, email, or write me directly to let me know what you did or didn't like about this book—as well as what we can do to make our books stronger.

Please note that I cannot help you with technical problems related to the topic of this book, and that due to the high volume of mail I receive, I might not be able to reply to every message.

When you write, please be sure to include this book's title and author as well as your name and phone or fax number. I will carefully review your comments and share them with the author and editors who worked on the book.

Fax: 317-581-4666

Email: certification@macmillanusa.com

Mail: Associate Publisher
         Que
         201 West 103rd Street
         Indianapolis, IN 46290 USA

Table of Contents

Introduction   1

I TOPIC OVERVIEW   7

1 General Network Overview   9
OSI Model   10
   Seven-Layer Model   10
   OSI Protocol Map   12
Switching Versus Routing   13
Tunneling   13
Layer 2 Standards   14
   802.3   14
   Ethernet   15
   802.2 (LLC)   15
   802.5   15
   802.6   16
   FDDI   16
Protocol Functions   17
   Connection-Oriented Versus Connectionless Protocols   17
   Handshaking   17
   ACKs   18
   Windowing   18
   Flow Control   18
   MTU   19
   Error Checking   19
   Termination   19
Interface Speeds   19
   LAN Interfaces   19
   WAN Interfaces   20
Summary   20

2 General Topic Overview   25
Binary, Decimal, and Hex   26
Access Lists   27
   IP Access Lists   29
      ICMP   31
      TCP and UDP   31
   IPX Access Lists   31
      SAP Filter   32
      NLSP Filter   32

AppleTalk Access Lists   32
   Network Filter   32
   Cable Range Filter   33
   Range Filter   33
   Zone Filter   33
   NBP Filter   33
Distribute Lists   33
Access Class   34
Performance Management   34
   Queuing   34
      Priority Queuing Commands   35
      Custom Queuing Commands   35
   Resource Reservation Protocol (RSVP)   36
   Compression   36
   Load Balancing   37
Security   37
   AAA   37
   TACACS   38
   RADIUS   38
   Firewalls   39
   Encryption Keys and DES   40
Multiservice Technologies   40
   H.323   41
   Codecs   41
   SS7   41
   Real-Time Transport Protocol (RTP)   42
Cisco Device Operation   42
   Router Infrastructure Review   42
   Router Management   43
   Cisco Discovery Protocol (CDP)   46
   Simple Network Management Protocol (SNMP)   47
   The Cisco Hierarchical Internetworking Model   48
Summary   48

II THE LAN   55

3 Ethernet   57
Definition and Architecture   58
Media Access Control Layer   59
Carrier Sense and Collision Detection   60

IEEE 802.3 MAC Frame and Address Format   62
Ethernet II Versus IEEE 802.3   63
Gigabit Ethernet   64
Limitations and Troubleshooting   65
Summary   65

4 Token-Ring and FDDI   71
Token-Ring   72
Token-Ring Operation   73
Frame Format   73
Token-Ring Fault-Management Mechanisms   75
Priority Scheme   76
Fiber Distributed Data Interface   76
FDDI Specifications   77
Physical Features   77
FDDI Fault-Management Features   78
Bandwidth Features   79
Frame Format   79

5 LANE—LAN Emulation   85
LANE Components   86
Virtual Connection Types for LANE   88
LANE Communications   90
LEC Setup   90
LEC Communication   92
Configurations   93
LEC Configuration   94
LES/BUS Configuration   94
LECS Configuration Example   94
Obtain LES NSAP Address Configuration   95
Simple Server Replication Protocol (SSRP)   95
Summary   97

III SWITCHING AND BRIDGING   103

6 LAN Switching   105
Transparent Bridging   106
Configuration of Transparent Bridging   107
Spanning Tree Protocol (STP)   107
Bridge Protocol Data Unit (BPDU)   108
Interface Modes   109

VLANs   111
Trunking   111
  Trunk Modes   112
  Trunk Configuration   112
EtherChannel   113
  EtherChannel Modes   113
  EtherChannel Configuration   113
VLAN Trunk Protocol (VTP)   114
  VTP Messages   115
  VTP Configuration   116
Multicast Management   116
  Internet Group Management Protocol (IGMP)   116
  Cisco Group Management Protocol (CGMP)   117
Summary   117

7   Other Bridging Technologies   123
Nonroutable Protocols   124
Concurrent Routing and Bridging   124
  Understanding CRB   125
  Configuring CRB   125
Integrated Routing and Bridging   126
  Understanding IRB   126
  Configuring IRB   127
Source-Route Bridging   127
  Understanding SRB   128
  Understanding RIF Fields   129
  Constructing a RIF   131
  Configuring Pure SRB   132
  Configuring Multiport SRB   133
Remote Source-Route Bridging   134
  Understanding and Configuring RSRB   134
Source-Route Transparent Bridging   135
  Configuring SRT   136
Source-Route Translational Bridging   136
  Understanding Ethernet to Token-Ring MAC Conversion   136
  Configuring Basic SR/TLB   137
Data-Link Switching   139
  DLSw Terms   139
  DLSw Operation   140
  Configuring DLSw   141
  Command Output Examples   142

IV ROUTING TCP/IP 149

8 TCP/IP   151

IP   152

Header Format   152

IP Addressing   154

Address Masks   156

Address Resolution Protocol (ARP)   158

Transmission Control Protocol (TCP)   160

Features   160

Header Format   161

TCP Connection Establishment   163

User Datagram Protocol (UDP)   163

Well-Known TCP/UDP Ports   164

Domain Name Service (DNS)   165

Internet Control Message Protocol (ICMP)   166

Hot Standby Routing Protocol (HSRP)   167

Dynamic Host Configuration Protocol (DHCP)   168

Network Address Translation (NAT)   169

Summary   171

9 Routing Concept Overview   179

Loop Prevention Techniques   180

Split Horizon   180

Poison Reverse   181

Other Mechanisms   182

Link State Versus Distance Vector   183

Classful Versus Classless Routing   184

Route Selection   184

Static and Default Routes   185

Default Administrative Distances   189

Summary   190

10 RIP   195

Routing Metrics   196

Route Updates   197

RIP Timers   198

RIPv1   199

RIPv2   200

Configuration Examples   202

Summary   205

11 **IGRP and EIGRP   209**

   IGRP   210
      Stability Features   211
      Route Metrics   212
      Route Updates   213
      Monitoring IGRP   214
      IGRP Configuration Example   216
   EIGRP   217
      Route Metrics   217
      Components   217
      Route Summarization   219
      Bandwidth Control   220
      Adjacency Process   220
      Route Convergence   220
      EIGRP Configuration Examples   221
         Sample Configuration   222
   Summary   223

12 **OSPF   227**

   OSPF Features   228
      Metric   228
      Bandwidth Conservation   229
      Fast Convergence   229
      Hierarchical Design   230
      VLSM Support   230
      Authentication   230
      Memory Requirements   230
      Processor Power   230
   OSPF Operation   231
      Establishing Neighbors   231
      DR and BDR Election   231
   Route Discovery   232
      Route Selection   232
      Route Maintenance   233
   Hierarchy and Components   233
      Area Types   233
      Router Types   234
      LSA Types   235
      Virtual Links   236

Configuration Examples 236
   Basic OSPF Configuration 236
   Stub Area Configuration 237
   Virtual Link Configuration 238
   Troubleshooting Commands 239
Summary 239

13 BGP 245
Design Elements and Definitions 246
Route Maps, Filters, and Neighbors (Peers) 247
   Route Maps 247
   Filters 248
      Filter by Route Example 248
      Filter by Path Example 249
      Filter by Community Example 249
   Neighbors/Peers 250
Decision Algorithm 250
Interior Border Gateway Protocol (IBGP) 252
Exterior Border Gateway Protocol (EBGP) 252
   CIDR (Classless Inter-Domain Routing) 253
Other BGP Associated Terms and Commands 254
   Autonomous System 254
   Neighbor Definition 254
   To Validate BGP Peer Connections 254
   Redistribution 255
   BGP Backdoor Command 255
   Multi-Exit Discriminator (MED) 255
   Methods of Route Manipulation 255
   Basics of Route Maps 255
   Communities 256
   Confederation 256
   Route Flap Dampening 256
   Route Reflectors 257
Summary 257

14 Managing Routing 261
Route Redistribution 262
   Metric Issues 262
   Summarization Issues 264
   Route Tagging 266

Route Management   267
  Passive Interfaces   *268*
  Distribute Lists   *268*
  Policy Routing   *270*
  Route Selection   *273*
Multicast Management   275
  Protocol Independent Multicast (PIM)   *275*
    Dense Mode   275
    Sparse Mode   275
    Sparse-Dense Mode   277
  Distance Vector Multicast Routing Protocol (DVMRP)   *278*
  Internet Group Management Protocol (IGMP)   *280*
  Cisco Group Management Protocol (CGMP)   *281*
Summary   281

V OTHER NETWORK PROTOCOLS   287

15 IPX: Internet Packet Exchange   289
Frame Format   290
IPX Addressing   290
Encapsulation Types   291
  Ethernet   *291*
  Token-Ring   *292*
  FDDI   *292*
  Serial   *292*
Service Advertisement Protocol (SAP)   293
Get Nearest Server   293
IPX Configuration Fundamentals   293
ipxwan   294
IPX Routing   294
  IPX RIP   *294*
  IPX EIGRP   *295*
  IPX NLSP   *295*
Basic IPX Configuration Example   295
  R1   *296*
  R2   *296*
  R3   *297*
  R4   *297*
  R7   *297*

Identifying Routes   297
Identifying Servers   299
Filtering IPX Network Traffic   300
Access Lists   300
Standard Access Lists   300
Extended Access Lists   300
SAP Filters   301
Summary   302

16 AppleTalk   307
AppleTalk Protocol Suite   308
Addressing   310
Addressing Structure   310
Address Assignment   311
Zones   312
Services   312
DDP   312
AARP   313
AEP   314
ATP   314
NBP   315
ZIP   315
ASP   316
ADSP   316
PAP   316
AFP   316
AppleTalk Routing   317
RTMP   318
AURP   318
AppleTalk EIGRP   319
Configuration Commands   319
Summary   320

17 Other LAN Protocols   325
DECnet   326
Addressing   327
Routing   327
Configuration   328
NetBIOS   330
Summary   331

VI THE WAN   337

18 ISDN and DDR   339

ISDN   340
ISDN Function Groups and Reference Points   340
ISDN Protocols (HDLC and LAPD)   342
PPP   345
PPP Features   345
PPP Frame Format   347
PPP Protocols   348
ISDN and DDR   349
  Interesting Traffic   350
Dialer Maps   351
ISDN Callback   352
ISDN and Dial Backup   352
More Examples   354
Example 1   354
Example 2   355
Example 3   356
Example 4   357
Example 5   357
Example 6   358
Example 7   358
Summary   359

19 X.25   365

Features   366
X.25 and the OSI Model   367
Addressing   368
X.25 Routing   369
Encapsulation   369
X.25 Over TCP/IP (XOT)   370
Route Tables   371
Link Access Procedure Balanced (LAPB)   372
Error Control/Recovery   374
Flow Control/Windowing   376
Sliding Window Flow Control   376
Buffering Flow Control   377
Source-Quench Messages   377

Signaling   377
Mapping   378
Switched Virtual Circuit (SVC)/Permanent
  Virtual Circuit (PVC)   380
Protocol Translation   383
Configuration Example   386
Summary   387

20 Frame Relay   393
Frame Relay Overview   394
Permanent Virtual Circuits and DLCIs   395
Link Management Interface (LMI)   396
Frame Relay and Layer 3 Addressing   398
    Inverse ARP   399
    Frame Relay Maps   400
    Subinterfaces   401
Frame Relay Traffic Management   403
Cisco's Implementation of Traffic Shaping   405
Summary   408

21 ATM: Asynchronous Transfer Mode   413
PVCs and SVCs   414
ATM Interfaces   414
    PNNI   415
    ATM Cell Header Format   416
    ATM Protocol Reference Model   416
    ATM Addressing   417
    ATM Signaling   418
ATM Features and Terminology   419
    Service Specific Convergence Protocol (SSCOP)   419
    Interim-Interswitch Signaling Protocol (IISP)   419
    Quality of Service (QoS)   419
Configuration Examples   420
    ATM Permanent Virtual Circuit (PVC) Configuration
      Examples Using AAL5snap and AAL5mux Encapsulations   420
    ATM Switched Virtual Circuit (SVC) Configuration
      Example   422
Summary   423

VII APPENDIXES   429

A Objectives Index   431

B Glossary   443

C CCIE Certification Process and Testing Tips   475

D Alternative Resources   481

E Using the CD-ROM   483

F Lab Exercises   485

For years now, data networks have become increasingly important. At first, networks were just a large corporate phenomenon. Now, almost any business with more than a few computers or more than one location has a data network. And now, with the growth of the Internet, many people's home computers are often connected to a network. As data networks grow in size and importance, there must be a corresponding growth of people required to design, build, and maintain them.

Cisco invented the router and has been selling networking products since 1986. Since then, the company has maintained a definitive lead in the data networking marketplace. Some people estimate that 85% of routers and switches are Cisco products. Regardless of the exact number (which is hard to definitively prove), Cisco is and probably will be a major player for a long time to come.

So, two factors should reinforce your decision to obtain Cisco certification:

- The continual rise in the importance of data networks
- Cisco's market leadership in much of this market

So, if you are an entrepreneurial individual who is interested in computers, you'll see these two factors and notice a growing employment market for people trained in Cisco networking products. Cisco certainly saw this, and that is why Cisco developed its certification series.

Intended Audience and Prerequisites

This book is written for intermediate to advanced network engineers who have at least some hands-on experience. Some topics, even some whole chapters, assume you have a certain familiarity with networks. We wrote this book like this for two reasons. First, the CCIE is one of the most advanced professional certifications in the world. It certainly is the most advanced network-related technical certification. It is unrealistic for an average person to be able to read a single book and be able to pass the CCIE Written Exam. Also, the amount of material that would be required to take a complete novice to the level of knowledge required to pass the CCIE Written Exam would not fit within the covers of a single book.

We recommend at least two years of solid hands-on data networking professional experience (that is, not just tech college, college, or university classes) before seriously pursuing the CCIE certification. You might be able to pass the written exam, but you'd have to take the lab exam within a year, and classroom experience is just not enough to offer you a reasonable chance of success.

However, if you have two years of experience, we strongly encourage you to take this big step in your career. CCIEs are in extremely high demand. Not only is a CCIE a great thing to put on your résumé, but it will help you immensely when it comes time to discuss your salary and benefits package!

Cisco Certifications and the CCIE

The CCIE was Cisco's original professional certification. The company wanted to design a program that would define people as definitive experts in the field of data networking with Cisco equipment. The program is designed to prevent people from successfully completing it if all they use for preparation is "book knowledge." Cisco wanted to ensure that people with a CCIE have knowledge *and* excellent hands-on ability (that is, experience). The company accomplished this by designing a two-step program: a written exam and a hands-on lab exam. The written exam could be taken at the same places as other certification exams (such as Microsoft's MCSE exams). But the lab exam was originally offered only at Cisco's headquarters in San Jose, California. The lab exam was (and is) a two-day hands-on affair. It is proctored and graded by a Cisco staff expert and includes configuration and troubleshooting of a variety of general and Cisco-specific technologies.

After the CCIE program was established and running, Cisco implemented a number of other certifications. Two of these, CCNA and CCNP, have a twofold purpose. First, they offer more people the chance to attain some level of certification at different knowledge and skill levels. Second, they form a track to prepare people for the CCIE. CCNA and CCNP certifications are not prerequisites for a CCIE, as some people think. However, they can be useful in your CCIE preparation, either as training or as validation of your skills before attempting the challenge of the CCIE. More information on these certifications can be found on Cisco's Web site:

```
http://cco-sj-2.cisco.com/warp/public/10/wwtraining/certprog/index.html
```

How to Use This Book to Prepare for the Exam

The initial table of contents was derived from Cisco's CCIE Exam Blueprint, which at the time of this publication is available at

`http://cco-sj-2.cisco.com/warp/public/625/ccie/rsblueprint.html`

We used all the same categories as Cisco's Exam Blueprint, with a few exceptions. These exceptions will be mentioned where appropriate throughout the book. Appendix A, "Objectives Index," lists the blueprint objectives and where they are discussed in this book. This will help you look up the chapter for any particular objective.

The book is designed to be read from beginning to end. It is organized to address topics roughly from simplest to most complex and, after Part I, "Topic Overview," from the bottom of the OSI model to the top. Although that approach was our overall goal, we could not adhere to these philosophies exclusively because so many topics are interrelated and need to be grouped together. In this way, it should be easier to read from start to finish or easier to skip through some sections if you are a highly experienced or knowledgeable professional.

The Flash Notes pull-out is a boiled-down version of the raw content of the each chapter. Call this your "Parking Lot Review," if you will. You can also use it before reading the book to see where your strengths and weaknesses are, so you can spend more time where needed and save time where you can.

There is also the Mastery Test CD. Unlike most test preparation CDs that are included with test preparation books, all questions on this CD are *different* from the questions in the printed book. This will prepare you to answer questions on a computer as if you were taking the actual exam.

There are also lots of great resources in the appendixes:

- Objectives Index—A mapping of the CCIE Written Blueprint and where the topic is addressed in the book.
- Glossary—Terms used in the book that are useful to have in one reference location.
- Certification Process and Testing Tips—How to register for the written test after completing this book. Also tips on your final preparation, strategy for taking the written test, and how to sign up for the lab exam.
- Alternative Resources—Resources where we got our information and other great sources for further study, if desired.
- Using the CD-ROM—How to install and use the CD-ROM included with this book.

- Moving on to the Lab—Some tips on how to prepare for the lab exam after you pass the written.
- Lab Exercises—Some exercises you can perform yourself, pulled from the configuration examples throughout the book.

How Each Chapter Is Organized

Each chapter has roughly the same format and teaching elements. The rough format for each chapter is

- Overview
- Details
- Configuration (where appropriate)
- Summary

Each chapter includes the following teaching elements to help guide and evaluate your reading:

- Prerequisites—What you should read or understand from this book before addressing these topics.
- "While You Read" chapter pretest—Open-ended questions that can serve two purposes: to guide your reading through the chapter or to help you decide whether you already know the material.
- Key Concepts—Concepts that are important enough for the exam that they are worth emphasizing in a summary sidebar.
- "While You Read" chapter pretest answers—The answers to the "While You Read" questions appear at the end of the chapter.
- Chapter practice test—Questions that are in the same style as you are likely to see on the actual exam. Each question also has an explanation of the answers—why the correct answers are correct and why the other answers are not.

Cisco Command Conventions

To communicate router or switch commands, we use the same formatting conventions as Cisco does in its IOS Command Reference (either hard copy or online). The following are these conventions:

- All commands will be presented in `monospace` type.
- **`Bold type`** commands are entered literally as shown.
- *`Italicized`* commands describe a value that you need to provide.

- Commands in squared-off brackets (`[brackets]`) are optional: Use if you desire the result, or skip.
- Commands separated by a bar (`|`) are required but exclusive: You must choose one.
- Commands in braces (`{braces}`) mean you must choose one of the commands within the braces: usually used with commands separated by bars (`|`).
- Braces within brackets (`[ {braces_in_brackets} ]`) indicate a required choice in an optional element: You must choose one if you desire this result (also often used with bars).

Summary

We hope you find this book easy to read and understand. Most importantly, we hope you find it valuable for helping you pass this difficult, but worthwhile, exam. Although this is just one step toward your CCIE, it is a very big one. Study hard, and good luck!

Topic Overview

1 General Network Overview

2 General Topic Overview

CHAPTER PREREQUISITE

Before reading this chapter, you must have a solid understanding of networking terminology and concepts. Your understanding should extend from LAN and WAN technology to how these network architectures compare with the Open System Interconnect (OSI) reference model. Subsequent chapters build on the overview presented in this chapter.

General Network Overview

WHILE YOU READ

1. Which layer of the OSI model is responsible for reliable connections?

2. Which layer of the OSI model did the IEEE redefine?

3. Why are some protocols unable to be routed?

4. What is the difference between acknowledgments and handshaking?

5. Which layer of the OSI model defines network addresses?

6. What does the abbreviation CSMA/CD stand for? What is its significance?

7. What happens when an FDDI network fails?

8. Does a Token-Ring network have collisions?

SEE
APPENDIX **F**

OSI Model

The International Standards Organization (ISO) developed the Open Systems Interconnection (OSI) Reference Model to define functional communications standards. This reference model is widely used by equipment manufacturers to assure their products will interoperate with products from other vendors.

Seven-Layer Model

The *OSI Model* is an architectural model that describes functional aspects of data communications. The model is composed of seven layers. Within each layer are defined functions that are performed within that layer. The model does not describe any specific protocols, only functions. Table 1.1 shows the seven layers defined by the OSI model and their relationship to one another.

 Key Concept

The OSI model is a functional model. It defines functions to be performed and the relationships between functions. The OSI model does not define any specific protocols.

Table 1.1   Layers of the OSI Model

Layer	Layer Function	Sublayer
Layer 7	Application	
Layer 6	Presentation	
Layer 5	Session	
Layer 4	Transport	
Layer 3	Network	
Layer 2	Data Link	LLC
		MAC
Layer 1	Physical	

The *Physical layer* defines the parameters necessary to build, maintain, and break the physical link connections. It defines the characteristics of the connectors, data transmission rates and distances, and the interface voltages.

The *Data Link layer* provides reliable transit of data across a physical network link. The Data Link layer also defines the physical network-addressing scheme, such as the MAC address on network interface cards in a workstation connected to a LAN. The Data Link layer also defines the topology of the network (bus, star, dual ring, and so on). Flow control at the Data Link layer is defined to ensure receiving stations are not overrun with data before they can process data already received.

The Institute of Electrical and Electronics Engineers (IEEE) has redefined the Data Link layer into two sublayers. The sublayers are the *Logical Link Control (LLC)* layer and the *Media Access Control (MAC)* layer. The LLC and MAC sublayers are defined in the IEEE 802.2 standards. The LLC manages communications between devices over a single link of a network. The MAC sublayer manages access to the physical medium from multiple upper-level protocols. The MAC layer also defines the MAC address, which uniquely identifies devices at the Data Link layer.

The *Network layer* defines routing services that allow multiple data links to be combined into an internetwork. The Network layer defines network-addressing schemes that logically identify network devices. The logical network addresses are different from the physical addresses defined at the MAC layer, and are used by routing protocols running at this level to transfer packets from one network to another. The most common network addressing protocols are IP, IPX, and AppleTalk. Typical routing protocols that run at this level are RIP, OSPF, IGRP, and NLSP.

Key Concept

Routing occurs at the Network layer. A protocol suite must have a Network layer to be routed. If a protocol does not have a Network layer, the protocol must be bridged.

The *Transport layer* implements reliable internetwork data transport services that are transparent to upper-layer protocols. The services include flow control, multiplexing, and error checking and recovery. If virtual circuits are needed for the communication to be accomplished, they are built and maintained at this layer. Flow control is responsible for making sure that a sending station does not transmit data faster than the receiving station can process it. Multiplexing allows multiple applications to share a common network interface. Error checking is implemented to discover errors on transmission and to provide a recovery mechanism when errors are found. Typical error recovery includes retransmission of the data.

Key Concept

Protocols used at the Transport layer will determine whether you are using connection-oriented or connectionless communications. Connection-oriented services are provided at this layer.

The *Session layer* is responsible for creating, managing, and terminating sessions that are used by entities at the presentation layer. The Session layer is responsible for coordinating the service requests and responses generated and received by a station when it is communicating with other entities on the internetwork.

The *Presentation layer* is responsible for encoding and decoding data that is passed from the Application layer to another station on the internetwork. This layer is responsible for encoding data in a format that the receiving station can interpret and for decoding data received from other stations. Data compression and encryption are accomplished at this layer. Typical coding schemes include ASCII, EBCDIC, MPEG, GIF, and JPEG.

The *Application layer* provides the interface to the user. Any user application that requires network communication accesses the communication resources through this layer. This layer also is responsible for finding and determining the availability of communication partners. Typical applications in the TCP/IP protocols are Simple Mail Transfer Protocol (SMTP), Telnet, and File Transfer Protocol (FTP).

A simple mnemonic will help you remember the order of the OSI Reference Model layers. Beginning at the lowest layer, the Physical layer, the initial character of each layer's name is extracted to form the string PDNTSPA. This same string results from taking the first letter from each word in the following sentence:

Please Do Not Throw Sausage Pizza Away.

OSI Protocol Map

Table 1.2 shows the OSI model and some common protocols that exist at each different layer.

Table 1.2   Mapping of Protocols to OSI Model Function Layers

OSI Model Layer	TCP/IP Protocols	Novell NetWare	Microsoft Windows	AppleTalk	DECnet
Application (7)	FTP, SMTP, Telnet	NDS	SMB	AFP	NICE
Presentation (6)	ASCII, MPEG, GIF, JPEG	NCP	NetBIOS	AFP	DAP, MAIL, CTERM
Session (5)		SAP	NetBEUI	ADSP, ZIP, ASP, PAP	SCP
Transport (4)	TCP, UDP	SPX	NetBEUI	RTMP, AURP, NBP, ATP, AEP	NSP

OSI Model Layer	TCP/IP Protocols	Novell NetWare	Microsoft Windows	AppleTalk	DECnet
Network (3)	IP	IPX	NetBEUI	DDP, AARP	DRP
Data Link (2)	Ethernet, 802.3, 802.5, FDDI, Frame Relay, ISDN	Ethernet, 802.3, 802.5, FDDI, Frame Relay, ISDN	Ethernet, 802.3, 802.5, FDDI, Frame Relay, ISDN	ELAP, LLAP, TLAP, FLAP	MOP, LAPB, DDCMP
Physical (1)	10BASE-T, 100BASE-T, UTP 4/16 Unshielded Twisted Pair, SONET	10BASE-T, 100BASE-T, UTP 4/16 Unshielded Twisted Pair, SONET	10BASE-T, 100BASE-T, UTP 4/16 Unshielded Twisted Pair, SONET	802.3, 802.5, FDDI, LocalTalk	Ethernet, Token-Ring, FDDI, x.21bis

Switching Versus Routing

The primary difference between switching and routing is that they operate at different layers in the OSI model. Switching is much simpler than routing and looks at the data link address (layer 2) to make forwarding decisions. There are limited filtering capabilities with switches. Switches keep track of the port from which they have seen a packet arrive and maintain a data link address to the port table, which is used to forward incoming packets. Routing occurs at the Network layer, or layer 3, in the OSI model. The routing algorithms use the network layer–assigned network addresses to make forwarding decisions. Routing provides a much greater filtering capability. Filtering can be accomplished based on network addresses, protocols, and so on using access control lists. Some protocols—for example, NetBIOS—do not have a network layer and cannot be routed; they must be bridged.

Key Concept

Switching services are defined at layer 2 in the OSI model. Routing services are defined at layer 3.

Tunneling

Tunneling is the technology used to "package" one network protocol inside another for delivery. The encapsulated protocol and data is carried as data in the encapsulating protocol. On the far end of the data transmission, the encapsulating protocol is stripped off and the encapsulated protocol and its data are processed as normal. This technology is used to reduce the number of networks deployed with different protocols. Common examples include the following:

- Tunneling serial network traffic in a packet-switched IP network
- Tunneling a nonroutable protocol inside a routable protocol
- Tunneling an IPX or some other protocol through an IP network or link

Tunneling can eliminate the need for separate serial and IP networks. Tunneling can also be referred to as encapsulation. Tunneling is usually deployed on the backbone of a network where transmission facilities are more expensive.

Key Concept

Tunneling, or encapsulation, is used to carry one network protocol within another. It is usually employed to keep from deploying multiple backbone networks.

Layer 2 Standards

Now that we have reviewed the Physical layer (Layer 1), we can move up the OSI model and discuss the common Data Link layer, or Layer 2, standards.

802.3

The 802.3 standard specifies the *Carrier Sense Multiple Access Collision Detect (CSMA/CD)* media-access technology over a variety of different cabling options. 802.3 technology is drawn from an earlier specification for Ethernet (see the section "Ethernet," later in the chapter). Both 802.3 and Ethernet define physical layer cabling; however, Ethernet is defined only on coaxial cable, whereas 802.3 is defined for multiple cabling options including coaxial and twisted pair. Both specifications implement CSMA/CD, which is designed for networks with sporadic volumes of data transmissions, with only occasional heavy traffic loads. 802.3 is far more common today.

The packet format specifications for 802.3 and Ethernet differ primarily at byte offset 19. 802.3 has a 2-byte field that contains the length of the data in the frame. The Ethernet frame has a 2-byte field with a code defining the upper-layer protocol to receive the data.

All stations on the segment see all the packets being transmitted, but they copy the packets onto local buffers only if the Data Link layer address in the packet matches the station's data link address. Stations transmit data whenever the network is quiet. If multiple stations transmit at the same time, a collision occurs. When the transmitting stations detect the presence of a collision, they stop sending, wait a random length of time, and transmit again.

Key Concept

802.3 has a 2-byte field that contains the length of the data in the frame. The Ethernet frame has a 2-byte field with a code defining the upper-layer protocol to receive the data.

Ethernet

The original (and literal) Ethernet specification defines a CSMA/CD protocol for coaxial transmission media (not twisted-pair or fiber-optic cabling as commonly used in today's networks). The Ethernet specification predates the 802.3 specification and was developed by Xerox in the 1970s. Today, the term "Ethernet" is used interchangeably to describe 802.3 and Ethernet networks.

Both 802.3 and Ethernet are discussed in more detail in Chapter 3, "Ethernet."

802.2 (LLC)

The *Logical Link Control (LLC)* sublayer provides a data-repackaging service for different types of networks. This service separates the upper layers from having to know what type of network is actually being used. The upper-layer protocols can then be moved to a different network topology and will not have to make any modifications. The LLC is the upper of the two sublayers defined by the IEEE for the OSI Data Link layer.

The 802.2 also implements a protocol header that is used in conjunction with the rest of the 802 protocols (802.3, 802.5, and so on). The 802.2 header defines *Service Access Point (SAP)* fields. The SAP identifies the upper-layer protocol that will receive or send the packet. There is a source and destination SAP field in each packet and each field is one byte long.

802.5

The *802.5* specifications define a token-passing network protocol commonly referred to as Token-Ring. In a Token-Ring network, a participating station must wait to acquire a token frame from the network before it can transmit data. The token is a special packet with a token bit set. When a station acquires the token, it can transmit until the token holding timer expires. At that point it must release the token and pass the token to the next station on the ring.

Token-Ring was originally specified on Type 1 cabling (older, heavy shielded twisted pair), but it is now usually implemented on Category 5 twisted-pair cabling.

Token-Ring networks are considered deterministic, in that it is guaranteed that each station will have the opportunity to transmit within a specific period. This contrasts with 802.3/Ethernet networks where each station is attempting to transmit and might collide with other stations transmitting at the same time.

The Token-Ring architecture distributes the responsibility for managing and maintaining the ring among all the participating stations. Because the network interfaces are more intelligent, they tend to be more expensive than Ethernet.

Token-Ring is discussed in more detail in Chapter 4, "Token-Ring and FDDI."

802.6

The 802.6 specification defines a *Distributed Queue Dual Bus (DQDB)* architecture used in a *Metropolitan Area Network (MAN)*. In this architecture, two unidirectional data buses pass cells in opposite directions. The cells are fixed in length at 53 bytes: five bytes for a header and 48 bytes for payload. One node is designated as the head of the bus and is responsible for generating the cells and setting the timing for both buses. If the node that is acting as the head of the bus fails, redundancy features switch the head of the bus's responsibilities to another node.

The MAN technology is usually implemented as an interconnection between LANs that are dispersed geographically. MANs can be configured to carry traffic at native LAN speeds, if the underlying transmission facilities are available. *Switched Multi-Megabit Data Service (SMDS)* is based on the 802.6 specifications, but it does not fully implement them. SMDS is seen as an intermediate step toward implementation of *Asynchronous Transfer Mode (ATM)*, which is discussed in more detail in Chapter 21, "ATM: Asynchronous Transfer Mode."

FDDI

The *Fiber Distributed Data Interface (FDDI)* specification describes a dual-ring architecture where the tokens on the rings rotate in opposite directions. FDDI uses a token-passing algorithm similar to Token-Ring to allow stations to transmit. The architecture provides fault tolerance in that each station has the capability to connect the two rings in a process called *wrapping*, which allows the network to continue passing data around a failed link or station. The fault tolerance is limited to a single fault; multiple faults will cause the ring network to break into smaller rings that are not interconnected. The specifications for FDDI were published by ANSI.

FDDI is discussed in more detail in Chapter 4.

Protocol Functions

Protocols are developed to define the behavior of communicating partners, such that desired functions can be performed. These functions are performed in protocol suites and not in individual protocols at specific layers of the OSI Reference Model.

Connection-Oriented Versus Connectionless Protocols

Connection-oriented protocols provide error checking, packet sequencing, and connection path setup and maintenance. When a connection is requested, the protocol establishes a fixed path from the source to the destination. During the time when the connection is in use, the protocol assures that the sequence of packets arrives in the proper order and that none of the packets is lost. If a packet is lost or arrives out of sequence, a retransmission is initiated to recover the missing packets. When the connection is no longer needed, the connection is torn down between the source and destination, and resources are freed for other connections. Connection-oriented protocols are also referred to as *reliable*.

A *connectionless protocol* does not provide any error checking and does not provide any assurance that data sent from the source reaches the destination. As data is transmitted by the source, the protocol makes a best effort to deliver the packets to the destination, but it does not guarantee delivery or correct sequence. Any error checking required by an application using a connectionless protocol should be provided by the application. Connectionless protocols are also called *unreliable*, although the network protocols usually deliver the packets.

An example of a connection-oriented protocol is TCP in the IP protocol suite, and UDP is an example of a connectionless protocol. See Chapter 8, "TCP/IP," for more information.

Key Concept

Connection-oriented protocols provide error checking and are also called *reliable*. Connectionless protocols do not provide error checking and are called *unreliable*. Connectionless communications depend on upper-layer protocols to do any necessary error checking.

Handshaking

A *handshake* is the exchange of control information during the session setup. A connectionless protocol, such as UDP, does not exchange control information (called a handshake) to establish an end-to-end connection before transmitting data. In contrast, a connection-oriented protocol, such as TCP, exchanges control information with the remote peer network layer to verify that it is ready to receive data before sending it. When the handshaking is successful, the peer network layers are said to have established a connection.

ACKs

ACKs, or *acknowledgments*, are part of a connection-oriented protocol that acknowledges to the sender that a packet has been received by the destination. The sender, on receiving the acknowledgment, knows that it can now send the next portion of the data stream. Acknowledgments can be affected by the window size.

Windowing

Windowing is a technique that improves the throughput of a connection-oriented proto-col. At the time the connection is established, the sender and receiver agree on the vol-ume of data that will be sent before the receiver acknowledges receipt. The volume of data is usually expressed as the number of packets that will be transmitted. The number of packets is called the *window size*. A large window size permits the sender to send more packets before waiting for an *acknowledgment* from the receiver. However, if there is an error in one of the packets within the transmitted window, the entire window is retrans-mitted, not just the erroneous packet. If retransmissions caused by marginal transmission facilities are common, a smaller window size should be configured.

Flow Control

Flow control is a process that regulates the volume and timing of data transmissions. The object is to make sure that the sending station does not overrun the receiving station with more data than it can process or store in its message queue. Typically a receiving station will queue incoming packets until they can be processed and sent to upper-layer proto-cols. If the receiver is busy completing other processing and the incoming queue fills up, the network protocols tell the senders to slow down or stop sending more packets. When the queue has been processed below a target level, the protocols tell the senders they can begin transmitting again.

Flow control can also be linked to windowing. Some flow-control algorithms use the win-dow size as a means of flow control. When a message queue begins to fill up, the receiv-ing station can reduce the window size in its responses to the sending station. The sending station then reduces the amount of data it sends. As the queue is processed, the receiver adjusts the window size and the sender increases the data volume.

MTU

The *Maximum Transmission Unit (MTU)* is the maximum size, in bytes, that a station's network interface can handle. The MTU has a default size for each type of interface, but the MTU can be adjusted on Cisco router interfaces. Packets that exceed the MTU are fragmented and sent as a series of packets on the network, if the packets are not marked as "don't fragment." If they are marked as "don't fragment" and the packet is larger than the MTU, the packets are normally dropped. This can be overridden by configuring MTU discovery on the interface.

Error Checking

Error checking on a connection-oriented link will examine packets and look for bytes that are lost, delayed, duplicated, or misread. The packets containing these bytes must then be retransmitted. A timeout mechanism allows devices to detect lost packets and request retransmission. *Checksums* are used to detect damaged packets. A checksum is a value that is calculated by the transmitting station and included in the packet. The receiving station recomputes the checksum on the data it receives and compares the resulting value to the value sent by the transmitter. If the checksums are the same, the packet is considered error-free.

Termination

When a network connection is no longer needed, the connection is terminated. If additional communications are required between the communicating parties, another communication path must be established.

Interface Speeds

Interface speeds vary depending on the type of technology used between communicating partners. Changing the configuration of the host can usually control the speed of an interface. Interface speeds are also called *link speeds*. Interface speeds are defined in Physical layer protocols.

LAN Interfaces

LAN interfaces are relatively fixed, as opposed to WAN interfaces where there are more options for setting link speeds. Token-Ring has been implemented at both 4 and 16MB/second. Fast Ethernet interfaces can usually automatically sense a 10MB or 100MB link, and can usually be forced to one of these speeds by configuration. Table 1.3 shows LAN interface types and the associated link speeds.

Table 1.3 Common LAN Interface Speeds	
Interface Type	Link Speed (per Second)
Token-Ring	4MB or 16MB
Ethernet	10MB
Fast Ethernet	100MB
Gigabit Ethernet	1000MB
FDDI	100MB

WAN Interfaces

WAN interfaces have more options for a link's speed configuration. Bonding multiple channels together, in the case of ISDN or T1 interfaces, can alter the overall link speed. Links speeds can also be affected by the bandwidth available from common carriers; for example, a fractional T1 will have one of a variety of links speeds depending on how the link was provisioned from the common carrier. Table 1.4 shows the type of WAN interfaces and the associated maximum link speeds.

Table 1.4 Common WAN Interface Speeds	
Interface Type	Maximum Link Speed (per Second)
ISDN - BRI	128KB
ISDN - PRI	1.536MB
TI	1.544MB
E1	2.048MB
High-Speed Serial	52MB
ATM - OC3	155.52MB
ATM - OC12	622MB

Summary

The OSI model describes the functions that are performed in data communications. The model architecture is seven layers, with each layer defining specific functions. Network protocols suites can be mapped to these layers; not all protocols, however, can be cleanly identified as belonging to a specific layer because they contain functions defined in multiple layers. And some protocol suites do not have a function for each layer.

Routing and switching are mechanisms for passing data between different segments. Routing uses network addresses and operates at layer 3 in the OSI model. Switching uses

MAC or DLC addresses and operates at layer 2 in the OSI model. Routing provides a broader range of traffic-filtering capabilities but generates more network traffic and is more complicated to deploy and maintain.

Two communicating peers can establish a connection-oriented or connectionless communication. Connection-oriented communications provide error, sequence, and flow controls. Connectionless communications are best efforts by the network and rely on applications for error checking.

QUESTIONS AND ANSWERS

1. Which layer of the OSI model is responsible for reliable connections?

   A: The Transport layer of the OSI model is responsible for reliable connections. Reliable connections are also called *connection-oriented*.

2. Which layer of the OSI model did the IEEE redefine?

   A: The IEEE redefined the Data Link layer. They broke the layer into two sublayers: the LLC and the MAC sublayers.

3. Why are some protocols unable to be routed?

   A: Protocols that do not have a network layer cannot be routed because routing occurs at the network layer.

4. What is the difference between acknowledgments and handshaking?

   A: Handshaking is used to negotiate the properties of a connection that is being established. Acknowledgments are used to tell the sender that data has been successfully received by the destination during the use of a connection.

5. Which layer of the OSI model defines network addresses?

   A: Network addresses are defined at layer 3, the network layer. Network addresses are used for routing. An IP address is an example of a network address.

6. What does the abbreviation CSMA/CD stand for? What is its significance?

   A: CSMA (Carrier Sense Multiple Access Detect) is how Ethernet works. Each station (carrier) senses traffic. When no traffic is sensed, it can access the media. It also detects any collisions and retransmits data if necessary.

7. What happens when an FDDI network fails?

   A: The ring "wraps" on itself, and the station transmits in the opposite direction on the second ring.

8. Does a Token-Ring network have collisions?

   A: No. Because there is only one token, only one station can transmit at any time.

PRACTICE TEST

1. The OSI model defines the protocols comprising the TCP/IP protocol suite.

    A. True

    B. False

Answer A is incorrect because the OSI model does not relate to any singular protocol or protocol suite. It is a functional model that describes functions and relationships between functions that are required for network communications. **Answer B is correct.**

2. Which of the following standards defines the specifications for FDDI?

    A. 802.2

    B. 802.3

    C. 802.5

    D. 802.6

    E. None of the above

Answer A is incorrect because 802.2 redefines the Data Link layer. Answer B is incorrect because 802.3 defines CSMA/CD similar to Ethernet. Answer C is incorrect because 802.5 defines a token-passing architecture similar to Token-Ring. Answer D is incorrect because 802.6 defines DQDB architecture for MANs. **Answer E is the correct answer.**

3. Which statement best describes tunneling?

    A. It is a key component in large database applications and interoperates with data mining.

    B. Tunneling is a technique of encapsulating a nonroutable protocol within a routable protocol so routers instead of bridges can pass the traffic.

    C. Tunneling is a technique of encapsulating one network protocol within another network protocol.

Answer A is incorrect because tunneling is unrelated to data mining. Answer B is incorrect because encapsulated protocols are not restricted to being nonroutable, although nonroutable protocols are frequently encapsulated. **Answer C is correct because tunneling allows one protocol to be carried by another protocol of the same OSI layer.**

4. At what layer in the OSI model would you find protocols such as RIP, OSPF, or NLSP?

    A. Session

    B. Transport

    C. Network

    D. Data Link

    E. Physical

The given protocols are all routing protocols, and routing occurs at the Network layer in the OSI model. Answers A, B, D, and E are incorrect because none of the other layers defines routing functions. **Answer C is correct because routing takes place at layer 3 of the OSI model, the Network layer.**

5. Which of the following are reliable connection-oriented protocols?

    A. UDP

    B. TCP

    C. SPX

    D. ATP

    E. None of the above

Answer A is incorrect because UDP is a connectionless protocol from the TCP/IP suite. The connection-oriented protocols are from the following suites: TCP—TCP/IP, SPX—Novell, and ATP—AppleTalk. **Answers B, C, and D are correct because they all rely on some form of acknowledgments.**

6. Which statement is true of switching?

    A. Switches are easier to configure than routers.

    B. Switches operate at layer 2 in the OSI model.

    C. Switches have extensive packet filtering capabilities, particularly on network addresses.

    D. None of the above

Answer A is correct because switches have a more limited array of options than a router. Answer B is correct because switches make forwarding decisions based on MAC addresses, which reside at layer 2 of the OSI model. Answer C is incorrect because switches do not have extensive packet filtering capabilities at the network layer because they operate at layer 2, not 3.

7. When a collision occurs on a CSMA/CD network, what happens to the packets being sent?

    A. The nearest router drops them, and a retransmission is requested.

    B. The sending stations recognize the collision, wait a random length of time, and attempt to resend the packets.

    C. The token is passed to the next station on the ring.

    D. The collision causes the router to identify the link as down and the routing table updates are sent to the neighbor routers.

Answer A is incorrect because the router interface sees the collision, but it does not request a retransmission. If the router is one of the sending stations, it follows the procedure in B. **Answer B is correct because this is the "carrier sense" aspect of CSMA/CD.** Answer C is incorrect because there is no token or ring on a CSMA/CD network. Answer D is incorrect because collisions are normal on CSMA/CD networks and do not cause routers to identify the link as down.

8. An unreliable transport protocol means the data packets will not likely reach the destination.
   A. True
   B. False

Answer A is incorrect because unreliable simply means that delivery is not guaranteed. **Answer B is correct because unreliable, or connectionless, transport protocols will not perform error checking, sequence checking, or request retransmissions.** The data usually will arrive at the destination, but the destination upper-layer protocols will have to perform any desired error checking.

9. What is the difference between an 802.3 frame and an Ethernet frame?
   A. The 802.3 frame has a length field, and the Ethernet frame has a type field.
   B. The 802.3 frame has a type field, and the Ethernet frame has a length field.
   C. The frames are completely different.
   D. The frames are exactly the same.

Answer A is correct. Answer B is incorrect because the differences are reversed. Answers C and D are incorrect because the frames are similar but not exactly the same.

10. At what layer of the OSI model does the File Transfer Protocol (FTP) run?
    A. Network
    B. Transport
    C. Session
    D. Presentation
    E. Application

Answers A through D are incorrect because FTP is an application. **Answer E is correct because FTP is an application that uses network communications. It runs at the Application layer.**

General Topic Overview

WHILE YOU READ

1. How can you convert hex characters to their binary equivalents?

2. What are the assigned Cisco Access List numbers?

3. What are the three types of queuing?

4. What is the purpose of RSVP?

5. What does AAA stand for?

6. What are the two most common AAA protocols?

7. What is DES?

8. The H.323 protocol is used for what?

9. What are some services made possible by SS7?

10. Where is the router configuration file stored?

Lab

SEE
APPENDIX **F**

This chapter provides an overview of topics that should be review for you or that do not require the same depth of coverage as other topics in the book. For example, as an intermediate-to-advanced professional, you should be familiar with the topic of Access Lists, so we didn't feel it was necessary to interrupt your study of other topics (IP, IPX, and so on) with Access List information. Also, most of the information is now in one location for easy reference when you are reviewing for the exam. The purpose of this chapter, in this case, is to summarize the information you should know, as an overview.

Other topics—such as performance management, security, and multiservice—are not covered in very much depth because it is not necessary. So we have put those topics here as well. In short, this chapter is a bit of a catchall for information that we felt didn't fit neatly anywhere else!

Binary, Decimal, and Hex

It is important to understand how binary 1s and 0s are converted to decimals or hex characters. This is crucial to fully understand addressing, subnetting, and RIF reading, and many other concepts.

Each bit can represent only two possible options: 1 or 0. However, two bits can represent up to four options (00, 01, 10, 11). The combinations double with the addition of each bit, so that eight bits represent up to 256 possible combinations of 1s and 0s. So, if a byte (eight bits) is all 0s, its decimal value is 0, and if it is all 1s, its decimal value is 255. One method of calculating the decimal value of a byte is to assign a value to each bit (if that particular byte is set to 1) in the following manner:

```
        1    1    1    1    1    1    1    1
       128   64   32   16    8    4    2    1      Sum = 255
```

For example, the byte

```
        0    1    1    0    0    1    1    0
equal   0   64   32    0    0    4    2    0      Sum = 102
```

Hex is based on the same basic principle of combinations of 1s and 0s. However, hex is designed so that each hex character represents four bits. This way, a byte is only two hex characters long. As you just saw, four bits have a maximum of 16 combinations (decimal 0–15). So, hex requires 16 characters, using 10 decimal characters (0–9) and six alphabetic characters (a–f). So letters a–f represent decimal values 10–15, as shown in Table 2.1.

Table 2.1   Binary Value of Hex Characters

Hex Character	Binary Value
0	0 0 0 0
1	0 0 0 1

Hex Character	Binary Value
2	0 0 1 0
3	0 0 1 1
4	0 1 0 0
5	0 1 0 1
6	0 1 1 0
7	0 1 1 1
8	1 0 0 0
9	1 0 0 1
a	1 0 1 0
b	1 0 1 1
c	1 1 0 0
d	1 1 0 1
e	1 1 1 0
f	1 1 1 1

In this way, you can now convert a byte of hex to binary and then to decimal:

Hex value = 3e

Binary value = 0 0 1 1 1 1 1 0

Decimal value = 62 (32+16+8+4+2)

From here, you should be able to convert to any form (binary, hex, or decimal) from any other form.

Access Lists

Access Lists allow an administrator to control where traffic flows in a network. They are typically implemented to restrict user access or limit traffic (preserve bandwidth).

There will likely be Access List questions on the exam that require you to proofread Access Lists. A question might include a description of what the hypothetical network admin is trying to accomplish. You would then choose from several configuration examples. So, you will need to know appropriate commands and syntax for the written exam. This section of the chapter should serve as a refresher for you.

As you might know, each type of Access List is assigned a number for clarity and ease of configuration. When you define a number at the beginning of the configuration command, the router will limit your syntax choices according to the number you entered. Table 2.2 shows the numbers, as of IOS 12.0.

Table 2.2 Cisco Access List Numbers	
Number	ACL Type
1–99	IP Standard Access List
100–199	IP Extended Access List
200–299	Protocol Type-Code Access List
300–399	DECnet Access List
400–499	XNS Standard Access List
500–599	XNS Extended Access List
600–699	AppleTalk Access List
700–799	48-bit MAC Address Access List
800–899	IPX Standard Access List
900–999	IPX Extended Access List
1000–1099	IPX SAP Access List
1100–1199	Extended 48-bit MAC Address Access List
1200–1299	IPX Summary Address (NLSP) Access List
1300–1999	IP Standard Access List (expanded range)
2000–2699	IP Extended Access List (expanded range)

Key Concept

Memorize the ACL numbers!

Configuring Access Lists is a two-step process. First is the writing of the Access List itself. Unlike other commands, Access List commands must be entered in the same order in which you want the router to make filtering decisions. That is to say that the router runs through an Access List in the entered order. As soon as a match is found, the router makes the corresponding forwarding decision (forward or filter) and does not examine the rest of the Access List commands. So, logically, you will want to enter commands from the most specific to the most general. The other step is applying the Access List to the desired interfaces. An Access List can be applied to affect an interface's incoming or outgoing traffic. Also, an Access List works for only one protocol.

Key Concept

An interface can have up to one Access List per direction (incoming/outgoing), per protocol.

Due to how Cisco routers receive commands for Access Lists, if you want to add a command anywhere except at the end of the list, the entire list must be deleted and re-entered (with the new command where appropriate). To get around this, you can copy the list from the router to a text editor and add the new commands there. You can then delete the Access List in the router and simply paste in the new one from your text editor. To delete an Access List, you do not need to delete each line. You can remove an entire list by entering

```
no access list access-list-number
```

Another way to deal with this feature is to add an entirely new Access List (with a new number) that includes your new commands. You can then apply it to the appropriate interfaces. Then, you simply "unapply" the old Access List. This way, you can quickly and easily revert to the previous Access List in case there is a problem with the new one.

By default, the router will filter (deny) any packet that is not expressly mentioned in an Access List. This is known as the *implicit deny* feature. Some people make sure to configure a "deny any" type statement at the end of their Access Lists so they don't forget this.

Key Concept

An implicit deny feature filters all unmentioned traffic of the appropriate type for an Access List.

The remainder of this chapter provides command syntax and examples of how to apply the most common types of Access Lists. All Access Lists have two steps to configuration. First, the Access List must be written. Second, the Access List must be applied to the desired interfaces.

IP Access Lists

There are two types of IP Access Lists: *standard* and *extended*. An IP Standard Access List filters based on the packet's source IP address. The source can be a specific host or a network. These Access Lists are assigned the 1–99 range. In later IOS versions, a second range is available (1300–1999) but rarely needed.

Before reviewing configuration, I should mention the *wildcard* mask. This is a 32-bit value that tells the router which bits of the preceding IP address should be ignored. See the following examples.

The IP Standard Access List command syntax is

```
access-list access-list-number {deny | permit} source [source-wildcard]
```

The command to apply a Standard IP Access List to an interface is

```
ip access-group {access-list-number | name}{in | out}
```

For example,

```
access-list 11 permit 10.1.11.0  0.0.0.255
ethernet0
  ip access-group 11 out
```

This configuration permits all IP traffic from the 10.1.11.0 network to go out the Ethernet0 interface. The wildcard mask defines all fourth-octet bits to be ignored for the purpose of filtering. All other IP traffic will be denied (implicit deny).

If you define a specific host address with an access-list command, you do not need to enter a wildcard mask. A wildcard of 0.0.0.0 (all bits are relevant) is assumed if the last octet of the IP address is not 0.

Key Concept

The wildcard mask instructs the router which bits of the IP address should be ignored for the purpose of filtering.

An extended IP Access List can filter on many other parameters. IP Extended Access Lists are assigned the range 100–199. In later IOS versions, a second range is available (1300–1999) but rarely needed.

The basic IP Extended Access List command syntax is

```
access-list access-list-number {deny | permit} protocol source source-wildcard
destination destination-wildcard
```

These Access Lists are used to filter based on source and destination. A further level of precision is offered by the "protocol" keyword. So, you can also filter a very specific *type* of traffic from a specific source to a specific destination. The options for the protocol keyword are eigrp, gre, icmp, igmp, igrp, ip, ipinip, nos, ospf, tcp, udp, or the IP protocol number, 0–255. Other command options become available, depending on the protocol keyword used. Some examples follow.

ICMP

```
access-list access-list-number {deny | permit} icmp source source-wildcard
destination destination-wildcard [icmp-type [icmp-code]] | icmp-message]
```

The `icmp-type` and `icmp-code` are numerical values (0–255) for the ICMP message type and code. Otherwise, the `icmp-message` name (that is, `echo`, `host-unreachable`, `ttl-exceeded`, and so on) can be used.

TCP and UDP

```
access-list access-list-number {deny | permit} tcp source source-wildcard
[operator port [port]] destination destination-wildcard [operator port
[port]] [established]
```

Here, based on the operator word used, you can filter source or destination TCP traffic in numerous ways:

- `eq`—TCP traffic of this port number
- `gt`—TCP port numbers greater than this
- `lt`—TCP port numbers less than this
- `neq`—All port numbers not equal to this
- `range`—All port numbers in this range

The established keyword is available only when TCP is the protocol defined. This keyword allows previously established sessions (UDP is connectionless, so there is no need to preserve sessions). The router will look for the ACK or RST bits to be set. This is useful when port numbers are renegotiated on session setup.

It will be useful for you to memorize some of the common port numbers for use in IP Extended Access Lists. This is covered in Chapter 8, "TCP/IP."

IPX Access Lists

Similar to IP Access Lists, IPX Standard lists filters based on network or node address. On the other hand, an IPX Standard Access List is different from an IP Standard Access List because the IPX list can filter based on source and destination network or node address, although source network is all that is required. The command syntax is

```
access-list access-list-number {deny | permit} source-network[.source-node
[source-node-mask]] [destination-network[.destination-node
[destination-node-mask]]]
```

An Extended IPX lists can filter based on the IPX equivalent of ports—that is, sockets. Some of the most common IPX sockets are discussed in Chapter 15, "IPX: Internet Packet Exchange." The command syntax is

```
access-list access-list-number {deny | permit} protocol [source-network]
[[[.source-node] source-node-mask] |
[.source-node source-network-mask.source-node-mask]] [source-socket]
[destination.network][[[.destination-node] destination-node-mask] |
[.destination-node destination-network-mask.destination-node-mask]]
[destination-socket]
```

The command to assign any IPX Access List to an interface is

```
ipx access-group {access-list-number | name} {in | out}
```

The other two main types of IPX filters are SAP filters and NLSP filters. SAP and NLSP are discussed more in Chapter 15. The command syntax is provided here to complete this reference of IPX Access Lists.

SAP Filter

Service Advertising Protocol (SAP) filters are given the range 1000–1199. The command syntax is

```
access-list access-list-number {deny | permit} network[.node]
[network-mask.node-mask] [service-type [server-name]]
```

NLSP Filter

NetWare Link Services Protocol (NLSP) filters are given the range 1200–1299. The command syntax is

```
access-list access-list-number {deny | permit} network network-mask
[ticks ticks] [area-count area-count]
```

AppleTalk Access Lists

There are many types of AppleTalk Access Lists. They all use the assigned range 600–699. The most basic type is a network filter. The different types are summarized here.

Network Filter

It filters traffic based on the source AppleTalk network number. Its command syntax is

```
access-list access-list-number {deny | permit} network network
```

Cable Range Filter

This filter is based on the AppleTalk cable range and operates the same way:

```
access-list access-list-number {deny | permit} cable-range cable-range
```

Range Filter

There is another command that can list a range of networks or cable ranges:

```
access-list access-list-number {deny | permit} includes cable-range
```

In this case, the `cable-range` value must specify a beginning and end of a range of networks or cable ranges, separated by a hyphen.

PART
I

CH
2

Zone Filter

To filter based on a source AppleTalk zone name:

```
access-list access-list-number {deny | permit} zone zone-name
```

NBP Filter

To filter based on the AppleTalk Name Binding Protocol (NBP) packet type. You will not see this on the written exam, but you should know that it is available. NBP is discussed more in Chapter 16, "AppleTalk."

Distribute Lists

A Distribute List is actually an Access List that is applied to the routing process. In this case, the Access List lists which networks the router will permit into its routing table or will advertise out a specific interface. When filtering incoming advertisements, the routing process has no knowledge of denied networks. When filtering outgoing advertisements, the specified routes will not be learned via that interface.

The command syntax for applying an Access List as a Distribute List is

```
distribute-list {access-list-number | name} in [interface-name]
```

If no `interface-name` is specified, the list will apply to all interfaces receiving routing updates.

A Distribute List is applied to the routing process as in this example:

```
router ospf 100
  distribute list 199 in ethernet0
```

With this, any network being filtered by Access List 199 will not be entered into the routing table.

Distribute Lists are discussed more in Chapter 14, "Managing Routing."

Access Class

To use an Access List to limit Telnet access, you can define an `access-class`. You can use a Standard or Extended IP `access-list` as an `access-class`. It is applied like the `access-group` command, except it is applied to the VTY lines, not an interface. It is configured in the following manner:

```
RTR (config)# line vty 0 4
RTR (config-line)# access-class access_list_number {in | out}
```

Performance Management

There are three types of queuing in Cisco routers: Weighted Fair queuing, Priority queuing, and Custom queuing. Each one is quickly reviewed here.

Weighted Fair queuing is the default on Cisco routers. During Weighted Fair queuing, all incoming packets are sent to the queue. They are transmitted in the order in which the last bit of each packet was received. This means that smaller packets are transmitted before larger packets.

Queuing

You must know the difference between the three types of Cisco queuing, and you will need to recognize a properly configured queue list. This section will provide a brief overview of this material.

Cisco's default queuing is *Weighted Fair queuing*. It operates by assigning a high priority to traffic that is low-volume in nature. This way, FTP transmissions will not cause other traffic, such as Telnet, to time out. Weighted Fair queuing is on by default for all interfaces with a 2.048Mbps or lower speed. It can be disabled on any interface by using the `no faire-queue` command.

Another queuing option is *Priority queuing*. There are four priority levels (high, medium, normal, and low). All traffic in the high queue will be sent before any traffic in the medium queue is sent. Likewise, the medium queue will be cleared before packets in the low queue are sent. Traffic must be administratively defined and assigned a queue priority. Traffic is defined by network protocol type (IP, IPX, and so on) or protocol characteristic (TCP port, packet size, Access List, and so on).

To further customize Priority queuing, you can define queue sizes and a default queue. The default queue will be used for all traffic that does not match any other queue statement.

Much like Access Lists, Priority queuing is configured by building one or more priority list. Each priority list defines the priority queue levels (high, medium, normal, and low) and traffic types for a particular queuing purpose. A priority list is then assigned to an interface by using the `priority-group` command. There can be up to 16 priority lists on a Cisco router.

Priority Queuing Commands

To configure a priority-list parameter, use this command (more than one parameter can make up each Priority queue):

```
RTR (config)# priority-list list-number {default | protocol protocol-name |
interface interface} {high | medium | normal | low}
```

To define the Priority queue sizes, use this command:

```
RTR (config)# priority-list list-number queue-limit high_limit  medium_limit
normal_limit  low_limit
```

To apply a Priority queue to an interface, use this command:

```
RTR (config-if)#priority-group list-number
```

The other type of queuing is *Custom queuing*. With Custom queues, you build your own queues and control the amount of bandwidth you would like a particular type of traffic to use. If the allocated bandwidth is not being used for Custom queue–defined traffic, other types of traffic can use it until it becomes needed for the Custom queue traffic. Each queue is configured with a maximum size (either number of packets or byte count). This defines how much traffic will be transmitted (and therefore, the bandwidth used) before the router moves on to the next queue. In Custom queuing, each queue is processed in order. Up to 16 queues can be defined in each Cisco router.

Custom queuing is configured by building one or more queue lists, much like Priority queuing or Access Lists. Each queue list will have the queues defined (numbered), allocated bandwidth defined (percentage), and the byte count of each queue defined. Then, to apply the Custom queue to an interface, use the `custom-queue-list` command.

Custom Queuing Commands

To configure a Custom queue protocol parameter, use this command (more than one parameter can make up each Priority queue):

```
RTR (config)# queue-list list-number protocol protocol-name queue-number
queue-keyword keyword-value
```

Choices for `queue-keyword` are gt (greater than), lt (less than), list (referring to an Access List), tcp (to define a TCP port), and udp (to define a UDP port).

To define the transmission for a queue, in either packets or byte count:

```
RTR (config)# queue-list list-number queue queue_number {limit packet_count |
byte-count bytes}
```

To define a queue for traffic that does not match queue-list parameters

```
RTR (confog)# queue-list list-number default queue-number
```

To apply a Custom queue to an interface

```
RTR (config-if)#custom-queue-list list-number
```

Key Concept

Weighted Fair queuing—By default, low-volume traffic gets higher priority.

Priority queuing—Traffic assigned one of four priority levels (high, medium, normal, and low) with priority lists.

Custom queuing—Traffic assigned a numerical importance (1–16) with queue lists. Bandwidth and byte count for each queue can be defined, as well.

Resource Reservation Protocol (RSVP)

Resource Reservation Protocol (RSVP) is currently being standardized by the IETF. It operates at the Transport layer of the OSI model. It enables applications on end stations to attain a particular Quality of Service (QoS) for a particular sending node to a single or multiple destination nodes. For multicast sessions, it works in conjunction with Internet Group Membership Protocol (IGMP).

RSVP works by obtaining routes from the routing protocols. It then joins a multicast group (via IGMP) and sends RSVP messages to RSVP-capable routers. Each RSVP-capable router then queues them in a packet scheduler, which establishes a route and level of QoS.

Not every router along the entire path needs to be RSVP-capable for RSVP to function. It's simply that the non-RSVP routers will be unable to reserve resources. In these cases, you would need to establish an RSVP tunnel through the non-RSVP environment.

Right now, all you should need to know are these basics about RSVP. If you're interested, more information about RSVP can be found at

```
http://www.cisco.com/univercd/cc/td/doc/cisintwk/ito_doc/rsvp.htm.
```

Compression

On point-to-point links, it is sometimes advantageous to compress traffic. Compression significantly raises the router's CPU utilization. HDLC, PPP, and LAPB can be compressed by using the following command in interface configuration mode:

```
compress {predictor | stac}
```

The predictor and stac keywords are used to define the compression algorithm to be used (RAND and Stacker, respectively). Both ends of a link must be configured the same to function properly.

Load Balancing

Load balancing is the capability of a network device (such as a router) to transmit packets over more than one path. Load balancing is implemented by numerous protocols and technologies (DLSW+, routing protocols, and so on) and takes different forms for each implementation. For the purpose of the CCIE Written Exam, you will need to know a little about a few of these different uses (for example, DLSW+). Therefore, the particular uses of load balancing features are discussed in conjunction with the associated protocols or technologies in this book.

Security

Security is an increasingly important subject. As the importance of the information crossing our networks increases, so does the price tag associated with potentially losing the data to business competitors or criminals. In general, Cisco routers are not designed to provide security features. However, they do integrate well with other security devices, such as AAA servers and firewalls.

AAA

AAA stands for *authentication, authorization, and accounting*. The industry recognizes these features as necessary for any general-security software package. A software package like this, such as CiscoSecure ACS, resides on a server, typically NT or UNIX. It interacts with network devices such as routers and Remote Access Servers (RASs) to

- Authenticate—Allow users into the network
- Authorize—Allow users access to specific resources or areas
- Account—Keep track of who or what is attempting to get in or accessing the network resources

The local Cisco router security features (local usernames, passwords, enable passwords) do not offer the same features as an AAA service.

 Key Concept

AAA is a standard security feature set that stands for authentication, authorization, and accounting.

The most common protocols for AAA are TACACS, RADIUS, and Kerberos. The first two are discussed in a bit more detail later in the chapter. Typically, a server will run services that communicate to network devices via one of these protocols. In this way, all the authentication requirements of the network can be configured in one central location. Also, servers can be implemented in a redundant manner so that if one server fails, other servers are available simply by configuring a list of the servers in the router.

AAA is enabled on Cisco routers with the aaa new-model command. Then, the specific *method list*, or list of authentication methods, is configured using aaa authentication, aaa authorization, and aaa accounting commands.

TACACS

Terminal Access Controller Access Control System (TACACS) is discussed in RFC 1492 and is used for AAA. Currently, there are three versions of TACACS: TACACS, TACACS+, and Extended TACACS. Each is a distinct protocol and is not interoperable with the others. TACACS can work with other protocols such as PAP and CHAP, which are discussed in Chapter 18, "ISDN and DDR."

The heart of TACACS communication is a request/response pair. Every request demands a response (permit or deny). The following are Request message types:

- AUTH—Asks for authentication
- LOGIN—Asks for authentication and, if successful, starts a connection
- CONNECT—Requests a TCP connection to a specific IP address and port (for existing connections)
- SUPERUSER—Requests superuser status on the terminal server (for existing connections)
- LOGOUT—Existing connection should be terminated
- SLIPON—Requests a specific SLIP address for the remote connection (for existing connection)
- SLIPOFF—Existing SLIP connection should be terminated

Response messages are simply "accepted" or "rejected" because Request messages are very specific requests.

TACACS uses TCP port 49. TACACS carries the username and password in clear text. There should be no need to memorize the packet format, but it is available in the RFC.

RADIUS

Remote Authentication Dial-In User Services (RADIUS) is discussed in RFC 2058. It is also used for AAA. Like a TACACS server, each RADIUS server holds a list of conditions that must be met for a user to be positively authenticated (username, password, port number, and so on). RADIUS can work with other protocols such as PAP and CHAP.

RADIUS clients and servers share a secret key, which is never transmitted over the network. In addition, passwords are encrypted using the MD5 algorithm.

When a client wants to authenticate, it sends an *access-request* message to the server. It is re-sent or sent to another specified server if no response is received in a specified time interval. At this point, there are four options for what can happen:

- If the client does not have the same shared secret, nothing will happen (= implicit deny).
- If a database condition is not met, an *access-reject* message is sent to the client.
- If database conditions are met, an *access-accept* message is sent to the client.
- If the server has been configured to request more information, an *access-challenge* message is sent to the client and (if supported) will be forwarded to the user. The user's response is then sent as another access-request message.

Key Concept

TACACS sends passwords in clear text, whereas RADIUS encrypts passwords with MD5.

Firewalls

A *firewall* is typically a designated box that limits the types of traffic allowed between a private and public network, such as a corporation and the Internet. Cisco's product is the PIX. It can filter incoming or outgoing traffic.

The PIX can operate as a *proxy firewall*—a firewall that acts as the remote destination to the internal client, so that there is not a direct connection through the firewall.

The PIX uses *Adaptive Security Algorithm (ASA)*, which tracks all sessions and stores this information in a database against which all traffic is compared.

The PIX can be implemented to access a TACACS or RADIUS server to authenticate users, as well. In this way, it acts as a "cut-through proxy" firewall. That is, it interrupts the setup of a session to authenticate the client with an AAA server. After the user is approved and policy established, the PIX will allow the client to communicate directly with the destination but still maintain all session information.

Encryption Keys and DES

Encryption is the use of a "scrambling" algorithm to decode data to its destination. The scrambling is achieved by applying a cryptography algorithm to the actual data before transmission. Many methods (algorithms) are available (and more are being invented all the time) to accomplish this. Some of the basic concepts or most common methods are discussed in this section, as they are relevant to the CCIE Written Exam.

A *key* is a variable that is added to a cryptography algorithm. If both ends possess, or know, the key, the message can be coded at one end and correctly decoded at the receiving end. In this way, an intercepted message is much more difficult to decode by the unintended reader. Even if they know the algorithm used, they would have to guess at the key. Keys are also referred to as *ciphers*. There are two basic methods used in cipher algorithms: stream ciphers and block ciphers. So, they are never transmitted. Stream ciphers encode each bit, whereas block ciphers encode chunks of data. These are secret key algorithms—both sides know the key in advance and maintain the keys, but the key cannot be securely transmitted. In this way, after an undesired source discovers or figures out the key, the encryption is useless until another secret key method can be reliably agreed on at both ends.

Keys can be transmitted using public and private keys. A public key is generated from a secret or private key. So the public key cannot be used to decipher data encrypted with a private key. In this way, a public key can be generated and transmitted securely, because the key itself needs deciphering before the key can be used to decipher the actual data. The algorithm used to generate public keys is the *Diffie-Hellman* algorithm.

The standard encryption-key algorithm used by the U.S. government is the Data Encryption Standard (DES). DES is also standardized by the IETF and ANSI. Original DES uses a 56-bit key (40-bit for export). This version was very secure until computers had the power to try all possible key combinations in a reasonable amount of time. The new DES standard, referred to as *Triple DES*, encrypts the original data three times with 56-bit keys. So it is the equivalent of up to a 168-bit key, while being backward compatible to original DES systems.

Multiservice Technologies

Multiservice technologies have to do with the transmission on voice (and data) over legacy data-only service circuits. The following are a few of the most common technologies. You need to be familiar with them only for the purpose of the CCIE Written Exam.

H.323

H.323 is an ITU-T standard protocol used for transmission of multimedia communications over packet-based networks. It has three main elements:

- H.245—Opening and closing of channels, flow control, and information messages
- Q.931—Call setup (protocol "borrowed" from ISDN)
- H.225—Handles authentication, authorization, and status. Used only when H.323 Gatekeepers (gateway) are present (optional).

H.323 supports data, video, and voice, including Voice Over IP.

Key Concept

H.323 is a standard protocol used for transmission of multimedia applications over packet-based networks and supports data, video, and voice.

Codecs

A *codec* is a coder-decoder, which sends a signal that represents the actual data. It is typically used when transmitting analog signals over data circuits. Codecs convert voice signals into digital signals, normally using the Pulse Code Modulation (PCM) technique. PCM is defined in ITU-T standard G.711.

Codecs are commonly used in Voice Over IP implementations.

SS7

SS7 (Signaling System 7) is used for signaling in the backbones of telecommunications systems around the world. It refers both to the protocol SS7 and to the network. SS7 provides out-of-band signaling on a logically separate network than voice traffic itself. However, SS7 traffic sometimes uses the same physical circuits as voice traffic. In this case, SS7 always has a dedicated timeslot within these facilities, so it remains logically separate.

SS7 is responsible for routing, link status, and connection control information in the network. There are many slightly different "standard" versions of SS7 throughout the world, but they are all largely interoperable. SS7 roughly corresponds to the OSI model and has capabilities at all equivalent layers, top to bottom.

SS7 enables services such as 1-800 calls, local number portability, portable phone roaming, in-network voice mail, and others.

Key Concept

SS7 provides out-of-band signaling in the telecommunications network; is responsible for routing, link status, and connection control; and enables services such as 1-800 calls, local number portability, portable phone roaming, and in-network voice mail.

Real-Time Transport Protocol (RTP)

Real-Time Transport Protocol (RTP) is a layer 4 (Transport) protocol designed to transmit extremely time-sensitive data, such as audio and video. It can operate over multicast or unicast network services. It is often used in conjunction with audio and video codecs, and in Voice Over or Video Over IP implementations.

RTP is also used to compress the packet header before transmission. It can usually compress a 40-byte header down to two-to-four bytes, thereby reducing your overhead. Payload is usually 20 to 160 bytes, so you can see a percentage difference in the overall packet size by using RTP headers for compression.

Cisco Device Operation

The following section is a review of the basic device-management tasks you must know to effectively manage a Cisco router.

Router Infrastructure Review

The main components of a Cisco router are

- ROM—Read-Only Memory
- RAM—Random-Access Memory (read/write capable)
- NVRAM—RAM that does not erase when power is lost
- Flash memory—Also known as EEPROM (Electronic Erasable Programmable Read-Only Memory) (read/write capable)

A Cisco router needs an *Internetworking Operating System (IOS)* to boot. The binary form of the IOS is most commonly stored in and loaded from flash memory. The router can also be configured to boot from an IOS image on a server somewhere (via TFTP, DECnet MOP, or RCP), or to boot from ROM. If no IOS is found, the router will boot from ROM by default. This is called ROM monitor mode. When it boots from ROM, only a limited feature set is available.

When the IOS loads during the boot process, it is loaded into RAM.

During the boot process, after the IOS is loaded, the router will look for its current configuration, which is stored in the router's NVRAM. If a configuration file is found, it will load this to RAM as well.

The router's *central processing unit (CPU)* is the "brain" that uses the IOS and configuration to process the bits through the router.

Configuration changes take place immediately on a Cisco router. When changes are made, they are made to the running image. This is the image currently in RAM. If the router were powered off, any changes would be lost unless you had written the changes to the startup configuration (in NVRAM).

A router with no configuration can be accessed via the console port on the router, or via a reverse Telnet session from another router's asynchronous port, directly connected to the new router's AUX (auxiliary) port.

Once online, the router can be accessed by using the console port, the VTY port (via Telnet), reverse Telnet, a terminal server, or a network-management station.

Router Management

This section briefly covers the options and commands for proper management of the boot process, IOS, configuration files, and basic router security. Again, this material should be familiar to you, but we wanted to include an overview of it in this book so it is a more complete reference for your exam preparation.

The configuration register is a four-character hex (16-bit) value that instructs the router how to boot itself. The default configuration register is expressed as four hex characters in the following manner: 0x2102. Any changes to the configuration register are done by using the `config-register` global configuration command followed by the value you desire—for example, `config-register 0x2101`.

One of the most important characters of the configuration register to know how to manipulate is the last character. This last character (the last, or lowest, four bits) is called the *boot field*. Table 2.3 shows the values, meanings, and results of the different setting for this field.

Table 2.3 Boot Field Values, Meanings, and Results

Boot Field Value (Hex)	Meaning	Result
0	Boot to ROM monitor mode	> or rommon> prompt
1	Boot from ROM	router (boot)> prompt
2–F	Boot from NVRAM	Boot any image found in NVRAM

The other important configuration register setting to know about is bit 6. This bit, when set, forces the router to boot up but ignore the contents of NVRAM (the saved configuration file). To do this, the third character in the configuration register needs to be a 4 or higher. So instead of the value being 0x2102, it would be 0x2142. This is very important to know so that you can recover lost passwords on Cisco routers.

Typically, to perform password recovery on a router, you break a bootup so the router boots into ROM monitor mode. Then, you change the configuration register to force the router to boot as normal but ignore the saved configuration in NVRAM. At this point you issue the show startup-config command to view the passwords or change the passwords. You will need to configure new passwords if the passwords are encrypted in the configuration file. Then, you can change the configuration register value back to boot from NVRAM, reboot the router, and use the viewed or new passwords. Just make sure that when you reboot, you boot from the startup config, not the running config. The running config is incomplete due to the limited feature set of ROM monitor mode!

As stated previously, the IOS is normally stored in flash memory and loaded to RAM during the boot process. The IOS also can be stored on a server and loaded via TFTP, DECnet MOP, or RCP. Of course, TFTP is by far the most common. A typical way to configure a router is to create a boot order list that tells the router to first boot from Flash, to then try to boot from an IOS image on a server, and to finally boot from ROM if both these fail. This can be done with these commands:

```
RTR (config)# boot system flash c2500-jos56i-1.120-7.bin
RTR (config)# boot system tftp c2500-jos56i-1.120-7.bin 10.10.10.1
RTR (config)# boot system rom
```

For this example, c2500-jos56i-1.120-7.bin is the IOS filename in flash memory. You can use the show flash command to discover the IOS image filename. The IP address 10.10.10.1 is the TFTP server's IP address. If IP domain lookup is enabled (which it is by default), you can use the TFTP server's hostname instead of an IP address.

To copy the IOS image to a TFTP server, use this command:

```
RTR# copy flash tftp
```

You will then be prompted for the IOS image filename, the TFTP server's hostname or IP address, and what you want the image to be called on the TFTP server.

Or, to copy an IOS image from a TFTP server, use this command:

```
RTR# copy tftp flash
```

You will then be prompted for the IP address or hostname of the TFTP server. If the server is found on the network, you will be prompted for the image filename you want copied to the router and for the name of the IOS image after it's copied into flash.

Likewise, you can load the configuration from NVRAM or from a TFTP server (or DECnet MOP server). It is common to configure a router to load the configuration in the same manner as it looks for the IOS:

```
RTR (config)# boot host RTR-config
RTR (config)# boot host tftp RTR-config 10.10.10.1
```

In this example, RTR-config is the name of the configuration file and 10.10.10.1 is the TFTP server's IP address.

To copy the configuration file to a TFTP server, use this command:

```
RTR# copy running-config tftp
```

You will then be prompted for the IP address or hostname of the TFTP server. If the server is found on the network, you will be prompted for what you want to name the configuration file on the TFTP server.

Or, to copy a configuration file from a TFTP server:

```
RTR# copy tftp running-config
```

You will then be prompted for the IP address or hostname of the TFTP server. If the server is found on the network, you will be prompted for the configuration filename.

The other important router-management task is password management. There are two main types of passwords for Cisco routers: the line password and the enable password. A line password allows access to the EXEC mode. Here you can enter configuration mode if you know the enable (privileged EXEC) mode password. Each type of line (port) needs passwords configured independently, including console, VTY (Telnet), and auxiliary lines.

To configure a password for the console:

```
RTR (config)# line console 0
RTR (config-line)# password 46hark89
RTR (config-line)# login
```

In the previous example, the password to enter EXEC mode when accessing the router via the console port is 46hark89. The login command tells the router to prompt for a password. The commands are the same to configure passwords for the VTY (Telnet) and auxiliary ports. You would just specify the desired ports in the first line. For example,

```
RTR (config)# line vty 0 4)
```

The enable password controls access to enable, or privileged EXEC, mode. There are two ways to configure the enable password. You can use the enable password command or the enable secret command. Cisco recommends the enable secret command because it provides security. When the enable password command is used, the enable password appears in clear text in the configuration file. When the enable secret command is used, the enable password appears in encrypted form in the configuration file. Enable password encryption is configured with one of the following commands:

```
RTR (config)# enable password 35look78
```

Or,

```
RTR (config)# enable secret 35look78
```

The enable and other (line) passwords can be encrypted by using this command:

```
RTR (config)# service password-encryption
```

If you use this command, you can still use the stronger encryption of the enable secret command for the enable password.

Cisco Discovery Protocol (CDP)

Cisco Discovery Protocol (CDP) is a Cisco proprietary (layer 2) protocol that provides information about directly connected Cisco routers and switches (if enabled on the switch). CDP messages are not forwarded and, of course, not routed (layer 2). The protocol operates transparently and is enabled by default on all Cisco routers. It can be useful if you are trying to troubleshoot a connectivity problem. If the Data Link layer is operating, you will see CDP information from all directly connected routers (and switches, if enabled) that also have layer 2 functionality. Here is the kind of information provided:

```
RTR1#show cdp neighbors detail
------------------------
Device ID: RTR3
Entry address(es):
  IP address: 10.10.10.2
  Novell address: a1.0090.ab80.5e0f
(Other configured network protocols would appear here)
Platform: cisco 2500,  Capabilities: Router
```

```
Interface: Serial0.103,  Port ID (outgoing port): Serial0.1
Holdtime : 151 sec

Version :
Cisco Internetwork Operating System Software
IOS (tm) 2500 Software (C2500-JOS56I-L), Version 12.0(7),
    RELEASE SOFTWARE (fc1)
Copyright (c) 1986-1999 by cisco Systems, Inc.
Compiled Thu 14-Oct-99 01:54 by phanguye
```

Key Concept

Cisco Discovery Protocol (CDP) is a Cisco proprietary (layer 2) protocol that provides information about directly connected Cisco routers and switches.

Simple Network Management Protocol (SNMP)

Simple Network Management Protocol (SNMP) operates over UDP (ports 161 and 162) and is used by one or more *Network Monitoring Stations (NMS)* to monitor and control network devices such as routers, switches, servers, and other equipment. An NMS is a server that sits on the network and monitors and collects data. It can also be used for accessing and controlling the devices. Each managed device must run an *SNMP Agent* with which the NMS communicates via a *Management Information Base (MIB)* that is provided by the network device manufacturer (such as Cisco) and is loaded directly on the NMS.

Key Concept

Simple Network Management Protocol (SNMP) operates over UDP.

Most of the time, the NMS initiates data gathering. If desired, you can have network devices report certain events. The type of events available depend on what features the manufacturer has built in to its product. These event-triggered reports to the NMS are called *traps*.

In order for the NMS and the device to communicate, they must share an access password called a *community string*. To set the community string on a Cisco router or switch, use these commands:

```
RTR (config)# snmp-server community community_string
SW> (enable) set snmp community {read-only | read-write | read-write-all}
community_string
```

To enable traps:

```
RTR (config)# snmp server enable traps [trap_type]
SW> (enable) set snmp trap server_address community_string
SW> (enable) set snmp trap {enable | disable} [trap_type]
```

With these trap commands, all traps are enabled if no specific trap type is specified.

The Cisco Hierarchical Internetworking Model

Cisco characterizes networks by using a three-level hierarchical model. This helps clarify the purpose of each device in the network. Cisco calls them the Access, Distribution, and Core levels. They are described here:

- Access level—Where end (user) nodes access the network. These are closet or desktop routers or switches. If the network is designed well, a good portion of the intra-workgroup traffic will remain at the Access level. VLANs are implemented at this level. Some basic filtering can happen here, but it is usually implemented at the distribution level. If there are WAN connections, they would connect the Access level to the Distribution level.

- Distribution level—Aggregates the Access level connections to the Core level. Oversubscription of bandwidth happens here (150 10Mbps access–level users do *not* require a T1 to the Core, because they will not all use this bandwidth at the same time). Most Access Lists, compression, and encryption should be implemented here. Devices at this level are almost exclusively routers.

- Core level—Concentrates all traffic that needs to transverse the network. The focus here is switching traffic as fast as possible. ATM, Gigabit, SONET, and other high-speed technologies are usually implemented here (although it is becoming more common to see higher speeds closer to the Access level, as equipment prices drop).

Summary

This chapter provides an overview of topics that should serve as a refresher for you or that do not require the same in-depth discussion as the topics in the remainder of the book. So, the information is presented here in an overview style for you to read now and reference later. From here, you should be ready to dive into the rest of the book.

Please do not take the fact that we are just summarizing these topics to mean that they are not important on the test! Many of them most certainly are, especially the topics that are foundational in nature. Although they are important to include here, we just could not commit the pages needed to cover these topics in further detail as if you had not studied them before. As stated numerous times, this book is for the intermediate-to-advanced professional. Many other sources (see Appendix D, "Alternative Resources") teach these topics from a more introductory stance.

On the other hand, you might not see any questions on some of the topics in this chapter (H.323, SS7, and SNMP). Regardless, they are mentioned in the CCIE Blueprint and sometimes appear on the test, even if in just a few questions. So, it would behoove you to understand this material before moving on.

QUESTIONS AND ANSWERS

1. How can you convert hex characters to their binary equivalents?

Hex Character	Binary Value
0	0 0 0 0
1	0 0 0 1
2	0 0 1 0
3	0 0 1 1
4	0 1 0 0
5	0 1 0 1
6	0 1 1 0
7	0 1 1 1
8	1 0 0 0
9	1 0 0 1
a	1 0 1 0
b	1 0 1 1
c	1 1 0 0
d	1 1 0 1
e	1 1 1 0
f	1 1 1 1

…continues

...continued

2.	What are the assigned Cisco Access List numbers?
Number	**ACL Type**
1–99	IP Standard Access List
100–199	IP Extended Access List
200–299	Protocol Type-Code Access List
300–399	DECnet Access List
400–499	XNS Standard Access List
500–599	XNS Extended Access List
600–699	AppleTalk Access List
700–799	48-bit MAC Address Access List
800–899	IPX Standard Access List
900–999	IPX Extended Access List
1000–1099	IPX SAP Access List
1100–1199	Extended 48-bit MAC Address Access List
1200–1299	IPX Summary Address (NLSP) Access List
1300–1999	IP Standard Access List (expanded range)
2000–2699	IP Extended Access List (expanded range)

3. What are the three types of queuing?

   A: Weighted Fair queuing, Priority queuing, and Custom queuing

4. What is the purpose of RSVP?

   A: Maintains a QoS for (time-sensitive) applications

5. What does AAA stand for?

   A: Authentication, authorization, and accounting

6. What are the two most common AAA protocols?

   A: TACACS and RADIUS

7. What is DES?

   A: Data Encryption Standard—a standard 56-bit encryption scheme

PART
I

CH
2

8. The H.323 protocol is used for what?

A: H.323 is used for multiservice (multimedia) applications, usually in a Voice Over IP environment.

9. What are some services made possible by SS7?

A: 1-800, local number portability, portable phone roaming, and in-network voice mail

10. Where is the router configuration file stored?

A: In NVRAM

PRACTICE TEST

1. What is the decimal equivalent of 0x2e?
   A. 00101110
   B. 11100010
   C. 46
   D. 226

Answers A and B are incorrect because they are binary, not decimal. **Answer C is correct.** Answer D is the decimal equivalent of e2.

2. What is the allocated range for IPX SAP Access Lists?
   A. 100–199
   B. 600–699
   C. 900–999
   D. 1000–1099
   E. 1100–1199

Answer A is IP Extended. Answer B is AppleTalk. Answer C is IPX Extended. **Answer D is correct.** Answer E is Extended MAC Addresses.

3. Which of the following are acceptable Access List commands?
   A. `access-list 1 deny 10.1.11.1`
   B. `access-list 1 permit 10.1.11.1 0.0.0.0`
   C. `access-list 100 permit 10.1.11.0 0.0.0.255`
   D. `access-list 101 permit tcp 10.10.1.1 0.0.0.0 eq telnet 10.10.2.2 0.0.0.0`
   E. `access-list 101 permit tcp 10.10.1.1 0.0.0.0 ip telnet 10.10.2.2 0.0.0.0`

Answer A is correct because you do not have to specify a mask when a host address is used. Answer B is correct because you can specify a mask of 0.0.0.0 if you like, for

administrative clarity. Answer C is incorrect because it is not an Extended IP list but has number 100. **Answer D is correct and is a good example of an IP Extended Access List.** Answer E is incorrect because there is no protocol keyword `ip` usable with a TCP Extended Access List.

4. What is the result of the following command?

```
access-list 199 permit tcp 10.10.1.1 0.0.0.0 eq 23 10.10.2.2 0.0.0.0
```

- **A.** Allows 10.10.1.1 to Telnet to 10.10.2.2
- **B.** Allows 10.10.1.1 to be Telnetted to from 10.10.2.2
- **C.** Denies 10.10.1.2 to Telnet to 10.10.2.2
- **D.** All of the above
- **E.** None of the above; this Access List does not deal with Telnet
- **F.** None of the above; this Access List command is not entered correctly

Answer A is correct because the TCP port equal to `eq 23` is Telnet. Answer B is incorrect because 10.10.1.1 is the source and 10.10.2.2 is the destination for this command, so the reverse would not work. **Answer C is correct because all hosts besides 10.10.1.1 would be denied.** Answer D is incorrect because B is incorrect. Answers E and F are incorrect because A and C are correct.

5. Priority Queuing has 16 possible priority levels.

- **A.** True
- **B.** False

Answer B (False) is correct—Custom queuing has 16 levels, Priority queuing has 4.

6. Which of the following are authentication, authorization, and accounting protocols?

- **A.** AAA
- **B.** Kerberos
- **C.** RADIUS
- **D.** RSVP
- **E.** RTP
- **F.** TACACS

Answer A is incorrect because AAA is simply the abbreviation for authentication, authorization, and accounting. **Answer B is correct. Answer C is correct.** Answer D is incorrect because it stands for Resource Reservation Protocol. Answer E is incorrect because it stands for Real Time Protocol. **Answer F is correct.**

7. Which of the following statements are true?

    A. TACACS operates over TCP.

    B. RADIUS operates over TCP.

    C. TACACS encrypts passwords before transmission.

    D. RADIUS encrypts passwords before transmission.

    E. TACACS can work with PAP and CHAP.

    F. RADIUS can work with PAP and CHAP.

PART
I

CH
2

Answers A, B, D, E, and F are true. Answer C is incorrect because TACACS sends passwords in clear text.

8. Where is the running configuration located?

    A. RAM

    B. ROM

    C. NVRAM

    D. Flash memory

Answer A is correct because the startup configuration is written to RAM during the boot process, which becomes the running configuration. Answer B is incorrect because ROM is what helps the router boot. Answer C is incorrect because NVRAM is where the startup configuration is stored. Answer D is incorrect because flash is where the IOS image is stored.

9. To force the router to ignore the configuration file in NVRAM, the configuration register should be set to which of the following:

    A. 0x2102

    B. 0x4102

    C. 0x2142

    D. 0x2101

Answer A is incorrect because it is the default setting. Answer B is incorrect. **Answer C is correct; the third character must be a 4 or higher because the sixth bit must be set.** Answer D is incorrect.

10. Given the following diagram of newly installed routers, which of the following statements are true regarding CDP:

Router 1   e0   e1   Router 2   e0   e1   Router 3

A. CDP will need to be enabled for CDP to function properly.

B. Router 1 should see both the other routers.

C. Router 2 should see both the other routers.

D. Router 3 should see both the other routers.

E. There are no IP addresses; no router will see any of the others.

Answer A is incorrect because CDP is on by default on Cisco routers. **Answer B is correct.** Answers C and D are incorrect because you can "see" directly connected devices only via CDP, and Router 3 is not directly connected. Answer E is incorrect because CDP works at layer 2 and therefore needs no network (layer 3) addresses to operate, although it will discover any network addresses configured on the attached router.

The LAN

3 Ethernet

4 Token-Ring and FDDI

5 LANE—LAN Emulation

CHAPTER

3

CHAPTER PREREQUISITE

Before reading this chapter you should read Chapter 1, "General Network Overview," to familiarize yourself with the OSI model and layer 2 standards.

Ethernet

——WHILE YOU READ——

1. What are the media speeds for Ethernet, Fast Ethernet, and Gigabit Ethernet?

2. What are the Ethernet connector types on the router?

3. Describe the difference between unicast, multicast, and broadcast traffic.

4. What field in the MAC address is used for universal administration?

5. Describe the operation of a CSMA/CD network.

6. What are the four different Ethernet IPX encapsulation types?

7. How do these encapsulations differ?

SEE
APPENDIX **F**

Definition and Architecture

Ethernet is a *local area network (LAN)* architecture that uses the *Carrier Sense Multiple Access/Collision Detection (CSMA/CD)* access method. Ethernet was originally developed by Digital Equipment Corporation, Intel, and Xerox (DIX). This standard is known as Ethernet Version II. Later, the Institute of Electrical and Electronics Engineers (IEEE) included Ethernet as part of the IEEE 802 standard. This standard is known as IEEE 802.3. To make things more confusing, the generic term "Ethernet" is used to describe both standards.

The IEEE 802.3 standard corresponds to layer 1 and part of layer 2 of the *Open Systems Interconnect (OSI)* Reference Model. IEEE 802.2 *Logical Link Control (LLC)* and IEEE 802.1d Bridging, also known as *Spanning Tree Protocol (STP)*, provide the missing parts of OSI layer 2. STP is described further in Chapter 6, "LAN Switching." The Ethernet Version II standard corresponds to layers 1 and 2 of the OSI/RM. The relationship between the OSI/RM, Ethernet Version II, and IEEE 802.3 is described in Figure 3.1.

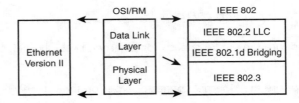

Figure 3.1
Relationship between OSI/RM, Ethernet Version II, and IEEE 802.

Key Concept

IEEE 802.3 supports all of layer 1 and part of layer 2 of the OSI model. Ethernet Version II supports both layer 1 and layer 2.

IEEE 802.3 has defined several media speeds as part of the physical layer. These speeds are as follows:

- 10Mb for Ethernet
- 100Mb for Fast Ethernet
- 1000Mb or 1Gb for Gigabit Ethernet

Just as there are different media speeds there are different types of physical media. IEEE 802.3 uses a designation for each combination of speed and physical media type. Appending the speed in megabits to the word *BASE* and then adding a designation for the physical media type forms this designation. As an example, *10BASE-T* designates 10Mb Ethernet over twisted-pair telephone wire. Following is a list of the commonly used physical media for Ethernet and Fast Ethernet:

- 10BASE-2 and 10BASE-5 use coaxial cable (also called thinnet and thicknet).
- 10BASE-T uses twisted-pair telephone wire with an RJ-45 connector.
- 100BASE-T is Fast Ethernet over twisted-pair telephone wire with an RJ-45 connector.
- 100BASE-FX is Fast Ethernet over optical fiber.

It is impractical to have a connector on the router for every possible physical media type. Hence, generic interfaces were developed that supported several physical interfaces. A transceiver is used to convert from the generic interfaces that follow to a specific physical interface:

- Attachment Unit Interface (AUI) for 10Mb Ethernet
- Media Independent Interface (MII) for 10Mb Ethernet and Fast Ethernet
- Gigabit Media Independent Interface (GMII) for Gigabit Ethernet

 Key Concept

> IEEE 802.3 supports multiple speeds (for example, 10Mb Ethernet, 100Mb Fast Ethernet, and 1000Mb Gigabit Ethernet). Ethernet Version II supports only 10Mb operation. Both standards support multiple physical media types.

Following is a sample router configuration for a 10Mb Ethernet interface with an AUI connector and a 100Mb Fast Ethernet interface with an MII connector:

```
interface Ethernet0
   media-type aui

interface FastEthernet0
   media-type mii
```

Media Access Control Layer

The MAC layer is responsible for transmitting LLC data between two stations over the physical media. This layer specifies the MAC address and frame format. Each frame will contain a destination and source MAC address. This address is 48 bits long.

PART

II

CH

3

The most significant bit of the MAC address is the *Individual/Group Address Bit (I/G Address Bit)*. If this bit is set to a zero, this is an individual address, which means that this frame is destined for a single station. This is also called *unicast* traffic. If the I/G Address Bit is set to 1, this is a group address meaning that the frame is destined for more than one station. There are two types of group addresses. Group addresses are either *functional addresses* or *broadcast addresses*. If all the bits of the MAC address are set to one, this is a broadcast address. If not, this is a functional or multicast address.

The second most significant bit of the MAC address is the *Universally or Locally Administered Address Bit (U/L Address Bit)*. If this bit is set to 0, the address is administered universally. The IEEE does this by assigning blocks of MAC addresses to the various Ethernet vendors. In this scheme, the first 24 bits of the MAC address are called the *Organizational Unique Identifier (OUI)*. OUIs are apportioned out to Ethernet vendors who then administer the last 24 bits to guarantee globally unique addresses. Individuals are not required to use the universally administered MAC address, also called the burned-in address. They locally administer the MAC address by setting the U/L Address Bit to 1. Locally administered MAC addresses must be unique.

Key Concept

MAC addresses must be unique for each station and support unicast, multicast, and broadcast traffic.

Carrier Sense and Collision Detection

Ethernet uses the CSMA/CD access method. CSMA/CD is best understood by breaking it down into its component parts:

- Carrier Sense
- Multiple Access
- Collision Detection

Carrier Sense means that the Ethernet stations monitor the Ethernet segment and don't transmit until they sense that no one else is transmitting. This is also called "listen before talk." This prevents one station from transmitting while another is already transmitting.

Multiple Access means that two or more stations share the same Ethernet segment. This is also called *shared media*. Shared media implies that on a 10Mb Ethernet segment with ten stations, all ten stations share the same 10Mb of bandwidth. This is also known as half-duplex operation. This is in contrast to full-duplex operation where two stations are connected point-to-point and are capable of using the entire bandwidth of the segment. Full-duplex operation also allows stations to transmit and receive at the same time. Chapter 6 discusses full-duplex operation in more detail.

In a half-duplex shared-media environment such as Ethernet, you have multiple stations competing for the same bandwidth. Even with Carrier Sense, two stations can transmit simultaneously. This will cause a collision on the Ethernet media, and both frames will be corrupted. The method used to determine that a collision has taken place is called *collision detection*. This means that the transmitting stations listen to the Ethernet segment for the frame that it just transmitted. If the frame was corrupted, the transmitting station will know this because the *Frame Check Sequence (FCS)* will be invalid. The station will continue to transmit for a specified period so that all the other stations on the segment detect that the frame is corrupted. This corruption of the frames is called a *collision*.

After a collision has occurred, the transmitting station will wait a random amount of time before retransmitting. This is called *random backoff*. If two stations are transmitting at the same time, detect a collision, and wait the same fixed amount of time before retransmitting, they will collide the next time they both try to transmit.

Key Concept

Ethernet is a CSMA/CD protocol supporting half- and full-duplex operation.

Fast Ethernet interfaces on the Cisco router support both half- and full-duplex operation. They also support auto-sensing of speed and duplex. Following is a sample router configuration of three Fast Ethernet interfaces—the first one is configured for 10Mb half-duplex operation, the second is configured for 100Mb full-duplex operation, and the third is configured for auto-sense of both speed and duplex:

```
interface FastEthernet0
  speed 10
  duplex half

interface FastEthernet1
  speed 100
  duplex full

interface FastEthernet2
  speed auto
  duplex auto
```

PART

II

CH

3

IEEE 802.3 MAC Frame and Address Format

Following is the IEEE 802.3 MAC frame format with the associated fields. The numbers within each field indicate the length of the field in octets or bytes. The IEEE 802.3 frame format is described in Figure 3.2.

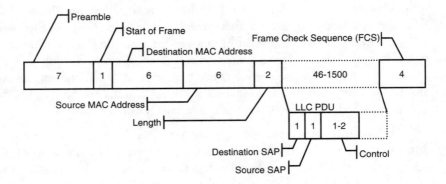

Figure 3.2
IEEE 802.3 frame format containing IEEE 802.2 LLC Protocol Data Unit (PDU).

The preamble field allows the hardware to establish the frame timing. The *Start of Frame (SOF)* is set to a bit pattern of 10101011 to delimit the start of the IEEE 802.3 frame. The destination and source MAC addresses follow the format described in Figure 3.3.

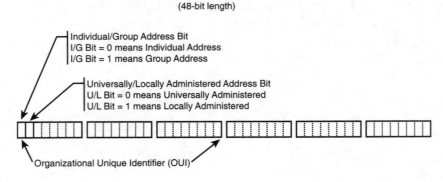

Figure 3.3
MAC address format including I/G Address Bit, U/L Address Bit, and OUI.

There is a minimum and maximum size for an Ethernet frame. The frame size starts at the first octet of the destination MAC address until the last octet of the FCS. The minimum frame size is 64 octets. If the frame is less than the minimum, padding is inserted after the last octet of data and before the FCS to bring the frame up to 64 octets. The maximum frame size is 1,518 octets.

The length field describes the size of the data after the length field and before the FCS. This is also called the transmission unit. There is a *Maximum Transmission Unit (MTU)* size of 1,500. This transmission unit also includes an IEEE 802.2 LLC *Protocol Data Unit (PDU)*.

Key Concept

The MTU for Ethernet is 1,500 octets. The minimum frame size is 64 octets, and the maximum frame size is 1,518 octets.

LLC provides an interface to the higher levels of the OSI/RM via a *Service Access Point (SAP)*. The SAP is a one-octet field used to direct the frame within the internal software of the station to the appropriate process or application. The LLC PDU contains a destination and source SAP and a one- or two-octet control field.

The FCS is a *Cyclic Redundancy Check (CRC)* to validate the integrity of the data transmitted.

Ethernet II Versus IEEE 802.3

The Ethernet Version II frame format is slightly different from the IEEE 802.3 frame format. The Ethernet Version II frame format is described in Figure 3.4.

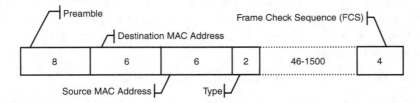

Figure 3.4
Ethernet Version II frame format.

With Ethernet Version II, there is no SOF field and the preamble is extended to eight octets. The IEEE 802.3 Length field becomes a type field to describe the protocol type of the frame. There is no LLC PDU.

The Cisco router supports four different frame types via the encapsulation command:

- ARPA for Ethernet Version II frames
- NOVELL-ETHER for IEEE 802.3 frames without an LLC PDU (default)
- SAP for IEEE 802.3 frames with an IEEE 802.2 LLC PDU
- *Subnet Access Protocol (SNAP)*, for IEEE 802.3 frames with an IEEE 802.2 LLC PDU and a SNAP header

The SNAP format is an extension of the IEEE 802.3 format to include a SNAP header after the LLC Header. The LLC header is specially encoded. The destination and source SAP are set to 0xAA, and the control field is one octet and set to 0x03. The SNAP header is five octets in length. The first three octets are set to 0 and the last two octets contain an EtherType that defines the appropriate protocol.

Key Concept

Ethernet allows multiple encapsulation types at the Data Link layer.

Following is a sample router configuration to set an Ethernet interface to SAP encapsulation and a Fast Ethernet interface to SNAP encapsulation:

```
interface Ethernet0
  encapsulation sap

interface FastEthernet0
  encapsulation snap
```

Gigabit Ethernet

Gigabit Ethernet is defined in the IEEE 802.3z extension to the IEEE 802.3 standard. The media speed is 1000Mb or 1Gb. It uses the same frame and MAC address formats as Ethernet. It operates in either half- or full-duplex mode. There is also an optional IEEE 802.3x flow control standard.

There are several different media types at the Physical layer:

- 1000BASE-LX using long-wave laser over single-mode or multimode fiber
- 1000BASE-SX using short-wave laser over multimode fiber
- 1000BASE-CX using balanced shielded 150-ohm copper cable
- 1000BASE-T using *Unshielded Twisted Pair (UTP)*

Gigabit Ethernet allows you to choose on a port-by-port basis what physical media type you will use via a *Gigabit Ethernet Interface Carrier (GBIC)*. There are different GBICs for each physical media type. GBICs plug directly into the router.

Key Concept

Gigabit Ethernet supports existing Ethernet frame formats and encapsulations. This means no changes to applications that already support Ethernet.

Limitations and Troubleshooting

The main limitation of CSMA/CD is collisions. Collisions occur more frequently as the utilization of the Ethernet segment increases. At very high levels of utilization, collisions become so bad as to affect the higher-level protocols. This will show up as applications timing out or as significant performance degradation. Attaching key servers and routers via a full-duplex connection to the network can alleviate this.

The most common problems tend to involve a mismatch of speed, duplex, or encapsulation type. An auto option on the speed and duplex commands allows the router to auto-sense the speed or duplex. It is best to check that both devices are negotiated to the appropriate speed and duplex. Some stations receive multiple encapsulation formats but only respond with a specific encapsulation. When using anything other than the default encapsulation type, be sure that all stations on the segment support the encapsulation that you are using.

Summary

Ethernet is a LAN architecture using the CSMA/CD access method. Two standards define Ethernet: Ethernet Version II (developed by DIX) and IEEE 802.3. Ethernet Version II corresponds to both layers 1 and 2 of the OSI/RM and a media speed of 10Mb. IEEE 802.3 corresponds to layer 1 and part of layer 2 of the OSI/RM and media speeds of 10Mb, 100Mb for Fast Ethernet, and 1000Mb for Gigabit Ethernet. IEEE 802.3 also defines different physical media types and generic interfaces to those physical media. MAC addresses uniquely define stations on the Ethernet segment. Bits in the MAC address define unicast, multicast, and broadcast traffic.

The CSMA/CD is the access method for the Ethernet physical media. Listening to the physical media before sending and then listening while sending to detect collisions characterize CSMA/CD. Ethernet also defines operation in a half-duplex shared-media environment and point-to-point full-duplex operation. Four different frame formats are allowed. They are specified in the router as ARPA, NOVELL-ETHER, SAP, and SNAP. Frames also have a 64-byte minimum and 1,518-byte maximum frame size. The MTU of Ethernet is 1,500 bytes. Gigabit Ethernet uses the existing frame formats from Ethernet and Fast Ethernet to allow for a clean migration path for users that need more bandwidth.

QUESTIONS AND ANSWERS:

1. What are the media speeds for Ethernet, Fast Ethernet, and Gigabit Ethernet?

    A: Ethernet media speed is 10Mb. Fast Ethernet media speed is 100Mb. Gigabit Ethernet media speed is 1,000Mb or 1Gb.

2. What are the Ethernet connector types on the router?

    A: ■ AUI
    ■ 10BASE-T for RJ-45 on 10Mb Ethernet
    ■ 100BASE-T for RJ-45 on Fast Ethernet
    ■ MII

3. Describe the difference between unicast, multicast, and broadcast traffic.

    A: Unicast traffic flows from a single source to a single destination MAC address. Multicast traffic flows from a single source MAC address to many destinations and uses a functional MAC address. Broadcast traffic is from a single source to all devices on the Ethernet segment. This is specified by a destination MAC address of all ones.

4. What field in the MAC address is used for universal administration?

    A: The *Organizational Unique Identifier (OUI)* field is the first 24 bits of the MAC address. OUIs are assigned to individual Ethernet adapter vendors. These vendors control the second half of the MAC address to make sure the total address is globally unique.

5. Describe the operation of a CSMA/CD network.

    A: Carrier Sense means that Ethernet stations listen to the Ethernet media to make sure that no other station is transmitting before they transmit. Multiple Access means that more than two stations share the same Ethernet media. This is also known as half-duplex operation or shared media. This differs from full-duplex operation on a point-to-point switched media. Carrier Detect means that the transmitting station monitors its own transmission to make sure that it can receive it without error. If an error occurs, that implies that another station was transmitting at the same time and collided with the first transmitting station.

6. What are the four different Ethernet encapsulation types?

    A: From the Cisco IPX encapsulation command they are ARPA, NOVELL-ETHER, SAP, and SNAP. ARPA corresponds to Ethernet Version II, NOVELL-ETHER corresponds to IEEE 802.3 without an LLC PDU, SAP corresponds to IEEE 802.3 with an IEEE 802.2 LLC PDU, and SNAP corresponds to an IEEE 802.3 frame with an IEEE 802.2 LLC PDU and an additional SNAP header.

7. How do these encapsulations differ?

    A: All three encapsulations start with destination and source MAC address fields. The Ethernet Version II or ARPA encapsulation then follows with a two-octet type field that specifies the upper-layer protocol. The NOVELL-ETHER and SAP encapsulations follow the destination and source MAC addresses with a two-octet length field. The SAP encapsulation adds an IEEE 802.2 LLC PDU. The SNAP encapsulation adds a SNAP header after the LLC PDU in IEEE 802.3 format. The destination and source SAP addresses in the LLC PDU are set to 0xAA, and there is a one-octet control field that is set to 0x03.

PRACTICE TEST

1. The CSMA/CD access method is defined by what IEEE standard?
    A. 802.1
    B. 802.2
    C. 802.3
    D. 802.4
    E. 802.5

Answer A is incorrect; 802.1 defines MAC Bridging. Answer B is incorrect; 802.2 defines LLC. **Answer C is correct; 802.3 defines the CSMA/CD access method.** Answer D is incorrect; 802.4 defines a token bus architecture. Answer E is incorrect; 802.5 defines a Token-Ring architecture.

2. IEEE 802.3 defines what portions of the OSI/RM?
    A. All of layer 1 and none of layer 2
    B. All of layer 1 and part of layer 2
    C. All of layer 1 and all of layer 2
    D. None of layer 1 and all of layer 2

Answer A is incorrect; this would be the OSI/RM Physical layer. **Answer B is correct; IEEE 802.3 defines all of layer 1 and part of layer 2 of the OSI/RM.** Answer C is incorrect; This is correct for Ethernet Version II but not for IEEE 802.3. Answer D is incorrect; this would be the Data Link layer of the OSI/RM.

3. IEEE 802.3 specifies what media speeds? (Choose all that apply.)

    A. 10Mb

    B. 16Mb

    C. 100Mb

    D. 155Mb

    E. 1,000Mb

Answer A is correct; 10Mb is an IEEE 802.3 media speed. Answer B is incorrect; 16Mb is an IEEE 802.5 media speed. **Answer C is correct; 100Mb is an IEEE 802.3 media speed for Fast Ethernet.** Answer D is incorrect; 155Mb or OC-3 is commonly used in ATM networks. **Answer E is correct; 1,000Mb is 1Gb is defined as an IEEE 802.3 media speed.**

4. Which traffic types are defined by the MAC address? (Choose all that apply.)

    A. Unicast

    B. Half-duplex

    C. Multicast

    D. Full-duplex

    E. Broadcast

Answer A is correct; I/G Bit equals zero defines unicast traffic. Answer B is incorrect; duplex is a Physical layer characteristic. **Answer C is correct; I/G Bit equals one and all bits not one define multicast traffic.** Answer D is incorrect; duplex is a Physical layer characteristic. **Answer E is correct; a MAC address of all ones defines broadcast traffic.**

5. Which statements apply to CSMA/CD half-duplex operation? (Choose all that apply.)

    A. Stations sense the media before transmission.

    B. Stations transmit while other stations are transmitting.

    C. Stations wait to transmit until other stations are not transmitting.

    D. Stations monitor the media for collisions.

    E. Stations retransmit after collisions at a fixed backoff time interval.

Answer A is correct; this is called carrier sense. Answer B is incorrect; this applies to full-duplex operation. **Answer C is correct; this is also part of carrier sense. Answer D is correct; this is collision detection.** Answer E is incorrect; if the backoff time is fixed in the network, collisions will recur. Random backoff times are used.

6. What is the MTU for Ethernet?

   A. 64

   B. 512

   C. 1,500

   D. 1,518

   E. 2,048

Answer A is incorrect; this is the minimum frame size. Answer B is incorrect; this is a valid transmission unit size but not the maximum. **Answer C is correct; the MTU for Ethernet is 1,500.** Answer D is incorrect; this is the maximum frame size. Answer E is incorrect; this values exceeds the maximum frame size.

7. The Ethernet Version II frame format contains which fields? (Choose all that apply.)

   A. preamble

   B. SOF

   C. destination/source MAC address

   D. length

   E. LLC PDU

   F. SNAP header

Answer A is correct; the preamble is a valid field. Answer B is incorrect; this only applies to IEEE 802.3. **Answer C is correct; the destination/source MAC addresses are required.** Answer D is incorrect; Ethernet Version II uses a type field instead of a length field. Answer E is incorrect; this is valid only for IEEE 802.3. Answer F is incorrect; this is valid only for the SNAP encapsulation type.

8. The IEEE 802.3 frame format contains which fields? (Choose all that apply.)

   A. preamble

   B. SOF

   C. destination/source MAC address

   D. length

   E. LLC PDU

   F. SNAP header

Answer A is correct; the preamble is a valid field. Answer B is correct; the SOF is a valid field. Answer C is correct; the destination/source MAC address are valid fields. Answer D is correct; IEEE 802.3 uses the length field. Answer E is correct; the LLC PDU is after the length field. Answer F is incorrect; this is valid only in the SNAP encapsulation type.

PART

II

CH

3

9. The SNAP encapsulation type contains which fields? (Choose all that apply.)
   A. preamble
   B. SOF
   C. destination/source MAC address
   D. length
   E. LLC PDU
   F. SNAP header

Answer A is correct; the preamble is a valid field. Answer B is correct; the SOF is a valid field. Answer C is correct; the destination/source MAC address are valid fields. Answer D is correct; IEEE 802.3 uses the length field. Answer E is correct; the LLC PDU is after the length field. Answer F is correct; this is valid only in the SNAP encapsulation type.

10. Which of the following statements are true about Gigabit Ethernet? (Choose all that apply.)
    A. Supports 1,000Mb media speed
    B. Allows for an optional IEEE 802.3x flow control
    C. Supports half- and full-duplex operation
    D. Uses extended super frame format
    E. Supports long-wave laser over single- and multimode fiber

Answer A is correct; 1,000Mb is 1Gb. Answer B is correct; this is not true for Fast Ethernet. Answer C is correct; Gigabit Ethernet supports half- and full-duplex operation. Answer D is incorrect; Gigabit Ethernet uses existing Ethernet frame formats.

CHAPTER

4

Token-Ring and FDDI

WHILE YOU READ

1. What are the main differences between Ethernet and Token-Ring/FDDI?

2. At what speeds do Token-Ring and FDDI operate?

3. What kinds of applications benefit most from token-based networks?

4. In a Token-Ring environment, how can a workstation be given a greater share of the network bandwidth?

5. What are the three major fault-management techniques employed by Token-Ring?

6. What network topology does a Token-Ring network employ?

7. In an FDDI environment, how can certain types of network traffic be given a greater share of the network bandwidth?

8. What network topology does an FDDI network employ?

9. What is the most significant aspect of FDDI?

10. What is the difference between a DAS and a SAS?

Lab

SEE
APPENDIX **F**

Unlike Ethernet, covered in Chapter 3, Token-Ring and *Fiber Distributed Data Interface (FDDI)* network stations rely on the possession of a token to transmit data on the media. Unless the workstation acquires the token as it circles the ring, it may not transmit any data. The highly rigid token-based protocols ensure that there will be no Ethernet-style collisions or bandwidth-hogging workstations. It virtually guarantees that every station will be given an equal chance to transmit data.

The term used for this kind of media access is known as *deterministic*, meaning that it is possible to determine the amount of time that will pass before a workstation will be able to transmit. Token-based networks also have priority systems and fault-management systems. These features taken together make token-based networks ideal for applications that are sensitive to delays and which require robust network operation.

Key Concept

Token-based networks require workstations to acquire the token before transmitting data and to employ systems for prioritizing traffic recovering from errors.

Because the underlying concepts of Token-Ring and Fiber Distributed Data Interface (FDDI) are similar, both technologies are covered in this chapter.

Token-Ring

The term *Token-Ring* describes both the original IBM specification and the subsequent IEEE 802.5 specification. The major difference is that 802.5 does not specify a physical topology, whereas IBM's Token-Ring specifies a star topology with all workstations connected to a multistation access unit (MAU). Token-Ring is often referred to as a *physical star* and a *logical ring*. Older MAUs were simply electromechanical devices without even a power cord. MAUs are linked together with patch cables, whereas workstations are attached to the MAUs with lobe cables. Newer Token-Ring implementations use twisted-pair cables connected to devices that are more intelligent. These include active MAUs and Token-Ring switches that have a similar function to the Ethernet switches covered in Chapter 6, "LAN Switching." All stations on the ring must run at either 4Mbps or 16Mbps.

Key Concept

Token-Ring and IEEE 802.5 operate in a physical star, but a logical ring runs at either 4Mbps or 16Mbps.

Token-Ring Operation

Regardless of physical connectivity or ring speed, all workstations in a Token-Ring LAN form a logical ring that forms a single closed loop. Around this ring, a small frame called a *token* is sequentially passed from workstation to workstation. To send data, a workstation must seize or acquire the token and flip one bit in the header, transforming it into a start-of-frame delimiter. Between this new header and the end-of-frame delimiter, it places the data to be transmitted. The completed *information frame* is then put out onto the wire and received only by the next station on the ring, also known as a *downstream neighbor.*

Each station is responsible for transmitting the frame to its downstream neighbor. This process continues until the frame gets to its destination. To indicate that it has received the frame, the destination host sets the A and C bits of the *frame status field* to 1 and sends the entire frame to its own downstream neighbor. When the original workstation receives the frame, it interprets the A and C bits to mean that the destination Acknowledged the frame as being addressed to its MAC address, and that it Copied the data to its buffers to be processed by the upper-layer protocols (including TCP, IPX, and NetBIOS). The sending station then places a new token on the ring, and the next station that has data to send repeats the entire process.

Key Concept

After seizing the token, a workstation creates a data frame that is passed from station to station around the ring until it reaches its destination. The destination marks the frame as copied, and it is then passed from station to station around the rest of the ring until it reaches the original source, which places another token on the ring.

An optional parameter may be configured on Token-Ring networks, which allows a token to be released by the sending workstation as soon as it has sent its data frame, rather than waiting for the frame to return from the destination. This is known as *early release.*

Frame Format

Figure 4.1 shows the token frame format and the data frame format.

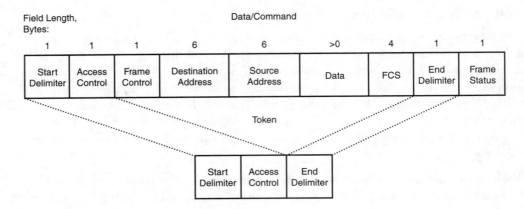

Figure 4.1
Token-Ring frame formats of the token frame and data/command frame.

Following is a summary of the fields shown in Figure 4.1:

- Start Delimiter—Signals the beginning of a token or data frame using patterns that are not allowed within the rest of the frame.
- Access Control—The attributes of the access control fields determine the type of access a Token-Ring device has to the media to transmit data.
  - Priority field (most significant three bits)—Allows the administrator to give certain stations to preempt other devices and have more frequent access to the media.
  - Reservation field (least significant three bits)—Used by stations configured with high priority to acquire the token after the priority has been raised.
  - Token bit—Distinguishes between a token frame and a data frame.
  - Monitor bit—Used by the active monitor to determine whether the frame is circling endlessly.
- Frame Control—Indicates whether the frame contains data or control information.
- Destination/Source Address—Contains the 6-byte MAC address of the source and destination workstations.
- Data—The maximum time a station can hold a frame determines the data field length.
- Frame Check Sequence (FCS)—Like Ethernet, the source and destination calculate this value to determine whether an error exists in the frame. Frames with errors are discarded.

- End Delimiter—Signals the end of the frame, as well as indications of damaged frames and whether the frame is the last of a logical sequence of frames.

- Frame Status—The most signification function is the A and C bits (*address-recognized indicator* and *frame-copied indicator* bits, respectively).

Token-Ring Fault-Management Mechanisms

Several mechanisms exist within the Token-Ring design to detect and correct network problems. Token-Ring's star topology contributes to its reliability. Because active MAUs (and Token-Ring switches) can see all data in a Token-Ring network, they can be programmed to check for problems and remove workstations from the ring if necessary.

Token-Ring attempts to correct certain other problems by using an algorithm known as *beaconing*. The most common reason for a workstation to send beacon frames is when it detects a serious problem, such as a cable break. It sends a beacon frame that identifies the station reporting the problem as well as its *nearest upstream neighbor (NAUN)*. Workstations that receive the beacon frame attempt to reconfigure the network around the problem, a process known as *auto reconfiguration*. An active MAU or Token-Ring switch can listen to the beacon and accomplish this through electrical reconfiguration.

PART

II

CH

4

Key Concept

A ring will beacon when a serious problem has been detected, such as a break in the cable.

The most sophisticated fault-management mechanism employs one workstation as the *active monitor*. Each workstation that enters the ring attempts to become the active monitor. The most prominent ring-management function of the active monitor is to remove continuously circulating frames from the ring. For example, if a station leaves the ring before removing its data frame from the ring and sends out a token, the data would circle endlessly and the ring would cease to operate. In this situation, the active monitor will remove the frame and place a new token on the ring.

Key Concept

The active monitor is responsible for removing orphaned data frames and placing a new token on the ring.

Priority Scheme

The Token-Ring specification provides administrators the option to configure certain stations to use the network more often than they ordinarily would. Two fields of a Token-Ring frame control priority: the *priority field* and *reservation field*, both within the access control byte (refer to Figure 4.1). Only stations with a priority equal to or higher than the priority field shown in the token are able to acquire the token and send data. When these data frames have been put onto the network, only stations with a priority equal to or higher than the priority field shown in the data frame are able to reserve the token for the next pass around the ring. When the token is put back on the ring, it is the responsibility of the high-priority station to either reinstate the previous priority level or leave it unchanged.

Key Concept

A workstation can be configured to access the network more often through the use of the priority and reservation fields within the token.

Fiber Distributed Data Interface

In the mid-1980s, the ANSI X3T9.5 standards committee released the Fiber Distributed Data Interface (FDDI) standard. Although it never gained the widespread following of Ethernet and Token-Ring, it has performance and reliability features that made it ideal as a backbone technology at that time. High-performance workstations also benefited from its unique features. Most recently, however, it was announced that FDDI chips would no longer be manufactured.

Like Ethernet and Token-Ring, the FDDI specification defines the Physical layer and media-access portion of the OSI/RM. However, at a time when Ethernet and Token-Ring were still providing only 10Mbps and 16Mbps of bandwidth, the FDDI standard specifies 100Mbps. Like Token-Ring, it employs a token-passing scheme but uses a second ring for redundancy. In addition, as the name implies, it relies on fiber-optic cables, which are nearly impervious to interference and offer increased security because they cannot be tapped. Some of the 100Mbps Ethernet standard was later built on the signaling specifications of FDDI (and *CDDI*, its copper cousin).

Key Concept

FDDI is a token-based network that uses dual, 100Mbps counterrotating rings for redundancy.

FDDI Specifications

The FDDI specification is composed of four areas, explained here along with their standard abbreviation, and beginning with the lowest layer. Figure 4.2 shows the relationship between the FDDI specifications and OSI Reference Model.

- Physical Layer Medium (PMD)—Specifies the characteristics of the cable, including connectors, power levels, bit error rates, and all optical components.

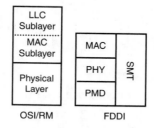

Figure 4.2
FDDI specifications and the OSI reference model.

- Physical Layer Protocol (PHY)—Specifies framing, data coding and decoding, and timing.
- Media Access Control (MAC)—Specifies how the media is accessed, including addressing, token passing, frame format, CRC checking, and other error-detection and recovery procedures.
- Station Management (SMT)—Specifies the station configuration, including station initialization, insertion, and removal; ring control and configuration; error detection and recovery; and statistics gathering.

Physical Features

The most significant feature of FDDI is its dual rings. Each ring carries traffic in opposite directions between end stations. The *primary ring* carries the data traffic, whereas the *secondary ring* is used for redundancy. FDDI stations are classified by how they connect to the rings. Class A or dual-attachment stations (DAS) connect to both rings. Class B or single-attachment stations (SAS) connect to a concentrator, which itself is a DAS. Typically, PCs connect to a concentrator so that the ring does not go down when the PC is frequently rebooted. Figure 4.3 shows the essential elements of an FDDI ring.

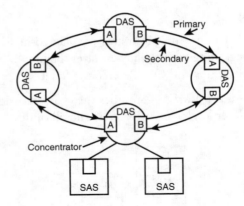

Figure 4.3
FDDI DAS, SAS, concentrator, and counterrotating rings.

 Key Concept

FDDI stations are either attached to both rings (DAS) or attached to a concentrator (SAS).

FDDI Fault-Management Features

FDDI's counterrotating rings are its most important fault-management feature. In the event of failure, such as a disconnected cable or a DAS hardware failure, the dual rings automatically wrap to form a single ring. In Figure 4.4, a DAS has failed, but ring operation is maintained. A failed cable would produce a similar recovery situation.

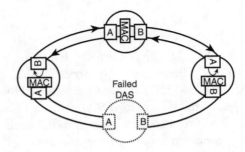

Figure 4.4
FDDI recovery from a failed DAS.

Key Concept

When a failure is detected in an FDDI network, the stations on each side of the failure "wrap" the network into one ring by using the secondary ring.

Larger networks face a much larger problem in the failure of more than one station or cable. In this case, the ring is separated into two partitions that are independent of each other. To avoid this situation, *optical bypass switches* may be used. If an interface that is connected to a bypass switch fails or shuts down, the bypass switch activates automatically and allows the light signal to pass directly through it, bypassing the failed interface completely.

Bandwidth Features

Like Token-Ring, FDDI's SMT specification defines a prioritization scheme. Traffic is classified as either synchronous or asynchronous. Part of the 100Mbps bandwidth may be dedicated to synchronous traffic and used for applications that require continuous data transmission such as voice and video. Asynchronous traffic consumes the remaining bandwidth and uses an eight-level priority scheme to determine bandwidth access.

Frame Format

The formats of the token and data frame are similar to Token-Ring. Figure 4.5 shows the token frame format and the data frame format.

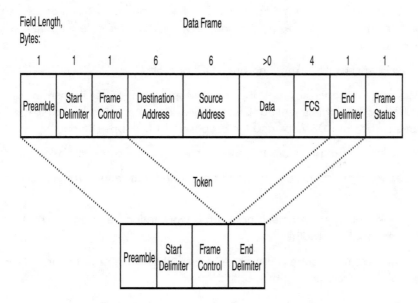

Figure 4.5
FDDI frame formats of the token frame and data frame.

Following is a summary of the fields shown in Figure 4.5:

- Preamble—Alerts the station about an upcoming token or data frame.
- Start Delimiter—Signals the beginning of a token or data frame using patterns that are not allowed within the rest of the frame.
- Frame Control—Indicates whether the frame contains data or control information, the length of the address fields, and whether the frame contains synchronous or asynchronous data.
- Destination/Source Address—Contains the 6-byte MAC address of the source and destination workstations.
- Data—Payload for an upper-layer protocol, or control information.
- Frame Check Sequence (FCS)—Like Ethernet and Token-Ring, the source and destination calculate this value to determine whether an error exists in the frame. Frames with errors are discarded.
- End Delimiter—Signals the end of the frame by using nondata symbols.
- Frame Status—The most signification function is the A and C bits (address-recognized indicator and frame-copied indicator, respectively).

QUESTIONS AND ANSWERS

1. What are the main differences between Ethernet and Token-Ring/FDDI?

    A: CSMA/CD governs media access in Ethernet and possession of a token governs media access in Token-Ring and FDDI. The result is deterministic media access.

2. At what speeds do Token-Ring and FDDI operate?

    A: Token-Ring operates at 4Mbps or 16Mbps, whereas FDDI operates at 100Mbps. (As of this writing, Cisco devices do not support higher Token-Ring speeds such as 100Mbps and the proposed 1,000Mbps standard).

3. What kinds of applications benefit most from token-based networks?

    A: Applications that are sensitive to delays and that require robust network operation.

4. In a Token-Ring environment, how can a workstation be given a greater share of the network bandwidth?

    A: This is done through a priority scheme that uses the priority and reservation bits of the access control byte of the frame.

5.   What are the three major fault-management techniques employed by Token-Ring?

     A: Star topology, beaconing, and active monitor.

6.   What network topology does a Token-Ring network employ?

     A: Physical star and logical ring.

7.   In an FDDI environment, how can certain types of network traffic be given a greater share of the network bandwidth?

     A: This is done through a priority scheme that defines traffic as either synchronous (that is, voice and video) or asynchronous.

8.   What network topology does an FDDI network employ?

     A: Physical star and logical ring.

9.   What is the most significant aspect of FDDI?

     A: Counterrotating rings that provide redundancy through "wrapping" around faults.

10. What is the difference between a DAS and a SAS?

     A: A DAS is connected to both rings; a SAS is connected to a concentrator.

PART

II

CH

4

PRACTICE TEST

1. To transmit data on a token-based network, a station must always possess a token.
    A. True
    B. False

Answer A (True) is correct. There is no other way for a workstation to transmit on a token-based network.

2. Which topology is specified in the IEEE 802.5 standard?
    A. Star
    B. Bus
    C. Hub-and-spoke
    D. None of the above

Answers A, B, and C are incorrect because they are not part of the 802.5 standard.
Answer D is correct because the IEEE 802.5 standard does not technically specify any topology.

3. Which Token-Ring entity performs ring maintenance functions such as removing circulating frames from the ring?

    A. Ring error monitor

    B. Ring parameter monitor

    C. Active monitor

    D. Standby monitor

    E. Configuration server

Answer C is correct. None of the other entities exists, except the standby monitor.

4. In a Token-Ring environment, which of the following statements are false?

    A. The destination station is responsible for removing any frames it receives from the ring.

    B. The ring monitor is responsible for removing all frames from the ring.

    C. The ring broadcast monitor is responsible for removing all broadcast frames from the ring.

    D. The source station is responsible for removing any frames it puts on the ring.

Answer A is correct. The destination merely changes two bits and puts the frame back on the network. Answer B is correct. There is no such thing as a ring monitor. Answer C is correct. There is no such thing as a broadcast monitor. Answer D is incorrect. This is the responsibility of the source station.

5. Which statements are true about FDDI bridging?

    A. In a translational FDDI bridge, an Ethernet's IP address is translated into an FDDI address.

    B. In a translational FDDI bridge, an Ethernet's MAC address is translated into an FDDI address.

    C. In an FDDI encapsulating bridge, an Ethernet frame is packaged into an FDDI frame.

    D. In an FDDI encapsulating bridge, an Ethernet frame is translated into an FDDI frame.

    E. An FDDI translational bridge only works with nonroutable protocols such as MOP and LAT.

Answer A is incorrect because IP is a layer-3 protocol and FDDI is a layer-2 protocol. **Answers B, C, and E are correct.** Answer D is incorrect because there is no translation.

6. You perform a show interface tokenring 0 and notice it is beaconing. Which of the following are not possible reasons?

    A. The router is configured for a different ring.

    B. A station is configured for early release.

    C. Another computer on the ring has the same MAC address.

    D. The router is configured for a different ring speed.

Answers A and C are correct (they are not possible reasons) because these options might cause bridging problems. Answer B is correct because it would have no effect. Answer D is incorrect (it is a possible reason) because beaconing is a layer-1 condition.

  7. Which ANSI standard defines FDDI?

    A. X.12

    B. X3T5.9

    C. XT39.5

    D. X3T9.5

Answer D is correct. Answers A, B, and C are incorrect because they don't define FDDI.

  8. An FDDI DAS operates at 100Mbps in half-duplex mode and 200Mbps in full-duplex mode.

    A. True

    B. False

Answer B is correct because FDDI operates only at 100Mbps; duplex modes are not defined.

  9. Which FDDI specification is responsible for framing, coding/decoding, and timing?

    A. PMD

    B. MAC

    C. PHY

    D. SMT

    E. PAS

Answer A incorrect because PMD defines cables, power, and optical components. Answer B is incorrect because MAC defines media access. **Answer C is correct.** Answer D is incorrect because SMT defines station-management functions. Answer E is incorrect because this is not part of the FDDI specification.

  10. Which of the following FDDI devices are connected to both rings?

    A. SAS

    B. DAS

    C. Concentrator

    D. MAS

Answer A is incorrect because single-attached stations (SAS) are only connected to a concentrator. **Answers B and C are correct because dual-attached stations (DAS) and concentrators are connected to both rings.** Answer D is incorrect because MAS is not part of the FDDI specification.

11. Under normal circumstances in an FDDI environment, which rings carry user traffic?

    A. The first one to activate

    B. Primary

    C. Secondary

    D. Options A and B

    E. Options B and C

    F. Options A, B, and C

Answer B is correct. Answer C is incorrect because the secondary ring carries user traffic only when the ring is wrapped.

12. When a failure occurs in an FDDI network, wrapping the ring is the responsibility of which FDDI specification?

    A. PHY

    B. MAC

    C. PMD

    D. SMT

    E. WRP

Answer A is incorrect because PHY defines framing, coding, and timing. **Answer B is correct.** Answer C is incorrect because PMD defines cables, power, and optical components. Answer D is incorrect because SMT defines station-management functions. Answer E is incorrect because this is not part of the FDDI specification.

LANE—LAN Emulation

WHILE YOU READ

1. Which ATM PVC is used for signaling?

2. Identify the virtual path identifier in the following ATM PVC: ATM PVC 15 0 6.

3. Identify the VCI in ATM PVC 4 0 4.

4. Which ATM PVC is used to obtain configuration and status information from the ATM switch?

5. What is the MTU size for an emulated Ethernet LAN?

6. Which LAN medium isn't supported in LANE?

7. LANE functions at which layer of the OSI model?

8. If a company has a VLAN A located in Los Angeles and a VLAN A also located in Detroit joined across a LANE network, what characteristics do they share?

9. Which protocols are permitted through an ATM LANE network?

SEE
APPENDIX **F**

LANE is a protocol that operates at layer 2 of the OSI model (Data Link layer) and was designed to connect local area networks together across an ATM network. LANE maps ATM (NSAP) addresses to MAC addresses. NSAP addresses are 20 bytes long and are used on private ATM networks (external ATM networks use ITU-T standard E.164 addresses). The NSAP is the ATM address defined for the ATM interface.

LAN Emulation (LANE) is the method of forwarding Data Link traffic over ATM. LANE extends existing LANs over a high-speed ATM backbone. LANE is multiprotocol. The medium is transparent, so any LAN protocol can transverse the ATM network. Traditional LAN applications can operate without any knowledge of the ATM network regardless of geographical location of the physical LAN media. The LAN devices will communicate as if they were on an actual local area network. Basically, an ATM interface looks like another LAN network interface with LANE.

Emulated LANs (ELANs) are the wide-area links that are used to connect LANs. LANE creates a separate ELAN for every VLAN that is created. In a LANE network, the VLANs that are connected across an ELAN form one IP subnet and a single broadcast domain. For example, a company in Chicago can have users on the same IP subnet and broadcast domain as users in New York on an ATM LANE network. Both locations will receive broadcast traffic as if they were attached to the same Ethernet or Token-Ring switch. LAN broadcasts are emulated as ATM multicasts.

LANE is supported for Ethernet IEEE 802.3 and Token-Ring IEEE 802.5, but there is no support for FDDI. FDDI packets must be mapped or bridged to Ethernet or Token-Ring ELANs. LANE can be implemented on directly attached ATM hosts, on layer-2 devices (switches), and layer-3 devices (routers). LANE hides the ATM network from the LAN components. LANE doesn't emulate every particular Physical/Data Link characteristic. For example, it does not support CSMA/CD for Ethernet or token passing for Token-Ring. LANE defines the MTU of the media that it emulates, so better performance is given to classical IP.

LANE Components

To facilitate communications, several functions must take place. If desired, a device can perform more than one component's function. Four different types of devices are specified to accomplish these tasks:

- LEC—LAN Emulation Client
- LECS—LAN Emulation Configuration Server
- LES—LAN Emulation Server
- BUS—Broadcast and Unknown Server

For an overview of the different LANE components and connections, see Figure 5.1.

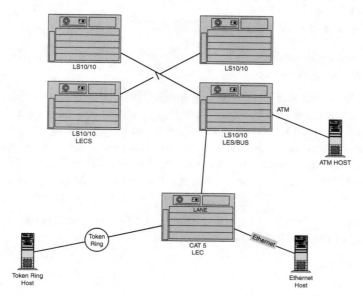

Figure 5.1
LANE components and connections.

The *LAN Emulation Client (LEC)* is a LANE end station where the LANE protocols run. Most commonly this is implemented in a Catalyst LANE module that is optimized for that purpose. The LEC is the interface that performs address resolution requests between ATM devices and non-ATM devices. The LANE client connects directly to the ATM switch, such as a Cisco LS1010. LANE uses a *LAN Emulation User-to-Network Interface (LUNI)* to communicate with LANE services or between LECs.

Key Concept

LANE clients are implemented in workstations, servers, ATM switches, routers, and ATM LAN switches.

The *LAN Emulation Configuration Server (LECS)* provides configuration services in the LANE environment. There is only one LECS per administrative domain. When the LECS receives a request from a LEC (LE_CONFIGURE_REQUEST), it responds with the following information (LE_CONFIGURE_RESPONSE):

- ATM address of LES
- ELAN name and assignment
- ELAN type and maximum frame size

The *LAN Emulation Server (LES)* is the central point of address and ELAN membership information for the LANE network.

First, it maintains a database of address mappings. The mappings it maintains are LEC ATM addresses and corresponding MAC addresses. Address resolution is supplied by the LES to an end station (LEC) that knows the MAC address of the device it wants to contact but does not know the ATM address. The service uses LE_ARP (LAN Emulation ARP). LE_ARP works similar to IP ARP. The difference is that IP ARP resolves IP (layer-3) addresses to MAC (layer-2) addresses, whereas LE_ARP resolves MAC to ATM addresses, which are both at layer 2.

Second, it maintains a list of all ELAN members. A LEC joins an ELAN by sending an LE_JOIN_REQUEST to the LES. This message contains

- ATM address
- ELAN name
- MAC address
- Maximum frame size

Most of the information in the LE_JOIN_REQUEST was obtained from the LECS. The LES then responds with an LE_JOIN_RESPONSE and adds the LEC to the Control Distribute VCC (see the section "Virtual Connection Types for LANE," later in this chapter, to learn more about the process).

The *Broadcast and Unknown Server (BUS)* is used when a LEC wants to send a broadcast or multicast to an unknown ATM address. This is similar to IP Broadcast addresses and IP Multicasting in an IP world, where end stations share an address for receiving traffic destined for a group of devices such as setup and status messages. The BUS handles sending data to multiple locations, thus emulating the effect of broadcasts and multicasts. In a LANE environment, the LES and BUS functions are typically implemented on one unit, referred to as the LES/BUS. There is only one active BUS per ELAN.

Virtual Connection Types for LANE

Virtual Circuit Connections (VCCs) provide communication paths from LEC to LEC and between LANE servers (LECS, LES, and BUS). Two types of VCCs are used for LANE communications: Control VCCs and Data VCCs. The LEC maintains Control and Data

VCCs separately. The Control VCCs are for control traffic and the Data VCCs are for user traffic. The number by each VCC corresponds to Figure 5.2.

Control VCCs

1. Configure Direct VCC—Bidirectional between LEC and LECS
2. Control Direct VCC—Bidirectional point-to-point between LEC and LES
3. Control Distribute VCC—Unidirectional point-to-multipoint between LEC and LES

Data VCCs

4. Multicast Send VCC—Bidirectional point-to-point between LEC and BUS
5. Multicast Forward VCC—Unidirectional point-to-multipoint between LEC and BUS
6. Data Direct VCC—LEC to LEC for data transfer between end stations

Figure 5.2 shows the different types of VCCs. The only VCC between clients is the Data Direct VCC.

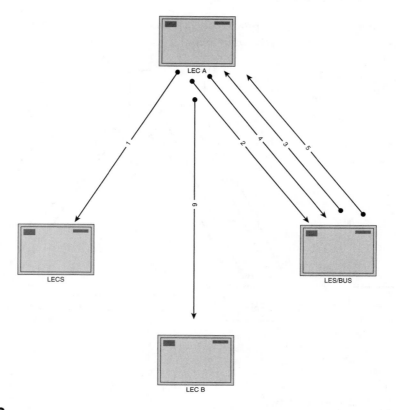

PART

II

CH

5

Figure 5.2
Virtual Circuit Connections (VCCs; compare the diagram with the numbered Control and Data VCCs).

LANE Communications

There are two types of communication in a LANE environment: LEC setup and LEC communication. Each LEC must be established in the ELAN before it can communicate in a normal manner.

LEC Setup

LANE setup has four major stages:

1. Initialization—The LEC contacts the LECS to determine the LES.
2. Registration—The LEC registers its MAC address and ATM address with its LECS.
3. Address resolution—The LEC requests the ATM address for a specified MAC address.
4. Data forwarding—When the LEC has the ATM address for the specified destination, data is carried from the source to the destination.

Figure 5.3 shows the step-by-step process of the LEC setup process. It will also help you understand the role of each LANE component.

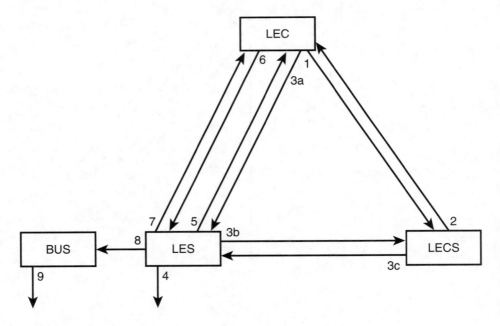

Figure 5.3
LEC setup process (logical view).

1. LEC contacts LECS for ELAN membership information (`LE_CONFIGURE_REQUEST`) using a Configure Direct VCC.
2. LECS responds to the LEC (`LE_CONFIGURE_RESPONSE`) with the ELAN configuration information and LES ATM address.
3. LEC attempts to join ELAN:
    a. LEC requests to join the ELAN from the LES (LE_JOIN_REQUEST).
    b. (Optional) LES checks with LECS whether to let the LEC join.
    c. (Optional) LECS responds.
4. LES adds the LEC to its Control Distribute VCC.
5. LES responds to the LEC confirming ELAN membership (`LE_JOIN_RESPONSE`).
6. LEC sends an `LE_ARP` to the LES for the ATM address of the BUS.
7. LES responds with the ATM address of the BUS.
8. LEC requests a Multicast Send VCC to be established with the BUS.
9. BUS adds LEC address to Multicast Send VCC.

At this point, the LEC is ready to operate normally in the ELAN. Figure 5.4 shows how the components might be physically implemented.

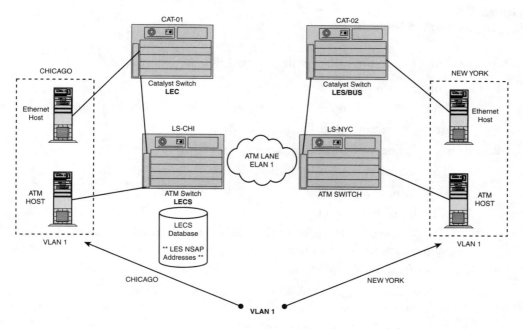

Figure 5.4
An example of the LANE communication environment.

LEC Communication

When the LEC is established in the ELAN, it can communicate with other members of the ELAN. Figure 5.5 shows this process.

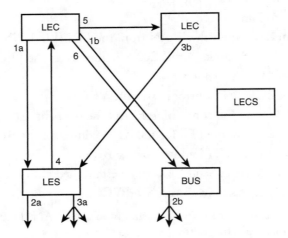

Figure 5.5
LEC communication (logical view).

When a LEC needs to communicate with another LEC, the following is the process:

1. Communication is initiated:
    a. An LE_ARP is sent to the LES requesting the destination's ATM address.
    b. At the same time, the data is sent to the BUS.
2. The next steps happen at the same time:
    a. The LES looks in its ARP database to find the appropriate address.
        i. If found, go to 4.
        ii. If not found, go to 3.
    b. The BUS sends the data out to all LECs via Multicast Forward VCC (this speeds communication but uses more bandwidth).
3. New address found (if needed; see step 2).
    a. LES sends out LE_ARP to all LECs via Control Distribute VCC to find the appropriate address.
    b. Destination LEC responds to LE_ARP.

4. LES sends the destination ATM address to the initiating LEC.

5. A Data Direct VCC is set up between the two LECs.

6. The initiating LEC sends a flush message to the BUS so it stops forwarding data to the other LECs.

Notice how the LECS is uninvolved with the LEC communication process; its job is to maintain and distribute ELAN configuration information.

Configurations

Following are some sample configurations for the LANE components and a diagram explaining connections and status inquiries. These are the required parameters to set up a basic LANE network with the LEC, LES/BUS, and LECS. Refer to Figure 5.6 for the diagram.

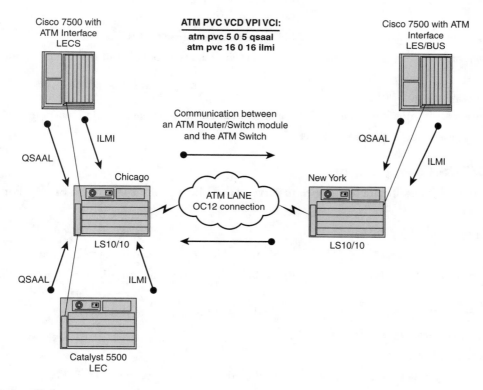

Figure 5.6
LEC, LES/BUS, and LECS configuration.

LEC Configuration

As stated earlier in the chapter, a LEC is typically a workstation, server, ATM switch, router, or ATM LAN switch. In a Catalyst switch, there is a special LANE module, which can be accessed and configured as follows. Each LANE component must have two PVCs defined for signaling and ILMI. Signaling is used for connection setup and termination. ILMI is used for configuration and status information from the ATM switch.

`Session #`	The # represents the ATM module in the Catalyst switch.
Interface ATM 3/0/0	The following command defines a PVC with a Virtual Circuit Descriptor (VCD) of 5, Virtual Path Identifier (VPI) of 0, and a Virtual Channel Identifier (VCI) of 5. Each is defined, respectively, following the command.
`atm pvc 5 0 5 qsaal`	Signaling for connections to remote ATM addresses
`atm pvc 16 0 16 ilmi`	Enables configuration and status information from the switch
`lane config cisco`	Binds the LECS database to this interface
`lane auto-config-atm-address`	Allows the automatic computation of NSAP addresses to be used for all subinterfaces
Interface ATM 3/0/0.1	
`lane client ethernet elan1`	Enables this interface to support the LEC function
`ip address 10.10.5.1 255.255.255.0`	

LES/BUS Configuration

It is normal to configure one device to serve as the LES and the BUS for an ELAN. For example,

Interface ATM 3/0/0	
`atm pvc 5 0 5 qsaal`	Signaling for connections to remote ATM addresses
`atm pvc 16 0 16 ilmi`	Enables configuration and status information from the switch
`lane config cisco`	Binds the LECS database to this interface
`lane auto-config-atm-address`	
Interface ATM 3/0/0.1	
`lane server-bus ethernet elan1`	Enables this interface to support LES/BUS
`ip address xxxxxxxxxxxxx`	

LECS Configuration Example

Here's an example of how to configure the LECS:

`lane database cisco`	Defines the lane database that stores LES ATM addresses
`name elan1 server-atm address` `47.00918100000001000020000.001007800841.01`	NSAP address for the LES
`Interface ATM 3/0/0`	
`atm pvc 5 0 5 qsaal`	Signaling for connections to remote ATM addresses
`atm pvc 16 0 16 ilmi`	Enables configuration and status information from the switch
`lane config cisco`	Binds the LECS database, defined earlier, to this interface
`lane auto-config-atm-address`	

Obtain LES NSAP Address Configuration

Issue the `show lane default` command on the device defined as the LES on the LANE network to obtain the ATM address (NSAP) address for the LES. This address is necessary and should be configured in the LECS database. The last two digits of this address should be the subinterface number for the interface that is defined as the LES in hexadecimal. Following is an example of a `show lane default` command issued from the LES/BUS. Remember that you will add the LES NSAP address with the subinterface in hex to the LECS.

```
LES-ROUTER#sh lane default-atm-addresses
interface ATM0/0/0:
LANE Client:        47.00918100000002000020000.00905F6E0000.**
LANE Server:        47.00918100000002000020000.00905F6E0001.**
LANE Bus:           47.00918100000002000020000.00905F6E0002.**
LANE Config Server: 47.00918100000002000020000.00905F6E0003.00
note: ** is the subinterface number byte in hex
```

Simple Server Replication Protocol (SSRP)

Cisco has introduced a proprietary protocol called the Simple Server Replication Protocol for LANE. It enables the existence of multiple LECS on the network. SSRP is enabled for LECS by creating a list of LECS in each ATM Switch and delivering this information to the end stations. SSRP is enabled for the LES/BUS by configuring the LES ATM address for each ELAN with an index priority, which specifies the order of operation.

 Key Concept

For SSRP it is important that each LEC has the same list of LECS addresses in the same order.

The simplest method for assigning LECS addresses to end stations is to configure the LECS address into the switch and let ILMI deliver that address to the end station. We will define the two LECS addresses, giving each one a priority. This is done in a similar way for the LES/BUS. Both LES ATM addresses will be defined identically in the LECS for redundancy.

Key Concept

The primary and backup servers communicate with each other with the LNNI protocol. Only one LECS and one LES are active within the LANE network per domain.

Figure 5.7 explains the configuration required for SSRP. The `lane database cisco` configuration defines the LECS database called `cisco`. The `name` command defines the elan1 and the NSAP address of the LES with a index priority of 1. A second LES also is defined in the database with an index priority of 2. The first LES configuration will have the priority because its index is set to 1.

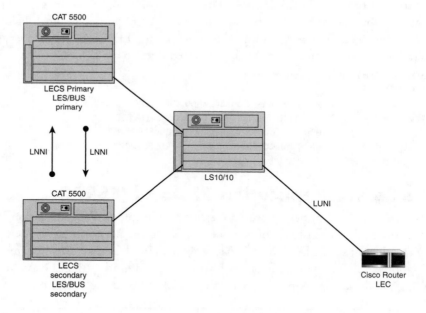

Figure 5.7
SSRP example.

The LECS could be configured for multiple LES/BUS components as follows:

```
LECS-ROUTER:config#lane database cisco
name elan1 server-atm add 47.009181000000010000020000.
001007800841.01 index1
(index 1 for SSRP priority)

name elan1 server-atm add 47.009181000000010000020000.
001007800876.04 index 2
(index 2 for SSRP priority)
```

SSRP confirmation for LES/BUS operation:

```
LECS-ROUTER#show lane database
LANE Config Server database table 'cisco'
bound to interface/s: ATM0/0/0
no default elan
elan 'cisco': un-restricted
server 47.009181000000010000020000.
001007800841.01  (prio 1) active
server 47.009181000000010000030000.
001014F3F841.C9 (prio 2) backup
```

The Cisco ATM Switch (LS10/10) can be configured for SSRP for multiple LECS components as follows:

```
ATM-Switch(config)#atm lecs-address-default
47.009181000000020000020000.00905F6E0003.00 1
ATM-Switch(config)#atm lecs-address-default
47.009181000000020000020000.00905F456373.00 2
```

Summary

ATM LANE was developed to connect Ethernet and Token-Ring LANs over an ATM core backbone. These connected LAN segments share the same IP subnet and broadcast/multicast domain as if they resided on the same physical switch. LANE emulates specific characteristics of local area networks, such as the maximum transfer unit (MTU). This makes classical IP a better choice for performance because of the reduced MTU size of LANs or emulated LANs compared to an ATM interface.

LANE operates at the Data Link layer of the OSI model. ATM uses the NSAP address for registration throughout the LANE network. The NSAP is a 20-byte address that is defined for ATM interfaces. During the process of LANE communication, when stations attempt connections, a MAC address to ATM address mapping process called LE_ARP is performed. The LES performs the address resolution or the LE_ARP for the LANE clients.

LANE is composed of four components:

- LEC—LANE Emulation Client
- LES—LANE Emulation Server
- BUS—Broadcast and Unknown Server
- LECS—LANE Emulation and Configuration Server

The communications from LEC to LEC and to LANE servers is provided by Virtual Circuit Connections (VCCs). There are two categories of VCCs: Data and Control. Each category has three types of VCCs.

The LECS and the LES are components that are supported by Simple Server Replication Protocol (SSRP). Only one LES or LECS device is active per domain, whereas the secondary resides in the background for redundancy. In LANE, the protocol used for ATM switch-to-switch communication is LANE NNI (LNNI). The communication from an end station to an ATM switch is LANE UNI (LUNI).

QUESTIONS AND ANSWERS

1. Which ATM PVC is used for signaling?

   A: The ATM PVC used for signaling is ATM PVC 2 0 5. The VCI defined as 5 is the key to this configuration and is defined for ATM signaling.

2. Identify the virtual path identifier in the following ATM PVC: ATM PVC 15 0 6.

   A: The VPI is 0 in the configuration. 15 is the virtual circuit, and 6 is the VCI.

3. Identify the VCI in ATM PVC 5 0 4.

   A: The VCI in the configuration is 4. 5 is the virtual circuit, and 0 is the VPI.

4. Which ATM PVC is used to obtain configuration and status information from the ATM switch?

   A: 16 is the correct answer. ILMI is received on this VCI, and the ATM switch sends the configuration and status information through ILMI.

5. What is the Maximum Transmission Unit (MTU) size for an emulated Ethernet LAN?

   A: The MTU size for an emulated LAN is the same MTU size of the actual LAN that it emulates.

6. Which LAN medium isn't supported in LANE?

    A: There is no concept for LANE for FDDI networks.

7. LANE functions at which layer of the OSI model?

    A: LANE operates at layer 2. The process involved is ATM address to MAC address mappings, which are Data Link processes.

8. If a company has a VLAN A located in Los Angeles and a VLAN A also located in Detroit joined across a LANE network, what characteristics do they share?

    A: LANE components will share the same broadcast domain and IP subnet but will have unique NSAPA addresses.

9. Which protocols are permitted through an ATM LANE network?

    A: ATM LANE is multiprotocol and permits all LAN protocols across the ATM cloud.

PRACTICE TEST

1. How many LESs are required per ELAN?
    A. One for each physical segment of the LANE network
    B. One LES per network
    C. Two: one as the primary and the other as the secondary

Answer A is incorrect; lane components are expanded beyond a physical segment of the network. **Answer B is correct; only one LES is required for the operation of a LANE network.** Answer C is incorrect; although two LESs can exist for the primary and secondary for the use of SSRP, only one is required to establish a operational LANE network.

2. When a device in a LANE network needs to know where a MAC address is located, it sends an LE_ARP to what device?
    A. LECS
    B. LES
    C. BUS

Answer A is incorrect; the LECS doesn't send an LE_ARP request. **Answer B is correct because the LEC sends an LE_ARP request to the LES for registration information.** Answer C is incorrect; the BUS responds to Broadcast and Unknown request and not to LE_ARP requests.

PART
II

CH
5

3. When frames for MAC Address and NSAPA are undefined, where are these frames forwarded?

   A. BUS
   B. LEC
   C. LECS

Answer A is correct because all broadcast and unknown inquiries are sent to the Broadcast and Unknown Server (BUS). Answer B is incorrect; the LEC is an end device on a LANE network. Answer C is incorrect; the LECS stores information about the LANE network within the database.

4. Which LANE device is the central point for an ATM network and stores ATM address information for other ATM devices?

   A. LES
   B. BUS
   C. LECS

Answer A is incorrect; the LES is the central point for all LECs but it is not the central point for the ATM LANE network. Answer B is incorrect; the BUS responds to Broadcast and Unknown request. **Answer C is correct because the LECS stores database information for the LANE network with information such as the NSAPA or ATM address of the LES.**

5. LE_ARP functions at which of the following OSI layers?

   A. Transport
   B. Data Link
   C. Network

Answer A is incorrect; LE_ARP is the mapping of ATM addresses to MAC addresses. **Answer B is correct; LE_ARP operates at the Data Link layer. Remember that LANE is a layer-2 protocol and the ATM address to MAC address mappings are done at layer 2.** Answer C is incorrect; LANE is a layer-2 protocol so the network layer has no concept in the LANE functions.

6. What type of information does the LECS store about the ELANS?

   A. NAME of the LES
   B. NSAPA address of the LES
   C. ATM PVC for ILMI

Answer A is incorrect; the name of the LES is not maintained, but the name of the ELAN is stored in the LECS database. **Answer B is correct; the LECS stores LANE database information that includes the NSAPA for the LES.** Answer C is incorrect; ATM ILMI information is required for the location of LECS, but this information is not stored in the LECS database.

7. Which device uses LE_ARP to find the ATM address to the LES?

  A. LEC

  B. LES

  C. LECS

Answer A is correct; the LEC uses the LE_ARP feature to find the LES for address resolution. Answer B is incorrect; the LES is the device that is being discovered. Answer C is incorrect; the LECS doesn't need to discover the MAC address of the LES.

8. Which LANE device handles LANE ARP requests and responses and provides address registration?

  A. Broadcast and Unknown Server

  B. LANE Server

  C. LANE Emulation Configuration Server

Answer A is incorrect; the BUS responds to broadcast and unknown requests. **Answer B is correct; the LANE Server handles all LE_ARP requests for address resolution for the LECs.** Answer C is incorrect; because the LECS is the central point of the LANE network, it does not respond to LANE ARP requests and responses nor does it provide address registration.

9. Which LANE devices are not supported by SSRP?

  A. LECS

  B. LEC

  C. LES

Answer A is incorrect; the LECS is supported by Cisco's Simple Server Replication Protocol (SSRP). Multiple LECSs are configured into the ATM Switch for redundancy with priorities that determine the priority of each. The LECS also provides redundancy for the configuration of LESs NSAP Address in multiple LECS databases. **Answer B is correct because SSRP is used for LANE redundancy and is configured for the LANE servers. The LEC doesn't require redundancy for the LANE network to continue to function.** Answer C is incorrect; the LES can be used for redundancy by supplying multiple LES NSAP addresses from different Lane Servers within the LECS database.

10. Select the protocol that is used for communication between primary and secondary SSRP components.

  A. LNNI

  B. LUNI

  C. PNNI

Answer A is correct; LNNI is the protocol used for communication between SSRP components and stands for LANE Network-to-Network Interface. Answer B is incorrect; LUNI is used for the connection between the LEC and the Lane Servers. Answer C is incorrect; PNNI is an advanced routing protocol used within ATM for private and public networks for ATM switch-to-switch connections.

Switching and Bridging

6 LAN Switching

7 Other Bridging Technologies

CHAPTER PREREQUISITE

Chapter 1, "General Network Overview," Chapter 2, "General Topic Overview," Chapter 3, "Ethernet," and Chapter 4, "Token-Ring and FDDI"

LAN Switching

WHILE YOU READ

1. What are the three main tasks of a transparent bridge?

2. What are the five STP port states?

3. How many instances of spanning tree can be present in a VLAN?

4. What are the two types of trunk encapsulation protocols?

5. How many VTP modes are there and what are they?

6. What are the requirements to implement EtherChannel?

7. What protocol is used to trunk FDDI VLANs?

8. What is the SAID value used for in a FDDI VLAN?

9. What does VTP Pruning do?

10. What does CGMP do that IGMP does not?

Lab

SEE
APPENDIX F

This chapter reviews a few of the basics related to switching and discusses different features and technologies that are used to enhance a switched network. In general, all the features discussed help to increase or preserve bandwidth. You should already be familiar with most of this material from past reading, training, certifications (such as CCNA), and experience. However, some of this material is presented here in greater detail than you might have learned before. This deeper understanding is necessary for the CCIE Written Exam. This chapter serves as a refresher for most of these topics.

Only basic configuration commands are discussed where appropriate. More complex configurations might be required of you for the lab exam. You might be asked to know or recognize these commands in the written test.

Switching, as you know, happens at layer 2 of the OSI model. So, this chapter focuses on layer-2 transparent bridging and technologies, such as Cisco's Catalyst switches and using routers as bridges.

Transparent Bridging

Like switches (discussed in Chapter 1, "General Network Overview"), a *transparent bridge* forwards frames based on a table of MAC addresses and outgoing ports on the device. Along the way, the packet is not altered in any way and is invisible (or transparent) to the sending and receiving devices. That is, a packet would never have the switch as its source or destination address. A transparent bridge is almost always Ethernet. A layer-2 switch, such as the Catalyst, is a transparent bridge. Therefore, in this chapter, the terms *transparent bridge* and *switch* are used interchangeably.

Key Concept

A transparent bridge and a switch are functionally the same.

A transparent bridge forwards, broadcasts, or filters incoming packets. For efficiency, a transparent bridge has three tasks:

- Learning—Passively entering the MAC addresses of all nodes on each segment (port) into its forwarding table.
- Forwarding—Sending a packet to the appropriate outgoing port or, if no outgoing port is known for the destination MAC address, broadcasting the packet out all ports (except the incoming port).
- Filtering—If more than one MAC address is learned for a single segment (port), packets between devices on that segment will be seen—and then dropped—by the switch (they do not need forwarding to a different port).

Note that the term *filtering* in context of a transparent bridge is different from filtering like an Access List. When a transparent bridge filters a frame, it does nothing with it, whereas Access Lists can selectively forward or drop, depending on the parameters you set.

Key Concept

The three tasks of a transparent bridge (switch) are learning, forwarding, and filtering. Packets are filtered only when a packet is bound for the same port on which it was received.

Routers can also be configured to perform transparent bridging. Of course, they have fewer ports and are not very cost-effective if this is their only purpose on the network. But you will probably need to enable bridging on a router if you want a nonroutable protocol, such as NetBIOS, to be transmitted over a routed network infrastructure; otherwise, there would be no way for a nonroutable protocol to transverse multiple networks.

Configuration of Transparent Bridging

Transparent bridging is what a layer-2 switch does by default and does not need to be configured, per se. Cisco switches use the IEEE spanning tree protocol, which can be turned on or off. However, transparent bridging does need to be configured on a router. Luckily, transparent bridging is simple to configure on Cisco routers. The only required tasks are to select and enable a spanning tree protocol on the router and assign any interfaces to the spanning-tree group. This is done with the following commands.

Transparent bridging related commands:

```
SW> (enable) set spantree {enable | disable} vlans
    RTR (config)# bridge bridge-group protocol {dec | ibm | ieee}
    RTR (config-if)#bridge-group bridge-group number
```

Spanning Tree Protocol (STP)

Spanning Tree Protocol (STP) is a protocol designed to prevent loops in a switched network. If a switch has multiple paths to the destination device, the switch would have two entries in its forwarding table. To prevent loops, only one path can be used for a given transmission. This section describes how STP achieves a loop-free environment.

Here's how loops occur. If there is more than one physical path to a destination, unknown unicast (unicast messages destined for an address the switch does not know about) and broadcast packets would (by default) get flooded out at all ports. Any attached switches would then do the same. The receiving switch would flood the packet out at all ports (except the receiving port). This means that if there were more than one link between the two switches, this would include sending the packets back to the original switch through the other links. So, the switches would send the packets back and forth indefinitely because they never reach a final destination. This loop could result in a *broadcast storm*—consumption of your network bandwidth by the continual regeneration of broadcast messages across all links. If we were discussing a routed environment, the Time to Live (TTL) field could be decremented at each device, and the packet would eventually die. But there is no mechanism in layer 2, so a different method is necessary to choose an effective single path to transmit unknown unicast and broadcast messages. This is the function of STP.

The detailed mechanics of how STP operates is very complex. This section provides an overview to the level required for the CCIE Written Exam.

As mentioned before, there are three main STP types: IEEE (802.1D), IBM, and DEC. IEEE 802.1D is used in all Cisco switches and is the most common type. So, from this point, assume that we are discussing the IEEE 802.1D protocol.

To achieve a loop-free, converged topology, STP goes through three steps:

1. Root bridge election (per spanning tree)
2. Root port election (per switch)
3. Designated port election (per segment)

Bridge Protocol Data Unit (BPDU)

At the heart of STP operation are frames called *Bridge Protocol Data Units* (*BPDUs*). One part of a BPDU is called the *Bridge ID (BID)*. The BID has two parts: a 2-byte bridge priority value (0-65,535) and the 6-byte MAC address of the switch. The default bridge priority value is 32,768.

The purpose of the BID is to determine the root of the bridged network. The lowest BID becomes the root of the spanning tree. A root bridge is the logical center of the bridged network. After the network is converged, BPDUs should emanate from the root.

Another function of BPDUs is to calculate and advertise the *path cost* to the root bridge. A path cost is a numerical value for the bandwidth of each link. For example, a 100Mbps link has a path cost value of 19. After the root bridge is elected (according to their BID), other switches must choose which port should be used to reach the root bridge. This is done by calculating the sum of the path costs of each link to the root bridge. The port with the lowest root path cost on a switch becomes the *root port*. The switch now knows which outgoing port to use to reach the root bridge.

At this point the spanning tree is almost built. But, what if a LAN segment is attached to two different switch ports (either on the same switch or on different switches)? Switches must delegate one incoming port for each LAN segment it services. The switch again uses path costs to select a *designated port* for each LAN segment.

Key Concept

Bridge Protocol Data Units (BPDUs) carry Bridge ID and path cost information. This information assists in

- Electing a root bridge for the network

- Selecting a root port for each switch

- Selecting a designated port for each LAN segment

The BPDUs that accomplish these tasks are called *configuration* BPDUs. The only other type of BPDU is a *Topology Change Notification (TCN)* BPDU. TCN BPDUs originate from nonroot bridges destined for the root bridge. They do what their name implies— they notify the root of a change in the spanning tree topology. This is caused by a port changing a port to blocking state or to forwarding state.

Figure 6.1 shows multiple paths to the root bridge. The cost of each link and the resulting root ports and designated port are labeled. There is one link that is 10MB. Note how the root port of that switch is the 100Mbps link, not the 10Mbps link.

Interface Modes

There are five possible states for bridge ports in an 802.1D spanning tree. Normally, ports that will end up as root ports or designated ports will start in the Blocking state and then move through the Blocking, Listening, and Learning states on the way to the Forwarding state. Other ports will stop at one of these states:

- Disabled—Manually shut down by the administrator.

- Blocking—Listening to BPDUs (right after port initialization) and sending no user data. Nonroot or designated ports are set to Blocking state.

- Listening—Sending and receiving BPDUs. Convergence process (previously listed) taking place.

- Learning—A port is building bridge tables and not sending user data.

- Forwarding—A designated or root port starts forwarding user data.

PART

III

CH

6

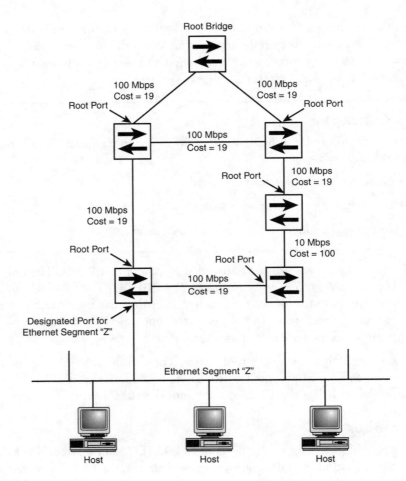

Figure 6.1
The root port for each switch is the port that has the least total path cost to the root bridge.

 Key Concept

The five STP port states are Disabled, Blocking, Listening, Learning, and Forwarding. User data is passed only when a port is in Forwarding state.

If a switch port has only one device on it, that port will be the designated port for that segment and end up in Forwarding state. This, of course, is known as micro-segmenting and is an increasingly popular network design. Micro-segmenting eliminates collisions. To limit broadcasts, *Virtual LANs (VLANs)* are usually employed.

VLANs

In many environments it is advantageous to implement VLANs to create smaller broadcast domains. Here is a quick refresher of the major issues and features of VLANs:

- By default, broadcasts and multicasts are flooded throughout a VLAN.
- Traffic between VLANs must be routed.
- Inter-VLAN traffic can be handled by an attached router or, if the Cisco switch supports it, by a Route Switch Module (RSM).
- Each VLAN has its instance of Spanning Tree Protocol (STP).

You might be asked to provide or identify basic VLAN configuration commands for a Catalyst switch. Here they are.

VLAN-Related Commands:

```
SW> (enable) set vlan {vlan_num} {mod/ports}
SW> (enable) clear vlan {vlan}
```

Trunking

When a port on a switch belongs to more than one VLAN, it is referred to as a *trunk*. Trunks are most commonly used to

- Connect a switch to a router (for inter-VLAN routing).
- Connect a switch to another switch for VLAN traffic (if they share a VLAN).
- Connect a resource node (such as a server) that must be accessed by multiple demand nodes from multiple VLANs in the switch (to keep traffic local, not traversing the core).

Two protocols are used to define Ethernet inter-VLAN trunking. Both of them define how to encapsulate and tag packets with VLAN information when transmitted over a trunk. Cisco has developed Inter-Switch Link (ISL) protocol. The IEEE standard is 802.1Q. ISL adds a 26-byte header and a 4-byte CRC to each frame. 802.1Q inserts a 26-byte tag between the Ethernet packet's SA and Type/Length fields. Either protocol can be used on most Catalyst switches.

FDDI trunks uses a different trunking protocol: IEEE 802.10. 802.10 allows the switch to treat the entire ring as a trunk. Part of the 802.10 encapsulation includes a clear header field. A portion of this clear header contains the 32-bit SAID value. The SAID value is important because the source VLAN number is carried in the SAID. Typically, the SAID value is the VLAN number plus 100,000 (unless configured otherwise—which is not necessary).

Key Concept

Trunks allow multiple VLANs to travel over a single link.

Trunk Modes

All trunk ports operate in a mode, which can be manually set by the administrator. There are five modes for trunk ports: on, off, desirable, auto, and negotiate. How these modes interact is very complex. Here is a summary of the effect of configuring the mode of a switch's trunk port:

- Off—Disables trunking and advertises its state out the port.
- On—Enables trunking and advertises its state out the port.
- Desirable—Advertises a desire to trunk. Other side must be on, auto, or desirable to enable trunking.
- Auto—Port receives, but never sends, requests to become a trunk. Other side must be on or desirable to enable trunking. (Catalyst default mode.)
- Negotiate—Enables trunking but does not advertise trunk configuration on the port. Other side must be on or desirable to trunk.

Trunk Configuration

Following is the main command needed to configure a trunk on a Catalyst 5000 switch. Note all the different parameters included in this one set trunk command. Each of these parameters can be entered or changed separately (that's why they are each shown as optional), but at least one of them must be entered each time you use the set trunk command.

Trunk-Related Commands:

```
    SW> (enable) Set trunk {mod_num / port_num}
[on | off | desirable | auto | negotiate] [vlans] [trunk_type*]
    * trunk type = isl, dot1q, dot10, lane, negotiate
```

EtherChannel

EtherChannel, otherwise known as Fast EtherChannel, enables you to combine two or more physical links between the same two devices (switches or routers) into a single logical link. Besides providing more bandwidth, EtherChannel provides a means to implement redundant (fault-tolerant) links without creating a spanning tree loop. Either Fast Ethernet or Gigabit Ethernet links may be used to create channels. Bundling ports together in a channel increases the total available bandwidth, not the speed.

There are several requirements for implementing EtherChannel. All ports in a channel must be members of the same VLAN or be trunk ports for the same VLANs. All ports must be the same speed and duplex. In Catalyst 5000 and 5500s, all ports must be contiguous in the switch, and you can bundle only two or four ports (not three). The Catalyst 6000 supports noncontiguous channel ports and channels of two, three, or four physical links. EtherChannel must be configured on the local switch and the switch or router on the other end of the channel.

Key Concept

All channel ports must belong to the same VLAN or must trunk the same VLANs. They must also be the same speed and duplex. (The Catalyst 5000 series has additional requirements.)

EtherChannel Modes

There are four modes for EtherChannel ports:

- On—Use this port as a channel port.
- Off—Never use this port as a channel port.
- Auto—Use this port as a channel port if the other end is on or desirable.
- Desirable—Use this port as a channel port if all requirements are met (as explained earlier in the chapter).

EtherChannel Configuration

Because channels are either switch-to-switch or switch-to-router, it is important to know the basic configuration commands for both devices. The relevant commands to enable EtherChannel are shown here. As you can see, configuration requires only one step on the switch, whereas on the router it is a two-step process: Create a port-channel interface and then assign interfaces to the channel.

PART
III

CH
6

EtherChannel-Related Commands:

```
SW> (enable)  set port channel port_list {on | off | auto | desirable}
RTR (config-if)# channel-group channel-number
RTR (config)# interface port-channel channel-number
```

VLAN Trunk Protocol (VTP)

VTP is a Cisco proprietary protocol designed to manage VLANs in a switched environment. It is a layer-2 multicast protocol. The purpose of VTP is to make administration of VLANs simpler and more secure by automatically propagating VLAN information throughout a switched environment. However, VTP will not assign specific ports to VLANs (this still must be done on each switch).

VTP works within a domain structure. All switches connected via trunks and configured with the same domain name will share a domain and, therefore, VTP messages. Switches will transmit VTP packets over all ISL or 802.1Q trunk ports, but no others. Routers, on the other hand, do not participate in VTP domains. Data in a VTP packet is configuration data for switches in a domain. This configuration information informs other switches of what VLANs need to be created. VTP shares this VLAN configuration information only within its own domain. So, if needed, there can be multiple VTP domains in a network.

Key Concept

VTP shares VLAN configuration information but does not assign switch ports to VLANs.

There are three possible VTP modes for a switch. The VTP mode will determine how a switch receives and processes a VTP message. The mode types are Server, Client, and Transparent. Table 6.1 shows a summary of the differences.

Table 6.1   VTP Mode Types

Function	Server	Client	Transparent
Ability to create and delete local VLANs	Yes	No	Yes
Generate and send new VTP messages	Yes	No	No
Act on received VTP messages	Yes	Yes	No

Function	Server	Client	Transparent
Forward received VTP messages	Yes	Yes	Yes
Remember own VLAN info (power cycle)	Yes	No	Yes

When a switch makes a change as a result of a VTP message, it increments a configuration revision number. This way, when a new message is received, the switch can compare the revision number to its own most configuration revision number to decide whether the information is truly new or not.

VTP Messages

There are four types of VTP messages:

- Summary Advertisements—Sent out every five minutes. Confirms the revision number and VTP membership information. Other switches can respond with an Advertisement Request message.
- Subset Advertisements—Sent out by a server due to a change made. Updates clients.
- Advertisement Requests—Sent by clients. Requests Summary and Subset Advertisement messages to be sent.
- VTP Join Message—Enabled with VTP Pruning. Advertises to other switches the VLANs for which the sending switch is interested in receiving traffic.

The final major feature of VTP is VTP Pruning. By default, a switch floods all packets for which it has no destination port in its table (unknown unicasts) and all broadcast frames. This includes flooding these frames out of the trunk ports, which then get flooded to all VLANs on the attached switches. *VTP Pruning* prevents frames from being flooded to a VLAN other than the source port's VLAN. With VTP Pruning, a switch will flood messages only to other switches that have advertised that VLAN in their VTP Join messages. Pruning can also be customized with the `pruneeligible` commands (see "VTP Configuration" later in this chapter).

 Key Concept

VTP Pruning prevents unknown unicasts and broadcasts from being flooded to other VLANs.

PART III

CH 6

Other VTP information:

- VTP travels only over the default VLAN for the media type (Ethernet = VLAN 1, FDDI = VLAN 1002, and so on).
- Default ELAN must be configured to transmit VTP over ATM.
- There is a VTP v.2 that enables Token-Ring VLAN configuration, which is impossible with the default VTP v.1.

VTP Configuration

Following are the main commands you need to configure the feature just discussed. You'll need to be able to recognize them for the test.

VTP-Related Commands:

```
SW> (enable) set vtp domain name
SW> (enable) set vtp mode {server | client | transparent}
SW> (enable) set vtp pruning enable
SW> (enable) set vtp pruneeligible vlan_range
SW> (enable) clear vtp pruneeligible vlan_range
```

Multicast Management

Multicasts, as you know, are messages sent to groups of addresses. Routers do not, by default, forward multicasts. However, switches do. Multicasts can result in a lot of bandwidth being wasted if the switches forward a multicast to all switched nodes when it needs to be transmitted to only a few.

There is a protocol (IGMP) that allows routers to selectively forward multicasts to appropriate end nodes. It is discussed here so that we can discuss CGMP, which interacts with IGMP.

Internet Group Management Protocol (IGMP)

Internet Group Management Protocol (IGMP) allows routers to track which hosts are interested in receiving traffic for a multicast group. IGMP is configured on routers, not switches. There are two versions of IGMP, and version 2 is backward compatible. Version 1 has two message types whereas version 2 has four. Version 2 is the default on Cisco routers.

In a switch, by default, IGMP messages are flooded to all ports. This unnecessary traffic can be limited by configuring static CAM (content addressable memory) table entries or by enabling *IGMP snooping*. The final way to limit unnecessary flooding of multicasts through a switch is to use Cisco Group Management Protocol (CGMP).

Key Concept

IGMP helps a router track hosts' multicast group membership.

IGMP-Related Commands:

```
RTR (config)# ip multicast-routing
SW>(enable) set igmp {enable | disable}
```

The first command enables multicast routing using IGMP in Cisco routers. The second turns IGMP snooping on or off.

Cisco Group Management Protocol (CGMP)

CGMP is a Cisco proprietary protocol that works with IGMP to control unwanted multicast flooding. It must be configured on all routers and switches you want to use CGMP.

When a CGMP-enabled router receives an IGMP message from a host, it sends a CGMP message back to the Catalyst switch. The switch then adds the host's MAC address to the address list for the multicast group in which the host wants to participate.

Key Concept

CGMP complements IGMP to limit flooding of multicasts in a switch.

CGMP-Related Commands:

```
SW> (enable) Set cgmp enable
SW> (enable) Set multicast router mod_num / port_num
RTR (config-if)# ip cgmp
```

These commands enable CGMP on Cisco switches. The `ip cgmp` command enables CGMP on selected router interfaces.

Summary

This chapter provided an overview of transparent bridging, which is necessary for the following chapter on bridging. It also summarized the switching topics outlined in the CCIE Routing and Switching Written Exam Blueprint. You should now understand the features, operation, and configuration of STP, VLANs, trunking, EtherChannel, VTP, IGMP, and CGMP.

PART

III

CH

6

This chapter explained the three tasks of a transparent bridge and that it operates without the knowledge of end nodes (hosts). You also learned how spanning tree works in conjunction with transparent bridges (and switches) to prevent loops in the bridged network.

After reading this chapter, you should know how Cisco switches, especially the Catalyst switches, implement technologies such as VLANs. For the test, know the difference between the possible switch port states for VLAN ports and EtherChannel ports. You also need to know what VTP does and the implications of the different VTP modes.

QUESTIONS AND ANSWERS

1. What are the three main tasks of a transparent bridge?

   A: Learning, Forwarding, Filtering

2. What are the five STP port states?

   A: Disabled, Blocking, Listening, Learning, Forwarding

3. How many instances of spanning tree can be present in a VLAN?

   A: One

4. What are the two types of Trunk encapsulation protocols?

   A: IEEE 802.1Q and Cisco's ISL

5. How many VTP modes are there and what are they?

   A: Three: Server, Client, and Transparent

6. What are the requirements to implement EtherChannel?

   A: All ports (up to four) in a channel must be members of all the same VLAN or be trunk ports for the same VLANs and must be the same speed and duplex. In Cat 5000s, only two or four ports can be used, and the ports must be contiguous.

7. What protocol is used to trunk FDDI VLANs?

   A: IEEE 802.10

8. What is the SAID value used for in a FDDI VLAN?

   A: To transmit the VLAN number in the clear header of the 802.10.

9. What does VTP Pruning do?

   A: Limits the flooding of unknown unicast and broadcast frames through a switch to the same VLAN as the source port.

10. What does CGMP do that IGMP does not?

    A: Enables the switch (not the router) to limit flooding of multicasts.

PRACTICE TEST

1. What is the `vlan_type` entered in the CLI of a Catalyst 5000 to change the encapsulation from ISL to 802.1Q?

    A. isl

    B. 802.1

    C. 802.1q

    D. dot1q

    E. 802dot1q

Answer A is incorrect because it would set the encapsulation to `isl`. **Answer D is correct because the command `dot1q` is used with the `set trunk` command.** Answers B, C, and E are bogus commands.

2. How many physical ports can be combined in an EtherChannel on a Catalyst 5000? (Choose all that apply.)

    A. 2

    B. 3

    C. 4

    D. 6

Answer A is correct, and it is the minimum number of ports to make an EtherChannel. Answer B is incorrect. The Catalyst 6000 can use three ports, but not the Catalyst 5000. **Answer C is correct because it is the maximum number of ports possible.** Answer D is incorrect because four is the maximum.

3. Which of the following are true regarding STP?

    A. A two-line channel can be treated as a loop.

    B. A VLAN can have multiple instances of STP.

    C. VTP eliminates the need for STP.

    D. STP is irrelevant in routed networks.

Answer A is incorrect because two lines can be treated as a loop only if the lines are not in a channel. Answer B is incorrect because a VLAN has only one instance of STP. Answer C is incorrect because VTP and STP have entirely different functions. **Answer D is correct because STP deals with layer 2 and routing happens at layer 3.**

PART

III

CH

6

4. There are two switches connected via an EtherChannel. All requirements have been met for the channel to function. You are now configuring the channel mode on one end. The other end is set to auto. Which of the following modes will enable the channel to work?

   A. On
   B. Auto
   C. Designated
   D. Desirable
   E. Negotiate

Answers A and D are correct because they are options to get the channel to function. Answer B is incorrect because, if both ends of a channel are set to auto, the channel will not work. Answer C is incorrect because there is no such mode as Designated. Answer E is incorrect because Negotiate is a trunk mode, not a mode for EtherChannel.

5. Which of the following are true about VTP mode Client?

   A. You can create local VLANs in this switch.
   B. This switch will send out its own VLAN information.
   C. This switch will remember its own VLAN configuration if power is lost.
   D. This switch will act on subset advertisement messages.
   E. This switch will forward advertisements to other connected switches.

Answer A is incorrect because VLANs can be created only on server and transparent switches. Answer B is incorrect because only VTP servers send out VLAN configuration information. Answer C is incorrect because only VTP Server and Transparent mode switches will retain their VLAN configuration if power is lost. **Answers D and E are correct; they are the only two functions of a VTP Client switch.**

6. The protocol used to trunk VLANs over FDDI is

   A. 802.1Q
   B. 802.1F
   C. ISL
   D. 802.10
   E. SAID

Answer A is incorrect because 802.1Q is the IEEE standard for trunking over Ethernet. Answer B is incorrect because there is no such thing as 802.1F. Answer C is incorrect—ISL is the Cisco proprietary Ethernet trunking protocol. **Answer D is correct.** Answer E is incorrect; the SAID is a field in the clear header of an 802.10 packet, which is the encapsulation for trunking over FDDI.

7. Which of the following are tasks of a transparent bridge?
- **A.** Listening
- **B.** Learning
- **C.** Forwarding
- **D.** Filtering
- **E.** Blocking
- **F.** Disabling
- **G.** Encapsulating

Answer A is incorrect; it is an STP mode state. **Answers B, C, and D are correct.** E is also incorrect; it is also an STP port mode. F and G are fictitious answers.

8. Which of the following are STP port states?
- **A.** Waiting
- **B.** Listening
- **C.** Learning
- **D.** Forwarding
- **E.** Routing
- **F.** Filtering
- **G.** Blocking

Answers B, C, D, F, and G are correct.

9. The three types of STP are IEEE, IBM, and _____.
- **A.** OSI
- **B.** VTP
- **C.** DEC
- **D.** RTP

Answer A is incorrect because OSI is a standards organization. Answer B is incorrect because VTP is VLAN Trunk Protocol. **Answer C is correct because the three spanning tree protocols are IEEE (802.1D), IBM, and DEC.** Answer D is incorrect because RTP is Reliable Transport Protocol.

10. What is the default bridge priority value?
- **A.** 0
- **B.** 16,384
- **C.** 32,768
- **D.** 65,535

Answer C is correct; 32,768 is the default Bridge Priority value. It is combined with the MAC address to make the Bridge ID (BID) field of the BPDU. Lowest BID is elected the root bridge. The others are bogus answers.

PART
III

CH
6

Other Bridging Technologies

─ WHILE YOU READ ─

1. What are the four primary nonroutable protocols?

2. How is CRB different from IRB?

3. What is the function of the BVI?

4. In an SRB environment, what device determines the data communications path between end stations?

5. What is the function of the explorer?

6. What is the function of the RIF?

7. How many bits does it take to specify the ring number?

8. What is the maximum hop-count in SRB environments?

9. What is the difference between RSRB and SRB?

10. In an SRT environment, what determines whether a frame enters the SRB domain?

SEE
APPENDIX **F**

Bridging operates at the Data Link layer of the OSI/RM, as opposed to routing, which operates at the Network layer. While Transparent bridging concepts are covered in Chapter 6, "LAN Switching," this chapter deals with the technologies that are used to transport nonroutable traffic through a network. More specifically, the types of bridging covered in this chapter require routers configured as bridges, and are most commonly used to transport SNA data to and from a mainframe.

Historically, bridging concepts have been weighed heavily on the CCIE written exam. Therefore, this area should be thoroughly understood in order to pass the exam.

Nonroutable Protocols

Although SNA probably accounts for the majority of bridging situations, it is by no means the only reason for bridging. Other protocols operate only at the Data Link layer of the OSI/RM. Listed here are the nonroutable protocols:

- DEC LAT (Digital Equipment Corporation Local Area Transport)
- DEC MOP (Digital Equipment Corporation Maintenance Operation Protocol)
- NetBIOS (Network Basic Input/Output System)
- SNA (Systems Network Architecture)

To transverse a network, NetBIOS is most commonly encapsulated into TCP/IP and, to a lesser extent, IPX. When NetBIOS is not encapsulated in a network layer protocol but runs on top of the LLC2 sublayer, it must be bridged. NetBIOS is also referred to as NetBEUI (NetBIOS Extended User Interface).

Key Concept

Major nonroutable protocols include SNA, NetBIOS, DEC LAT, and DEC MOP.

Concurrent Routing and Bridging

Cisco's *CCIE Blueprint* lists *Concurrent Routing and Bridging (CRB)* as a required knowledge area for certification. CRB employs a single router to bridge a routable protocol on one group of interfaces and concurrently to route that protocol on another group of interfaces. CRB differs from Integrated Routing and Bridging (discussed later in the chapter) in that routing and bridging functions are not performed on the same interfaces.

Understanding CRB

The diagram in Figure 7.1 illustrates this concept using IP as an example of a routable protocol. The interfaces shown on the left are routing interfaces, whereas the ones shown on the right are transparent bridging interfaces. The CRB process does not affect non-routable protocols; they are bridged according to the bridge-group commands.

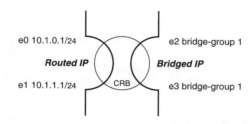

Figure 7.1
Routing and bridging processes are separate in CRB.

Traffic from each group of interfaces cannot be switched between groups unless either of the following conditions exists:

- The bridged interfaces are given a network-layer configuration (that is, configured with IP)
- The routed interfaces are added to the same bridge group as the bridged interfaces

With CRB, if e0 and e1 were also in `bridge-group 1` (to allow NetBEUI to be bridged, for example), the router would also bridge the IP traffic. To cause the router to route IP, an explicit bridge route command must be configured.

 Key Concept

CRB is concurrently routing on one group of interfaces while bridging on another group. Traffic from one group is prohibited from crossing to the other group.

Configuring CRB

Here is how the router in Figure 7.1 would be configured:

```
interface Ethernet0
 ip address 10.1.0.1 255.255.255.0
```

```
interface Ethernet1
 ip address 10.1.1.1 255.255.255.0

interface Ethernet2
 no ip address
 bridge-group 1              (assigns the interface to transparent bridge group 1)

interface Ethernet3
 no ip address
 bridge-group 1              (assigns the interface to transparent bridge group 1)

bridge crb                   (enables CRB functionality)
bridge 1 protocol ieee    (bridge 1 will use the spanning tree protocol)
bridge 1 route ip         (specifies that IP traffic on bridge 1 will be routed)
```

Listed here is a command related to CRB, which shows statistics about CRB interfaces:

```
rtr# show interfaces crb
```

Integrated Routing and Bridging

Whereas CRB does not combine the routing and bridging process, *Integrated Routing and Bridging (IRB)* employs a single router to integrate its routing and bridging process on the same interfaces. This is done through configuring a *Bridge Virtual Interface (BVI)* that represents the bridging interfaces to the routing process. For a successful IRB configuration, the number of the BVI must match the number of the bridge-group (that is, `bridge-group 1` and `bvi1`).

Understanding IRB

The diagram in Figure 7.2 illustrates the IRB BVI concept using IP as the routable protocol. The interfaces shown on the left are routing interfaces, whereas the ones shown on the right are transparent bridging interfaces. Nonroutable protocols are not affected by the IRB process; they are bridged according to the bridge-group commands.

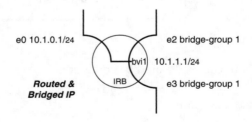

Figure 7.2
Routing and bridging processes are integrated in IRB.

The bridged segments e2 and e3 are both represented by the IP network configured in bvi1. Hosts on either segment will use bvi1 as their default gateway for network-layer communication with the rest of the network. Network layer protocols are bridged by default when IRB is enabled. Therefore, an explicit route statement is necessary to configure routing for that protocol (in the earlier example, bridge 1 route ip).

Key Concept

IRB integrates groups of routed interfaces with groups of bridged interfaces. The BVI is a virtual interface in the bridged group that allows traffic to be routed into the routed group.

Configuring IRB

Here is how the router in Figure 7.2 would be configured:

```
interface Ethernet0
 ip address 10.1.0.1 255.255.255.0

interface Ethernet2
 no ip address
bridge-group 1            (assigns the interface to transparent bridge group 1)

interface Ethernet3
 no ip address
bridge-group 1            (assigns the interface to transparent bridge group 1)

interface BVI1            (creates an interface to represent bridge group 1 to the
                                routing process)
 ip address 10.1.1.1 255.255.255.0

bridge irb                (enables IRB functionality)
bridge 1 protocol ieee    (bridge 1 will use the spanning tree protocol)
bridge 1 route ip         (specifies that IP traffic on bridge 1 will be routed)
```

Listed here is a command related to IRB, which shows statistics about IRB interfaces.

```
rtr# show interfaces irb
```

Source-Route Bridging

Pure *Source-Route Bridging (SRB)* concepts are completely different from those of transparent bridging and related derivatives such as LAN switches, IRB, and CRB. The SRB algorithm was developed by IBM in the mid-1980s as a way to bridge multiple Token-Ring LAN segments to IBM mainframes. Along with Token-Ring, SRB is now part of the IEEE 802.5 specification.

PART
III

CH
7

SRB was not designed with very large networks in mind. IBM specifications state that there can be no more than eight rings and seven bridges between any two devices (this is often referred to as a seven-hop limit). The IEEE 802.5 specification now allows up to 14 rings and 13 bridges, although Cisco generally follows the original IBM recommendation.

Understanding SRB

The name SRB is an apt one, given that the source is required to preselect the best route across the network of rings and bridges to reach its communication partner. It then places this information in the header of each Token-Ring frame. Consider Figure 7.3.

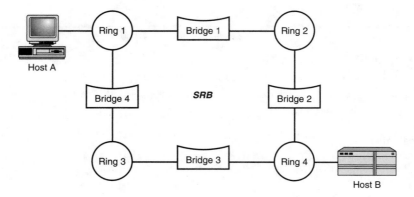

Figure 7.3
SRB networks are composed of alternating rings and bridges.

If Host A does not know the route to destination B, it first assumes the destination is local and sends out a test frame on its local Token-Ring segment (Ring 1). If the test frame returns from the destination, communication can begin. If the test frame is not received by the sending station, the source must send out an explorer frame to determine to which remote segment the destination is attached (in this case, Ring 4). The explorer, and any frame destined for a remote ring, must have the group/individual bit set to 1. This is the first bit in the MAC address and is also known as the *multicast bit*.

Each bridge that receives the explorer will forward it out its ports and add its routing information to the explorer frame. In the example shown in Figure 7.3, as Host B receives each explorer frame, it learns the route the frame took to reach it and now knows both routes back to Host A. Using this information, Host B then sends a reply to each explorer frame back to Host A. From the replies to its explorer frames, Host A has now learned two routes to Host B:

- Ring 1, Bridge 1, Ring 2, Bridge 2, Ring 4
- Ring 1, Bridge 4, Ring 3, Bridge 3, Ring 4

Host A must now choose a route to Host B. Because the IEEE 802.5 standard does not mandate the methodology for route selection, most hosts use the route contained in the first returned explorer they receive. Host A can now begin communication with Host B by placing the route to Host B in the *Route Information Field (RIF)* of the Token-Ring frame. The RIF is only present in a Token-Ring frame when the frame is destined for a remote LAN (that is, ring).

Understanding RIF Fields

Although being able to construct a RIF might not always help you configure SRB, it *will* help you pass the CCIE written exam, because you will be required to build and read RIFs in order to answer questions correctly. Therefore, an explanation of each field appears in Figure 7.4, followed by an example.

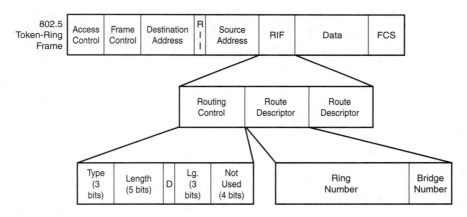

Figure 7.4
Token-Ring frame with Route Information Field.

If the *Ring Information Indicator (RII)* of the Token-Ring frame is set to 1, this indicates that the frame will have a RIF and is therefore destined for another ring.

Key Concept

The Ring Information Indicator (RII) bit of a 802.5 Token-Ring frame is set to 1 if a RIF is present in the frame.

Each RIF consists of a single *routing control* field and one *route descriptor* for each ring-bridge pair necessary to specify the route to the destination host. The routing control field consists of four subfields:

- Type—Specifies three types of routes:
  - Specifically routed (000)—Used when the end station knows the route to the destination.
  - Spanning-tree explorer (110)—Used by NetBIOS hosts to find the best path to the destination. Only bridges in the source's spanning tree forward the explorer (also known as single-route broadcast).
  - All routes explorer (100)—Used by SNA to find all paths to the destination (also known as all routes broadcast).
- Length—Specifies the total RIF length in bytes (2 to 18).
- D—Direction bit specifies the direction (forward or reverse) the frame should travel through the rings and bridges (0 = read left to right; 1 = read right to left).
- Largest Frame Size—Specifies the largest acceptable frame to the workstation (that is, MTU). Bridges are able to modify the frame size along the route to accommodate smaller MTUs along the path. The following table shows the MTU values associated with each bit combination:

Bits	MTU
000	Up to 516 bytes
001	1500
010	2052
011	4472
100	8144
101	11407
110	17800
111	Used in all-route broadcast frames

The route descriptor field consists of two subfields:

- Ring number (12 bits)—Specifies a value that must be unique within the network
- Bridge number (4 bits)—Specifies a value that must only be unique between rings

Key Concept

Know how to build and read RIFs. You must know what every bit of the RIF is used for!

Constructing a RIF

The route that the workstation specifies in the route descriptor field of the RIF is an alternating series of ring and bridge numbers. The route begins with the ring number of the source host and ends with the ring number of the destination host (to fill out the fields, the last bridge number is always set to 0). The following example shows how to build a RIF for the network shown in Figure 7.5.

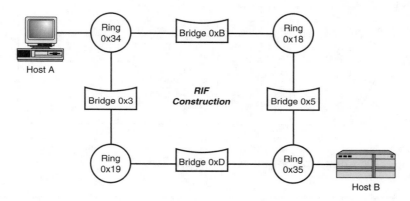

Figure 7.5
Network topology used in constructing a RIF using hexadecimal ring and bridge numbers.

In this scenario, four routes are possible for Host A to reach Host B. (Note that the ring and bridge numbers are given in hexadecimal while IOS configuration files show the values in decimal.) Table 7.1 shows four possible RIFs necessary for Host A and B to communicate. Note that in paths 3 and 4, the direction bit is set so that the RIF is read right to left.

Table 7.1	RIFs Necessary for Communication Between Host A and Host B	
Path	Route	RIF in Hexadecimal
1	Host A to Host B via Ring 34, Bridge B, Ring 18, Bridge 5, Ring 35	0830.034B.0185.0350
2	Host A to Host B via Ring 34, Bridge 3, Ring 19, Bridge D, Ring 35	0830.0343.019D.0350
3	Host B to Host A via Ring 35, Bridge 5, Ring 18, Bridge B, Ring 34	08B0.034B.0185.0350
4	Host B to Host A via Ring 35, Bridge D, Ring 19, Bridge 3, Ring 34	08B0.0343.019D.0350

PART

III

CH

7

The RIF for path 1 is explained in the Figure 7.6. The RIF is shown in Hex in the top line, followed by the binary representation of the hex values. Next, the length of each field is given in bits along with the corresponding field names. Underneath the field names, the function of each field is shown.

Hex:	0	8	3		0	034	B	018	5	035	0
Binary:	000	0 1000	0	011	0000						
Length:	3	5	1	3	4	12	4	12	4	12	4
Field Name:	Type	Length	D	Lg.	Unused	Ring	Bridge	Ring	Bridge	Ring	Bridge
Meaning:	Specifically Routed	RIF is 8 bytes long	Direction: left to right	Largest Frame MTU is 4136	Unused	Ring 52 (decimal)	Bridge 11 (decimal)	Ring 24 (decimal)	Bridge 5 (decimal)	Ring 53 (decimal)	(last bridge is always set to 0)

Figure 7.6
Constructing a RIF using topology shown in Figure 7.5.

Key Concept

An SRB network requires the source to know the route to the destination. The network comprises rings (for example, Token-Ring) with unique numbers, and bridges with numbers that need only be unique between bridges. To learn the route, the end station sends out an explorer frame and waits for it to return. To specify the route, the end station places a series of ring and bridge numbers into a part of the Token-Ring frame known as a RIF (route information field). Bridges then read the RIF to forward the frame.

Configuring Pure SRB

The diagram in Figure 7.7 gives a simple illustration of SRB, followed by the corresponding IOS configuration. (Note that the ring and bridge numbers in this example are given in hexadecimal while the IOS configuration file shows the values in decimal.)

Here is how the router/bridge in Figure 7.7 would be configured:

```
interface TokenRing0
  source-bridge 52 11 24          (local ring, bridge number, target ring)

interface TokenRing1
  source-bridge 24 11 52          (local ring, bridge number, target ring)
```

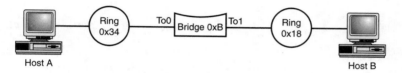

Figure 7.7
Network topology used in configuring the SRB example.

Configuring Multiport SRB

According to IEEE 802.5 specifications, a pure SRB cannot have more than two interfaces per bridge. To overcome this limitation, the Cisco IOS can be configured with a virtual ring to which all interfaces point. Consider Figure 7.8 with the configuration
example that follows. (Note that, in this example, ring and bridge numbers are given in
decimal on the diagram and configuration.)

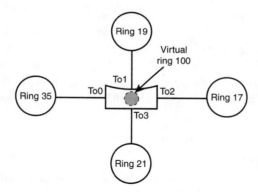

Figure 7.8
Network topology with virtual ring used in configuring multiport SRB example.

Here is how the router/bridge in Figure 7.8 would be configured. The primary difference
between this example and the pure SRB example in Figure 7.7 is that all the Token-Ring
interfaces use the virtual ring.

```
source-bridge ring-group 100    (establishes virtual ring)

interface TokenRing0
  source-bridge 35 1 100          (local ring, bridge number, virtual/target ring)

interface TokenRing1
  source-bridge 19 1 100          (local ring, bridge number, virtual/target ring)
```

```
interface TokenRing2
  source-bridge 17 1 100              (local ring, bridge number, virtual/target ring)

interface TokenRing3
  source-bridge 21 1 100              (local ring, bridge number, virtual/target ring)
```

Key Concept

A bridge can have more than two ports by specifying a virtual ring inside the router to which all other interfaces point.

Remote Source-Route Bridging

Another limitation of SRB is that it must run over Token-Ring networks. Cisco IOS can overcome this limitation in several ways, including *Source-Route Transparent Bridging (SRT), Source-Route Translational Bridging (SR/TLB),* and *Remote Source-Route Bridging (RSRB)*. RSRB is typically an SRB implementation over a WAN network (although it could be over any non–Token-Ring media). In this configuration, the virtual ring concept (described earlier in the chapter) is extended over the WAN interfaces, making them appear to be part of one Token-Ring segment. The primary command that distinguishes an RSRB configuration is source-bridge remote-peer. Along with this statement is a transport type, typically TCP, which causes all the SRB data in the virtual ring to be encapsulated into TCP/IP as it traverses the WAN.

Key Concept

RSRB allows an SRB network to exist over non–Token-Ring media by creating a virtual ring that spans the non–Token-Ring network. This ring must be the same on both routers. SRB data is then encapsulated by the sending router, and de-encapsulated by the receiving router before being placed on the target Token-Ring segment.

Understanding and Configuring RSRB

Consider the example in Figure 7.9 with corresponding IOS configuration.

Here is how the routers/bridges in Figure 7.9 would be configured. The primary difference between this example and the RSRB example in Figure 7.8 is the remote-peer statements that configure the virtual Token-Ring over the WAN link via TCP/IP encapsulation.

R1

```
source-bridge ring-group 100              (establishes virtual ring)
source-bridge remote-peer 100 tcp 10.1.100.2   (specifies RSRB peers,
source-bridge remote-peer 100 tcp 10.1.100.1    virtual ring & encapsulation)

interface Serial0
 ip address 10.1.100.1 255.255.255.252

interface TokenRing0
 source-bridge 20 1 100        (local ring, bridge number, virtual/target ring)
```

R2

```
source-bridge ring-group 100              (establishes virtual ring)
source-bridge remote-peer 100 tcp 10.1.100.1   (specifies RSRB peers,
source-bridge remote-peer 100 tcp 10.1.100.2    virtual ring, & encapsulation)

interface Serial0
 ip address 10.1.100.2 255.255.255.252

interface TokenRing0
 source-bridge 30 2 100        (local ring, bridge number, virtual/target ring)
```

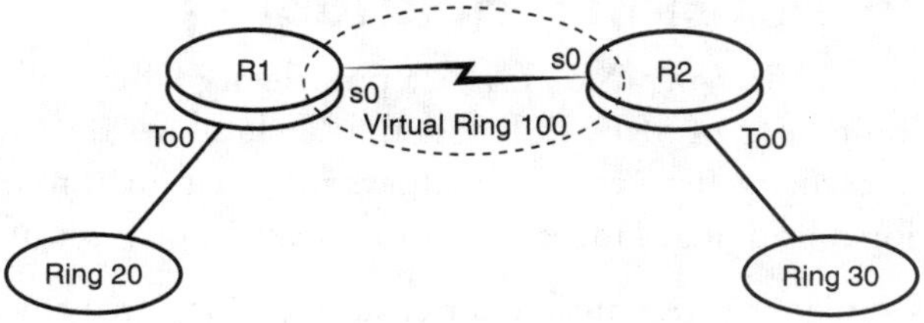

Figure 7.9
Network topology used in configuring RSRB example.

Source-Route Transparent Bridging

Source-Route Transparent Bridging (SRT) allows SRB and transparent bridging to happen within the same router. If the frame contains a RIF, the SRB process handles it; otherwise, the frame is transparently bridged. As in CBR (discussed at the beginning of this chapter), the two processes do not communicate with each other. In addition, Ethernet to Token-Ring communication (translational bridging) is not provided by SRT.

Configuring SRT

Configuration is a straightforward combination of SRB and translational bridging commands. Each interface that needs SRT enabled is configured with both the SRT and SRB commands, as shown in previous examples.

```
interface TokenRing0
  source-bridge 52 11 24          (local ring, bridge number, target ring)
  bridge-group 1            (assigns the interface to transparent bridge group 1)

interface TokenRing1
  source-bridge 24 11 52          (local ring, bridge number, target ring)
  bridge-group 1            (assigns the interface to transparent bridge group 1)

bridge 1 protocol ieee          ( bridge 1 will use the spanning tree protocol)
```

Key Concept

SRT combines the elements of SRB and transparent bridging, integrating them on one router. When the router detects the existence of a RIF field, the frame will enter the SRB domain.

Source-Route Translational Bridging

Source-Route Translational Bridging (SR/TLB) is a proprietary Cisco solution that eases some of the major limitations of SRB, RSRB, and SRT. It allows the SRB and transparent bridging processes to exchange frames. It also allows Ethernet hosts to enter the SRB domain via translational bridging. However, it introduces its own set of challenges.

- The network designer is responsible for ensuring a loop-free environment between the transparent bridging and SRB domains because spanning tree protocol packets will not cross between the two processes.
- MTU sizes are different between Ethernet and Token-Ring.
- Ethernet frames do not support RIFs.
- Token-Ring and Ethernet use a different bit order in the MAC addressing scheme

Understanding Ethernet to Token-Ring MAC Conversion

The bit-ordering differences between Ethernet and Token-Ring require a more detailed discussion for the CCIE candidate. Although both Ethernet and Token-Ring use a 48-bit MAC address, the primary difference is the bit order within the individual bytes. Ethernet devices read all the bits and bytes from left to right (in *canonical* order). Like Ethernet,

Token-Ring devices also read the bytes from left to right. However, within each byte, Token-Ring devices read the bits from right to left (in *noncanonical* order). This will cause the hex value of the MAC address for the same end node to look completely different on a Token-Ring segment than on an Ethernet segment. Following is an example of the reversed bit order within each byte:

Ethernet: 00000000.01010111.01100010

Token-Ring: 00000000.11101010.01000110

As a second example, an Ethernet MAC address from a Cisco router (0000.0c13.d717) will be used to demonstrate the conversion process (see Figure 7.10).

Ethernet	Hex	0 0	0 0	0 c	1 3	D 7	1 7
	Binary	0000 0000	0000 0000	0000 1100	0001 0011	1101 0111	0001 0111
Token Ring	Binary	0000 0000	0000 0000	0011 0000	1100 1000	1110 1011	1110 1000
	Hex	0 0	0 0	3 0	C 8	E B	E 8

Figure 7.10
Converting an Ethernet MAC address to a Token-Ring MAC address.

From this example, we see that the Ethernet address of 0000.0c13.d717 converts to a Token-Ring address of 0000.30c8.ebe8.

Key Concept

When data is exchanged between Ethernet and Token-Ring networks, the bit order of every packet is changed, most notably the MAC addresses.

Configuring Basic SR/TLB

Configuring SR/TLB involves configuring multiport SRB and transparent bridging (both described earlier). After this is finished, the primary command that distinguishes an SR/TLB configuration is the source-bridge transparent statement, which links the SRB environment with the transparent bridge environment. The full syntax is explained here:

`source-bridge transparent` ring-group pseudo-ring bridge-number tb-group

- ring-group is the virtual ring group created by the source-bridge ring group command.

- pseudo-ring is the ring number that represents the transparent domain to the SRB domain.

- `bridge-number` is the bridge that leads to the transparent domain from the SRB domain.
- `tb-group` is the number of the transparent bridge-group that should be tied to the SRB domain.

The diagram and IOS configuration listing in Figure 7.11 provide an additional explanation.

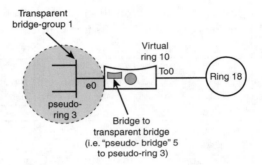

Figure 7.11
Network topology used in configuring SR/TLB example.

In Figure 7.11, a RIF showing the route from the Token-Ring segment to the Ethernet segment would show ring 18 to bridge 7 to ring 10 to bridge 5 to ring 3.

Here is how the router/bridge in Figure 7.11 would be configured for SR/TLB:

```
source-bridge ring-group 10          (establishes virtual ring)
source-bridge transparent 10 3 5 1   (specifies ring-group, pseudo-ring,
                                      bridge-number, & transparent bridge-group)

interface Ethernet0
 bridge-group 1                (assigns the interface to transparent bridge group 1)

interface TokenRing0
 source-bridge 18 7 10         (local ring, bridge number, virtual/target ring)
 source-bridge spanning        (enables NetBIOS spanning explorers)

bridge 1 protocol ieee         (bridge 1 will use the spanning tree protocol)
```

Key Concept

SR/TLB allows an Ethernet segment to be part of the SRB domain, identified by the pseudo-ring.

Data-Link Switching

Data-Link Switching (DLSw), described in RFC 1795, provides a method for forwarding SNA and NetBIOS traffic over TCP/IP networks using Data Link layer encapsulation and switching. DLSw uses *Switch-to-Switch Protocol (SSP)* instead of SRB, eliminating the major limitations of SRB, including hop-count limits, broadcasts and unnecessary traffic, timeouts, lack of flow control, and lack of prioritization schemes. SSP is used to locate resources, establish connections, forward data, and handle flow control and error recovery. In contrast to SRB and its derivatives, DLSw also natively switches between diverse media. However, the primary advantage of DLSw over SRB is that it locally terminates data-link connections (DLCs), such as LLC2. By terminating DLCs locally, DLSw eliminates DLC timeouts and keeps unnecessary traffic—such as link layer acknowledgments, keepalives, and polling—off the WAN. Because of these and other advantages over SRB, Cisco recommends DLSw implementations over SRB.

DLSw Terms

DLSw routers are referred to as *peers*. The connection between two DLSw routers is referred to as a *peer connection*. A single peer connection can carry multiple circuits. A DLSw *circuit* comprises the following:

- The data-link control connection between the originating SNA device and the originating router
- The TCP connection between the two routers
- The data-link control connection between the target router and the destination SNA device

The diagram in Figure 7.12 illustrates the essential DLSw terms and concepts.

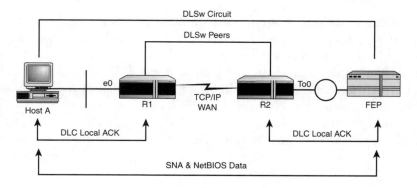

Figure 7.12
DLSw terms and concepts.

DLSw Operation

Before any end-system communication can occur over DLSw, the following must take place:

- Establish peer connections (IOS command: `show dlsw peer`)
- Exchange capabilities (IOS command: `show dlsw capabilities`)
- Establish circuit (IOS command: `show dlsw circuit`)

A peering relationship is established as soon as there is TCP/IP connectivity between the two routers and DLSw is configured on both routers. A single router may have multiple DLSw peers, also called partners. After the TCP connections are established, the routers exchange their capabilities. These include the DLSw version number, initial pacing windows (receive window size), NetBIOS support, list of supported link service access points (SAPs), and the number of TCP sessions supported.

Circuit establishment between a pair of end systems includes locating the target resource (based on its destination MAC address or NetBIOS name) and setting up data-link control connections. This process is transparently "spoofed" by the DLSw SSP process, with the DLC connections actually being established between each end system and its local DLSw router. From our discussion on SRB, we know that SNA devices find each other by sending an explorer frame (a TEST or an exchange identification [XID] frame) with the MAC address of the target SNA device. When a DLSw router receives an explorer frame, the router sends a `canureach` frame to each of its DLSw peers. If one of these partners can reach the specified MAC address, it replies with an `icanreach` frame. The specific sequence includes a `canureach ex` (explorer) to find the resource and a `canureach cs` (circuit setup) that triggers the peering routers to establish a circuit. DLSw will cache this information so that subsequent searches for the same resource do not result in the sending of additional explorer frames.

After the circuit is established, SNA information frames can flow over the circuit, while DLC layer ACKs continue to be handled by the routers on each side of the circuit. To the end stations, the network appears to have only one bridge between them. To the DLSw process, this circuit is uniquely identified by the source and destination circuit IDs, which are carried in all steady state data frames in lieu of data-link control addresses such as MAC addresses. Each circuit ID is defined by the destination and source MAC addresses, destination and source link service access points (LSAPs), and a data-link control port ID. The circuit concept simplifies management and is important in error processing and cleanup.

Key Concept

DLSw, with its peers and circuits concepts, replaces SRT, RSRB, and SR/TLB. With local ACK of layer-2 frames, it is able to preserve bandwidth and reduce timeouts associated with bridging over a WAN.

Configuring DLSw

There are some similarities between configuring DLSw and RSRB. Although there are many options to the `dlsw remote-peer` statement, the ones used here demonstrate the essential concepts. The following example relates to Figure 7.12.

```
R1

dlsw local-peer peer-id 10.1.10.1          (specifies local DLSw address)
dlsw remote-peer 0 tcp 10.1.20.1           (remote DLSw address & encapsulation)
dlsw bridge-group 1                      (bridge 1 is part of the DLSw process)

interface Loopback0
 ip address 10.1.10.1 255.255.255.252    (creates local DLSw interface
                                           to be used in peering)

interface Ethernet0
 bridge-group 1              (assigns the interface to transparent bridge group 1)

bridge 1 protocol ieee          (specifies that bridge 1 uses
                                  the spanning tree protocol)

R2

source-bridge ring-group 100              (establishes virtual ring)
dlsw local-peer peer-id 10.1.20.1 promiscuous    (specifies local DLSw address
                                                    and allows multiple peers)
dlsw duplicate-path-bias load-balance      (per circuit load balancing)

interface Loopback0
 ip address 10.1.20.1 255.255.255.252    (creates local DLSw interface
                                           to be used in peering)

interface TokenRing0
 source-bridge 17 1 100        (local ring, bridge number, virtual/target ring)

interface TokenRing1
 source-bridge 19 1 100        (local ring, bridge number, virtual/target ring)
```

PART
III

CH
7

In this example, SNA and NetBIOS traffic on e0 of R1 are tied to the DLSw process via the `bridge-group 1` statements. The configuration shown in R2 adds additional features not shown in the diagram. The `promiscuous` statement allows any DLSw router to become a partner without modification of R2's configuration. It is common in large enterprise networks to have a Front End Processor (FEP) on two different rings (often with the same MAC address configured on multiple NICs). For redundancy in the router, a second Token-Ring interface is used along with `dlsw duplicate-path-bias load-balance`. This command allows the router to load-balance between the two Token-Ring segments on a per-circuit basis, not on a per-packet basis. In the event of failure associated with one ring, traffic would be quickly switched to the other ring. In an SRB environment, the stations would then have to rediscover the route to the destination. However, this redundancy is handled by the DLSw process; the end stations are unaware of these events and therefore suffer no ill effects.

Command Output Examples

The three major `show` commands are provided to further demonstrate the DLSw concepts.

```
R1#show dlsw peer
Peers:              state    pkts_rx   pkts_tx  type  drops ckts TCP  uptime
   TCP 10.1.20.1    CONNECT  13817927   760164  conf      0    2   0    3w1d
```

Output from this command shows that R1 has established a peering relationship with R2. Other important statistics are shown, such as how long they have been partners (counters are reset if the connection is unavailable), the number of circuits between them (2), and how many packets have been sent and received.

```
R1#show dlsw reachability
DLSw Remote MAC address reachability cache list
Mac Addr          status    Loc.    port             rif
0000.8124.1106    FOUND     LOCAL   TBridge-001    --no rif--
0002.f682.c4e3    FOUND     LOCAL   TBridge-001    --no rif--
4000.7000.0003    FOUND     REMOTE  10.1.20.1(2065)
```

Output from this command shows the MAC addresses of SNA devices, both local and remote. This information is shared between DLSw peers and helps reduce DLSw explorer packets.

```
R1#show dlsw circuits
Index           local addr(lsap)     remote addr(dsap)   state
1040187525      0002.f682.c4e3(18)   4000.7000.0003(04)  CONNECTED
520093825       0002.f682.c4e3(04)   4000.7000.0003(04)  CONNECTED
```

Output from this command shows the two circuits, the local MAC address (in Token-Ring format), the local service access point (LSAP), the remote MAC address (in Token-Ring format), the destination SAP, and the state of the connection. When "CONNECTED" is shown, this indicates that a circuit has been established and data may now be exchanged between the two end stations.

QUESTIONS AND ANSWERS

1. What are the four primary nonroutable protocols?

    A: SNA, NetBIOS, DEC LAT, DEC MOP

2. How is CRB different from IRB?

    A: In CRB, the routing and bridging processes are separate, whereas in IRB they are integrated.

3. What is the function of the BVI?

    A: The BVI represents the bridging interfaces to the routing process.

4. In an SRB environment, what device determines the data communications path between end stations?

    A: Unlike a routed environment, in which the end stations only need to know about the gateway, an SRB environment requires that the source host specify the route through the network to the destination host.

5. What is the function of the explorer?

    A: In an SRB environment, an end station sends out an explorer to discover the route to the destination host.

6. What is the function of the RIF?

    A: The Route Information Field (RIF) is used by the source to specify the route through the network to the destination host.

7. How many bits does it take to specify the ring number?

    A: The short answer is three. This question is intentionally somewhat vague to represent those on the test that are equally vague and could be interpreted in a few different ways.

8. What is the maximum hop-count in SRB environments?

    A: The short answer is seven. Like the previous question, it is somewhat vague. Both the original IBM standard and Cisco's recommendations state seven. However, the IEEE 802.5 standard now allows for 15 hops.

9. What is the difference between RSRB and SRB?

    A: RSRB is a Cisco-proprietary function that allows an SRB domain to exist over non–Token-Ring network, such as a WAN.

10. In an SRT environment, what determines whether a frame enters the SRB domain?

    A: If the Ring Information Indicator (RII) field is set to 1 and the frame contains a RIF, the frame enters the SRB domain. If these conditions are not met, the frame is transparently bridged.

PART

III

CH

7

PRACTICE TEST

1. In a bridged network, end stations always communicate with the actual MAC address of their partners.

   A. True
   B. False

Answer A is correct because in a routed network, end stations communicate with the actual MAC address of partners on the local segment only. For off-segment traffic, the end stations communicate with the MAC address of the gateway (router) on their local segment. Ethernet to Token-Ring bridging is not an exception because the bits are simply read in a different order, not changed. Answer B is incorrect because bridges cannot communicate with anything other than a MAC address.

2. In source-route bridging (SRB), what specifically indicates that a frame is destined for a remote ring?

   A. The multicast bit in the source address field is set to 0.
   B. The multicast bit in the source address field is set to 1.
   C. The explorer bit is set to 0.
   D. The explorer bit is set to 1.
   E. The routing information field contains route designators.

Answer A is incorrect because if the bit were set to 1, it would be a multicast. **Answer B is correct because a value of 1 indicates "on," so this is a multicast, which is how a remote ring will be found.** Answers C and D are incorrect because the explorer bit does not indicate anything about a destination. Answer E is incorrect because, although the presence of route designators in the RIF (Answer E) would be the most obvious indication that the frame is destined for a remote ring, the frame will not make it past the local ring if the multicast bit is not set to 1, so does not in itself indicate the packet's destination.

3. Which is not a valid bridge number in a route designator?

   A. 0x3
   B. 0x7
   C. 0xb
   D. 0xf
   E. 0x11

Answers A through D are incorrect because the bridge number always appears as a two-character value when shown in hex, which the "0x" indicates. **Answer E is correct; because the field length is four bits long, the maximum value it can contain is F (15). It could also**

be argued that the IBM specification only allows for a maximum of seven bridges, a value Cisco recommends. The vagueness of the question is in line with Cisco's test.

4. In CRB, the command `no ip routing` is required to bridge routable protocols.

   A. True

   B. False

Answer A is incorrect because if the command is entered, the interface that is routing IP would be disabled from routing IP. **Answer B is correct because this command would disable the routing functions of CRB, and no routing would take place.**

5. Which statements are not true of a BVI?

   A. It translates between Ethernet and Token-Ring.

   B. It represents the bridging domain to the routed domain.

   C. It bridges IP by default.

   D. It bridges traffic only from the bridge group it represents.

   E. All traffic routed to the BVI is forwarded to the corresponding bridge group as bridged traffic.

Answer A is correct because it does not translate between media. Answer B is incorrect because it is a true statement. **Answer C is correct because a BVI routes; it does not bridge. Answer D is correct because a BVI routes, not bridges traffic.** Answer E is incorrect because this text comes directly from Cisco documentation.

6. A bridge that connects dissimilar media is called a

   A. Transparent bridge

   B. Source-route bridge

   C. Source-route transparent bridge

   D. Translational bridge

   E. Translating bridge

Answer A is incorrect because a transparent bridge connects Ethernet to Ethernet or Token-Ring to Token-Ring. Answer B is incorrect because a source-route bridge by definition can only use Token-Ring media. Answer C is incorrect because source-route transparent bridging is blending both technologies in one device. **Answer D is correct because translation means to convert data into a different media type.** Answer E is incorrect because a "translating bridge" is not a defined term.

7. Which types of bridges do not encapsulate the data into a different protocol?

   A. Source-route bridging

   B. Remote source-route bridging

   C. Transparent bridging

   D. Translational bridging

PART

III

CH

7

Answer A is correct because SRB is all Token-Ring. Answer B is incorrect because RSRB allows the definition of a virtual ring-group to allow the SRB domain to cross a non–Token-Ring network by means of encapsulation into a different protocol (that is, over a TCP/IP WAN link). **Answer C is correct because it is all Ethernet. Answer D is correct because it does not encapsulate anything; it converts data into a different media type.**

Refer to the following output from a show interface command for the next three questions:

TokenRing0 is up, line protocol is up

    Hardware is TMS380, address is 0000.30a0.a66f (bia 0000.30a0.a66f)

    MTU 4464 bytes, BW 16000 Kbit, DLY 630 usec, rely 255/255, load 1/255

    Encapsulation SNAP, loopback not set, keepalive set (10 sec)

    ARP type: SNAP, ARP Timeout 04:00:00

    Ring speed: 16 Mbps

    Multiring node, Source-Route Transparent bridge capable

    Source bridging enabled, srn 30 bn 2 trn 100 (ring group) proxy explorers enabled, spanning explorer disabled, NetBIOS cache enabled

    Group Address: 0x00000000, Functional Address: 0x0800011A

    Ethernet Transit OUI: 0x000000

8. From the output shown above, which of the following statements are not true?
   - A. The presence of the Encapsulation SNAP statement indicates that this interface is part of a transparent bridge configuration.
   - B. The presence of the multiring node statement indicates that this interface will translate Token-Ring to a FDDI DAS.
   - C. NetBIOS explorers are not supported.
   - D. Packets received on this interface without a RIF will be transparently bridged.
   - E. The presence of the ring group statement indicates that this interface is part of an RSRB configuration.

Answer A is correct because the encapsulation type has no relationship to transparent bridge configurations. Answer B is correct because the multiring node designation simply enables collection and use of RIF information. Answer C is incorrect because spanning explorers are disabled, so NetBIOS will not be able to send explorers. **Answer D is correct because an interface will report that it is SRT capable, but without knowing the router's configuration, it is impossible to tell from this output whether frames can be**

transparently bridged anywhere. **Answer E is correct because the existence of a ring group does not necessarily indicate an RSRB configuration. For example, a multiport SRB configuration would require the existence of a ring group.**

9. According to information shown above, this interface is capable of SRT. This means that which of the following is true?

   A. Token-Ring using SNAP encapsulation to Token-Ring using 802.3 encapsulation.

   B. Routing Information Fields (RIF) will be added or removed as necessary when going between the different media types.

   C. This interface can only forward traffic to Ethernet segments.

   D. The router will source-route transparently bridge Token-Ring frames to FDDI.

   E. Packets received on this interface without a Routing Information Field (RIF) can be transparently bridged.

Answer A is incorrect because this is a nonsense answer. Answer B is incorrect because the question asked about SRT (transparent bridging), not translational bridging. Answer C is incorrect because this is also a nonsense answer. Answer D is incorrect because a Token-Ring to FDDI bridge would be a translational bridge. **Answer E is correct because this is the exact interpretation.**

10. What is the Ethernet Transit OUI used for?

    A. Identifies bridge frames that are to be routed out this interface.

    B. Used when an Ethernet frame is translated to a Token-Ring SNAP frame.

    C. Used when bridging NetBIOS frames to non-IBM environments to mask out the vendor ID field.

    D. Provided for backward compatibility with Token-Ring to Ethernet repeaters.

    E. Used as the bridge number when traversing virtual rings.

Answer B is correct.

PART

IV

Routing TCP/IP

8 TCP/IP

9 Routing Concept Overview

10 RIP

11 IGRP and EIGRP

12 OSPF

13 BGP

14 Managing Routing

CHAPTER PREREQUISITE

You must understand the following chapters before moving on to this chapter: Chapter 1, "General Network Overview," Chapter 2, "General Topic Overview," and Chapter 3, "Ethernet."

TCP/IP

— WHILE YOU READ —

1. What does the TTL field of an IP packet header do?

2. What does the ACK field in the TCP packet header do?

3. What is the difference between TCP and UDP?

4. Telnet runs on TCP port ___ and FTP runs on TCP port ___.

5. What is HSRP?

6. What three Cisco commands are required to configure HSRP?

7. How do you enable the forwarding of DHCP broadcasts on a Cisco router?

8. What is the difference between a Public IP address and a Private IP address?

SEE
APPENDIX **F**

This chapter reviews TCP/IP and some of its common services. An understanding of the header details for both IP and TCP is critical in passing the CCIE written exam. In addition, understanding network address masks and how to subnet a network level address into smaller subnetworks is a must for the CCIE candidate.

IP

IP is defined as a connectionless, Network-layer (layer-3) protocol. IP was created as a way to hide the complexity of physical addressing by creating a virtual addressing scheme that is independent of the underlying network. Just try to imagine managing a network based on MAC addresses instead of IP addresses. In addition to addressing, IP provides for packet fragmentation and reassembly. IP does not ensure that data is delivered to the application in the appropriate order; that responsibility is left to upper-layer protocols such as TCP and UDP.

Key Concept

IP is a connectionless, Network-layer protocol.

Header Format

An IP header contains several pieces of information. The majority of the information is used in the process of routing data from source to destination. The minimum length of the header is 20 bytes and the maximum length of the header is 24 bytes, depending on whether the *options* field is used (see Figure 8.1).

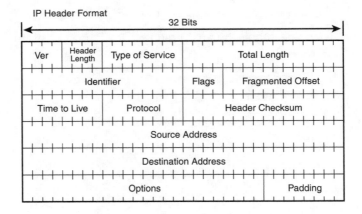

Figure 8.1
IP packet header.

IP Header fields:

- Ver (Version)—Identifies the version of IP implemented. In almost all cases, this value will be set to 0100, which indicates version 4. This value will not change until IPv6 is implemented.

- Header Length—Describes the length of the header in 32-bit words. The minimum length of an IP header is 20 bytes, which translates to a Header Length value of (20 bytes × 8 bits/byte) ÷ 32 bits/word = 5. This is represented in binary form as 0101. The maximum length is 24 bytes, which equates to a Header Length value of 6 or in binary, 0110.

- Type of Service—This field is assigned by upper-layer protocols that instruct IP how they would like the data within the packet handled. IP Precedence is on such upper-layer protocols.

- Total Length—Specifies the number of bytes within the IP packet (header plus data).

- Identifier—A unique number assigned by the sender that is used to reassemble a fragmented datagram. Fragments of a datagram all have the same value in the Identifier field.

- Flags—Made up of three bits.
  - Bit 0 = reserved
  - Bit 1 = Don't Fragment Bit (DF): 0 = may fragment, 1 = don't fragment
  - Bit 2 = More Fragment Bit (MF): 0 = last fragment, 1 = more fragments

- Fragmented Offset—Indicates where a fragment fits within a fragmented datagram. Value is represented in units of 64 bits.

- Time to Live (TTL)—Indicates the maximum time that a packet can be on the network. Each router that processes this packet decrements the TTL value by 1. If the value reaches 0, the packet is discarded from the network. The purpose of this field is to eliminate the possibility of a packet endlessly traversing across the network.

- Protocol—Indicates the upper-layer protocol that will handle the packet after the IP portion is process. Some well-known values are

1	Internet Control Message Protocol (ICMP)
6	Transmission Control Protocol (TCP)
17	User Datagram Protocol (UDP)
88	Interior Gateway Routing Protocol (IGRP)
89	Open Shortest Path First (OSPF)

- Header Checksum—Provides error control for the integrity of the IP header only.
- Source Address—32-bit address originating the packet.
- Destination Address—32-bit address of the packet's destination.
- Options—Variable length field that might be used. Usually not used.
- Padding—If an option is used, the datagram is padded with zeros to bring the total length of the IP header that is a multiple of 32 bits.

IP Addressing

An IP address is 32 bits long. The bits can be broken down into four bytes. Each byte is expressed in decimal form and separated from other bytes by a dot (that is, *x.x.x.x*). This is called *dotted-decimal* format. Each bit within a byte carries a binary weight (starting from left to right) of 128, 64, 32, 16, 8, 4, 2, 1. If you add up these values, you get a range of 0–255 for each byte.

For example, one byte can be translated from binary format to decimal format as follows:

```
128   64   32   16   8   4   2   1
 0     1    0    1    1   0   0   1  =  0 + 64 + 0 + 32 + 16 + 0 + 0 + 1 = 113
```

IP addressing has been broken down into five separate classes based on the number of maximum hosts required by the network (see Figure 8.2).

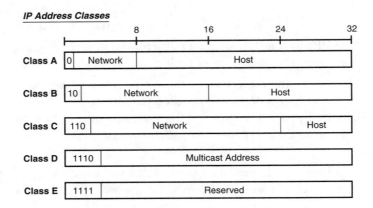

Figure 8.2
IP address classes.

You can see from Figure 8.2 that each address class contains a network portion and a host portion. The network portion identifies the data link that is in common with all the devices attached to that network. This is the portion of the address that is used to make routing decisions as the packet traverses between networks. The host portion uniquely identifies an end device connected to the network.

An easy way to determine the class of network that you are looking at is to examine the value of the first few bits of the address. Class A addresses always begin with the first bit set to 0, Class B addresses have the first two bits set to 1 0, and Class C are set to 1 1 0. However, humans don't think of IP addresses in their binary format, so it is simply easier to just memorize the information in Table 8.1.

Table 8.1 IP Address Classes

Class	Decimal Value of First Byte	Purpose	Max. Hosts
Class A	0–127	Large organizations	16,777,214
Class B	128–191	Medium-sized organizations	65,543
Class C	192–223	Small organizations	254
Class D	224–247	Multicast addresses	n/a
Class E	248–255	Experimental	n/a

Class A, B, and C addresses are most commonly known for their availability for commercial use. Within these three classes, we can make a further distinction between public address space and private address space. Private address space is not recognized by the Internet and can be used by anyone for use within a private network. Public address space, on the other hand, is a unique address that is assigned to a company. Within Classes A, B, and C the following ranges have been defined by RFC 1597 as private address space:

Starting Address	Ending Address
10.0.0.0	10.255.255.255
172.16.0.0	172.31.255.255
192.168.0.0	192.168.255.255

 Key Concept

Make sure you have the Private Address ranges memorized.

Each network has two addresses that are reserved and cannot be used for host addresses. The first address of the network range is the address of the network itself. The last address of the network range is the broadcast address, used to contact all hosts on that network. Take, for example, the Class C private network 192.168.1.0–192.168.255.255. The address 192.168.1.0 is the address of the network (used for routing) and the address 192.168.1.255 is the broadcast address for this network.

Address Masks

The network mask is used in conjunction with an IP address to delineate the network portion of an IP address from the host portion. Each major network address within its designated class has a standard network mask:

Address Class	Network Mask
Class A	255.0.0.0
Class B	255.255.0.0
Class C	255.255.255.0

A major network address can be further divided into smaller networks by using a technique called *subnetting*. When a major network is subnetted, the address can be broken into three parts:

- The network portion
- The subnet portion
- The host portion

When a network mask is varied into further subnets like this, it is commonly referred to as a *Variable Length Subnet Mask (VLSM)*.

Cisco often represents the subnet mask by identifying the number of bits used as the mask. For example, 192.174.10.0/30 would represent network 192.174.10.0 255.255.255.252. The value of 30 represents the number of bits used for the network portion of the address; in binary format, 30 would be

```
255.255.255.252 = 11111111.11111111.11111111.11111100 = 30
```

Let's look at another example. Given the following 170.130.0.0/21, what is the subnet mask?

```
21 = 11111111.11111111.11111100.00000000
```

The network address and mask are

```
170.130.0.0 255.255.248.0.
```

Understanding how to derive the network address and broadcast address when given an IP address and mask is critical to passing the CCIE Written Exam. Let's say that we want to determine the network address, the broadcast address, and the available addresses that correspond with the given IP address:

```
150.34.74.53    255.255.240.0
```

1. Convert the IP address and its address mask into binary format.

```
150.34.74.53  =    10010110    00100010    01001010    00110101
255.255.240.0 =    11111111    11111111    11110000    00000000
```

2. Perform a logical AND between the IP address and the mask.

A logical AND is a digital math operation that compares two bits of data to each other. The result of the operation is as follows:

0 and 0 = 0

0 and 1 = 0

1 and 0 = 0

1 and 1 = 1

So,

```
Host Address:       10010110    00100010    01001010    00110101
Mask:               11111111    11111111    11110000    00000000
Logical AND Result: 10010110    00100010    01000000    00000000
```

3. Convert the results of the logical AND back into decimal format; this is the network address:

```
10010110    00100010    01000000    00000000    = 150.34.64.0
```

4. Calculate the broadcast address.

Remember that the network mask is used to delineate the network portion of an IP address from the host portion. Mask bits are set to 1 if the corresponding bit in the IP address should be considered part of the network address and 0 if part of the host address.

```
150.34.74.53  =    10010110    00100010    0100      1010      00110101
255.255.240.0 =    11111111    11111111    1111      0000      00000000
                   Network Bits                      Host Bits
```

To determine the broadcast address, we need to replace each bit available within the host portion of the IP address with a value of 1.

So, the broadcast address of the network for the host 150.34.74.53 is

```
150.34.79.255 =    10010110    00100010    0100      1111      11111111
                   Network Bits                      Host Bits
```

Summary:

Given the IP address and address mask: 150.34.74.53 255.255.240.0, we have determined the following:

Network Address =	150.34.64.0
Broadcast Address =	150.34.79.255
Available Addresses =	150.34.64.1–150.34.79.254 (for a total of 4,078 hosts)

Key Concept

An address whose host bits are all 0s represents the network address. An address whose host bits are all 1s represents the broadcast address. Hosts on the same physical network must use the same address mask.

Address Resolution Protocol (ARP)

On a single physical network, hosts know of one another by their MAC address. As I mentioned earlier, IP addressing provides a more-logical and more-manageable host addressing scheme than does the 48-bit MAC address. The *Address Resolution Protocol (ARP)* provides dynamic address resolution between the MAC address of a host and its administered IP address.

The idea behind ARP is simple. Following Figure 8.3, when Host A wants to communicate with Host B, Host A must somehow learn the MAC address associated with Host B's physical adapter. This is where ARP comes in. The upper-layer application running on Host A knows the IP address of Host B; however, the lower-link-layer protocols need to associate this IP address with the physical MAC address of Host B. First, Host A looks within its ARP cache to see whether there is already a mapping between the IP address of Host B and a MAC address. If there is a mapping, IP hands the packet down to the link-layer protocol and the frame is written to the destination MAC address associated with Host B's IP address.

Key Concept

ARP maps MAC address to known network (IP) address.

If there isn't a mapping within Host A's ARP cache, Host A sends out a link-layer broadcast message. All hosts on the physical network forward this message up to the IP layer.

After Host B receives the broadcast message, the frame is handed off from the link layer to the Network layer or IP. Host B sees that the broadcast has an IP destination of itself. So, Host B responds directly to Host A. After Host A receives the response to the ARP message, a mapping that associates the IP address to the MAC address is entered into Host A's ARP cache. The ARP cache is then used for subsequent transactions. Entries in the ARP cache are usually flushed after a period of inactivity.

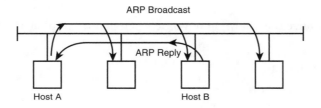

Figure 8.3
ARP operation.

If the destination host is not on the same network, a router will respond to Host A's ARP request. This is called *proxy ARP* and is shown in Figure 8.4. In this case, if the router has Host B's MAC address in its ARP cache, the router will respond to Host A's ARP request. The router will respond with the MAC address of the port that is on Host A's segment. If the router does not have Host B's MAC address in its ARP cache, the router will send out an ARP request to discover Host B's MAC address. After Host B responds to the router, the router can cache the address and respond to Host A.

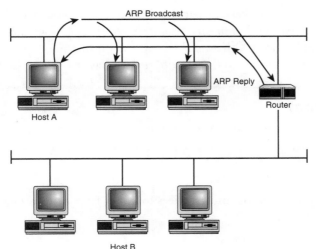

Figure 8.4
Router proxy ARP.

On a Cisco router, the default ARP cache timeout is set to four hours. If a mapping is not used for four hours, it will be removed from the cache. The default can be administratively controlled through the Cisco interface command:

```
arp timeout {#_of_seconds}
```

An arp timeout with a value of 0 on a Cisco router indicates that the ARP cache never times out. After an entry is entered into the ARP table, the entry is there until the router is reloaded.

You might often notice the following response when you try to ping a device from a Cisco router:

```
router>ping 192.168.10.3
```

Type escape sequence to abort.

```
Sending 5, 100-byte ICMP Echos to 192.168.10.3, timeout is 2 seconds:
.!!!!
```

The ping will return a value of a "dot" for the first ICMP echo request that it sends because there isn't an entry with the routers ARP cache associated with the IP address pinged. The "dot" represents the ARP broadcast message that was sent to resolve the MAC address associated with this IP address. By the time the second ping is sent (two seconds later), ARP has done its job and all subsequent pings are successful.

Transmission Control Protocol (TCP)

As previously discussed, the IP protocol does not provide reliable, connection-oriented, error-free delivery of data packets. In a routed network, this can result in the delivery of duplicate packets, corrupted packets, or packets that are out of sequence. In order to resolve these inefficiencies, the *Transmission Control Protocol (TCP)* was defined in RFC 793. TCP provides applications with a reliable, connection-oriented (end-to-end) data delivery service. TCP corresponds to the Transport layer (layer 4) of the OSI model.

 Key Concept

TCP is a reliable, connection-oriented Transport-layer protocol.

Features

To provide reliable, connection-oriented services to upper-layer applications, TCP provides the following features:

- Data Segmentation—Applications do not have to be concerned with breaking up data streams into the appropriate MTU (maximum transmission unit) supported by the underlying layer-2 protocols. During the setup of a TCP connection, the TCP protocol determines its maximum segment size based on the lowest MTU across the network.

- Reliability—Each transmitted TCP segment is assigned a sequence number, from which an acknowledgment (ACK) is required. If an ACK is not received within a specified time interval, the data is retransmitted. In addition to guaranteeing delivery of the data, the sequence number is also used to ensure that the original data stream is delivered to the upper-layer application in the same order in which it was sent.

- Flow Control—The TCP "window size" ensures that the TCP sender does not overflow the TCP receiver with data that the receiver cannot buffer.

- Multiplexing—The use of TCP ports enables a client to run multiple network applications simultaneously.

- Full Duplex—TCP provides for concurrent data transfer in both directions.

Header Format

Figure 8.5 shows a TCP packet header. It is important to know the fields of the header to fully understand how TCP operates.

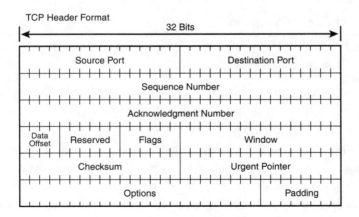

Figure 8.5
TCP segment header.

TCP Header fields:

- Source/Destination Port—Identifies the upper-layer applications that TCP is servicing (see section "Well-Known TCP/UDP Ports" later in this chapter for further discussion).

- Sequence Number—Specifies the sequence number assigned to the first byte following the TCP header (the encapsulated data). Each byte of a data steam delivered from an upper-layer protocol to TCP is assigned a sequence number. For example, if the sequence number were 1400 for a segment containing 600 bytes of data, the next segment would have a sequence number of 1400 + 600 + 1 = 2001.

- Acknowledgment Number—This field contains the value of the next sequence number the sending device expects to receive.

- Data Offset—Identifies the beginning of the data field by indicating the length of the header in 32-bit groups. This field is necessary because the options and padding fields are not included unless a specific option variable is used.

- Reserved—These bits are reserved for future use and always have a value of 0.

- Flags—Six one-bit fields used to tell how to interpret the contents of the header. The six fields are
    - URG—Urgent Pointer field significant
    - ACK—Acknowledgment field significant
    - PSH—Push Function
    - RST—Reset the connection
    - SYN—Synchronize sequence numbers
    - FIN—End of data stream

- Window—Indicates the number of octets that the receiver of this segment can transmit before it has to stop and wait for an acknowledgment.

- Checksum—Verifies the integrity of the segment.

- Urgent Pointer—Instructs TCP where the "urgent data" ends so that any interrupted data streams can continue. Whenever the URG bit is set, the data within the segment is given priority over any other data stream.

- Options—Specifies various TCP options, the most common of which is the "Maximum Segment Size."

- Padding—The options field is a multiple of eight bits; therefore, bit padding is necessary to ensure that the TCP header ends at a 32-bit boundary.

TCP Connection Establishment

To establish an end-to-end connection-oriented session, TCP uses a "three-way hand-shake" mechanism. Figure 8.6 shows the simplest example.

Key Concept

TCP uses a "three-way handshake" when setting up a TCP connection.

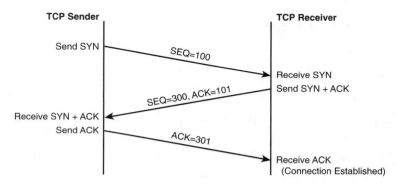

Figure 8.6
TCP handshake.

The TCP Sender begins the handshake by sending a SYN segment (SYN bit set to 1) indicating that it will use sequence numbers starting with 100. After the TCP Receiver processes the SYN segment, it responds with its own SYN and also includes an ACK (SYN and ACK bits set to 1) that indicates to the TCP Sender that the TCP Receiver is ready for the next segment. After the TCP Sender receives the SYN + ACK from the TCP Receiver, it turns around and sends an ACK (ACK bit set to 1) that acknowledges the TCP Receiver's SYN.

User Datagram Protocol (UDP)

Like TCP, *User Datagram Protocol (UDP)* is a layer-4 (Transport-layer) protocol that provides IP with an interface to upper-layer applications. The difference between TCP and UDP is that TCP is a connection-oriented protocol that provides error recovery and UDP is a connectionless protocol that doesn't provide error recovery. The benefit of UDP over TCP is that the header of UDP is significantly smaller than TCP.

Key Concept

UDP is an unreliable, connectionless, Transport-layer protocol.

Figure 8.7 shows a UDP packet header. It is important to know the fields of the header to fully understand how UDP operates.

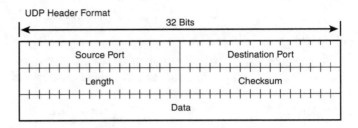

Figure 8.7
UDP segment header.

UDP Header fields:

- Source/Destination Port—Identifies the upper-layer applications that TCP is servicing.
- Length—Length in bytes of the UDP segment including data and header.
- Checksum—Verifies the integrity of the segment. Provides error detection, not correction.

Well-Known TCP/UDP Ports

TCP and UDP have defined port numbers for some common applications. Knowing some of the more common port numbers is helpful in defining and understanding extended IP access-lists which will very likely be on the test. Also, don't be surprised if you get a question or two on the written exam that explicitly asks you what the port number is for an application. Table 8.2 should help you prepare for such questions.

Table 8.2   Well-Known Port Numbers

Well-Known Port Number	Application
21	FTP
23	Telnet
25	SMTP
53	DNS
67/68	BootP

Well-Known Port Number	Application
69	TFTP
80	HTTP
123	NTP

Domain Name Service (DNS)

Domain Name Service (DNS) is used within a network to map an IP address to a machine's hostname. It is obviously quite a bit easier to remember a device's hostname (provided the naming scheme has some logic to it) than it is to remember it by its IP address. DNS is a hierarchical naming scheme used by the Internet and internal corporate intranets. Within the DNS hierarchy, the top level is always the "root" of the domain and is represented within a domain name with a dot. From the root domain, the hierarchy branches down into nodes or subdomains. Each node or subdomain is represented by a simple name. The domain name is actually the sequence of nodes, separated by dots, to the root domain.

Figure 8.8 shows an example.

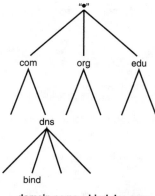

domain name = bind.dns.com.

Figure 8.8
DNS naming hierarchy.

DNS is based on a client/server paradigm. When a client queries a DNS server for the IP address associated with a domain name, the client generally sends out what is called a *recursive query*. The recursive query instructs the receiving DNS server that the client is requesting one of three responses:

- The IP address associated with the domain name
- Error stating that the DNS server can't respond to the request
- Message stating the domain name doesn't exist

If the DNS server is *authoritative*, meaning the server's database contains data for the requested domain name, the server responds directly to the client with the IP address associated to the domain name. If the DNS server is *nonauthoritative*, the server typically sends out an *iterative query* to DNS servers that it knows about. The iterative query tells the receiving DNS server to respond with the "best" information it has on the requested domain name. Sometimes this is the IP address for the domain name; other times it is the IP address of another server that might be better qualified to answer the query.

Internet Control Message Protocol (ICMP)

Internet Control Message Protocol (ICMP) is a Network-layer protocol within IP that provides an error-reporting mechanism. ICMP messages are always sent within the data portion of an IP packet. The ICMP echo request-reply is the most common message and is generated by executing the ping command on Cisco hardware. In response to an ICMP echo request, a router or host might respond with any of many different ICMP messages. Table 8.3 identifies the meaning of the various responses possible when issuing the ping command from a Cisco router.

Table 8.3   Common Ping Results

Ping Result	Description
!	Indicates successful receipt of an ICMP echo-reply
.	Indicates that there was a complete route to the host, but an ICMP echo-reply was never generated
U	Destination Unreachable—There is no route to the final destination network in the routing table
N	Network Unreachable—There is a route, but there was some kind of routing failure
P	Protocol Unreachable—Generally means that the receiving host does not support the upper-layer protocol specified with the Protocol Field of the IP header
Q	Source Quench—Means the neighboring router doesn't have the buffer space required to queue the packet for output to the next network
M	Could Not Fragment—Don't fragment bit is set within the IP header, however, fragmentation of the packet is required

Ping Result	Description
A	The destination is Administratively Unreachable. The path is blocked by an interface that is Administratively down or an ACL.
?	Unknown packet type

Hot Standby Routing Protocol (HSRP)

Hot Standby Routing Protocol (HSRP) is a Cisco proprietary protocol that brings routing functionality to end devices that would otherwise be incapable of taking advantage of redundant network connections. HSRP enables a pair of Cisco routers to work together to present the appearance of a single virtual default-gateway to end devices on a LAN segment. When you configure HSRP, the administrator assigns the virtual IP address whereas the Cisco IOS chooses a MAC address that falls within Cisco's MAC address block.

HSRP uses a priority scheme that enables routers within the same *standby group* to determine which is the *Active router* and which is the *Standby router*. The router with the highest priority is designated as the Active router; this would be the router that will forward all traffic. The mode of the router (Active/Standby) is communicated among routers within the same HSRP group through the HSRP Hello Protocol. A router that is a member of an HSRP group assumes it is in the Active mode until it hears an HSRP Hello that contains a priority that is higher than that configured on its interface. By default, the HSRP Hellos are sent out every 3 seconds and the hold timer is 10 seconds. If an HSRP router in Standby mode misses three consecutive HSRP Hellos, the router will assume that the Active router is finished and will transition into Active mode.

Figure 8.9 illustrates the configuration of a typical HSRP scenario. Each physical Ethernet interface on Router A and Router B is assigned an IP address and the virtual standby IP address that is shared between the two routers. The configuration of the virtual standby IP address is accomplished with the following command:

```
standby 1 ip 192.168.10.1
```

In this command, 1 is the HSRP standby group number and 192.168.10.1 is the standby IP address that is shared between Router A and Router B. The group number enables you to configure multiple standby IPs on a single interface.

For each segment attached to Router A and Router B, we can control which is the Active router and which is the Standby router. This flexibility provides load-balancing capabilities. Controlling the Active and Standby routers is done with the command

```
standby 1 priority 200/100
```

The interface with the highest priority is always the active router (the default value of the priority is 100). So, in Figure 8.9 we can see that Router A would be the Active router and Router B would be the standby router.

To ensure that Router A is always the Active router, the following command is required:

```
standby 1 preempt
```

This command guarantees that if Router A ever loses its Active status, it will regain the Active status from Router B when Router A comes back online. The command is included in Router B's configuration so that it knows that it should give up its Active router status if a higher priority interface is online.

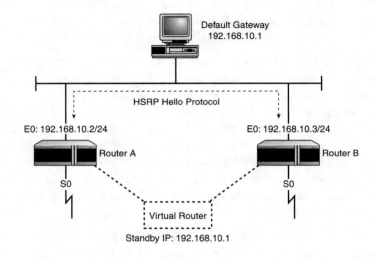

Figure 8.9
Simple HSRP example.

Dynamic Host Configuration Protocol (DHCP)

The *Dynamic Host Configuration Protocol (DHCP)* provides a mechanism to automate the assignment of IP addresses within a network. DHCP is a client/server paradigm. When a client workstation needs to connect to the network, it sends out a UDP-based broadcast message called a `DHCPDISCOVER`. The receiving DHCP server responds with a `DHCPOFFER` message that contains an IP address and other IP configuration parameters that the client workstation needs to configure its IP software.

In a routed network, the `DHCPDISCOVER` broadcast message is handled like every other broadcast, in that the router doesn't forward it. To handle the forwarding of such broadcasts properly, you must configure the router to provide this function. The following Cisco interface configuration would enable a Cisco router to forward a UDP-based DHCP broadcast to the remote DHCP server:

```
interface ethernet 0
   ip address 192.168.10.1 255.255.255.0
   ip helper-address 192.168.1.1
```

The `ip helper-address` command is used to direct a DHCP broadcast to the DHCP server. The IP address specified in the command is the IP address of the remote DHCP server. By default, the `ip forward-protocol udp` command is enabled when the `ip helper-address` command is executed. When configured separately, the `ip forward-protocol udp` command enables the forwarding for ports associated with the following protocols:

■ Trivial File Transfer Protocol

■ Domain Name System

■ Time service

■ NetBIOS Name Server

■ NetBIOS Datagram Server

■ Boot Protocol

■ Terminal Access Controller Access Control System

To enable forwarding for other ports, you must specify them as arguments to the `ip forward-protocol udp` command.

Network Address Translation (NAT)

Network Address Translation (NAT) is defined in RFC 1631 and provides a mechanism for solving address depletion. NAT enables a company to use private addressing and still connect to the Internet. Remember that the Internet does not recognize private addressing space. With NAT, companies can run their private network using the same private address scheme as another company. Routers running NAT convert the *private address* space (local) into unique *global address* space that is recognizable to the Internet. NAT works by creating a table on the router that maps the local (private) address space to the global address space. Figure 8.10 illustrates the configuration of NAT on two routers from two different companies connecting to the Internet.

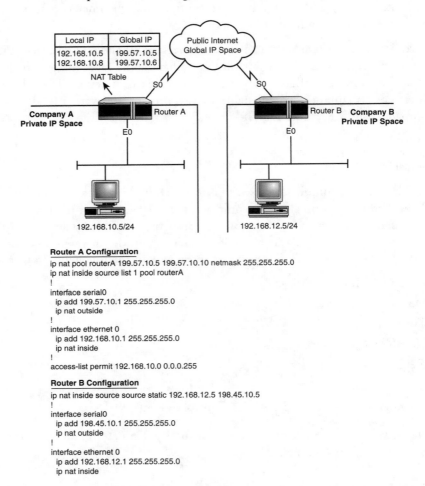

Local IP	Global IP
192.168.10.5	199.57.10.5
192.168.10.8	199.57.10.6

NAT Table

Router A Configuration
ip nat pool routerA 199.57.10.5 199.57.10.10 netmask 255.255.255.0
ip nat inside source list 1 pool routerA
!
interface serial0
  ip add 199.57.10.1 255.255.255.0
  ip nat outside
!
interface ethernet 0
  ip add 192.168.10.1 255.255.255.0
  ip nat inside
!
access-list permit 192.168.10.0 0.0.0.255

Router B Configuration
ip nat inside source source static 192.168.12.5 198.45.10.5
!
interface serial0
  ip add 198.45.10.1 255.255.255.0
  ip nat outside
!
interface ethernet 0
  ip add 192.168.12.1 255.255.255.0
  ip nat inside

Figure 8.10
A simple NAT configuration example.

Figure 8.10 illustrates the configuration of two routers that connect users to the Internet using NAT. Router A is using dynamic address translation and Router B is using static mapping. Looking at Figure 8.10, let's say that Host A would like to send data to Host B. When Host A sends a packet to Host B, Host A will send the packet to the globally unique address of 198.45.10.5 instead of 192.168.12.5. Host A sends the packet with the source/destination pair 192.168.10.5/198.45.10.5 to Router A. Because the packet sourced from 192.168.10.5 passes the defined access-list defined on Router A, the packet is translated into the first available global address within the NAT pool of addresses. Router A then forwards the packet to the Internet with the source/destination pair 199.57.10.5/198.45.10.5. After Router B receives the packet, the destination address gets translated by the static mapping from 198.45.10.5 to 192.168.12.5, so the source/destination address pair that Host B would see is 199.57.10.5/192.168.12.5.

The Cisco specific configuration is explained as follows. The `ip nat inside` and `ip nat outside` commands denote the interface connected to the local address space and the interface connected to the global address space. Access-list 1 permit 192.168.10.0 0.0.0.255 instructs the router to forward any packets sent to or from network 192.168.10.0 to the NAT processes. The NAT process then references the command `ip nat source list 1 pool routerA` that determines which pool of addresses this packet should be translated into (there can be multiple pools). In this example, there is only one pool of addresses named Router A. The translation of the local address is then performed through the command `ip nat pool routerA 199.57.10.5 199.57.10.10 netmask 255.255.255.0` which creates a pool of addresses within the range 199.57.10.5–199.57.10.10. After the translation is made, an entry is created in the NAT table that records the mapping of the local IP address to the global IP address.

Summary

This chapter reviews the TCP/IP protocol and services it offers. For the exam, you need a complete understanding of the IP, TCP, and UDP packet headers. You should also know the differences between TCP and UDP. Be familiar with the well-known TCP/UDP port numbers highlighted in the chapter. Configuration of HSRP and NAT will also be covered on the exam, so you should understand the Cisco configuration specifics of each. In addition to the contents of this chapter, be sure to understand the various IP access-list configurations possible with a Cisco router.

QUESTIONS AND ANSWERS

1. **What does the TTL field of an IP packet header do?**

    A: The TTL field indicates the maximum time that a packet can be on the network. Each router that processes this packet decrements the TTL value by 1. If the value reaches zero, the packet is discarded from the network. The purpose of this field is to eliminate the possibility of a packet endlessly traversing the network.

2. **What does the ACK field in the TCP packet header do?**

    A: The ACK field contains the value of the next sequence number the sending device expects to receive.

3. **What is the difference between TCP and UDP?**

    A: The primary difference between TCP and UDP is that TCP is a connection-oriented protocol and UDP is a connectionless protocol.

4. **Telnet runs on TCP port ___ and FTP runs on TCP port ___.**

    A: Telnet runs on port 23 and FTP runs on port 21.

5. **What is HSRP?**

    A: HSRP, or the Hot Standby Routing Protocol, is a Cisco proprietary protocol that brings routing functionality to end devices that would otherwise not be capable of taking advantage of redundant network connections. HSRP enables a pair of Cisco routers to work together to present the appearance of a single virtual default-gateway to end devices on a LAN segment.

6. **What three Cisco commands are required to configure HSRP?**

    A: The three commands required to configure HSRP are

    ```
    standby 1 ip x.x.x.x
    standby 1 priority Y
    standby 1 preempt
    ```

7. **How do you enable the forwarding of DHCP broadcasts on a Cisco router?**

    A: The following interface command enables the forwarding of DHCP broadcasts:

    ```
    ip helper-address x.x.x.x, where x.x.x.x is the
                        IP address of the DHCP server
    ```

8. What is the difference between a Public IP address and a Private IP address?

A: Public address space is a unique address that is assigned to a company. Private address space is not recognized by the Internet and can be used by anyone within their private network. RFC 1597 defines private IP address space as falling within the following ranges:

Starting Address		Ending Address
10.0.0.0	-	10.255.255.255
172.16.0.0	-	172.31.255.255
192.168.0.0	-	192.168.255.255

PRACTICE TEST

1. Which of the following is the well-known TCP port for SMTP?

A. 23

B. 21

C. 67

D. 123

E. 25

Answer A is incorrect because it is telnet. Answer B is incorrect because it is FTP. Answer C is incorrect because it is BootP. Answer D is incorrect because it is NTP. **Answer E is the correct answer.**

2. What is the network address, broadcast address, and usable address range given the IP address and mask, 172.130.1.10 255.255.255.240?

A. 172.130.0.0

B. 172.130.1.0

C. 172.130.1.255

D. 172.130.1.8

Answer A is incorrect because its network mask would be 255.255.0.0. **Answer B is correct because of the following explanation:**

Breaking the IP address and mask into binary format, we have

```
172.130.1.10 =      10101100    10000010   00000001   0000      1010
255.255.255.240 =   11111111    11111111   11111111   1111      0000
                      Network Bits                            Host Bits
```

Determine the network address by ANDing the results. So,

```
10101100    10000010    00000001    00001010
11111111    11111111    11111111    11110000
10101100    10000010    00000001    00000000 = 172.130.1.0 Network Address
```

Answer C is incorrect because it is not in the same network range given the 255.255.255.240 mask. Answer D is incorrect because it is a node address.

3. What address mask is associated with the following, 172.240.1.10/22?

   A. 255.255.255.0
   B. 255.255.252.0
   C. 255.255.255.252
   D. 255.255.255.248
   E. 255.255.255.224

Answer A is incorrect because

```
255.255.255.0 = 11111111.11111111.11111111.00000000 = 24 bit mask
```

Answer B is the correct answer, as shown here:

```
255.255.252.0 = 11111111.11111111.11111100.00000000
because counting up all the values of 1 = 22
```

Answer C is incorrect because

```
255.255.255.252 = 11111111.11111111.11111111.11111100 = 30 bit mask
```

Answer D is incorrect because

```
255.255.255.248 = 11111111.11111111.11111111.11111000 = 29 bit mask
```

Answer E is incorrect because

```
255.255.255.224 = 11111111.11111111.11111111.11100000 = 27 bit mask
```

4. Which of the following addresses are not recognized by the Internet and therefore would not be routed through the Internet?

   A. 10.130.55.6
   B. 172.16.38.5
   C. 172.30.38.5
   D. 192.168.54.1
   E. 192.168.33.1
   F. None of the above

Answer F is correct because RFC 1597 defines the following address ranges as private address space and are not routed by the Internet:

Starting Address		Ending Address
10.0.0.0	-	10.255.255.255
172.16.0.0	-	172.31.255.255
192.168.0.0	-	192.168.255.255

5. The _____ command is used to enable the forwarding of DHCP broadcast messages on a Cisco router's interface.

    A. `dhcp server (server_address)`

    B. `ip helper address (server_address)`

    C. `ip forward (server_address)`

    D. `ip helper-address (server_address)`

Answer A is incorrect because it is not a supported command. Answer B is incorrect because it is missing the hyphen between `helper` and `address`. Answer C is incorrect because it is not a supported command. It is similar to the `ip helper-address` command issues at the interface level for forwarding of UPD packets. **Answer D is correct and will forward all DHCP requests to the server specified.**

6. What is the default setting on a Cisco router for HSRP hello messages?

    A. 5 seconds

    B. 7 seconds

    C. 10 seconds

    D. 15 seconds

    E. 20 seconds

Answer C is the correct answer. When HSRP is configured on a Cisco router, HSRP hello messages are sent out in 10-second increments. The HSRP hello message is used as a keepalive between two routers.

7. Given the following configurations, under normal operating conditions which would be the active HSRP router?

    A. interface e0

```
ip address 192.168.10.2 255.255.255.0
standby 1 ip 192.168.10.1
standby 1 preempt
standby 1 priority 200
```

    B. interface e0

```
ip address 192.168.10.3 255.255.255.0
standby 1 ip 192.168.10.1
standby 1 preempt
```

C. interface e0

```
ip address 192.168.10.4 255.255.255.0
standby 1 ip 192.168.10.1
standby 1 preempt
standby 1 priority 75
```

D. interface e0

```
ip address 192.168.10.5 255.255.255.0
standby 1 ip 192.168.10.1
standby 1 preempt
standby 1 priority 125
```

Answer A is correct. Remember that in HSRP, the router with the highest priority will be designated the Active Router. Answer B is incorrect because a priority wasn't explicitly configured in the configuration for answer B; therefore, the default priority is equal to 110. Answers C and D are incorrect because the priorities are lower than answer A.

8. Which field in the IP header is used to prevent an IP packet from continuously looping through a network?

A. Time-to-Live (TTL)

B. Header Checksum

C. Identifier

D. Hop Count

Answer A is correct; the TTL value decrements as the IP packet is passed through a router. After the value hits 0, the packet is discarded from the network. Answer B is incorrect because the Header Checksum is used to verify the integrity of the IP packet. Answer C is incorrect because the Identifier is used to reassemble fragmented packets. Answer D is incorrect because the Hop Count is not a valid field in the IP header.

9. What do the following "ping" results indicate?

```
router>ping 192.168.10.3

Type escape sequence to abort.
Sending 5, 100-byte ICMP Echos to 192.168.10.3, timeout is 2 seconds:
.UU
```

A. There is no route within the routing table to the specified host.

B. There is a route to the specified host, but there was some kind of routing failure.

C. The specified host is not connected to the network.

D. The specified host is connected to the network but did not reply for some reason.

E. The neighboring router doesn't have the buffer space required to queue the packet for output to the next network.

Answer A is correct. Answer B would be correct if the value returned by the router were "N". Answer C would be correct if the value returned by the router were "…". Answer D would be correct if the value returned by the router were "…". Answer E would be correct if the value returned by the router were "Q".

10. Which of the following Cisco commands creates a pool of addresses within the range 192.168.10.5–192.168.10.50 that would be used by NAT to translate a local IP address?

A. `ip nat pool routerA 199.57.10.5 199.57.10.10 netmask 255.255.255.0`

B. `ip nat pool routerA 192.168.10.5 192.168.10.50 prefix-length 24`

C. `ip pool routerA 192.168.10.5 192.168.10.50 255.255.255.0`

D. `nat ip pool router A 192.168.10.5 192.168.10.50 255.255.255.0`

Answer A is incorrect because the addresses defined within the pool are incorrect. Note that the `netmask 255.255.255.0` keywords are valid syntax and have the same meaning as `prefix-length 24`. **Answer B is correct. The command defined in answer B creates a static NAT pool named "Router A" with a range of available addresses from 192.168.10.5–192.168.10.50.** Answer C is incorrect because the command syntax is incorrect. Answer D is incorrect because the command syntax is incorrect.

CHAPTER PREREQUISITE

A good understanding of IP addressing as covered in Chapter 8, "TCP/IP," is required to fully understand the topics of this chapter. Specifically, you should know how to recognize node addresses versus network addresses and how subnet masks work.

Routing Concept Overview

WHILE YOU READ

1. How does Split Horizon work?

2. How does Poison Reverse work?

3. What type of routing protocol maintains neighbors?

4. When does a distance vector send out routing table updates?

5. What are the most common Link State routing protocols?

6. What type of routing protocol is EIGRP?

7. What is the command to send all traffic destined for 10.2.2.0/24 to router 10.1.1.1/24?

8. What command can be added to a static route to make sure it stays in the routing table even if its associated interface goes down?

9. What is the administrative distance of OSPF?

10. What is the range of values for administrative distance?

Lab

SEE
APPENDIX F

This chapter is intended to be an overview of basic routing principles. Much of this material should be review for you if you are preparing for your CCIE. However, this material is included here to frame the topics of the next five chapters and to present some material that is new or particularly relevant to the CCIE Written Exam.

All routing protocols provide the same functions to achieve the same goal: a converged network. All routing protocols need to provide these functions:

- Determine the intended destination of the data
- Determine where the routing information is coming from
- Determine all possible routes to a destination
- Determine the best route to the destination
- Keep the routing information up to date

The only thing that makes routing protocols different from one another is *how* they accomplish these functions. The details of each major protocol are discussed in the following chapters of this part of the book. This chapter lays the conceptual foundation for those discussions.

Loop Prevention Techniques

As you know, the goal of any routing protocol is to reach convergence—for every router to "agree" where to send addressed packets. When routers "disagree," loops can occur. Routing loops would occur easily in most any network if there were not any techniques to prevent them. Split Horizon and Poison Reverse are two common techniques used to prevent routing protocols from creating loops.

Split Horizon

Split Horizon is a technique that prevents a router interface from advertising a route back in the direction of its source. This prevents one router from telling another router that it has the route to what is actually the other router's destination network (see Figure 9.1). Distance Vector protocols send routing updates according to this rule.

In Figure 9.1, Router 1 learns of routes to Net X, Net Y, and Net Z from Router 2. It will then advertise those routes out all other working interfaces (in this case, just one), but not back to Router 2. Likewise, Router 2 does not advertise to Router 1 that it knows how to get to Net A. The dotted line represents the virtual "horizon." Note how Router 2 does not advertise to Router 1 that it knows how to get to Net A, and Router 1 does not advertise to Router 2 that it knows how to get to Nets X, Y, and Z.

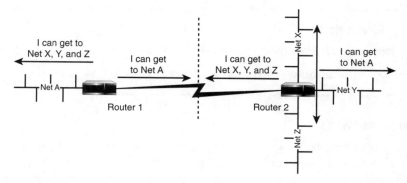

Figure 9.1
An example of how Split Horizon works.

Poison Reverse

Poison Reverse has the same end result as Split Horizon. However, instead of not advertising the route back in its originating direction, a router will advertise the router as *unreachable* back in the direction it was received. The Poison Reverse technique is used by several routing protocols, which are discussed in the following chapters. Right now, it is just important to understand how the technique works.

As you can see, Figure 9.2 is almost identical to Figure 9.1. Look at the differences in the routing messages. Note how the routes are advertised as unreachable in the direction from which they were received.

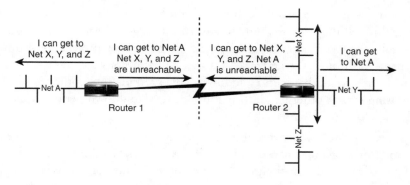

Figure 9.2
An example of how Poison Reverse works.

PART
IV

CH
9

Key Concept

Split Horizon does not advertise routes back to their source.

Poison Reverse advertises routes as unreachable back to their source.

Other Mechanisms

Other mechanisms are employed by routing protocols, such as Count to Infinity, Holddown Timers, and Triggered Updates. Their specific implementations will be discussed with their associated routing protocols later in this book. To provide context for these later discussions, here is a brief description of each.

- Count to Infinity—This mechanism limits the maximum number of hops. When the maximum value is reached, it is considered to be infinitely far away and, in effect, unreachable. When routing updates get forwarded through a network, each time a router forwards the route, it adds 1 to the hop count. If the update keeps being forwarded in a loop, the hop count could increment indefinitely. Count to Infinity prevents this by capping the maximum value (especially in Distance Vector protocols, such as RIP).

- Holddown Timer—When a router finds out about a bad route, it will wait to advertise the bad route (downed link) to other routers. This is the function of the *Holddown Timer.* Several benefits are provided by the Holddown Timer. It prevents routes from being advertised as down, when the interface might just be *flapping* (going up and down frequently) or just down for a few seconds. This, in turn, prevents many routers from recalculating their routing tables more frequently than necessary. It also saves bandwidth that might be wasted by advertising the bad route through the network, only to advertise it as good again a few seconds later. Basically, the Holddown Timer helps prevent bad route information from being propagated through the network. A router will also not accept any route information about a route that is in Holddown. This prevents some other router from confusing it with other bad information for the Holddown period. Many protocols use Holddown Timers.

- Triggered Update—When a routing protocol sends updates due to a change in its network topology information, this is called a *Triggered Update.* That is, the process of sending out an update is triggered by an event in the network. This is the opposite of *Timed Updates* that send updates on a chronologically scheduled basis (for example, every 60 seconds). RIP is an example of a Timed Update protocol. Triggered Updates save bandwidth and router CPU cycles. If a network is converged and stable, updates get sent out very rarely. Therefore, bandwidth is not used for unnecessary updates and routers save CPU cycles by not recalculating their routing tables. EIGRP is an example of a protocol that uses Triggered Updates.

Link State Versus Distance Vector

In determining the best route to a destination, different routing protocols use a number of different measurements. These measurements are called *metrics*. Each routing protocol uses one or more metric to calculate the best route to a particular destination. The most common metrics include path length (hop count), reliability, delay, bandwidth, load, and financial cost of a link. One or more metric is the raw information a protocol uses in order to calculate the quality of a route.

Another major difference between routing protocols is how they handle updating each other with current information. There are many methods of doing this.

Given these major differences, routing protocols are broken into two main categories: *Distance Vector* and *Link State*. Here is a summary of the major differences between these two types of protocols. This is by no means an exhaustive reference, but is good enough to serve as a refresher before we discuss individual protocols in more detail in the following chapters.

- Distance Vector Protocols—Distance Vector protocols include RIP (IP and IPX), RTMP, and IGRP. They send their entire routing tables out in all directions at regularly scheduled intervals. There is no method for identifying neighbors. Distance Vector protocols learn of new or downed routes when an update is *not* received. Less complex metrics are used to determine the best single path using the Bellman-Ford algorithm.

- Link State Protocols—Link State protocols include OSPF, NLSP, BGP, and IS-IS. They send partial routing tables (of their own networks) to everyone and then send updates when necessary. Link State protocols keep established relationships with their neighbors. More complex metrics are used to determine the best paths. These are sometimes referred to as Shortest Path First (SPF) algorithms, such as the Dijkstra algorithm.

Key Concept

Distance Vector Protocols are RIP (IP and IPX), RTMP, and IGRP.

Link State Protocols are OSPF, NLSP, BGP, and IS-IS.

EIGRP is a hybrid.

EIGRP is the only major routing protocol not mentioned earlier. That is because it is classified as a hybrid protocol. It is proprietary to Cisco and uses an algorithm called the *Diffusing Update Algorithm (DUAL)*. It calculates its route metrics in a similar manner to IGRP (a Distance Vector protocol) but maintains neighbor states and sends updates such as a Link State protocol. See Chapter 11, "IGRP and EIGRP," for further discussion).

Classful Versus Classless Routing

As you know already, IP addresses are separated into classes. Class A, B, and C addresses are the most common. See Chapter 8, "TCP/IP," for further discussion of address classes and the class boundaries. Routing protocols can handle network addresses according to these class boundaries (classful) or not (classless).

A *classful* routing protocol abides strictly to the bit boundaries of the IP address classes. For example, the 10.0.0.0 network—a Class A network—cannot be advertised as anything other than a route to 10.0.0.0, since the default network mask of a Class A network is 255.0.0.0. In other words, VLSMs are effectively useless. This is because the routing update packet has no field for subnet mask, so the default mask according to the class is assumed. Classful routing protocols include RIP v1 and IGRP.

It follows that a *classless* routing protocol does not need to abide by the bit boundaries of the IP address classes. The routing update packet includes a field for subnet mask. VLSMs can be used practically at will. Classless routing protocols include RIP v2, OSPF, EIGRP, IS-IS, and BGP.

Route Selection

Routing protocols will help a router determine the best path to each network address in the internetwork. The end result of a routing protocol is to create a routing table for each router. After a Cisco router establishes its routing table, and all metrics are equal, it needs a method to select a route to get the packet to its final destination. It does this by selecting the most specific route available.

Figure 9.3 is an example of how more than one possible route to a destination could exist in a router's routing table. In the diagram, Router B is summarizing its attached networks. Therefore, instead of advertising four routes to Router A, it will just advertise network 10.2.8.0/21, since this network address includes all the smaller network addresses (summarization will be discussed in greater detail in Chapter 14, "Managing Routing"). Meanwhile, Router C will advertise 10.2.10.0/24 to Router A. Note that network 10.2.10.0 is also within the range of 10.2.8.0/21. So, which route will the router choose to send packets destined for network 10.2.10.0?

The router will always choose the most specific route to a destination. So, Router A will send packets destined for 10.2.10.0 out its Ethernet 1 (E1) interface. This is because 10.2.10.0 is a more specific route than 10.2.8.0/21. The same is true for any packets destined for any of Router B's networks. Router A would use the 10.2.8.0 route for a packet destined for 10.2.13.0 because it is the most specific route available for that network.

Figure 9.3
An example of when a router could have two possible routes.

Static and Default Routes

Static routes are routes that are administratively configured in routers. They are typically used when dynamic protocols are either unnecessary or unwanted. For instance, if a branch office has a single-router LAN and is connected into the corporate WAN via a dial-on-demand ISDN line, using a dynamic routing protocol would be both unnecessary and unwanted. It is unnecessary because there is only one route. It is unwanted because the routing protocol could require the ISDN line to stay up, eliminating the benefits of a dial-on-demand link (you might as well use a leased line service).

A *static route* is manually configured and normally supersedes all other dynamically learned routes. So, unless configured otherwise (see the discussion of administrative distance, later in this chapter), the only route that will supersede a static route is a network on a directly attached interface.

The command to configure a static IP route is

```
RTR(config)#ip route   destination   mask {next_hop | outgoing_interface}
            [admin_distance] [permanent]
```

This command should be familiar to you as a prerequisite for this book. Just remember that the permanent tag means that you want the route to stay in the router's routing table even if the applicable interface goes down.

The admin_distance tag allows the administrative distance to be configured. This value is discussed later in this chapter.

Figure 9.4 is an example of static routing. Both main methods of configuring static routes—next_hop and outgoing_interface—are shown. That is, the static route can point traffic to either the next router (next hop) or the router interface out of which you want to send traffic. Note how static routes are configured in both directions between the hub Router C and the other routers.

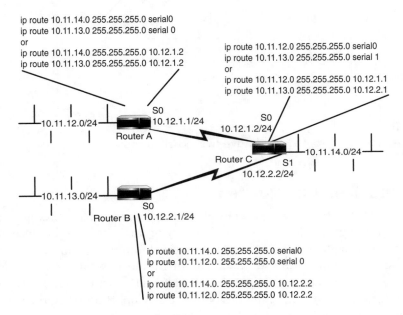

Figure 9.4
An example of the two main methods of configuring static routes.

 Key Concept

Static routes must always be configured in both directions (on both routers on each end of the route). That is, two routers that route to each other via static routes must point traffic to each other.

A *default route* is just a type of static route. Effectively, it is a static route that states, "If you don't have a route for this destination, send it here." Another way of thinking about a default route is "If you can't find it in this network, send it out this way." Since we already know that a router will always choose the most specific route from its routing table (if all else is equal), we want to be as general as possible when configuring a default route. So, in effect, what we want to say with the default route is "Transmit packets to every unknown destination via this place." So, the command would look like this:

```
RTR(config)#ip route 0.0.0.0  0.0.0.0 {next_hop | outgoing_interface}
[admin_distance] [permanent]
```

Defining the address 0.0.0.0 with a mask of 0.0.0.0 means that all IP addresses with any mask will match this statement. Since 0.0.0.0 is the most general possible address and mask, it would only be used if a better (more specific) match is not found.

Two common uses of default routes are to send traffic to the Internet or in a hub-and-spoke environment. To route Internet-bound traffic, you would configure the next_hop or outgoing_interface to point to your router that is connected to the Internet. This prevents each router on your network from having to keep a routing table for the entire Internet! Figure 9.5 is an example of using default routes in a hub-and-spoke environment. It is almost identical to Figure 9.4, which shows static routes. However, in this case, the administrator knows that Router C will soon be attached to a much bigger network. The administrator is willing to add all the static routes to Router C, but it would be very labor-intensive and error-prone to enter all the static routes into all the spoke routers, too. Each existing spoke router would need one new entry for each new spoke router. Note how much simpler the routes in Router A and Router B are in Figure 9.5.

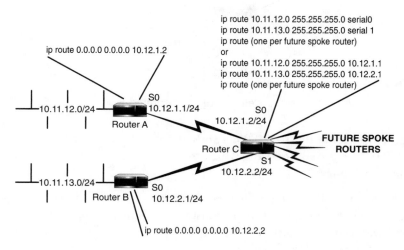

Figure 9.5
Using default routes instead of static routes in a hub-and-spoke environment.

Default routes are advertised by default via RIP, IGRP, and EIGRP and can be advertised by OSPF and IS-IS, if configured to do so. This will be discussed further in Chapter 10, "RIP," Chapter 11, "IGRP and EIGRP," and Chapter 12, "OSPF."

The other way to configure default routes is by using the ip default-network command. This defines an entire network to be used for the destination instead of a route. Therefore, a router must know about the route from some other source: a direct connection, a dynamic routing protocol, or a static route. The default network will then be advertised to other routers who will then add a route to 0.0.0.0 in the direction of the router from which the default route was received. In Figure 9.6, Router A will advertise the network 11.0.0.0 as the default network. It will advertise this route to all other routers in the 10.0.0.0 network.

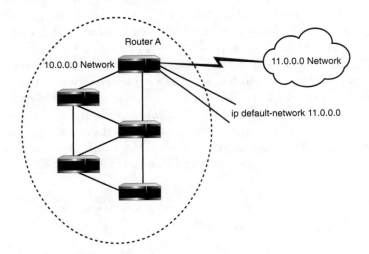

Figure 9.6
An example of when to use the default-network command.

All the other routers in the 10.0.0.0 network will then have an entry in their routing table to 0.0.0.0 via the address from which they received the advertisement (the next hop address toward Router A).

Static and default routes are typically used to work in conjunction with one or more dynamic routing protocol. There are few instances where an entire network should be configured with static routes. But by properly using static and default routes, you can add stability and reliability to your network.

Default Administrative Distances

If a router learns of different types of routes to the same destination (statically configured or advertised via a dynamic routing protocol), it must select which route to include in its routing table. Typically, only one route to a specific destination (same address and mask) is in a router's routing table. One method of route "selection" is accomplished by comparing the *administrative distance* of all the routes to the same destination. Administrative Distance is a value, which rates the reliability of the source of the route. If the source that provides a route to a router is considered to be less reliable—less trustworthy—it receives a higher administrative distance value. The lowest administrative distance becomes the preferred route entered in the routing table.

Administrative distance values range from 0 to 255. If desired, the administrator can configure administrative distances so that the default administrative distance is not used. It is important to know the default administrative distances in order to analyze routing functions and avoid problems, especially when redistributing routing protocols (see Chapter 14) into one another.

Table 9.1 shows the default administrative distances you should know.

Table 9.1   Default Administrative Distances

Source of Route Information	Default Administrative Distance
Attached Interface	0
Static Route Entry	1
EIGRP Summary Route	5
eBGP	20
EIGRP Internal Route	90
IGRP	100
OSPF	110
IS-IS	115
RIP	120
EGP	140
EIGRP External Route	170
iBGP	200
Unknown Source	255

 Key Concept

Make sure you memorize the Administrative Distance default values, because they are likely to appear on the exam.

For example, let's say a router's primary route is supplied by a dynamic protocol (say, over a leased line). There is also a modem attached to the router as a backup in case the primary route interface goes down. One way you can tell the router to use the backup modem line only when the primary goes down is to configure a static route with a higher administrative distance than the dynamic routing protocol is using. This way, the primary route will be used (lower administrative distance) until it goes down, in which case the static route to the interface with the backup modem will be used. This is called a floating static route because "it just floats there" until the primary goes down.

Chapter 14, "Managing Routing," provides more details about the issues involved in customizing the administrative distances of routing protocols.

Summary

This chapter provides a refresher in Routing Concepts necessary for an intelligent discussion of the routing protocols covered in the CCIE Written Exam.

Make sure that you understand the principles of routing protocol loop prevention techniques. You should be able to describe each one if asked. You also must know the main differences between Link State and Distance Vector protocols.

When working with Cisco routers, it is important to know how the router chooses what routes to use from the ones in the routing table. To this end, you must understand how to configure static and default routes and what effect administrative distances have on routing decisions.

QUESTIONS AND ANSWERS

1. How does Split Horizon work?

   A: A router *does not advertise* a route back in the direction from which it was received.

2. How does Poison Reverse work?

   A: A router *advertises a route as unreachable* in the direction from which it was received.

3. What type of routing protocol maintains neighbors?

   A: Link State.

4. When does a distance vector send out routing table updates?

   A: At a scheduled time interval.

5. What are the most common Link State routing protocols?

   A: OSPF, NLSP, and IS-IS.

6. What type of routing protocol is EIGRP?

   A: Hybrid.

7. What is the command to send all traffic destined for 10.2.2.0/24 to router 10.1.1.1/24?

   A: `ip route 10.2.2.0 255.255.255.0 10.1.1.1`

8. What command can be added to a static route to make sure it stays in the routing table even if its associated interface goes down?

   A: `permanent`

9. What is the administrative distance of OSPF?

   A: 110

10. What is the range of values for administrative distance?

    A: 0–255

PRACTICE TEST

1. Which of the following are Distance Vector protocols?
   A. IPX RIP
   B. IP RIP
   C. NLSP
   D. EIGRP
   E. IS-IS
   F. RTMP
   G. IGRP
   H. OSPF

Answers A, B, F, and G are Distance Vector protocols. Answer D is incorrect because EIGRP is a hybrid protocol. Answers C, E, and H are incorrect because these are Link State protocols.

2. Which of the following are Link State Protocols?

   A. IPX RIP

   B. IP RIP

   C. NLSP

   D. EIGRP

   E. IS-IS

   F. RTMP

   G. IGRP

   H. OSPF

Answers C, E, and H are correct because they are Link State protocols. Answer D is incorrect because EIGRP is a hybrid. Answers A, B, F, and G are incorrect because they are Distance Vector protocols.

3. What is DUAL?

   A. A Cisco proprietary routing protocol

   B. A routing algorithm

   C. A mnemonic device for configuring default routes

   D. A loop prevention technique

   E. A computer chip in Cisco routers for route selection

Answer A is incorrect because DUAL is not a routing protocol. **Answer B is correct because DUAL is a routing algorithm. EIGRP is the Cisco proprietary routing protocol that uses DUAL.** Answers C and E are incorrect because none of them has anything to do with routing, which DUAL does. Answer D is incorrect because the DUAL algorithm is not used to prevent routes.

4. Which of the following are Loop Prevention techniques?

   A. Count to Infinity

   B. Convergence Timers

   C. Queue Timers

   D. Holddown Timers

   E. Cascade Advertisements

   F. Triggered Updates

Answers A, D, and F are Loop Prevention techniques. The other answers are facetious or unrelated.

5. Number these in order of default administrative distance value, lowest to highest:

   A. OSPF

   B. RIP

C. eBGP

D. IGRP

E. Static Route

- **F.** Unknown Source

Answer: Static Route (1), eBGP (20), IGRP (100), OSPF (110), RIP (120), Unknown Source (255)

6. Distance Vector protocols use what algorithm?

A. DUAL

B. FIFO

C. Bellman-Ford

D. SPF

Answer A is incorrect because DUAL is the EIGRP algorithm. Answer B is incorrect because FIFO means "First In, First Out" and is unrelated to any routing protocols. **Answer C is correct because Distance Vector protocols use the Bellman-Ford algorithm.** Answer D is incorrect because SPF is the Link State Algorithm.

7. What does the command `ip route 0.0.0.0 0.0.0.0 ethernet0 permanent` do?

A. Nothing; there is an error in the command

B. Nothing; the route to 0.0.0.0 is a route to "nowhere"

C. Sends packets the router doesn't know where else to send to `ethernet0` interface

D. Turns on IP routing on interface `ethernet0`

E. Sends all traffic to `ethernet0`

Answer C is correct. The `permanent` command means this (default) route will stay in the routing table even if interface `ethernet0` goes down.

8. When configuring a static route, what information must come directly after `ip route 10.5.6.0 255.255.255.0` (more than one answer is possible)?

A. Nothing; the command could be complete as it is.

B. The administrative distance of the route

C. The next router's address where you want this network's traffic to go

D. The outgoing interface's IP address

E. The outgoing interface's name

Answer A is incorrect because entering just the command in the question would result in an error if entered as is. Answer B is incorrect because the administrative distance can be entered after the next hop or outgoing interface. **Answers C and E are both correct because these are the two methods for configuring a static route.** Answer D is incorrect because entering the outgoing interface's IP address will cause the route to fail because the destination address of the packet will be that interface (any other routers will send the packet back to it).

9. A router has a route to 10.0.0.0 255.0.0.0 via RIP. It also has a route to 10.6.0.0 255.255.0.0 via IGRP. It wants to send a packet to 10.6.12.3. How will the packet be sent?

A. Via the RIP route

B. Via the IGRP route

C. It will not be sent

D. It will be sent to the default route

E. It will be out to both destinations

Answer A is incorrect because RIP has a higher administrative distance than IGRP. **Answer B is correct because it will be sent out via the IGRP-provided route. It is more specific and has a lower administrative distance.** Answer C is incorrect because the router has a valid route. Answer D is incorrect because the question does not indicate that there is a default route. Answer E is impossible.

10. How do routers running Distance Vector protocols find out about downed routes?

A. By receiving a special type of routing update

B. By sending a query packet

C. Via Hello packets

D. When no update is received

Answer A is incorrect because Distance Vector protocols have only one type of update, sent at regularly scheduled intervals. Answer B is incorrect because there is no such thing as a query packet. Answer C is incorrect because Hello packets are associated with Link State protocols. **Answer D is correct because Distance Vector protocols require updates (Hellos) to keep the route up.**

CHAPTER PREREQUISITE

Before you read this chapter you must understand the material in Chapter 9, "Routing Concept Overview." You should have a good understanding of loop prevention techniques, link state versus distance vector, and route selection.

RIP

WHILE YOU READ

1. Does RIPv1 support variable length subnet masking?

2. The maximum hop count in a RIP network is _____.

3. RIP will send automatic updates every _____ seconds.

4. After the garbage collection timer has run out, will the route be deleted?

5. Cisco uses the _____ to help stabilize the routing table.

6. To avoid routing loops, RIP implements _____ with _____.

7. Are RIP packets TCP based?

8. There are _____ possible values for the command field.

9. Four of the extensions added in RIPv2 are _____, _____, _____, and _____.

Routing Information Protocol (RIP) is a distance vector algorithm that has been in use since the early days of the ARPAnet. One of the earliest versions of RIP was a Xerox protocol called GWINFO, which later became known as *Routed* (pronounced "Route Dee," the *d* representing the UNIX term *daemon*) and was distributed with Berkeley's UNIX in the early 1980s. There are currently two versions of RIP, known simply as version one and version two. RIPv1 (RFC1058) differs from RIPv2 (RFC 1723) in that it is a classful routing protocol, whereas v2 is classless. RIPv2 will support *Variable Length Subnet Mask (VLSM)*.

RIP was designed for small to medium-sized networks. Updates containing a full routing table are sent to all nodes every 30 seconds. This traffic could add a great deal of extra load on a large network, especially over WAN links. The other reason RIP is best suited for small networks is because of its relatively slow convergence time, since updates are only sent every 30 seconds.

Key Concept

Because RIP sends updates containing full routing tables every 30 seconds, a great deal of extra load can be placed on the network. Therefore, RIP should be used on small to medium-sized networks.

The purpose of any routing protocol is to provide information necessary for each router to calculate the best direction to route traffic through a network. Each router needs to store the following information about each destination on the network (in RIP terminology):

- The IP address of the destination.
- The IP address of the nearest gateway to reach the destination.
- The interface used to reach the gateway.
- The distance metric.
- The route timers.
- The route change flag.

The routers receive this information through routing protocol updates.

This chapter will take a closer look at RIP updates, timers, and the metric used by RIP.

Routing Metrics

The *metric* is a method of measuring the best route through a network that has multiple routes to the same location. The *metric* can be one of several variables such as hop count, bandwidth, or timing, or it can be a combination of variables.

RIP uses only one metric: hop count. Each hop to an adjacent gateway is counted as one. To prevent routing loops, RIP limits the maximum number of hops in a network to 15 (the Count to Infinity technique). A hop count of 1 indicates that the gateway is directly connected, whereas a hop count of 16 indicates *infinity*—that is, the gateway is unreachable.

Key Concept

RIP uses Hop Count as its only metric. The maximum number of hops in a RIP network is 15: One hop is a directly connected network, and 16 hops is an unreachable network. See Chapter 9, "Routing Concept Overview," for more information on routing metrics.

Route Updates

Every 25.5 to 30 seconds (time varies to avoid *update synchronization*, as discussed later in this chapter), a Cisco router will send a RIP update out every interface that has a RIP network attached to it. This variance in time between the updates (25.5–30 seconds) is called RIP_JITTER. Each update contains the entire routing table of the sending router. When another router on the network receives the update, it adds any new routes to its routing table or will replace a route if the update has a lower hop count for that route. As stated previously, when a router receives an update with a route having a hop count as 16, the route is flagged as unreachable.

Key Concept

RIP updates are sent out every 30 seconds. Cisco alters this with RIP_JITTER to make it every 25.5–30 seconds.

As mentioned earlier in this chapter, RIP uses RIP_JITTER to randomize the exact time interval between transmitting route updates to avoid a condition called *update synchronization*. Update synchronization is a problem that can occur on Ethernet backbones. If routing updates are all sent at the exact same time, they tend to "synchronize," or collide.

There are two RIP message types, *request messages* and *response messages*. A router that has just joined the network will send a *request* for route updates and all adjacent routers will *respond* by sending their route tables. A *response* packet can also be an update generated by the sender. When the new router receives the updates, it enters the new routes and the IP address of the responding routers into its routing table.

When a router makes a metric change, it sends triggered updates, which contain only the information about the network that caused the update. Triggered updates help with quicker network convergence because the routers don't need to wait for the full update.

RIP Timers

Standard RIP uses two timers to ensure that invalid routes are removed from a table:

- The first is called *timeout,* or *expiration timer.* Cisco IOS calls this the *invalid timer.* The timeout is first set when a new route is added to a table; it is reset every time an update is received for the route.

- The other timer is the *garbage collection,* or *flush timer.* If the timer is not reset for a route within 180 seconds, the garbage collection timer is started. The garbage collection timer will run for 60 seconds (even though the RFC-defined interval is 120 seconds) after the timeout expires. During this period, the route is advertised as unreachable (metric of 16).

If no update is received by the time the timer expires, the route is deleted.

Cisco implements one other timer associated with updates, the *holddown timer.* When an update for a route has a higher metric than what is currently in the table, the holddown timer prevents any changes in the table until the specified timer runs out. This feature helps to stabilize the routing table.

Key Concept

RIP timers:

- Timeout (also known as *expiration* or *invalid*)—How long since the last update for this route was received (default = 180 seconds)

- Garbage Collection (also known as *flush*)—After timeout expires, advertises the route as unreachable. Route removed when it expires (Cisco default = 60 seconds, RFC = 120 seconds)

- Holddown—Wait period before changing the routing table when a metric for a route changes (default = 180 seconds)

If an update is sent out an interface containing information on routes learned through that interface, a condition called *reverse route* occurs. Reverse route can cause routing loops and network convergence problems. RIP implements s*plit horizon with poisoned reverse* to avoid this situation. Basically, when an update is sent out an interface, any routes learned from that interface are flagged as unreachable.

RIPv1

RIP messages are UDP packets and use UDP port 520 for all communications. All packets sent to another host's RIP processor are sent to port 520. All packets leaving a RIP processor use port 520. Packets sent in response to a request are sent to the port where the packet originated.

The RIPv1 packet contains nine fields:

1. Command
2. Version number
3. Unused—Must be zero
4. Address family identifier
5. Unused—Must be zero
6. IP address
7. Unused—Must be zero
8. Unused—Must be zero
9. Metric

Figure 10.1 shows the RIPv1 packet.

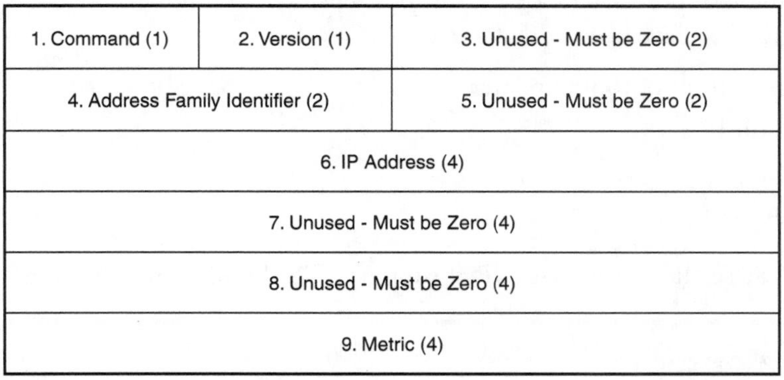

1. Command (1)	2. Version (1)	3. Unused - Must be Zero (2)
4. Address Family Identifier (2)		5. Unused - Must be Zero (2)
6. IP Address (4)		
7. Unused - Must be Zero (4)		
8. Unused - Must be Zero (4)		
9. Metric (4)		

Figure 10.1
The RIPv1 packet. The number following each field represents the number of octets (bytes). The maximum size of the packet is 512 octets.

The command and version fields are each one octet. It is important to note that fields 4 though 9 can repeat up to 25 times. Each of these 20-byte sections can advertise one route. So, a RIP datagram can contain up to 25 routes. Therefore, the maximum size of the message is 504 octets ($25 \times 20 + 4$). With the eight-byte UDP header, the entire datagram can be up to 512 bytes.

PART
IV

CH
10

Key Concept

The only fields used in a RIP v1 packet are Command, Version, Address Family Identifier, IP Address, and Metric.

The command field indicates the packet's intended purpose. There are five possible values for the command field:

- Request—Request for a routing table.
- Response—This could be in response to a request or a poll, or it could be an update.
- Traceon—No longer used.
- Traceoff—No longer used.
- Reserved—Used by Sun Microsystems.

RIPv2

RIPv2 has several extensions or improvements over RIPv1. However, the RIP packet does not change per se. The first four octets of the packet still contain the RIP header, whereas the remainder of the packet contains route entries (20 octets each). The improvements are placed after the RIP header and are meant to extend RIP's usefulness. The most important extensions that have been added are

- Authentication of route updates
- Next hop IP address
- Route tags
- Subnet mask

The effect of these changes is that RIPv2 support VLSM and authentication.

Key Concept

RIPv2 supports VLSM and authentication. RIPv1 does not.

All the other functions of RIP have not changed.

The RIPv2 packet contains nine fields:

1. Command
2. Version number

3. Unused—Must be zero

4. Address family identifier

5. Route Tag

6. IP address

7. Subnet Mask

8. Next Hop

9. Metric

Figure 10.2 shows a RIPv2 Packet. Note that the basic structure of the packet has not changed. The RIPv2 packet has a maximum size of 512 octets.

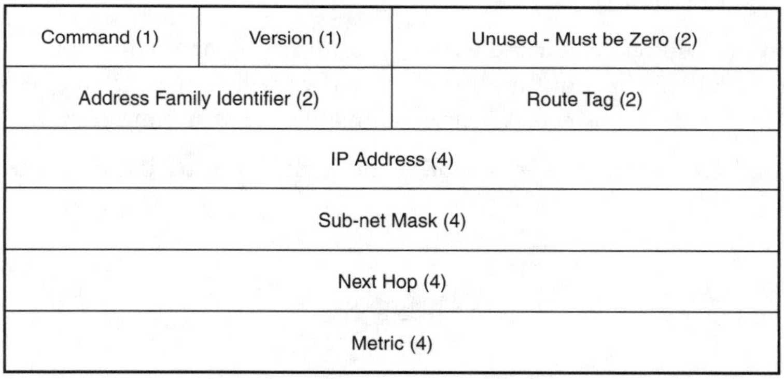

Command (1)	Version (1)	Unused - Must be Zero (2)	
Address Family Identifier (2)		Route Tag (2)	
IP Address (4)			
Sub-net Mask (4)			
Next Hop (4)			
Metric (4)			

Figure 10.2
The RIPv2 packet. Three fields added to RIPv1: route tag, subnet mask, and next hop.

Route tags are used to separate internal RIP routes from external RIP routes.

- Internal routes are within the RIP domain.
- External routes might have been imported from a BGP or another IGP.

The subnet mask field identifies the network and subnet of the IP address. This field has made it possible for RIP to become a *classless* routing protocol and support VLSM.

The next hop IP address is the address that the packet should be forwarded to, for the best route to the destination.

Key Concept

The difference between a RIPv1 and a RIPv2 packet is the addition of the Route Tag, Subnet Mask, and Next Hop fields.

Authentication is a method used to avoid updates from unauthorized sources. Hackers sometimes use routing updates to gain access into a network. This is because occasionally, a malfunctioning gateway can send erroneous updates. Authentication is one tool to help alleviate these problems. It is implemented by using what normally would be the first routing update's space as authentication. The receiving router knows that authentication information is present by reading the Address Family Identifier, which will be set to a specific value.

Configuration Examples

RIP is very simple to configure. All you need to do is enable RIP and add each network that uses RIP. However, RIPv2 has a few more possible commands; we will use two of them: version and no auto-summary.

Because the router will by default use RIPv1, you must use the version command to tell the router to use RIPv2. In addition, by default RIPv2 will summarize major networks across boundaries. Use the no auto-summary command to stop summarization.

Figures 10.3 and 10.4 show simple network configurations using RIPv1 and RIPv2, respectively.

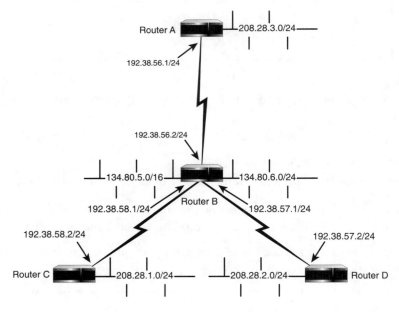

Figure 10.3
A simple RIPv1 network.

In Figure 10.3, each router simply needs RIP enabled and its attached networks defined under the routing protocol. Remember that the 134.80.x.x range is a Class B address (due to the value of the address's first byte). Notice the network address for the 134.80.x.x networks attached to Router B. The networks can be defined at the interface as having a 24-bit mask or one that's any other length. Router B will know where to send packets for the 134.80.5.x and 134.80.6.x networks, but this is not a function of the routing protocol; it's the router itself. Router B will only *advertise* the Class B network 134.80.x.x to other routers. In fact, when defining the RIP network, if you were to enter 134.80.5.0 as the network address, the router will assume 134.80.0.0, which will appear when you view the configuration. This is because RIPv1 is constrained by the classful address scheme, and the 134.80.x.x range is a Class B address (due to the value of the address's first octet).

```
Router A (config)#router rip
Router A (config_router)#network 208.28.3.0
Router A (config_router)#network 192.38.56.0

Router B (config)#router rip
Router B (config-router)#network 134.80.0.0
Router B (config-router)#network 192.38.56.0
Router B (config-router)#network 192.38.57.0
Router B (config-router)#network 192.38.58.0

Router C (config)#router rip
Router C (config-router)#network 192.38.58.0
Router C (config-router)#network 208.28.1.0

Router D (config)#router rip
Router D (config-router)#network 192.38.57.0
Router D (config-router)#network 208.28.2.0
```

Notice in Figure 10.4, the use of VLSMs for the WAN (serial) connections. Compared to the configuration shown in Figure 10.3, notice how much address space is saved! Also notice how the 134.80.x.x attached to Router B networks (as defined under the RIP routing process) are no longer constrained by the classful boundary. Even though the first octet is in the Class B range, they are subnetted to look like Class C networks, again preserving address space. With RIPv2, Router B will advertise the full 24-bit routes of 134.80.5.0 and 134.80.6.0. Of course, you still have the option of entering the Class B range 134.80.0.0 under the router rip process, but that means Router B should be the gateway for all 134.80.x.x addresses in the entire network—not a very flexible design!

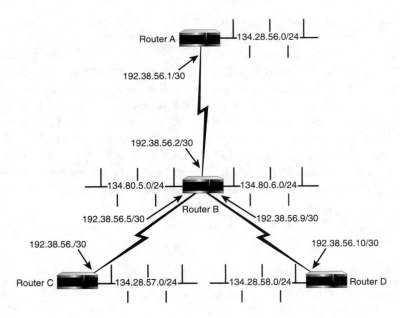

Figure 10.4
A simple RIPv2 configuration.

The following are the router configurations for the network in Figure 10.4.

```
Router A (config)#router rip
Router A (config-router)#version 2
Router A (config-router)#network 134.28.56.0
Router A (config-router)#network 192.38.56.0
Router A (config-router)#no auto-summary

Router B (config)#router rip
Router B (config-router)#version 2
Router B (config-router)#network 134.80.5.0
Router B (config-router)#network 134.80.6.0
Router B (config-router)#network 192.38.56.0
Router B (config-router)#network 192.38.56.4
Router B (config-router)#network 192.38.56.8
Router B (config-router)#no auto-summary

Router C (config)#router rip
Router C (config-router)#version 2
Router C (config-router)#network 134.28.54.0
Router C (config-router)#network 192.38.56.4
Router C (config-router)#no auto-summary
```

```
Router D (config)#router rip
Router D (config-router)#version 2
Router D (config-router)#network 134.28.58.0
Router D (config-router)#network 192.38.56.8
Router D (config-router)#no auto-summary
```

Summary

RIP is one of the oldest distance vector algorithms; it comes in two flavors: RIPv1 and RIPv2. RIPv1 is a classful protocol, whereas RIPv2 is classless and supports VLSM. Support of VLSM is made possible by the addition of the subnet mask field in the RIP packet. Both versions use split horizon with poison reverse to avoid reverse route and routing loops.

RIP uses hop count as a metric. The maximum number of hops in a RIP network is 15: A hop count of one is a directly attached network, and a metric of 16 indicates an unreachable network.

Cisco implementation of RIP uses three timers: invalid timer, flush timer, and holddown timer. The invalid timer and flush timer are used to remove invalid routes from the table. The holddown timer is for table stabilization.

The RIP packet is a maximum of 512 octets for both RIPv1 and RIPv2. The only difference between the two versions is the addition of three fields in the packet: next hop, route tags, and subnet mask. There are two types of RIP messages: request and response.

PART
IV

CH
10

QUESTIONS AND ANSWERS

1. Does RIPv1 support variable length subnet masking?

    A: No

2. The maximum hop count in a RIP network is ___.

    A: 15

3. RIP will send automatic updates every _____ seconds.

    A: 25 to 35 seconds

4. After the garbage collection timer has run out, will the route be deleted?

    A: Yes

5. Cisco uses the _____ to help stabilize the routing table.

    A: holddown timer

6. To avoid routing loops, RIP implements _____ with _____.

   A: split horizon, poison reverse

7. Are RIP packets TCP based?

   A: No; UDP port 520

8. There are _____ possible values for the command field.

   A: 5

9. Four of the extensions added in RIPv2 are _____, _____, _____, and _____.

   A: authentication, next hop, route tags, VLSM

PRACTICE TEST

1. Which of the following statements regarding RIP are true?
   - **A.** RIP is a distance vector algorithm.
   - **B.** RIP is best suited as an IGP.
   - **C.** There are two versions of RIP.
   - **D.** All of the above

Answer D is correct because RIP is a distance vector algorithm, there are two versions of RIP (RIPv1 and RIPv2), and RIP is best suited as an IGP.

2. The *metric* used by RIP is
   - **A.** Distance
   - **B.** Length
   - **C.** Hops
   - **D.** Loops
   - **E.** Address Family Identifier

Answer C is correct because RIP uses hop count as a metric. Answers A, B, and D are not valid responses. Answer E is incorrect because it is a field in a RIP packet.

3. In a RIP routing table, a route with a hop count of ____ indicates that the network is unreachable.
   - **A.** 0
   - **B.** 15
   - **C.** 1
   - **D.** 16

Answer A is incorrect because a hop count of 0 does not exist. Answer B is incorrect because 15 is the maximum number of hops in a RIP network. Answer C incorrect because 1 represents a directly connected network. **Answer D is correct; 16 is used so that the gateways will stop counting to infinity as soon as possible, speeding up convergence.**

4. Triggered updates occur

A. Every 25.5 to 35 seconds

B. When a new gateway is added to the network

C. When a gateway changes the metric for a route

D. All of the above

Answer A is incorrect because 25.5 to 35 seconds is the time span for normal updates. Answer B is also incorrect because a gateway that has been added to the network will send out a request, and then all participating gateways on the network will respond. **Answer C is correct because triggered updates contain only the information about the network that caused the update.**

5. To ensure that invalid routes are flushed from the routing tables, RIP uses two timers; they are _____ and Garbage Collection.

A. Flush

B. Holddown

C. Reverse Route

D. Invalid timer

E. Countdown

Answers A and B are incorrect because they are other timers used by other algorithms. Answer C is not a timer. **Answer D is correct because the invalid timer is first set when a new route is added to a table; it is reset every time an update is received for the route. ("Expiration" and "timeout" are other names for it.)** Answer E is incorrect because there is no such thing as a Countdown timer.

6. The holddown timer is implemented by Cisco to____

A. Speed up network convergence.

B. Avoid update synchronization.

C. Damper triggered updates.

D. Stabilize the routing table.

Answer A is incorrect because triggered updates help speed up network convergence. Answer B is also incorrect because RIP uses a random variable in the update timer to avoid update synchronization. Answer C is incorrect because RIP has no feature used to damper triggered updates. **Answer D is correct because the holddown timer prevents any changes in the table until the specified timer runs out.**

7. RIP is a UDP-based protocol that uses port _____ for all communications.

    A. 512

    B. 520

    C. Both A and B

    D. Neither A nor B

Answer B is correct. Answers A, C, and D are incorrect.

8. Name five possible values for the command field in a RIPv1 packet.

    A. Request, response, traceon, traceoff, and ping

    B. Request, response, host address, subnet number, and network number

    C. Host address, subnet number, network number, ping, and default

    D. None of the above

Answer D is correct: the five possible values for the command field are request, response, traceon, traceoff, and reserved.

9. The maximum size of a RIPv2 packet is ____.

    A. 512

    B. 520

    C. 504

    D. None of the above

Answer A is correct; just as with the RIPv1 packet, the RIPv2 packet is 512 octets, including the UDP header. Answer B is incorrect because this is RIP's UDP port number. Answer C is incorrect because the RIP message part can be up to 504 bytes.

10. VLSM is possible with ____.

    A. RIPv1

    B. RIPv2

    C. Both A and B

    D. Neither A nor B

Answer B is correct. The Variable Length Subnet Mask (VLSM) can only be implemented with RIPv2. The addition of the subnet mask field in the RIP packet has made VLSM possible.

CHAPTER PREREQUISITE

Read and understand the following chapters before reading this chapter: Chapter 8, "TCP/IP," Chapter 9, "Routing Concept Overview," and especially Chapter 10, "RIP," because IGRP and RIP are similar, as you will see in this chapter.

IGRP and EIGRP

WHILE YOU READ

1. What type of routing protocols are IGRP and EIGRP?

2. What four primary metrics are used in IGRP and EIGRP?

3. Of the four primary metrics used by IGRP and EIGRP, which two are most important?

4. What prevents regular update messages from reinstating an IGRP route that may have gone down?

5. What prevents route updates from being advertised back to the router from which they originated to prevent routing loops?

6. Do IGRP and EIGRP support multipath routing?

7. What is the frequency of an IGRP route update?

8. What are the four timers that IGRP employs to control performance?

9. Why is EIGRP considered a hybrid distance-vector routing protocol?

10. Does EIGRP perform route summarization of subnet routes into network-level routes?

The Interior Gateway Routing Protocol (IGRP) and Enhanced IGRP (EIGRP) are routing protocols developed in the mid-1980s and early 1990s, respectively, by Cisco Systems, Inc., to overcome the inadequate routing flexibility of RIP. More specifically, RIP's single metric and hop-count limit of 16, which does not scale well in complex environments, was overcome by IGRP's combination of metrics.

This chapter reviews the basic operations, protocol characteristics, and network configuration of Cisco System's proprietary routing protocols, IGRP, and Enhanced IGRP.

IGRP

IGRP is a distance-vector routing protocol, which calls for each router to send all or a subset of its routing table in a routing-update message to each of its neighboring routers at periodic intervals. As these updates proliferate through the network, routers can calculate distances to all nodes within an internetwork. IGRP uses a combination of metrics:

- Internetwork delay
- Bandwidth
- Reliability
- Load

All these metrics are factored into IGRP's routing decision. These metrics have default values or can be set by the administrator.

IGRP separates different administrative domains by using autonomous system (AS) numbers. Routing updates are not shared between routers in different autonomous systems.

Key Concept

IGRP supports multiple IGRP routing protocols running between routers through autonomous system (AS) numbers. All routers that need to exchange route information must be configured with the same AS number.

For example, in Figure 11.1, location A (on the left) and location B (on the right) are two separate networks connected via a WAN link. Route information will not be broadcast between the two networks because they are in different autonomous systems (location A is using AS 10 and location B is using AS 20). For location A and location B to exchange route information, they must both use the same AS number.

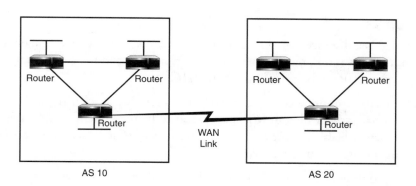

Figure 11.1
Two IGRP autonomous systems.

Stability Features

IGRP also incorporates some stability features over other distance-vector routing protocols. These features include

- Holddowns—Holddowns are used to prevent regular update messages from reinstating a route that might have gone down. If a route goes down during convergence, it will prevent routers that haven't been informed of the network failure from sending a regular route update message to a device that has already been informed of the network failure. Holddowns tell routers to hold down any changes that might affect stated routes for some period of time. This period usually is calculated to be just greater than the time required to update the entire network with a routing change.

- Split-horizons—Split-horizons are used to keep route updates from being advertised back to the router from which it originated to prevent routing loops. Although holddowns should prevent this, IGRP implements split-horizon to provide better algorithm stability.

- Poison reverse updates—Poison reverse updates are employed by IGRP to defeat larger routing loops. When increases in routing metrics occur, generally indicative of a routing loop, poison reverse updates are sent to remove the route and place it in holddown.

- Multipath routing—Multipath routing enables dual paths of equal bandwidth support to form a single stream of traffic in a round-robin manner. This feature is designed to enhance performance and redundancy if a line fails.

Route Metrics

Like RIP, IGRP is a distance-vector interior routing protocol. However, unlike RIP, IGRP can be used in larger autonomous systems due to its large maximum hop-count limit of 255, compared to RIP's maximum hop count of 16.

Additionally, IGRP uses more complex metrics that allow IGRP to distinguish between physically unequal paths, which to RIP may appear to be the same. Understanding these metrics is important because some of the characteristics of IGRP, such as unequal cost load balancing, are based on these metrics.

When making routing decisions, IGRP takes the following factors into consideration for its metrics:

- Metrics (also known as *administrative distance*)—These can be between 1 and 255 and set by the administrator to influence route selection.
- Delay—The speed of the medium in units of 10 milliseconds (typically any value from 1 to 2 to the 24th power). For 10Mbps Ethernet, the delay is 100, or 1ms.
- Bandwidth—Can take on values reflecting speeds from 1200bps to 10Gbps.
- Reliability—Represented in fractions of 255 (where 255 is optimal).

Although it is unnecessary to memorize the algorithm, it is useful to see how it works so you can better understand IGRP's features and scalability. IGRP uses the following formula for calculating route metrics:

$$\text{Metric}_{IGRP} = (K_1 * Bw) + ((K_2 * Bw) / (256 - \text{Load})) + (K_3 * \text{Delay}) * (K_5 / (\text{Reliability} + K_4))$$

Bw is the IGRP Bandwidth of the path and is calculated as follows: $Bw = 10^7 / Bw_{min}$. Bw_{min} is the minimum logical bandwidth of the path expressed in kilobits per second (Kbps). Logical bandwidth is a static parameter configurable on an interface using the command bandwidth in interface configuration mode. The bandwidth on each interface on a router reflects the actual bandwidth of the interface. However, for serial interfaces this defaults to 1544.

Delay is the IGRP delay of the path (sum of the delays of all segments along the path) expressed in 10-microsecond units.

Load is the IGRP load of the corresponding interface measured dynamically with an integer range of 1 to 255; 1 is minimally loaded, and 255 is a 100%-loaded interface.

Reliability is the IGRP reliability of the corresponding interfaces segment measured dynamically with an integer range of 1 to 255; 1 is minimally reliable, and 255 is a 100%-reliable segment.

K_1 - K_5 are administratively configurable IGRP weights with default values as follows:

K_1	1
K_2	0
K_3	1
K_4	0
K_5	0

When the default values of the IGRP weights are used, the formula for calculating the IGRP metrics is as follows: **Metric$_{igrp}$ = Bw + Delay**

Key Concept

In most cases, IGRP metric equals *Bandwidth + Delay*, except when the default metrics (K_1-K_5) are changed.

To verify the logical values used by IGRP in metric calculations (current bandwidth, delay, reliability, and load on an interface), use the show interface command. Example:

```
RTR# show interfaces serial 1
Serial1 is up, line protocol is up
    Hardware is HD64570
    Internet address is 200.100.0.1/24
    MTU 1500 bytes,   BW  1544 Kbit,  DLY 2000 usec,  rely  255/255,
  ➥load    1/255
```

Note the bandwidth (BW), delay (DLY), reliability (rely), and load values shown in the example.

Route Updates

Because IGRP is a distance-vector interior gateway protocol, it is required to send all or a portion of its routing table in a routing update message at regular intervals to each of its neighboring routers within the same autonomous system. The default time interval is every 90 seconds.

To control the performance and stability of route updates, IGRP provides a number of timers and variables with default settings for each of the following:

- Update timer—This specifies how frequently IGRP routing messages will be sent. The default is 90 seconds.

- Invalid timer—This specifies how long a router should wait in the absence of a routing-update message of a specific route before declaring it invalid. The default is three times the Update timer, 270 seconds.

- Holddown timer—This specifies the holddown period. The default is three times the update timer plus 10 seconds, 280 seconds.
- Flush timer—This indicates how much time should pass before an IGRP route is flushed from the routing table. The default is seven times the routing update period, 630 seconds.

IGRP advertises three types of routes:

- Interior routes—Between subnets
- System routes—Routes to networks within an autonomous system
- Exterior routes—Routes to networks outside the autonomous system

IGRP does not advertise interior routes if a network is not subnetted. System routes do not include subnet information. IGRP uses the list of exterior routes to determine the gateway of last resort for a specific router.

Finally, routes are entered into a route table based on the source's reliability. As mentioned in Chapter 9, "Routing Concept Overview," the administrative distance is used to rate the reliability of the source of the route. Every type of route and routing protocol is assigned a default administrative distance. The lowest administrative distance becomes the preferred route entered in the routing table.

Monitoring IGRP

To monitor IGRP on your Cisco routers, you can use the following commands:

- `show ip route`
- `show ip protocol`
- `show ip interfaces`
- `debug ip igrp`
- `trace`

The `show ip route igrp` command will list only the IGRP routes found. For example,

```
RTR# show ip route igrp
200.100.0.0    255.255.255.0  is subnetted,  4 subnets
I    200.100.50.0  [100/11828]  via 200.100.20.2,  00:00:55,  Serial0
I    200.100.40.0  [100/11828]  via 200.100.20.2,  00:00:55,  Serial0
I    200.100.30.0  [100/11828]  via 200.100.20.2,  00:00:55,  Serial0
```

The `show ip protocol` command shows IGRP protocol specific information such as AS number, route update information (invalid, holddown, update, and flush timers), and the IGRP metric weight (K_1–K_5) as mentioned earlier. For example,

```
RTR# show ip protocol
Routing Protocol is "IGRP 10"
    Sending updates every 90 seconds, next due in 55 seconds
    Invalid after 270 seconds, hold down 280,  flushed after 630
    Outgoing update filter list for all interfaces is not set
    Incoming update filter list for all interfaces is not set
    Default networks flagged in outgoing updates
    Default networks accepted from incoming updates
    IGRP metric weight K1=1,  K2=0,  K3=1,  K4=0,  K5=0
    IGRP maximum hopcount 100
    IGRP maximum metric variance 1
    Redistributing:  IGRP 10
    Routing for Networks:
        200.100.0.0
    Routing Information Sources:
        Gateway         Distance        Last Update
        200.100.20.2              100         0:00:05
    Distance:  (default is 100)
```

The show ip interfaces command shows you the current status of the interface, global parameters associated with each interface, interface configuration information, and routing protocol information. For example,

```
    RTR# show ip interface
 Ethernet0 is up,  line protocol is up
        Internet address is 100.200.50.1 255.255.255.0
        Broadcast address is 255.255.255.255
        Address determined by non-volatile memory
        MTU is 1500 bytes
        Helper address is not set
Directed broadcast forwarding is enabled
        Outgoing access list is not set
        Inbound access list is not set
        Proxy ARP is enabled
        Security level is default
        Split Horizon is enabled
        ICMP redirects are always sent
            ICMP unreachables are always sent
        ICMP masks are never sent
            IP fast switching is enabled
            IP fast switching on the same interface is disabled
        IP SSE switching is disabled
        Router Discovery is disabled
        IP output packet accounting is disabled
        TCP/IP header compression is disabled
        Probe proxy name replies are disabled
```

Unlike debug ip rip, the debug ip igrp command has two options: events and transactions. The command debug ip igrp events displays information about IGRP routing updates being received. The command debug ip igrp transactions displays the contents of the routing updates in detail.

Key Concept

In the debug output, you will see the sources of routing updates, even if they are from the wrong network or subnet, *a hint that something may be wrong*.

The trace command can be used to check the path a packet takes to get to the final destination. For example,

```
RTR# trace 100.200.50.2

Type escape sequence to abort.

Tracing route to 100.200.50.2

  1   100.200.20.2   20 msec   20  msec   20  msec
  2   100.200.30.2   36 msec   36  msec   42  msec      (Router2)
  3   100.200.50.2   32 msec   30  msec   30  msec      (Router3)
```

This shows us that to get from RTR to the device on Network 50 the packet went through the routers named Router2 and Router3.

IGRP Configuration Example

Configuring IGRP is similar to configuring RIP in that after the router command you must specify only directly connected (system routes) networks. The only difference is in the command to enable the routing protocol. You must specify an AS number when enabling IGRP. The AS number parameter specifies the autonomous system number that is supported by this IGRP process and allows multiple IGRP processes to run on a single router. The AS number can be between 1 and 65,655.

For example,

```
RTR(config)# router igrp 10
RTR(config-router)# network 200.40.0.0
RTR(config-router)# network 200.30.0.0
```

Key Concept

Unlike RIP, IGRP does not advertise individual host addresses. Instead, IGRP always summarizes routing updates on the classful boundary. Additionally, IGRP does not send routing updates for the secondary IP addresses configured on any interface.

EIGRP

Enhanced IGRP (EIGRP) is an enhanced version of IGRP developed by Cisco Systems, Inc. It is considered a hybrid because it employs distance vectors to determine the best paths to destination networks, but it resembles a link-state protocol in the way it uses topology changes to trigger routing table updates. EIGRP's convergence and operating efficiencies are far superior to IGRP. It employs an algorithm referred to as the *Diffusing Update Algorithm (DUAL)* that guarantees loop-free operation at every instant. It does this throughout a route computation and allows all devices involved in a topology change to synchronize at the same time. Routers that are not part of a topology change are not involved in the route computations.

Additionally, Cisco added the capability for EIGRP to handle routes for multiple networking protocols, including IP, AppleTalk, and IPX. Therefore, a single protocol engine can collect topology information and update the routing tables for all protocols. This conserves network bandwidth, router memory, and router CPU cycles.

Route Metrics

EIGRP uses the same metrics that IGRP uses—bandwidth, delay, load, reliability, and MTU (as mentioned in the previous section)—but it also multiplies IGRP metrics by 256. EIGRP metrics are as follows:

$$\text{Metric}_{EIGRP} = \text{Metric}_{IGRP} * 256$$

Where

$$\text{Metric}_{IGRP} = (K_1 * Bw) + ((K_2 * Bw) / (256 - Load)) + (K_3 * Delay) * (K_5 / (Reliability + K_4))$$

 Key Concept

Because EIGRP uses the same metric as IGRP, and the metric equation and coefficients are also the same, bandwidth and delay are the only two components that determine the final metric.

It is interesting to notice that like IGRP, metric coefficients must be the same on all routers running EIGRP.

Components

Enhanced IGRP (EIGRP) provides the following components and features:

■ Neighbor Discovery/Recovery—The process that EIGRP routers use to dynamically learn of other routers on their directly attached networks. Unlike IGRP, EIGRP does not send regular routing updates containing the whole routing table.

Instead, neighbor discovery/recovery is achieved with low overhead by periodically sending small hello packets to its neighbors. The purpose of the hello messages is to determine whether its neighbors are alive. If a physical interface goes down, or if the router misses three subsequent hello messages from a neighbor, a topology change is detected and EIGRP allows the router to send routing updates to the affected network.

■ Reliable Transport Protocol—This is responsible for guaranteed, ordered delivery of EIGRP packets to all neighbors. It supports intermixed transmission of multi-cast and unicast packets. Some EIGRP packets must be transmitted reliably, whereas others need not be. On multiaccess networks such as Ethernet, it is not necessary to send hellos reliably to all neighbors separately. Instead, EIGRP sends a single multicast hello with an indication in the packet informing the receivers that the packet need not be acknowledged. On the other hand, updates require acknowledgment and are indicated in the packet. The EIGRP reliable transport has a provision to send multicast packets quickly when there are unacknowledged packets pending. This helps ensure that convergence time remains low.

■ Diffusing Update Algorithm—The finite state machine that embodies the decision process for all EIGRP route computations. It tracks all routes advertised by all neighbors using the distance information (metric) to select efficient, loop-free paths. DUAL selects routes to be inserted into a routing table based on feasible successors. A *successor* is a neighboring router used for packet forwarding that has a least-cost path to a destination that is guaranteed to be loop free. If there are no feasible successors, but there are neighbors advertising the destination, a recompu-tation must occur to determine a new successor. The time it takes to recompute the route affects the convergence time; therefore, it is advantageous to avoid recomputation.

Key Concept

When a topology change occurs, DUAL test for feasible successors to avoid unnecessary recomputation.

■ Passive and Active Router—EIGRP provides the ability for automatic redistribu-tion of IGRP routes into EIGRP, and EIGRP routes redistributed into IGRP. However, this will happen only if you use the same AS number for IGRP and EIGRP. If desired, you can turn off redistribution. You can also completely turn off EIGRP and IGRP on the router or on individual interfaces (a combination of passive-interface and distance commands must be used to disable EIGRP on indi-vidual interfaces).

- VLSM—EIGRP supports full variable-length subnet masks (VLSM) operation by propagating the route and its mask together. By default, routes are summarized to classful addresses at network boundaries. EIGRP also makes it possible to propagate the subnets of a network by using the router subcommand `no auto-summary`. Using this command, you can avoid the problem of discontiguous subnets because all subnet information is propagated into the adjacent network.

- IPX/AppleTalk EIGRP—Unlike IGRP, EIGRP has the capability to handle routes for multiple networking protocols, including IP, AppleTalk, and IPX. Therefore, a single protocol engine can collect topology information and update the routing tables for all three protocols. This conserves network bandwidth, router memory, and router CPU time.

Route Summarization

By default, EIGRP performs route summarization of subnet routes into network-level routes. For example, you can configure subnet 100.200.50.0 to be advertised as 100.200.0.0. Automatic summarization is performed when two or more network router configuration commands are configured for the EIGRP process. The command `no auto-summary` prevents EIGRP from summarizing the routes on the classful boundary. For example,

```
RTR(config)# router eigrp 10
RTR(config-router)# network 100.200.0.0
RTR(config-router)# no auto-summary
```

This configuration disables auto-summarization.

A powerful feature of EIGRP is manual route summarization. To enable manual route summarization use the command:

```
RTR(config-if)# ip summary-address eigrp {AS Number} {IP Address} {Subnet Mask}
```

This will stop the router from sending regular EIGRP routing updates and instead advertises the summary address as specified in the parameters {IP address} {Subnet Mask}.

To force EIGRP to summarize network 10.0.0.0 out Ethernet interface 0 only, use the following command:

```
RTR(config)# interace ethernet 0
RTR(config-interface)# ip summary-address eigrp 10 10.0.0.0 255.0.0.0
```

Key Concept

It is a good idea to always accompany manual route summarization with the command `ip classless`.

Bandwidth Control

Output rate queues on each interface are used to prevent overloading links when a network topology change causes a burst of routing protocol traffic. EIGRP packets consume a maximum of 50% of the link bandwidth by default. You can change this value if a different level of link utilization is required or if the configured bandwidth does not match the actual link bandwidth (which may have been configured to influence route metric calculations). This can be accomplished by using the following command:

```
RTR (config-if)# ip bandwidth-percent eigrp {AS Number} {Percent}
```

For example,

```
RTR(config)# interace Serial 0
RTR(config-interface)# bandwidth 56
RTR(config-interface)# ip bandwidth-percent eigrp 10 75
```

Adjacency Process

The EIGRP hello protocol is used to establish neighbor relationships between routers. Hello packets are sent every five seconds by default on LAN media and every 60 seconds on WAN media. The information is stored in the router's EIGRP neighbor table. This table stores the identity of each neighbor, its hold time, and the sequence number and acknowledgments used to ensure the reliable delivery of updates to and from that neighbor.

The neighbor table can be viewed with the show ip eigrp neighbor command.

It is recommended that when configuring EIGRP you enable the logging of neighbor adjacency changes to monitor the stability of the routing system and to help you detect problems.

Key Concept

A router that is constantly resetting the uptime value in the neighbor table indicates a neighbor relationship that is constantly being restarted.

Route Convergence

Route convergence is the time that begins when a topology change occurs and ends when all the routers have recomputed routes based on the new topology. During this time, routing in the network is disrupted, from minimally to severely, depending on the topological change. By nature, link state-protocols will converge more quickly than distance vector protocols because of looping and the fact that distance vectors must be computed before a router can pass route information.

As stated earlier, the time it takes to recompute an EIGRP route affects the convergence time. The convergence time of EIGRP is considerably faster than that of other distance-vector protocols like RIP and IGRP. Convergence time is measured in tens of seconds for EIGRP compared to minutes for RIP and IGRP.

EIGRP Configuration Examples

EIGRP's basic configuration is identical to that of IGRP. You will see in the following configurations that, like IGRP, only the networks that are directly connected to each router are listed in the network statement of EIGRP. Also, the network statement tells the router which interfaces should be running EIGRP.

Remember, two key EIGRP configuration items must match in order for adjacent routers to pass route information properly. The first is the autonomous systems number, and the second is the metric equation coefficients (K1, K2, K3, K4, and K5), which must be the same on all routers within an autonomous system.

Figure 11.2 will be used for an example for the configurations.

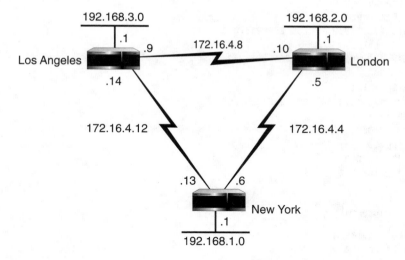

Figure 11.2
A sample EIGRP network.

Sample Configuration

New York router:

```
hostname NewYork
interface Ethernet0
  ip address 192.168.1.1   255.255.255.0
interface Serial 0
  ip address 172.16.4.13   255.255.255.252
  bandwidth 1544
interface Serial 1
  ip address 172.16.4.6   255.255.255.252
  bandwidth 1544
  clockrate 1300000
router eigrp 10
  network 172.16.0.0
  network 192.168.1.0
ip classless
```

London router:

```
hostname London
interface Ethernet0
  ip address 192.168.2.1   255.255.255.0
interface Serial 0
  ip address 172.16.4.5   255.255.255.252
  bandwidth 1544
interface Serial 1
  ip address 172.16.4.10   255.255.255.252
  bandwidth 1544
  clockrate 1300000
router eigrp 10
  network 172.16.0.0
  network 192.168.2.0
ip classless
```

Los Angeles router:

```
hostname LosAngeles
interface Ethernet0
  ip address 192.168.3.1   255.255.255.0
interface Serial 0
  ip address 172.16.4.9   255.255.255.252
  bandwidth 1544
interface Serial 1
  ip address 172.16.4.14   255.255.255.252
  bandwidth 1544
  clockrate 1300000
router eigrp 10
  network 172.16.0.0
  network 192.168.3.0
ip classless
```

PART IV

Summary

This chapter summarizes the characteristics of IGRP and EIGRP. After reading this chapter, you should thoroughly understand both IGRP and EIGRP. You should be able to identify the characteristics and features of each protocol such as route metrics, associated stability features (holddowns, split-horizons, and poison reverse updates), and timers. You should also be able to identify the similarities and differences between these protocols and how they are implemented in Cisco routers.

QUESTIONS AND ANSWERS

1. What type of routing protocols are IGRP and EIGRP?

    A: Distance-vector routing protocols

2. What four primary metrics are used in IGRP and EIGRP?

    A: Delay, Bandwidth, Reliability, and Load

3. Of the four primary metrics used by IGRP and EIGRP, which two are most important?

    A: Bandwidth and Delay

4. What prevents regular update messages from reinstating an IGRP route that may have gone down?

    A: Holddowns

5. What prevents route updates from being advertised back to the router from which they originated to prevent routing loops?

    A: Split-horizon

6. Do IGRP and EIGRP support multipath routing?

    A: Yes

7. What is the frequency of an IGRP route update?

    A: 90 seconds

8. What are the four timers that IGRP employs to control performance?

    A: Update, Invalid, Holddown, and Flush timer

9. Why is EIGRP considered a hybrid distance-vector routing protocol?

A: EIGRP is considered a hybrid distance-vector routing protocol because it resembles a link-state protocol in the way it uses topology changes to trigger routing table updates.

10. Does EIGRP perform route summarization of subnet routes into network-level routes?

A: Yes

PRACTICE TEST

1. What is the routing algorithm used by IGRP?

A. Routed Information

B. Link State

C. Distance Vector

D. Link Together

Answers A and D are incorrect because they are invalid terms. Answer B is incorrect because it is not a link-state protocol. **Answer C is correct because IGRP uses the distance-vector algorithm.**

2. Which command can you use to verify the broadcast frequency for IGRP?

A. `show ip route`

B. `show ip protocol`

C. `show ip broadcast`

D. `debug ip igrp`

Answer B is correct because the `sh ip protocol` command will display the broadcast frequency for IGRP. Answers A, C, and D are incorrect. Even though they are valid commands, the required information is not displayed with them.

3. What are the routing metrics used by IGRP? (Choose all that apply.)

A. TTL

B. Hop count

C. Count to Infinity

D. Bandwidth, Reliability, MTU, Delay, and Load

Answer A is incorrect because it is not a routing metric; it is a Time to Live field. Answer B is incorrect because it is the metric used by RIP. Answer C is incorrect because it is a loop-prevention technique employed by some routing protocols. **Answer D is correct because IGRP uses Bandwidth, Reliability, MTU, Delay, and Load for its routing metric.**

4. Holddowns are used for what?

A. To prevent a regular update message from reinstating a route that has gone down.

B. To prevent regular update message from reinstating a route that has just gone up.

C. To hold down the protocol from going to the next hop.

D. To prevent an irregular update message from reinstating a route that has gone down.

Answer A is correct because holddowns prevent regular update messages from reinstating a route that has gone down. Answers B, C, and D are incorrect because they are not functions of any protocol's feature set.

5. What is the default administrative distance for IGRP?

A. 90

B. 100

C. 120

D. 220

Answer A is incorrect because it is the administrative distance for EIGRP internal routes. **Answer B is correct because 100 is the administrative distance for IGRP**. Answer C is incorrect because it is the administrative distance for RIP. Answer D is not the administrative distance for anything.

6. What are the three types of routes that IGRP advertises?

A. Interior

B. Dynamic

C. Exterior

D. System

Answers A, C, and D are correct because they are the three type of routes that IGRP advertises. Answer B is incorrect and is not a route type for any protocol.

7. What is true about link-state networks?

A. They use RIP timers.

B. They don't use convergence.

C. They maintain a more complex table than distance-vector–based networks.

D. They maintain a less complex table than distance-vector–based networks.

Answer A is incorrect because RIP is a distance-vector protocol. Answer B is incorrect because convergence is not "used"; networks achieve convergence when all routing tables agree. **Answer C is correct because link-state networks maintain a more complex table than distance-vector–based networks.** Answer D is incorrect because distance-vector protocols are usually simpler than link-state protocols, resulting in simpler routing tables.

8. What is convergence time?

   A. The holddown update time

   B. The time it takes all routers to update their routing tables when a change takes place

   C. The time it takes to boot a router

   D. The time it takes a packet to get from destination host to receiving host

Answer B is correct because convergence time is the time it takes all routers to update their routing tables when a change takes place. Answers A, C, and D are incorrect and nonsensical answers.

9. Which command prevents EIGRP from summarizing the routes on the classful boundary?

   A. `auto-summary`

   B. `no auto-summary`

   C. `ip summary-address eigrp`

   D. `no ip summary-address eigrp`

Answer A is incorrect because it would allow, not prevent, summarizing. **Answer B is correct because the command `no auto-summary` in the configuration router mode will prevent EIGRP from summarizing the routes on the classful boundary.** Answers C and D are related but incorrect. They enable and disable manual route summarization of a specific set of routes.

10. What is the metric limit for link-state protocols?

   A. 16

   B. 255

   C. 6,500

   D. 65,533

Answers A, B, and C are incorrect; they are simply random numbers that look like feasible answers if you do not know the correct answer. **Answer D is correct; 65,533 is the metric limit for link-state protocols.**

CHAPTER PREREQUISITE
You should read and understand
the following chapters before
reading this chapter: Chapter 1,
"General Network Overview,"
Chapter 8, "TCP/IP," Chapter 9,
"Routing Concept Overview," and
Chapter 10, "RIP."

OSPF

— WHILE YOU READ —

1. What algorithm does OSPF use to compute its route table?
2. What three tables does an OSPF router build?
3. What is the significance of the DR and BDR?
4. How are the DR and BDR selected?
5. How is the router ID determined?
6. What is an ABR?
7. What is an ASBR?
8. What is a stub area?
9. What is a totally stubby area?
10. What is a virtual link?

SEE
APPENDIX **F**

Open Shortest Path First (OSPF) is an Interior Gateway Protocol (IGP) designed to correct the shortcomings of earlier routing protocols such as RIP. OSPF is characterized as a link-state routing protocol because of the way it learns route information. RIP, as you know, is a distance-vector routing protocol. The term *open* in OSPF refers to the fact that OSPF is open standard, unlike other routing protocols such as IGRP and EIGRP, which are Cisco proprietary. Shortest path first refers to the *shortest path first (SPF) algorithm*, also known as the *Dijkstra algorithm*, which OSPF uses to compute its route table.

Key Concept

OSPF is a link-state protocol, and it uses the shortest path first algorithm, also known as the Dijkstra algorithm, to compute its route table.

The overriding benefit of OSPF, when compared to other routing protocols, is scalability. OSPF possesses many features that make it quite suitable for large, growing internetworks.

OSPF Features

Following is an overview of features that distinguish OSPF from other routing protocols:

- OSPF's metrics
- OSPF's capability to conserve bandwidth
- Fast network convergence
- Hierarchical design
- VLSM support
- Authentication capability

This section also discusses OSPF's requirements of memory and processor power.

Metric

OSPF uses a metric called *cost*. By default on Cisco routers, the cost of a route is based on bandwidth. The route with the lowest cost—or, inversely, the highest bandwidth—to a destination becomes the preferred route and is the one that is inserted into the routing table.

This contrasts with RIP, which uses hop count as its metric and has a hop count limit of 15. Thus, in a RIP network, routers with more than 15 hops between them will be unable to communicate with each other. This obviously poses a serious problem to the operation of large internetworks, which can easily surpass this 15 hop-count diameter. With the OSPF cost metric, however, there are virtually no distance limitations on the size of the internetwork.

Key Concept

OSPF has no hop-count limitation because it does not use hop count in its route calculations; it uses cost as its metric.

Furthermore, the OSPF cost metric generally makes a lot more sense than a simple hop-count metric. Consider the case of two links, one a 56k and the other a T1, connecting two routers. RIP would treat both these links as the same, whereas OSPF would prefer the faster T1 circuit.

Bandwidth Conservation

Instead of broadcasting its entire routing table to all neighbors periodically like distance-vector routing protocols, OSPF multicasts its routing updates to selected routers only when changes occur in the internetwork topology. In addition, OSPF sends only information about the change that occurred and not its entire routing table in these updates. These features make OSPF much less of a bandwidth hog compared to typical distance-vector routing protocols.

Key Concept

OSPF multicasts routing updates only when changes occur in the internetwork and sends information about only that change, not its entire routing table.

Fast Convergence

When a change in the internetwork occurs, such as a link going down, this information is immediately flooded to all routers that need to know about this change, but *only* to the routers that need to know. After flooding this information to the appropriate routers, OSPF routers then recalculate their routing table. Because all routers affected by a change in a link's state are quickly notified of the change, all affected routers are able to gain an accurate view of the internetwork in a very short time. Thus, the internetwork converges much faster in an OSPF network than in a typical distance-vector network.

Hierarchical Design

OSPF allows for an internetwork to be broken up into groups of networks called *areas*. Areas allow for routing information to remain localized within that area, thereby reducing the amount of overhead traffic that flows across the entire internetwork. When combined with proper route summarization, areas also help reduce the size of routing tables and reduce the frequency of SPF algorithm recalculations.

VLSM Support

OSPF supports IP Variable-Length Subnet Masking (VLSM). This helps network administrators conserve IP address space and allocate address space in a flexible, logical manner. OSPF carries subnet mask information in its routing updates and is thus completely suitable for an internetwork that employs VLSM. Distance vector routing protocols such as RIP and IGRP, however, do not carry subnet mask information in their routing updates and thus would not be a good choice for deployment in an internetwork that uses VLSM.

Authentication

OSPF provides for authentication between routers. In large IP networks, it is often critical that only authorized routers within the administrator's domain are allowed to provide routing updates. Administrators can use authentication to ensure that unwanted updates that could degrade network performance are prevented.

Memory Requirements

Like anything, the benefits of OSPF do come at a price. Specifically, OSPF requires more router memory than distance-vector routing protocols. This is largely due to the fact that OSPF maintains three distinct, and often large, tables to allow it to make routing decisions. A *neighbor* or *adjacencies database*, a *link-state* or *topological database*, and the routing table all need to be maintained by an OSPF router. These are explained further, later in the chapter.

Processor Power

In addition to taxing a router's memory, OSPF also takes its toll on the router's CPU. The shortest path first algorithm is processor intensive. This is because OSPF frequently recalculates its route table, requiring the frequent running of the SPF algorithm. If the CPU is not powerful enough, this could hamper the router's capability to perform other key functions such as forwarding data packets. This is one reason steps should be taken in the design of an OSPF network to try to minimize the need for unnecessary route table recalculation.

OSPF Operation

Before routing tables are built, OSPF goes through a series of events when a new router or network is brought online. These stages are described later in the chapter.

Establishing Neighbors

Each router exchanges packets called *hello packets* with other routers attached to its network. This exchanging of hello packets is referred to as the *hello protocol.* After hello packets have been exchanged and parameters agreed on, the routers are considered to have established bidirectional communication and are now *adjacent.* Adjacencies must be established between routers before they can exchange link-state information.

Key Concept

Adjacencies must be established (via the hello protocol) between routers before they can exchange link-state information.

DR and BDR Election

A Designated Router (DR) and Backup Designated Router (BDR) are elected on multiaccess OSPF networks, such as Ethernet, Token-Ring, and FDDI LANs. Note that on nonbroadcast multiaccess (NBMA) networks such as Frame Relay, manual configuration might be necessary for the DR and BDR to work properly. On point-to-point networks, there is no concept of the DR and BDR because they are not necessary.

The DR and BDR serve as a point of contact for all routers attached to the network. Instead of having all routers exchanging link-state information with all other routers on the network, which would consume considerable bandwidth, OSPF routers on multiaccess networks exchange routing information only with the DR and BDR. It is the DR's job to distribute this routing information to the rest of the routers on the network. Should the DR go offline, the BDR will take over its responsibilities and become the DR. A new BDR would then be elected.

The DR and BDR are elected based on *router priority.* The router with the highest priority will become the DR, whereas the router with the second highest priority will become the BDR. By default, all routers have a router priority of 1. To break ties, OSPF uses *router ID.* The highest router ID is the highest IP address. Usually the IP address for OSPF router ID is configured on the virtual loopback interface of the router. Because this interface never goes down, DR and BDR elections should occur less frequently. If no loopback interface is configured on the router, the router ID is the highest IP address configured on any physical interface of the router. Thus, if all routers on the network have equal priority, the one with the highest router ID will be elected the DR.

You can also manually configure router priority. To ensure that a router does not become a DR or BDR, it should be configured with a router priority of 0.

Key Concept

The OSPF router ID is defined as the highest IP address on a router's loopback interface. If no loopback interface is configured on a router, the router ID is the highest IP address configured on any of the router's physical interfaces.

Route Discovery

Routes are discovered between OSPF routers via an exchange protocol. After adjacencies have been established and a DR and BDR elected for multiaccess networks, OSPF routers are ready to learn about the state of the internetwork. Link-state information is exchanged between routers through the transmission of *Link State Updates (LSUs)*. LSUs contain *Link State Advertisements (LSAs)* that describe the state of all links, or networks, that each router knows about. All this LSA information is stored in a link-state database, sometimes referred to as a topological database. This link-state database is the router's view of the internetwork. All routers within an OSPF area should have identical link-state databases.

Key Concept

LSUs contain LSAs, which describe links in the internetwork. LSAs are stored in the topological database.

Route Selection

Given the information in the link-state database, OSPF runs the SPF algorithm on the database to compute the route table. The SPF algorithm is a somewhat complex process. In summary, though, the router computing the route table will consider itself as the root of a tree and calculate costs to destination networks. The route with the lowest total cost to a destination network is selected for entry into the route table. By default on Cisco routers, cost depends on bandwidth. The higher the bandwidth, the lower the cost, and the more preferable a route becomes.

Key Concept

By default on Cisco routers, the OSPF cost metric is inversely proportional to bandwidth.

Route Maintenance

Two issues must be addressed with regard to route maintenance:

- Routers must hear about routes within a specified time or the route will age out of the topological database.
- Routers must know when changes to routes occur.

When a link-state changes, routers flood the LSA about that change within a LSU to appropriate routers within the area. A receiving router then adds this information to its link-state database, sends the LSU to other routers if necessary, and recomputes its route table. LSAs in the topological database need to be refreshed every 30 minutes. If a route ages out of the topological database, the router that originated the LSA will retransmit the LSA again to all necessary routers.

Hierarchy and Components

OSPF provides many hierarchical features, allowing it to scale very well for large internetworks. These hierarchical features are realized by grouping routers into areas. Areas allow for routing information to remain localized within the area and summary routes to be passed between areas. This way, link-state changes in one area do not cause route table recalculations in other areas, and bandwidth across the entire internetwork is spared consumption by numerous routing updates. Also, effective route summarization reduces the size of routing tables. The different types of areas, routers, and LSAs are described later in the chapter.

Area Types

Areas are an OSPF mechanism for administratively defining routing areas within a large internetwork, as described earlier. There are a number of different areas possible for an OSPF internetwork.

- Backbone Area
- Stub Area
- Totally Stubby Area
- Not-So-Stubby Area

The most important area is the backbone, which is always Area 0. All other areas need to connect to Area 0. All traffic travelling between areas flows through the backbone area. If only one area is configured in the internetwork, it needs to be configured as Area 0.

Key Concept

All areas must connect to Area 0. On the exam, if you are shown a network topology for an OSPF network, one thing to look for is that all routers connect to Area 0, via either a direct connection (shared router) or a virtual link (discussed later in the chapter).

A stub area is an area that does not accept routing updates from external autonomous systems (systems outside the OSPF internetwork). A default route is used to reach any external autonomous system.

A totally stubby area is an area that does not accept routing updates from any external areas, OSPF or otherwise. Thus, a totally stubby area uses a default route to reach any destinations outside its area.

A not-so-stubby area (NSSA) is a hybrid stub area, meaning that this area accepts some types of LSAs from external autonomous systems. The NSSA option was designed so that small branch offices running a routing protocol other than OSPF would be able to easily connect to an OSPF network.

Router Types

As logic would dictate, if there are different area types, the routers in them have different operations. OSPF routers can be characterized relative to their area location, as illustrated in Figure 12.1. The types of routers used in an OSPF network are

- Internal Router
- Backbone Router
- Area Border Router (ABR)
- Autonomous System Boundary Router (ASBR)

For example, a router with all its interfaces within a single area is called an *Internal Router*. A router with any one of its interfaces connected to Area 0 is called a *Backbone Router*.

A router with one interface connected to one area and another interface connected to another area is termed an *Area Border Router (ABR)*. And similarly, a router with one interface connected to one Autonomous System (AS) and another interface connected to another AS is deemed an *Autonomous System Boundary Router (ASBR)*.

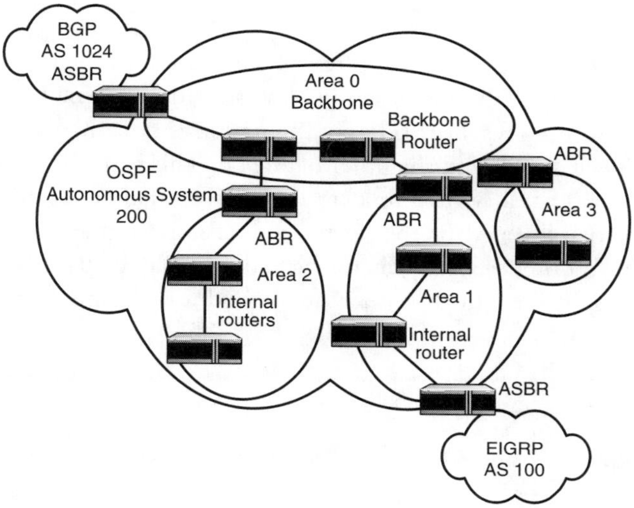

Figure 12.1
OSPF routers are characterized relative to their position in an area.

LSA Types

Link State Advertisements (LSAs) are the updates sent by routers describing the status of internetwork links. There are seven different types of LSAs. These LSAs are grouped based on where they originate and what they describe.

Key Concept

For the CCIE Written Exam, you should know the following:

- Type 1 and Type 2 LSAs are flooded only within a single area.
- Type 3 and Type 4 LSAs describe links in others areas and are flooded between areas.
- Type 5 LSAs describe routes external to the autonomous system.

Note that totally stubby areas do not accept Type 4 and Type 5 LSAs, and stub areas do not accept Type 5 LSAs. Type 7 LSAs are used for the NSSA option.

Virtual Links

Sometimes it is impossible for an area to have a physical connection to the backbone Area 0. Virtual links are designed to remedy this situation. A virtual link is like a tunnel through which OSPF can travel to reach Area 0. Configuration is done between two ABRs—one of the unconnected Area and the other of Area 0. This way, the area not physically connected to Area 0 has a "virtual link" to Area 0. The main condition for the creation of a virtual link is that both ABRs that form the link must connect to the same area that is between them. Another scenario when a virtual link may be used is to connect an Area 0 that has become split (but this is not a wise method for administering your routing domain).

Key Concept

Virtual links are used to link areas to Area 0 that have no physical connection to the backbone.

Configuration Examples

The key commands needed to configure OSPF and its features are described in the following section, along with examples.

Basic OSPF Configuration

At a minimum, the following commands are needed to configure OSPF:

```
RTR (config)# router ospf {process id}
RTR (config-router)# network {network} {wildcard mask} area {area-id}
```

{process id} is a number to distinguish one OSPF process from another OSPF process that might be running on a router. It is not recommended to run more than one OSPF process on a router in any case because of the overhead required to support OSPF. The process IDs do not need to be the same on routers within the same OSPF network.

{network} specifies which attached router interfaces will run OSPF. *{wildcard mask}* is used to specify the network. And *{area-id}* is just a number to identify the OSPF area. As an example, review Figure 12.2 and the accompanying configuration.

The relevant OSPF configuration on router R1, which by the way is both an ABR and a backbone router, would look as follows:

```
R1 (config)# router ospf 1
R1 (config-router)# network 10.5.5.0 0.0.0.255 area 0
R1 (config-router)# network 10.5.10.1 0.0.0.0 area 1
```

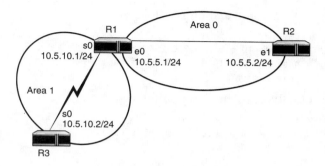

Figure 12.2
A basic multiarea OSPF scenario.

Note that a wildcard mask of 0.0.0.0 can be used to identify a specific interface, instead of a less-specific wildcard mask such as 0.0.0.255. In any case, the result is the same as both the e0 and s0 interfaces participate in the OSPF process on this router.

Stub Area Configuration

To configure an OSPF stub area, the following command needs to be entered under the OSPF process router configuration mode on all routers within the stub area:

```
RTR (config-router)# area {area-id} stub
```

To configure a totally stubby area, the following command needs to be entered only on the ABR that is connected to the totally stubby area:

```
RTR (config-router)# area {area-id} stub no-summary
```

Figure 12.3 provides an example of a stub area, using the same topology as in the previous example. The only difference is that area 1 is now configured as a stub area.

PART

IV

CH

12

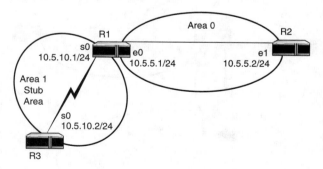

Figure 12.3
A stub area scenario.

Router R1's relevant OSPF configuration is as follows:

```
R1 (config)# router ospf 32
R1 (config-router)# network 10.5.5.0 0.0.0.255 area 0
R1 (config-router)# network 10.5.10.0 0.0.0.255 area 1
R1 (config-router)# area 1 stub
```

Router R3's relevant OSPF configuration is as follows:

```
R3 (config)# router ospf 57
R3 (config-router)# network 10.5.10.0 0.0.0.255 area 1
R3 (config-router)# area 1 stub
```

To configure area 1 as a totally stubby area, R3 would have the same configuration as in the stub area case, but R1's configuration would change slightly. The following shows the relevant configuration needed on R1 to configure area 1 as a totally stubby area.

```
R1 (config)# router ospf 32
R1 (config-router)# network 10.5.5.0 0.0.0.255 area 0
R1 (config-router)# network 10.5.10.0 0.0.0.255 area 1
R1 (config-router)# area 1 stub no-summary
```

Notice that the only change to R1's configuration is the addition of the keyword no-summary to the area stub command.

Virtual Link Configuration

To configure a virtual link, the following command must be entered in router configuration mode on both routers forming the link:

```
RTR (config-router)# area {area-id} virtual-link {router-id}
```

The *router ID* is the router ID of the other router with which the virtual link is being formed.

Figure 12.4 provides an example of a case when a virtual link is needed.

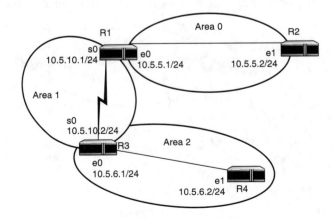

Figure 12.4
An OSPF topology in need of a virtual link.

In the case shown in Figure 12.4, Area 2 does not have a physical connection to the backbone Area 0. Thus, a virtual link is needed to connect Area 2 to the backbone area. The following configuration shows the relevant commands needed on routers R3 and R1 to form the virtual link. (For the sake of determining router IDs, it is assumed that the only interfaces on these routers, either physical or logical, are the ones shown in the diagram.)

R3's configuration:

```
R3 (config)# router ospf 15
R3 (config-router)# network 10.5.6.1 0.0.0.0 area 2
R3 (config-router)# network 10.5.10.2 0.0.0.0 area 1
R3 (config-router)# area 1 virtual-link 10.5.10.1
```

R1's configuration:

```
R1 (config)# router ospf 23
R1 (config-router)# network 10.5.5.1 0.0.0.0 area 0
R1 (config-router)# network 10.5.10.1 0.0.0.0 area 1
R1 (config-router)# area 1 virtual-link 10.5.10.2
```

Troubleshooting Commands

The Cisco IOS provides numerous show and debug commands for troubleshooting OSPF. Some useful show commands specific to OSPF are

- `show ip ospf neighbor detail`—Displays a list of neighbor routers and their state
- `show ip ospf database`—Displays contents of OSPF database, router-ID, and process ID
- `show ip ospf interface`—Shows the areas to which interfaces have been assigned

As for debug commands, there is really just one that has many options:

- `debug ip ospf`—Provides many optional keywords for debugging OSPF operation

PART
IV

CH
12

Summary

OSPF is a link-state routing protocol designed to address the shortcomings of earlier distance-vector routing protocols such as RIP. OSPF uses the shortest path first algorithm, also known as the Dijkstra algorithm, to compute its route table. Scalability is the key feature OSPF provides, as OSPF is well suited for large, complex internetworks. Related benefits of OSPF include no hop count limitation, bandwidth conservation, fast convergence, and VLSM support.

Before OSPF can begin to create its routing table, it goes through a series of steps to build its adjacencies and topological databases. Routers in large OSPF internetworks can be grouped into hierarchical areas to minimize overhead from consuming internetwork bandwidth and router resources.

QUESTIONS AND ANSWERS

1. What algorithm does OSPF use to compute its route table?

   A: OSPF uses the shortest path first (SPF) algorithm, which is also known as the Dijkstra algorithm.

2. What three tables does an OSPF router build?

   A: OSPF routers build an adjacencies database, a link-state or topological database, and a route table.

3. What is the significance of the DR and BDR?

   A: A DR, or Designated Router, serves as a point of contact for an OSPF router on a multiaccess network, because the DR is responsible for collecting routing updates from routers on the link and distributing these updates to all other routers on the link. If the DR goes offline, the BDR, or Backup Designated Router, takes over the DR's functions.

4. How are the DR and BDR selected?

   A: The DR and BDR are selected based on router priority. If there is a tie, the router with the highest router ID is preferred.

5. How is the router ID determined?

   A: The router ID is the highest IP address configured on any of the router's loopback interfaces. If no loopback interface is configured on the router, the router ID is the highest IP address configured on any of the router's physical interfaces.

6. What is an ABR?

   A: An ABR, Area Border Router, is a router with interfaces that connect to more than one area.

7. What is an ASBR?

   A: An ASBR, Autonomous System Boundary Router, is a router with interfaces that connect to more than one autonomous system.

8. What is a stub area?

   A: A stub area is an area that does not accept routing updates from outside its autonomous system.

9. What is a totally stubby area?

   A: A totally stubby area is an area that does not accept routing updates from outside its area.

10. What is a virtual link?

    A: A virtual link logically connects an ABR that does not physically connect the backbone Area 0 to another ABR that does connect to the backbone area, thereby linking an entire area to the backbone area.

PRACTICE TEST

1. Which of the following describe the OSPF routing protocol? (Choose all that apply.)
   A. Supports VLSM
   B. Uses hop-count metric
   C. Hierarchical
   D. Broadcasts routing table to neighbors
   E. Establishes adjacencies with neighboring routers

Answers A, C, and E correctly describe OSPF. Answers B and D are incorrect because these describe RIP.

2. Why is OSPF considered more scalable than RIP? (Choose all that apply.)
   A. No hop-count limitation
   B. Can be grouped into areas
   C. Sends routing updates every 30 seconds
   D. Converges faster

Answers A, B, and D are correct because these are accurate reasons for why OSPF is considered more scalable than RIP. Answer C is incorrect because this is a characteristic of RIP and periodic routing updates consumes bandwidth unnecessarily.

3. OSPF uses which of the following tables? (Choose all that apply.)
   A. Cost table
   B. Adjacencies database
   C. Hierarchy database
   D. Topological database
   E. Route table

Answers B, D, and E are correct because OSPF can use each of these tables. Answers A and C are fictitious and, therefore, incorrect.

4. Under what circumstances would LSAs need to be sent between routers? (Choose all that apply.)
   A. To verify that the neighboring router is still online
   B. A new router has just come online
   C. To agree on OSPF operational parameters
   D. A change has occurred in the state of an internetwork link
   E. LSAs have aged out of the topological database

Answers B, D, and E are correct because they require that LSAs be sent between routers. Answers A and C are incorrect because they refer to OSPF's hello protocol, which is needed to form adjacencies.

5. Which of the following statements are true? (Choose all that apply.)

   A. An internal router can also be an ABR.

   B. A backbone router can also be an ABR.

   C. A backbone router can also be an internal router.

   D. An ASBR can also be a backbone router.

   E. An ASBR can also be an internal router.

Answer A is false because an internal router by definition has all its interfaces within a single area, whereas an ABR connects to two different areas. **Answer B is true because an ABR that connects to the backbone Area 0 is both a backbone router and an ABR. Answer C is true because a backbone router with all its interfaces inside of Area 0 fits this criterion. Answer D is true because an ASBR that connects to the backbone Area 0 is both a backbone router and an ASBR.** Answer E is false because by definition an internal router has all its interfaces within a single area whereas an ASBR has at least one interface connecting to an external autonomous system.

6. Out of the following configurations, which is the only one that could possibly be correct?

   A. `router ospf 1`
      `network 133.17.45.48 255.255.0.0 area 0`

   B. `router ospf 0`
      `network 133.17.45.48 255.255.0.0 area 1`

   C. `router ospf 0`
      `network 133.17.45.48 0.0.255.255 area`

   D. `router ospf 1`
      `network 133.17.45.48 0.0.255.255 area 0`

Answer A is incorrect because its mask is not a wildcard mask. Answer B is incorrect because its mask is not a wildcard mask and the OSPF process ID needs to be a positive integer. Answer C is incorrect because an area-ID is not specified and the OSPF process ID needs to be a positive integer. **Answer D is correct because it is the only valid configuration. It has all the proper elements; it defines an area ID for the OSPF process, defines a network with a correct mask, and assigns the network to an area.**

7. Which of the following does not accept LSAs from any external autonomous systems?

   A. Backbone Area

   B. Totally Stubby Area

   C. Stub Area

   D. NSSA

Answer B is correct because a totally stubby area is the only option that does not accept LSAs from an external AS.

8. Which LSA types will not be allowed into a stub area?

A. LSA Type 1
B. LSA Type 2
C. LSA Type 3
D. LSA Type 4
E. LSA Type 5

Answers A, B, and C are incorrect because they all describe links within the OSPF autonomous system. **Answer E is correct because LSA Type 5 describes links in other autonomous systems and stub areas do not care about LSAs regarding external autonomous systems.**

9. Given the following interfaces and IP addresses on a router, what will be this router's router-ID?

```
interface ethernet 0
ip address 192.168.5.5 255.255.255.0
interface serial 0
ip address 192.168.6.6 255.255.255.0
interface loopback 0
ip address 192.168.4.3 255.255.255.0
interface loopback 1
ip address 192.168.3.4 255.255.255.0
```

A. 1
B. 0
C. 192.168.6.6
D. 192.168.3.4
E. 192.168.4.3

Answers A and B are incorrect because they are not IP addresses residing on any of the router's interfaces. Answer C is incorrect because physical interfaces are not considered for the router ID when loopback interfaces are configured on a router. Answer D is incorrect because it is a lower IP address than 192.168.4.3. **Answer E is correct because 192.168.4.3 is the highest IP address configured on one of the router's loopback interfaces.**

10. Given an internetwork consisting of only one OSPF area, what should be the area-ID of this area?

A. Area 1
B. Area 100
C. Area 0
D. Area OSPF

PART IV

CH 12

Answers A and B are incorrect because only area ID 0 can be used to identify the backbone area. **Answer C is correct because if only one area exists in an internetwork, it must be the backbone area, which is always designated Area 0.** Answer D is incorrect because OSPF area IDs must be an integer or dotted-decimal number.

CHAPTER PREREQUISITE

Chapter 1, "General Network Overview," Chapter 2, "General Topic Overview," Chapter 8, "TCP/IP," Chapter 11, "IGRP and EIGRP," and Chapter 12 "OSPF."

BGP

WHILE YOU READ

1. What is an Autonomous System?

2. For what purpose was BGP created?

3. What protocol and port number does BGP use as its transport?

4. What is the proper sequence of the BGP path-selection process?

5. What is the default version of BGP?

6. The lower a protocol's distance, the _____ the priority.

7. What is an Autonomous System Number?

8. How is a BGP session established between two routers?

This chapter covers *Border Gateway Protocol (BGP)*, as defined in RFC 1771. BGP was designed to create loop-free interdomain routing between autonomous systems. An autonomous system is a set of routers under a single technical administration, such as an internal corporate network. Routers in an Autonomous System (AS) can use one or more interior gateway protocols (such as RIP, IGRP, or OSPF) to exchange routing information inside the AS and an exterior gateway protocol (such as BGP) to route packets outside the Autonomous System.

BGP uses TCP as its transport protocol (port 179). Two BGP-speaking routers (routers with BGP setup) form a TCP connection between one another (peer routers) and exchange messages to open and confirm the connection parameters. By default, BGP sessions begin using BGP Version 4 and negotiating downward to earlier versions if necessary.

BGP routers will exchange network reachability information; this information is mainly an indication of the full paths (BGP AS numbers) that a route should take to reach the destination network. This information will help in constructing a graph of Autonomous Systems that are loop free and where routing policies can be applied to enforce some restrictions on the routing behavior.

BGP exchanges routing information in the form of routing updates that include the following information:

- Network number
- List of autonomous systems that the routing information has traversed (the Autonomous System path)
- List of path attributes

Key Concept

The Transport protocol and port number used by BGP is TCP (port 179).

Design Elements and Definitions

- BGP Next Hop—The *BGP nexthop* attribute is the next-hop IP address that is going to be used to reach a certain destination.
- EBGP Multihop—For EBGP, the next hop is always the IP address of the neighbor specified in the neighbor command. In some special cases, the Cisco router could be running external BGP with a third-party router that does not allow the two external peers to be directly connected. In this case, *EBGP multihop* is used to allow the

neighbor connection to be established between two indirectly connected external peers. The multihop is used only for external BGP and not for internal BGP.

■ Redistribution—Redistribution of your IGP (IGRP, OSPF, RIP, EIGRP, and so on) into BGP is possible. This might sound scary because now you are dumping all your internal routes into BGP; some of these routes might have been learned via BGP and you do not need to send them out again. Careful filtering should be applied to make sure you are sending to the Internet-only routes that you want to advertise and not everything you have.

■ Loopback Addressing—The BGP network IP address or neighbor's IP address could be the address of any of the router's interfaces, such as Ethernet, Token-Ring, or serial. Keep in mind that the stability of the neighbor connection will rely on the stability of the IP address you choose.

If the IP address belongs to an Ethernet segment that is unstable, the neighbor connection-routing updates will suffer. Cisco has introduced a loopback interface; this is actually a virtual interface that is supposed to be up all the time. Tying the neighbor to a loopback interface will make sure that the session is not dependent on any hardware interface that might be problematic.

Key Concept

Using the loopback interface is considered more stable than any other interface.

■ Overlapping Protocols/Backdoors—With different IGPs and EGPs working together to achieve routing, networks can learn via different protocols. Choosing one protocol over the other affects how your traffic flows. Different protocols might well have differing routes. The lower a protocol's administrative distance, the higher the priority. See Chapter 9, "Routing Concept Overview," for further discussion of Administrative Distances.

Route Maps, Filters, and Neighbors (Peers)

Filtering of routing information allows for control of path selection used by a router to forward received packets. A router must be selective in which sources of information it receives and what routes to believe.

Route Maps

In the BGP context, route maps are a method used to control and modify routing information. This is done by defining conditions for redistributing routes from one routing protocol to another or controlling routing information when injected in and out of BGP.

Filters

BGP updates can be controlled by different filtering methods. BGP updates can be filtered based on route information, on path information, or on communities. All methods will achieve the same results; choosing one over the other depends on the specific network configuration. Traffic filters apply to incoming traffic only.

Filter by Route Example

To restrict the routing information that the router learns or advertises, you can filter BGP based on routing updates to or from a particular neighbor. To achieve this, an Access List is defined and applied to the updates to or from a neighbor (see Figure 13.1). Use the following command in the router configuration mode:

```
RTR (config)# neighbor {ip-address|peer-group-name} distribute-list
➥access-list-number {in | out}
```

In the following example, RTR2 originates network 160.10.0.0 and sends it to RTR3. If RTR3 wanted to stop those updates from propagating to AS100, we would have to apply an Access List to filter those updates and apply it when talking to RTR1:

```
RTR3 (config)# router bgp 300
RTR3 (config)# network 170.10.0.0
RTR3 (config)# neighbor 3.3.3.3 remote-as 200
RTR3 (config)# neighbor 2.2.2.2 remote-as 100
RTR3 (config)# neighbor 2.2.2.2 distribute-list 1 out
RTR3 (config)# access-list 1 deny 160.10.0.0 0.0.255.255
RTR3 (config)# access-list 1 permit 0.0.0.0 255.255.255.255
(filter out all routing updates about 160.10.x.x)
```

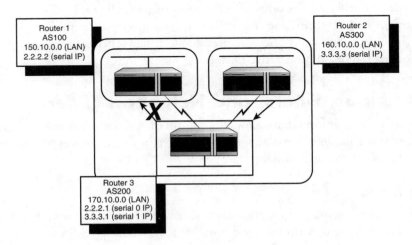

Figure 13.1
A basic BGP topology.

Filter by Path Example

Command syntaxes used:

```
ip as-path access-list access-list-number {permit|deny} as-regular-expression
neighbor {ip-address|peer-group-name} filter-list access-list-number {in|out}
```

The following example will stop RTC from sending RTA updates about 160.10.0.0:

```
RTR3 (config)# router bgp 300
RTR3 (config)# neighbor 3.3.3.3 remote-as 200
RTR3 (config)# neighbor 2.2.2.2 remote-as 100
RTR3 (config)# neighbor 2.2.2.2 filter-list 1 out
(filter-list 1 refers to the access list number below)
RTR3 (config)# ip as-path access-list 1 deny ^200$
RTR3 (config)# ip as-path access-list 1 permit .*
```

In this example (refer to Figure 13.1), `access-list 1` states: "Deny any updates with path information that starts with 200 (^) and ends with 200 ($)." The `^200$` is called a regular expression, with ^ meaning "starts with" and $ meaning "ends with." Because RTR2 sends updates about 160.10.0.0 with path information starting with `200` and ending with `200`, this update will match the Access List and will be denied. The `.*` is another regular expression with the dot meaning any character and the * meaning the repetition of that character. So `.*` is actually any path information, which is needed to permit all other updates to be sent.

Filter by Community Example

```
RTR2 (config)# router bgp 200
RTR2 (config)# network 160.10.0.0
RTR2 (config)# neighbor 3.3.3.1 remote-as 300
RTR2 (config)# neighbor 3.3.3.1 send-community
RTR2 (config)# neighbor 3.3.3.1 route-map setcommunity out
RTR2 (config)# route-map setcommunity
RTR2 (config)# match ip address 1
RTR2 (config)# set community no-export
RTR2 (config)# access-list 1 permit 0.0.0.0 255.255.255.255
```

Note that we have used the `route-map setcommunity` command to set the community to `no-export`. Note also that we had to use the `neighbor send-community` command to send this attribute to RTR3. Refer to Figure 13.1.

When RTR3 gets the updates with the attribute `no-export`, it will not propagate them to its external peer

PART

IV

CH

13

You can specify an Access List on both incoming and outgoing updates based on the BGP autonomous system path information. Filtering and route manipulating a route or a set of routes involves three actions:

- Identifying routes
- Permitting or denying the routes
- Manipulating attributes

Key Concept

When preparing for the exam, know the three actions associated with filtering and route manipulation: identifying routes, permitting or denying the routes, and manipulating attributes.

Neighbors/Peers

Any two routers that have formed a TCP connection to exchange BGP routing information are called *peers*. They can also be called *neighbors*. Because BGP uses TCP instead of broadcasts (like other interior routing protocols), neighbor routers do not have to be adjacent.

Two BGP routers become neighbors or peers after they establish a TCP connection between one another. The TCP connection is essential for the two peer routers to start exchanging routing updates.

Two BGP-speaking routers trying to become neighbors will first bring up the TCP connection between one another and then send open messages to exchange values such as the AS number, the BGP version they are running (version 3 or 4), the BGP router ID, the keepalive hold time, and so on. After these values are confirmed and accepted, the neighbor connection will be established. Any state other than established is an indication that the two routers did not become neighbors and hence the BGP updates will not be exchanged.

Decision Algorithm

After BGP receives updates about different destinations from different autonomous systems, the protocol will have to decide which paths to choose to reach a specific destination. BGP will choose only a single path to reach a specific destination. Because BGP chooses the single best route, this makes BGP incapable of load balancing across multiple routes.

The decision process is based on different attributes, such as next hop, administrative weights, local preference, the route origin, path length, origin code, metric, and so on. BGP will always propagate the best path to its neighbors.

It is possible for a routing table to contain multiple routes to the same destination. The BGP decision process uses the following rules (tie-breakers) to choose between two equal BGP routes:

- BGP Path Selection starts; if the next hop is inaccessible, do not consider it.
- Consider larger BGP administrative weights first.
- If the routers have the same weight, consider the route with higher local preference.
- If the routes have the same local preference, prefer the route that the specified router originated.
- If no route was originated, prefer the shorter AS path.
- If the AS paths are of the same length, prefer external paths over internal paths.
- If all paths are external, prefer the lowest origin code (IGP [Interior Gateway Protocol] <EGP <INCOMPLETE).
- If origin codes are the same, prefer the path with the lowest MULTI_EXIT_DISC METRIC. A missing metric is treated as zero.
- If IGP synchronization is disabled and only an internal path remains, prefer the path through the closest IGP neighbor.
- Prefer the route with the lowest IP address value for the BGP router ID.

Key Concept

Understand the decision process used by BGP in choosing between two equal routes. The decision process is based on the following factors (in order):

- Next hop
- Weights
- Local preference
- Route that the specified router originated
- Shorter AS path
- External paths over internal paths
- Lowest origin code
- Lowest Multi-Exit-Disc Metric
- Closest IGP neighbor
- Lowest IP address

Refer to Figure 13.1. The following are other points to keep in mind:

- Communications between RTA and RTB use EBGP.
- Communications between RTA and RTC use IBGP.
- Communications between RTA and RTD use EBGP Multihop.

Interior Border Gateway Protocol (IBGP)

IBGP is used if one AS wants to act as a transit system to other Autonomous Systems. You might ask, why couldn't we do the same thing by learning via EBGP redistributing into IGP and then redistributing again into another AS? We can, but IBGP offers more flexibility and more efficient ways to exchange information within an AS; for example, IBGP provides us with ways to control what is the best exit point out of the AS by using local preference. If a border router belongs to the same AS as its peer, the peer is an internal border router.

The address to which BGP points as an IBGP neighbor must also be reachable. This can be by a directly connected network or static routes, but can also be reachable by the internal routing protocol. Because other routers in our AS can usually be reached by multiple paths, a loopback address is generally used. This would eliminate the possibility that a downed interface would cause the network to be inaccessible, thus causing the network to flap.

Exterior Border Gateway Protocol (EBGP)

An internal routing protocol is not exchanged with External BGP Neighbors. The address to which your router points must be reachable without using a routing protocol. This can be accomplished either by pointing at an address that is reachable by a directly connected network or by using static routes to that IP address. Generally, the neighbor address that is used is a directly connected address of the other router. BGP does not advertise the routes learned from IBGP to other EBGP neighbors, thus the importance of having your EBGP networks fully meshed. EBGP is used between different Autonomous Systems (see Figure 13.2).

Key Concept

IBGP Peers/Neighbors are in the same Autonomous System.

EBGP Peers/Neighbors are in different Autonomous Systems.

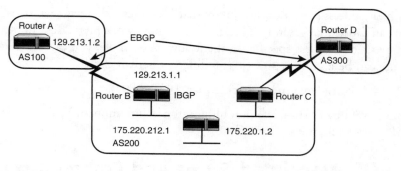

Figure 13.2
An integrated EBGP and IBGP topology.

In the show ip bgp command, the i means that the entry was learned via an internal BGP peer (see Figure 13.3). The i at the end indicates the origin of the path information to be IBGP. For example, network 128.213.0.0 is learned via path 200 with a nexthop of 128. 213.63.2. Note that any locally generated entry such as 203.250.15.0 has a nexthop of 0.0.0.0.

```
table version is 4, local router ID is 203.250.15.2 Status
codes: s suppressed, d damped, h history, * valid, > best, i - internal
Origin codes: i - IGP, e - EGP, ? - incomplete

   Network        Next Hop        Metric LocPrf Weight  Path
*i128.213.0.0    128.213.63.2        0    100     0 200  i
*i192.208.10.0   128.213.63.2             100     0 200  400 500 30
*i195.211.10.0   128.213.63.2             100     0 200  400 500 i
*i200.200.10.0   128.213.63.2             100     0 200  400 i
*>i203.250.13.0  203.250.13.41       0    100     0 i
*>i203.250.14.0  203.250.13.41       0    100     0 i
*>203.250.15.0   0.0.0.0             0          32768 i
```

Figure 13.3
Output from a show ip bgp command.

The > symbol indicates that BGP chose the best route based on the list of decision steps that I explained earlier in this chapter, in the section "Decision Algorithm." BGP will pick one best path to reach a destination, will install this path in the ip routing table, and will advertise it to other BGP peers.

CIDR (Classless Inter-Domain Routing)

CIDR is a way to allocate and specify the Internet addresses used in interdomain routing, offering more flexibility than the original Internet Protocol (IP) address classes. Using

CIDR, each IP address has a network prefix that identifies either aggregation of network gateways or an individual gateway. The length of the network prefix determines whether a route is more specific or less specific. In the following example, you can see that the less specific route can be used to represent 255 different networks:

192.165.242.0 is considered more specific than 192.165.0.0.

CIDR is supported by BGP-4, the prevailing exterior (interdomain) gateway protocol. Lesser BGP versions do not support CIDR.

Other BGP Associated Terms and Commands

Part of what makes BGP so complex is the vast amount of terminology that is unique to BGP. Therefore, the important terms and configuration commands are summarized for you here. You should be familiar with the following BGP terms and Cisco commands.

Autonomous System

- One contiguous network.
- A set of networks sharing the same routing policy.
- Range from 1 to 65,535 (64,512 through 65,535 are set aside for private ASNs).
- Enables BGP Routing.

Neighbor Definition

- Activates BGP Session.
- Use extended ping to verify connection.
- Local peer definition unnecessary.
- EBGP peers must be directly connected. Otherwise, use ebgp multihop command.
- IBGP peers need not be directly connected if an IGP is running between them.

To Validate BGP Peer Connections

- show ip bgp neighbor

  Any state other than "established" indicates peers are not up.

  Increasing table version indicates route flapping.
- clear ip bgp {*|address}

  Resets BGP connections.

  Use after changing BGP configuration.

Redistribution

- Redistribution of BGP into an IGP is discouraged.
- Distribution of IGP into BGP should be used with Access Lists to avoid redistribution loops.
- Requires conversion of metrics. Default metric is required.
- Distribution of IGP routes into BGP should be discouraged because this can lead to route flapping.

BGP Backdoor Command

Defined as an IGP connecting two BGP Autonomous Systems when a BGP path already exists.

- Suboptimal routing might result.
- Solution is to add the `backdoor` command.

Multi-Exit Discriminator (MED)

Used to influence inbound traffic preference exchanged between Autonomous Systems.

- Lower value preferred.
- MED is set using the `set metric` command.
- MED also set using `default-metric` command.
- Affects all routes from same AS path.
- Advertised to external neighbors.
- Lower MED value is preferable.

Methods of Route Manipulation

- Set Route Attribute.
- Route Aggregation.
- Route Maps.
- Distribute Lists.

PART

IV

CH

13

Basics of Route Maps

- Defines conditions for route redistribution between protocols.
- Route maps use a combination of `match` and `set` commands.
- When a defined condition is matched, a defined condition is set.
- Unmatched routes are dropped!

Communities

Grouping destinations into a community for applying a common policy.

- Each destination can belong to multiple communities.
- Must be set using route maps.
- Local AS: Do not advertise outside local AS.
- No-export: Do not advertise to external peers.
- No-advertise: Do not advertise to any peer.

Confederation

The major benefit is that setting up a confederation can solve an IBGP mesh problem.

- Collection of AS—sub-AS
- Visible to outside world as single AS
- Uses reserved AS numbers for internal sub-AS
- Sub-Autonomous Systems are fully meshed
- EBGP between sub-AS

Route Flap Dampening

When a route connection goes up and down (flaps), BGP imposes penalties that affect your network availability. Additional penalties are assessed with each flap as the penalties are exponentially increased.

- Route flap
  Interfaces/Peers going up and down of path
  Change in attribute
- Ripples through the entire Internet
- Wastes Router CPU
- Reduce scope of route-flap propagation
- Fast convergence for normal route changes
- History predicts future behavior
- Suppress oscillating routes
- Advertise stable suppressed routes

Route Reflectors

Route Reflectors are used to enable the advertisement of IBGP routes (reflected) within an Autonomous System. As described earlier, BGP does not advertise routes advertised by another IBGP speaker to a third IBGP speaker, thus the need to reflect routes to non-neighboring routers.

Summary

By now, you should be well prepared to answer any questions about BGP that might be on the CCIE Written Exam. The chapter covered how BGP works, how BGP routers communicate, and much of how BGP is configured. You might be required to identify a proper IBGP or EBGP configuration, so this is important.

You should know that BGP sends network number, Autonomous Systems, and path attributes in its routing updates. The chapter defined a wide array of BGP-related terms such as confederations, route flapping, and route reflectors. It also explained how to deal with route redistribution issues in relation to BGP.

By now, you should know what CIDR is. You should also know how route maps control and modify routing information. Finally, you should be familiar with what attributes BGP considers in its decision algorithm.

┌─ QUESTIONS AND ANSWERS ──────────────

1. What is an Autonomous System?

    A: A set of routers under a single administration

2. For what purpose was BGP created?

    A: BGP was created to provide loop-free interdomain routing between autonomous systems.

3. What protocol and port number does BGP use as its transport?

    A: TCP port 179

4. What is the proper sequence in the BGP path-selection process?

    A: Next hop

    Weights

    Local Preference

    Route that the specified router originated

    Shorter AS path

External paths over Internal paths

Lowest origin code

Lowest Multi-Exit-Disc Metric

Closest IGP neighbor

Lowest IP address

5. What is the default version of BGP?

A: Version 4, thus the term BGP4

6. The lower a protocol's distance, the _____ the priority.

A: higher

7. What is an Autonomous System Number?

A: A set of routers under a single administration

8. How is a BGP session established between two routers?

A: Two BGP speaking routers (routers with BGP setup) form a TCP connection between one another (peer routers) and exchange messages to open and confirm the connection parameters.

PRACTICE TEST

1. You would use _____ to communicate with a peer in the same AS.
   A. loopback
   B. IBGP
   C. EBGP
   D. DEM

Answer A is incorrect because it is a logical interface. **Answer B is correct because it offers more flexibility and more efficient ways to exchange information within an AS.** Answer C is incorrect because it is used to communicate between Autonomous Systems. Answer D is incorrect because it is a fictitious answer.

2. Multihop commands can only be used with _____.
   A. EBGP
   B. IBGP
   C. AS
   D. reflectors

Answer A is correct because multihop allows neighbor connections to be established between two indirectly connected external (not internal) peers. Answers B and C are both incorrect because IBGP and AS cannot use this command. Answer D is incorrect because it is fictitious.

   3. What is the administrative default protocol distance for EBGP?

   A. 10

   B. 20

   C. 200

   D. 110

Answer A is incorrect because 10 is not a valid default for any protocol. **Answer B is correct because the administrative distance for EBGP is 20.** Answer C is incorrect because it is used as a default for IBGP and BGP local. Answer D is incorrect also because 110 is the default for OSPF.

   4. You are examining the results of a show ip BGP command. The (i) means that a route was learned how?

   A. Via an internal BGP peer

   B. Via an external BGP neighbor

   C. Via static route

   D. Via PGP

Answer A is correct because "i" stands for "internal." Answer B is incorrect, because for it to be correct the question would have used instead of (i). Answers C and D are both incorrect because they are not valid results to the sh ip BGP command.

   5. What interface on a router is considered the most stable?

   A. FDDI

   B. Ethernet

   C. Serial

   D. Loopback

Answer A is correct because of FDDI's dual-ring topology. Answers B, C, and D are incorrect because they are physical hardware interfaces that are prone to failure.

   6. When looking at a BGP router configuration, what configuration statement would give you the next hop network?

   A. Route-map statement

   B. MED

   C. route-map statement

   D. neighbor statement

Answer A is incorrect because it uses AS numbers. Answer B is incorrect because it is fictitious. Answer C is incorrect because it is fictitious. **Answer D is correct because a neighbor is the same as the next hop.**

PART

IV

CH

13

7. What could cause a route to flap?
    A. A downed interface
    B. Router being powered off
    C. Circuit outage
    D. All of the above

Answer D is correct because flaps are caused when part of the network is no long accessible; this can be caused by a downed interface, hardware device, or circuit outage.

8. Which item does not belong in the BGP path-selection process?
    A. Next hop
    B. Weights
    C. Local Preference
    D. Route that the specified router originated
    E. Highest Multi-Exit-Disc Metric
    F. Shorter AS path

Answers A, B, C, and D are incorrect because all are used in the path-selection process. **Answer E is correct because the decision algorithm does not use something called "shortest AS path."**

9. Which command would you use to enable BGP on a router?
    A. `router bgp #200`
    B. `router bgp-200`
    C. `router bgp 200`
    D. `router bgp enable`

Answers A and B are improper syntax and, thus, incorrect. **Answer C is correct because it follows the correct syntax of enabling a BGP process.** Answer D is incorrect because this command does not exist.

10. Communities must be set using which command?
    A. Access lists
    B. Route Maps
    C. no-export
    D. IBGP

Answer A is incorrect because it is used for filtering traffic. **Answer B is correct because route maps are a method used to control routing information that, in turn, creates communities.** Answers C and D are incorrect because they are not commands.

CHAPTER PREREQUISITE

Read and understand the following chapters before reading this chapter: Chapter 9, Chapter 10, Chapter 11, Chapter 12, and Chapter 13. In particular, you should be familiar with default administrative distances defined for each IP routing protocol.

Managing Routing

WHILE YOU READ

1. How do you prevent an interface from sending routing updates?

2. Can policy routing be fast switched?

3. Can you redistribute a VLSM-aware routing protocol into a classful routing protocol?

4. How do you set the administrative distance for routes determined by a specific IP routing protocol?

5. How do you set the administrative distance for a specific route learned via a specific routing protocol?

6. How do sparse-mode PIM and dense-mode PIM differ from each other?

7. What is a rendezvous point?

8. What is CGMP and what hardware components are required when implementing this protocol?

Route Redistribution

Route redistribution is the method by which routes learned using one protocol are advertised to routers via a different routing protocol. This is needed when multiple IP routing protocols are in use but routes need to be known by routers running each protocol. In many cases, this occurs at administrative boundaries where an internal IP routing protocol such as OSPF ends, and an external IP routing such as BGP begins. Multiple IP routing protocols can also be found in networks that were formed as the result of the merging of several networks or in which multiple vendors' products have been used. In these cases, it is often required or desirable to maintain multiple routing protocols while allowing all protocols to have a complete picture of the IP network. This is where route redistribution is implemented.

When an autonomous system boundary dictates a change in routing protocol, redistribution from the interior routing protocol to the external routing protocol will allow the external network to reach your network. Where default routing is not desired, redistribution between the external routing protocol and the interior routing protocol will allow your network to reach the external networks. In the case of merging networks currently using differing interior routing protocols, redistribution between the two protocols at the boundaries will allow communication from one network to the other. In the final case, you might decide that you want to deploy VLSM techniques to conserve IP address space and have chosen EIGRP as your routing protocol, yet you have legacy routing equipment that only understands RIPv1, a non-VLSM aware routing protocol. Redistribution between the EIGRP and RIP protocols will be required to allow the legacy equipment to be reachable from the VLSM-aware network. Keep each of these three cases in mind while reading the following sections.

Metric Issues

When redistributing routes from one IP routing protocol to another, a mapping of metrics must occur because the protocols use different metrics. So the router must understand how to use the metrics of the incoming protocol when the router must advertise those routes via another protocol. For some routing protocols, such as IGRP and EIGRP processes, Cisco provides an automatic mapping. For all other common cases, you must define the metrics that will be used when a route is redistributed from one IP routing protocol to another. The actual commands used to accomplish this are protocol-dependent. This difference is due to the fact that each routing protocol uses its own set of metric definitions. To review, the following metrics are used by the various IP routing protocols discussed here:

- RIP—Hop Count
- IGRP/EIGRP—Bandwidth, Delay, Reliability, Load, MTU
- OSPF—Cost

For redistribution into RIP, static routes are by default assigned a metric of directly connected. Routes from all other sources must be explicitly assigned a metric via one of these methods:

- A `redistribute` command using the `metric` option
- A `redistribute` command using the `route-map` option
- A `default-metric` command in the router rip stanza

Without at least one of these statements, no other routes are redistributed.

For redistribution in either direction between IGRP and EIGRP, some special cases exist. When both an IGRP and an EIGRP process exist with the same autonomous system number within a router, automatic redistribution occurs between these processes and all metrics are preserved. When both an IGRP and an EIGRP process exist with differing autonomous system numbers within a router, metrics are preserved but redistribution must be explicitly requested. For redistribution of static routes into IGRP or EIGRP, a metric equivalent to a directly connected route is assigned.

Redistribution into BGP is a special case that does not require a metric translation, because BGP does not generally pass routing metrics.

OSPF treats redistributed routes as external routes. As a result, the defined metric is identified in terms of external cost. This is true regardless of the source of the external route, including another OSPF routing processes within the same router.

Although not specifically a metric issue, the `redistribute static` command is not required for static routes pointing to an interface as opposed to those defining a next hop IP address. This is because static routes defined to an interface are "connected" as long as that interface would normally participate in the routing process via its associated network commands. If not, these interface routes will not be redistributed without the `redistribute static` command.

For all other redistribution scenarios, one of the following types of commands is necessary:

- A `default-metric` command
- A protocol-specific `redistribute metric` command
- A `redistribute route-map` command with an associated set `metric` command in the referenced route map

To define a default metric for all redistributed routes, the following router command is used:

```
RTR (config-router)# default-metric {metric}
```

For any redistributed route, the metric value will be assigned to outbound routing updates. Keep in mind that this metric might be a single digit, as in the case of hop count for RIP, or a sequence of numbers to define all aspects of the metric, as in EIGRP. This metric will be used when no other more specific metric mappings exist. If you want a specific metric to be applied based on the routing process that sourced the route, an extension to the redistribute command is used:

```
RTR (config-router)# redistribute ospf {area#} metric {metric}
```

This variation will cause all routes learned via the OSPF process to be redistributed with the defined metric. This value is used in preference to the default metric value but can be overridden by a set metric command within a designated route map. If you desire to set the metric based on information above and beyond the source routing process, a route-map is employed as in the following example:

```
RTR (config)# router rip
RTR (config-router)# network 10.0.0.0
RTR (config-router)# redistribute eigrp 200 route-map eigrp2rip

RTR (config)# route-map eigrp2rip permit 10
  match interface Ethernet 0
  set metric 2
RTR (config)# route-map eigrp2rip permit 20
  set metric 5
```

This example shows that routes from EIGRP autonomous system 200 will be defined a metric based on the interface that the next hop for this route will be. If the route has a next hop interface of Ethernet 0, the metric will be set to 2. For all other routes, the metric will be set to 5. This type of metric setting can be used in complex redistributions that require redistributed routes to possibly override a natively learned route.

Key Concept

Metrics for redistributed routes can be set based on a routing process default metric, by a default metric assigned on the basis of the source routing process, or via a set command within an associated route-map statement within the redistribute command. The metric assigned via a route-map set command will take highest priority followed by a routing protocol–specific default-metric command with the non-protocol specific default-metric command having the lowest priority.

Summarization Issues

Redistribution of routes between VLSM-compatible protocols is relatively straightforward. The only option usually is whether to summarize the routes when redistributing.

The only routing protocol that addresses this issue is OSPF. When redistributing into OSPF, the subnets option at the end of the redistribution command indicates that all subnet information is to be included in the redistributed announcements. Without that option, the redistributed information will be summarized to the classful network level.

For redistribution of routes from classful routing protocols into a VLSM-compatible protocol, no specific action needs to be taken. Every subnet identified from that routing process would be assigned a mask appropriate to the mask being used by the classful protocol.

When redistributing from a VLSM-compatible protocol into a classful protocol, some interesting issues can occur. The general rule of thumb is that masks that are too long should be truncated, and masks that are too short should result in multiple entries. This same situation exists when redistributing between classful protocols with different subnet masks, just that all entries will either be longer or shorter than the destination protocol. Let's say that you have the following routes being delivered via EIGRP into the router (next hops have been eliminated for clarity):

Route 1: 10.1.1.0	255.255.255.0
Route 2: 10.2.0.0	255.255.0.0
Route 3: 10.3.3.128	255.255.255.128

You want to redistribute these routes into RIPv1 where the classful 10.0.0.0/8 network is defined as having a subnet mask of 255.255.255.0. Route 1 will be redistributed as is without any summarization occurring as expected. Route 2, having a shorter mask, should result in 256 routes being entered into the routing table, one for each /24 route being covered. However, the Cisco IOS drops this route because it does not have the mask expected by the destination routing protocol. Route 3, with a longer mask, should result in the route 10.3.3.0/24 being entered into the RIP update, possibly obscuring the real route to 10.3.3.0/25. Again, the Cisco IOS drops this route because it does not have the mask expected by the destination routing protocol. As a result, the information for Route 2 and Route 3 is lost when redistributing into RIPv1. To reach these networks from the RIPv1 portion of the network, the routers in the RIPv1 network must either have defined static routes or be receiving routing information via a VLSM-aware routing protocol that contains this information running within the RIPv1 portion of the network.

Key Concept

Redistributing from a VLSM-aware routing protocol, such as EIGRP or OSPF, into a non–VLSM-aware routing protocol, such as RIPv1 or IGRP, might result in loss of routing information.

PART

IV

CH

14

All routing protocols generally summarize routes at classful network boundaries. For classfull routing protocols, such as RIPv1 and IGRP, this behavior cannot be disabled. For classless protocols, such as OSPF, RIPv2, and EIGRP, the following router command will disable this automatic summarization:

```
RTR (config-router)# no auto-summary
```

When this command is in effect for a classless routing protocol, subnet information will be provided in all routing updates, even those that cross natural classful network boundaries.

Route Tagging

Route tagging is a means of communicating information about a route in addition to the normal information passed by the routing protocol. By default, the tag for any given route in the routing table will be set to 0. However, the tag value can be set when redistributing routes such that information about the source of the route can be communicated into the new routing process. This gives you a powerful tool to control the redistribution of routes based on tag values that have previously been assigned to a route. This feature can greatly simplify the redistribution process when multiple routing sources must be considered.

For tags to be useful a tagging scheme needs to be created and a method for setting of the tags is required. The tagging scheme can be somewhat arbitrary, or in the case of tag exchange between OSPF and BGP, it can be well defined and well standardized. As long as you understand the meaning of the tags within your administrative control, the tags can carry significant and valuable information.

To assign a tag to a static route,

```
RTR (config)# ip route {address} {mask} {distance} tag {tag}
```

The tag value, a number between 0 and 4294967295, will be used to identify the tag associated with this static route.

Although BGP does not transmit tags to its neighbors, you can control what tag is identified with a route entered into the routing table from a BGP process. The default action is to set the value of the tag to 0 for BGP routes. You can use the table-map command to set a specific tag using the command

```
RTR (config)# router bgp 104
   ...(other routing process commands)
RTR (config-router)# table-map {route-map}
```

The referenced route-map can then contain an explicit set tag command based on one or more match criteria. Another possibility is that the command set automatic-tag is used. This sets the tag based on RFC 1403, "BGP OSPF Interaction." This setting allows an

IGP, such as OSPF, to carry information concerning the autonomous system that sourced the route.

OSPF carries tags associated with external routes throughout the enterprise but does not explicitly set the tag value when a route is entered into the routing table. For the tag to be set, the OSPF process that learns the external route must set a tag on the route before advertising it. This is accomplished by identifying a `route-map` in the `redistribute` command. The following example shows importing routes from a RIP process into OSPF:

```
RTR (config)# router ospf 100
RTR (config-router)# network 10.0.0.0
RTR (config-router)# redistribute rip route-map rip2ospf

RTR (config)# route-map rip2ospf
RTR (config-router)# set tag 1000
```

In this example, assuming that 1000 is a unique tag value within the enterprise, any time an OSPF external route is encountered elsewhere in the network, a tag value of 1000 will indicate that it originated from this router.

IGRP, EIGRP, RIP, and IS-IS do not carry tag values in their updates. As a result, setting tag values when redistributing into these routing protocols has no effect.

To control redistribution based on tags, the following commands are used:

```
RTR (config)# router eigrp 100
RTR (config-router)# network 10.0.0.0
RTR (config-router)# redistribute ospf 100 route-map ospf2eigrp

RTR (config)# route-map ospf2eigrp permit 10
RTR (config-router)# match tag 345
RTR (config)# route-map ospf2eigrp deny 20
```

In this example, routes from OSPF process 100 with a tag value of 345 will be redistributed into EIGRP autonomous system 100.

Route Management

The managing of routes being received, advertised, or used by the IP forwarding process is accomplished through the use of four key concepts within a Cisco router. These concepts are

- Passive Interfaces
- Distribute Lists
- Policy Routing
- Route Selection

You can apply any one or a combination of these concepts to administratively control what routes are available or are used by specific IP packets entering the router.

Passive Interfaces

In some cases, you might be required to receive routing updates via an interface but not provide any updates through that interface. The `passive-interface` command can be used to accomplish this. It is important to note that the `passive-interface` command does not prevent the identified interface from receiving and processing routing updates. This activity must be controlled through the use of a distribute-list. To configure an interface as passive, use the command

```
RTR (config-router)# passive-interface {type} {number}
```

The interface defined by the {type} and {number} arguments will no longer provide routing updates. The following example shows this use:

```
RTR (config)# router rip
RTR (config-router)# network 10.0.0.0
RTR (config-router)# passive-interface serial 0
```

This example allows the router to listen to RIP updates on interface Serial 0 without sending any routing updates out this interface.

A special case exists for OSPF and IS-IS, where the interface identified by the passive interface command does not actively participate in the routing protocol at all. For OSPF, the attached network is treated as a stub network; whereas in IS-IS, the route is advertised out other active interfaces but IS-IS does not run on the interface.

The concept of passive interfaces does not apply to BGP. This is because BGP works on a defined neighbor relationship without regard to what interface will be used for communication between neighbors.

Distribute Lists

Distribute lists are used to determine what routes will either be accepted or advertised by a specific routing protocol. Distribute lists are constructed using standard IP Access Lists. You would use distribute lists when you want to control the information being provided to or received from a specific routing protocol. This works for all protocols except OSPF and IS-IS, where this practice will only apply to external routes.

To control which routes are received by a routing protocol, the following command is issued in router configuration mode:

```
RTR (config-router)# distribute-list {access-list} in
```

The routes allowed into the routing process are determined by the IP Access List defined by the {access-list} argument. An example using this command is as follows:

```
RTR (config)# router igrp 1000
RTR (config-router)# network 10.0.0.0
RTR (config-router)# distribute-list 90 in

RTR (config)# access-list 90 permit 10.200.0.0 0.0.255.255
RTR (config)# access-list 90 deny any
```

This sequence of commands allows IGRP updates to be received only if they are for routes in the 10.200.0.0/16 network. All other routes will be dropped. This command is applied to all updates independent of what interface they are received on. If you desire to filter only those routes that are received via a specific interface, the following version of the distribute-list in command can be used:

```
RTR (config-router)# distribute-list {access-list} in {type} {number}
```

Now instead of applying the Access List to all interfaces, this command isolates the Access List to one interface defined by the {type} and {number} values. The following example shows its usage:

```
RTR (config)# router igrp 1000
RTR (config-router)# network 10.0.0.0
RTR (config-router)# distribute-list 90 in Ethernet 0/0

RTR (config)# access-list 90 permit 10.200.0.0 0.0.255.255
RTR (config)# access-list 90 deny any
```

In this case, the same Access List and restrictions are defined, but they apply only to routes received via Ethernet 0/0. All routes will be accepted from any other interface on the router. Note that the use of the interface extension is invalid for OSPF.

To control which routes are advertised by a routing protocol, the following command is issued in router configuration mode:

```
RTR (config-router)# distribute-list {access-list} out
```

Similar to the inbound list, the Access List defined by the {access-list} argument is used to filter all outbound routing updates regardless on interface. The following example shows how this command would be implemented:

```
RTR (config)# router rip
RTR (config-router)# network 172.16.0.0
RTR (config-router)# network 10.0.0.0
RTR (config-router)# distribute-list 91 out

RTR (config)# access-list 91 permit 172.16.0.0 0.0.255.255
RTR (config)# access-list 91 deny any
```

PART

IV

CH

14

In this case, the RIP routing process has been set up to participate on both the 10.0.0.0/8 and 172.16.0.0/16 networks. For some reason, however, there is a requirement that only routes in the 172.16.0.0/16 network be advertised in RIP updates. This was accomplished by using the `distribute-list out` command. Like the `distribute-list in` command, it is likely that this policy must be applied to only a particular interface. If this is the case, use the following version of the `distribute-list out` command:

```
RTR (config-router)# distribute-list {access-list} out {type} {number}
```

Like the inbound filter, instead of applying the Access List to all interfaces, this command isolates the Access List to one interface defined by the {type} and {number} values. Extending the previous example provides the following configuration:

```
RTR (config)# router rip
RTR (config-router)# network 172.16.0.0
RTR (config-router)# network 10.0.0.0
RTR (config-router)# distribute-list 91 out Serial 0/3

RTR (config)# access-list 91 permit 172.16.0.0 0.0.255.255
RTR (config)# access-list 91 deny any
```

As was the previous case, the RIP routing process has been set up to participate on both the 10.0.0.0/8 and 172.16.0.0/16 networks. However, in this case the requirement is that the routes advertised only on interface Serial 0/3 be filtered. This was accomplished by using the `distribute-list out` command with an interface defined. All routes will be advertised from any other interface on the router. Note that the use of the interface extension is again not valid for OSPF.

Key Concept

The `distribute-list in` and `distribute list out` commands enable you to control what routes are received and advertised by a specific routing protocol.

Policy Routing

In traditional IP routing, the routing table provides a mapping between destination IP networks and next-hop IP addresses. As networks become more complex, you might need to specify next-hop IP addresses based on parameters other than destination IP address. Other possible parameters contained within the IP header are

- Source Address
- Incoming Interface
- Transport Protocol (UDP, TCP)

- Packet Length
- Application Type (Source or Destination Port Numbers)

You can use policy routing to accomplish this task. Policy routing is enabled on a per-interface basis by using the `interface` command:

```
RTR (config-if)# ip policy route-map {map-name}
```

The argument {map-name} is the name of a route map containing the policy. This command is applied to the source interface of the packets to be policy routed. The default behavior of this statement is to follow the traditional routing table if the packet does not match any of the route map entries.

The identified route map will usually define a series of match statements followed by a series of set statements that control the mapping of next-hop addresses. The simplest form of a route map entry contains no match statements followed by a sequence of set statements. This is the default action if none of the other route map entries are matched.

In the most common usage, policy routing is used to set a next-hop IP address based on destination address, source address, and application type. Figure 14.1 shows an example of policy routing.

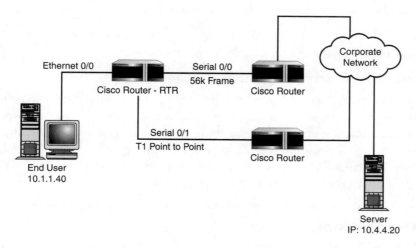

Figure 14.1
An example of a policy-routing implementation.

```
RTR (config)# interface Ethernet 0/0
RTR (config-if)# description Remote Branch LAN
RTR (config-if)# ip address 10.1.1.1 255.255.255.0
RTR (config-if)# ip policy route-map interactive
```

PART

IV

CH

14

```
RTR (config)# interface Serial 0/0
RTR (config-if)# description Low Cost, Low Speed WAN
RTR (config-if)# ip address 10.2.2.1 255.255.255.0

RTR (config)# interface Serial 0/1
RTR (config-if)# description High Cost, High Speed WAN
RTR (config-if)# ip address 10.3.3.1 255.255.255.0

RTR (config)# route-map interactive permit 10
  match ip address 101
  set ip next-hop 10.3.3.2

RTR (config)# access-list 101 permit tcp 10.1.1.0 0.0.0.255
    eq any host 10.4.4.20 eq telnet

RTR (config)# ip route 0.0.0.0 0.0.0.0 10.2.2.2
```

In this example, all hosts on the remote branch LAN will normally use a default IP route with a next-hop of 10.2.2.2. This network device would be reached via the Low Cost, Low Speed network on interface Serial 0/0. However, for those packets that have a destination IP address of 10.4.4.20 with a TCP destination application port of telnet (tcp port 23), the next-hop IP address will be set to 10.3.3.2 that would be reached via the High Cost, High Speed network on interface Serial 0/1.

By default, enabling policy routing disables fast switching on an interface. To enable fast switching while policy routing, use the following command:

```
RTR (config-if)# ip route-cache policy
```

You must keep in mind a couple caveats when enabling fast switching while policy routing is enabled: First, the set ip default command is not supported in a policy route-map. Second, the set interface command in a route map will be processed differently. When process-switched policy routing is used, the normal routing table is consulted to make sure that the identified interface is on a reasonable path to the destination IP address. In fast-switched policy routing, this check is bypassed.

Key Concept

Policy routing allows the next-hop IP address and IP precedence of a routed IP packet to be set independently of the current routing table based on most of the information contained in the header of the IP packet or the length of the packet itself.

Route Selection

When policy routing is not in effect, route selection is based only on metrics and administrative distances using the following rules:

- Routes with the lowest administrative distance are always preferred over those with higher administrative distance regardless of metric.
- If two or more routes are identified as having the same administrative distance, the route having the lowest cost metric is installed in the routing table.
- If equal costs metrics are encountered, all equal cost routes will be installed in the routing table up to the default of 4, except for BGP where the default number of installed paths is 1. This is configurable between 1 and 6 concurrent routes. The command used to define this in router configuration mode is

```
RTR (config-router)# maximum-paths {max}
```

In most cases, these rules are sufficient to properly route traffic. However, there might be cases where a route received from a routing protocol that by default has a lower administrative distance might be preferable to the more attractive route. The simplest case is where you need to adjust the administrative distance for all routes received by a particular routing process. The following router command is used in these cases:

```
RTR (config-router)# distance {weight}
```

The defined administrative distance, given by the value {weight}, is between 10 and 255. 0 through 9 are reserved for use by Cisco. Examples of the reserved distances are 0 for directly connected and 1 as the default for statically defined routes.

An example of where this command could be used is when you need all RIP-derived routes to override a similar route received via EIGRP. Under normal circumstances, the default administrative distance for RIP is 120 where EIGRP is 90. As such, the EIGRP will normally be preferred. To make RIP derived routes override EIGRP routes, the distance command is used as follows:

```
RTR (config)# router rip
RTR (config-router)# network 10.0.0.0
RTR (config-router)# distance 70

RTR (config)# router eigrp 200
RTR (config-router)# network 10.0.0.0
```

This sets the administrative distance for all routes received via RIP to have an administrative distance less than EIGRP. These routes are now, therefore, preferable to the EIGRP-derived routes. Remember that any routes received via EIGRP that are not overlapped exactly by RIP-derived routes will still be installed in the routing table. You might determine that only routes received from a specific neighbor or set of neighbors running RIP will need to override those learned via EIGRP. You can achieve this by using the following extensions to the `distance` command:

```
RTR (config-router)# distance {weight} {ip-address} {mask}
```

The weight parameter is the same, with the `{ip-address}` and `{mask}` options defining what range of neighbor IP addresses will be assigned the new administrative distance. The mask used here is similar to an Access List mask where a "1" in the mask indicates a "don't care" for matching. Multiple instances of this command can be used to set administrative distances for different sets of neighbors. Assuming that the neighbors on the 10.1.1.0/24 network are the only ones that need to override the EIGRP routes, the following configuration is used:

```
RTR (config)# router rip
RTR (config-router)# network 10.0.0.0
RTR (config-router)# distance 70 10.1.1.0 0.0.0.255

RTR (config)# router eigrp 200
RTR (config-router)# network 10.0.0.0
```

The most complete form of the `distance` command includes an Access List and becomes

```
RTR (config-router)# distance {weight} {ip-address} {mask} {access-list}
```

This form enables the administrative distance to be set based not only on neighbor address, but also on specific routes from specific neighbors based on the Access List defined by the value `{access-list}`. As a final extension to the example, you can now prefer RIP-derived routes for the 10.1.0.0/16 network and the 172.16.0.0/16 network over similar EIGRP routes. The following example uses `access-list 92` to define these routes:

```
RTR (config)# router rip
RTR (config-router)# network 10.0.0.0
RTR (config-router)# distance 70 10.1.1.0 0.0.0.255 92

RTR (config)# router eigrp 200
RTR (config-router)# network 10.0.0.0

RTR (config)# access-list 92 permit 10.1.0.0 0.0.255.255
RTR (config)# access-list 92 permit 172.16.0.0 0.0.255.255
RTR (config)# access-list 92 deny any
```

 Key Concept

The route used by the router will be determined first based on the lowest administrative distance followed by the best routing metric. Administrative distance can set based on the routing process, the neighbor from which the information was received, or for a specific route or set of routes from a specific neighbor.

Multicast Management

IP multicast traffic is primarily routed within a Cisco network using the Protocol Independent Multicast (PIM) routing protocol. To provide connectivity with non-PIM speaking routers, Cisco routers can send and receive multicast routes using the Distance Vector Multicast Routing Protocol. Interaction with the end users, whether they be multicast senders or receivers, is accomplished using the standard Internet Group Membership Protocol. Finally, Cisco routers and Catalyst switches can communicate group membership information between each other using the Cisco Group Membership Protocol.

Protocol Independent Multicast (PIM)

Protocol Independent Multicast (PIM) is a routing protocol used between routers to determine which multicast groups need to be forwarded between those routers and their connected interfaces. This protocol operates independent of any unicast protocols that might be used on the routers. In order to accomplish this task, PIM has three distinct modes of operations: dense mode, sparse mode, and sparse-dense mode. Each mode has specific characteristics that make it appropriate for different locations in the networks.

Dense Mode

Dense mode is the simplest mode in that it assumes that all other routers in the network will want to forward any multicast packets received. As such, a router operating in dense mode will forward all multicast packets to all its PIM neighbors. If a router receives a packet and has no directly connected host requiring the group or PIM neighbors, a prune message is sent back to the source of the packet. Additional packets for this group are not flooded after this occurs. In dense mode, PIM uses a source-based multicast distribution tree. To configure dense mode PIM on an interface, the following commands need to be configured on the router:

```
RTR (config)# ip multicast-routing

RTR (config)# interface serial 0
RTR (config-if)# ip pim dense-mode

RTR (config)# interface ethernet 0
RTR (config-if)# ip pim dense-mode
```

Sparse Mode

Sparse-mode operation assumes exactly the opposite of dense mode—that is, that all connected routers do not want to forward multicast packets for any given group unless there is a specific request for the traffic. Figure 14.2 shows an example of a sparse-mode implementation. These requests come in the form of a PIM join message directed back to a specific router known as the rendezvous point (RP). The RP is aware of all multicast sources on the network since the first-hop routers of all sources register that source with the RP. Using the knowledge of multicast sources, the RP forwards a PIM join request back to the source along a shared distribution tree.

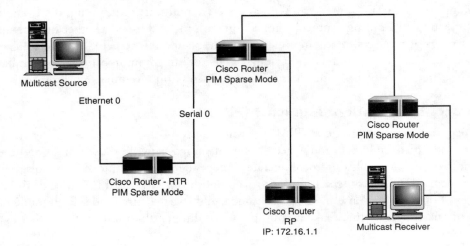

Figure 14.2
An example of sparse-mode PIM.

To configure sparse-mode operation, the following commands are required:

```
RTR (config)# ip multicast-routing

RTR (config)# ip pim rp-address 172.16.1.1

RTR (config)# interface serial 0
RTR (config-if)# ip pim sparse-mode

RTR (config)# interface ethernet 0
RTR (config-if)# ip pim sparse-mode
```

In sparse mode, the only possible additional information required beyond dense mode is the identification of an RP, as shown in the example using the ip pim rp-address command. This identification is required only in leaf routers where either multicast senders or listeners are attached. Sparse-mode routers with no need to handle host join requests do not need an RP defined.

Key Concept

At least one statically defined RP must be configured for all routers with sparse-mode interfaces that have hosts attached to them.

Sparse-Dense Mode

Sparse-dense mode is a hybrid mode where the interface in question can operate in both modes depending on the mode of the multicast group itself. That is, if the group is advertised to the RP, a sparse-mode connection can be established. If the RP is unaware of the group, a dense-mode connection might be available. In general, the configuration is similar to both dense and sparse mode with the addition of a new feature pertaining to RPs. In a sparse-mode environment, a default RP is required, as shown in the previous example. In sparse-dense mode, the use of the Auto-RP feature eliminates the need to statically define a default RP at each leaf router. For each non-RP router, the configuration simplifies to the following:

```
RTR (config)# interface ethernet 0
  ...(other interface configuration commands)
RTR (config-if)# ip sparse-dense mode
```

For the routers that are now acting as RPs, the following configuration command is required:

```
RTR (config-if)# ip pim send-rp-announce {interface} scope {ttl}
 group-list {access-list}
```

The following are descriptions for each parameter used in this command:

- The {interface} parameter defines the IP address that will be used to communicate with this RP.
- The {ttl} value limits the announcement to this number of hops from the RP.
- The {access-list} value points to a standard IP Access List to determine the groups for which this router will agree to be an RP.

In order for RPs to not overlap each other and potentially end up duplicating resources for a specific multicast group, an RP mapping agent is required. An RP mapping agent identifies which RPs will agree to accept which groups and then creates an RP to group mapping that is unique. The mapping agent then sends this information to all PIM

PART

IV

CH

14

routers so that they can select the correct RP for a given group. The global command to enable this feature is

```
RTR (config)# ip pim send-rp-discovery scope {ttl}
```

The {ttl} parameter limits the number of hops outgoing announcements will make. Because an RP can also act as an RP mapping agent, this final basic configuration will enable the use of the Auto-RP feature in a sparse-dense mode environment:

```
RTR (config)# ip multicast-routing
RTR (config-if)# ip pim send-rp-announce Ethernet 0/0 scope 5 group-list 1
RTR (config-if)# ip pim send-rp-discovery scope 5

RTR (config)# access-list 1 permit 224.0.0.0 15.255.255.255
```

This example shows the use of both the RP announce and RP mapping features on the same router. The scope, or hop count, is limited to five routers with the group list consisting of all multicast groups. Note that although it is possible and advisable to then define additional RPs for redundancy or load sharing, only one mapping agent can exist in the network. A typical scenario is to map locally scoped groups to one RP in the center of the network and another RP for globally scoped groups to an RP near the edge of the network.

Key Concept

PIM sparse-dense mode can take advantage of Auto-RP enabling automated redundancy and load sharing for RP activities.

Distance Vector Multicast Routing Protocol (DVMRP)

The *Distance Vector Multicast Routing Protocol (DVMRP)* is used by many non-Cisco multicast routers to forward multicast traffic. The most common implementation of the DVMRP protocol in non-Cisco equipment is based on the publicly available *mrouted program.* The mrouted program is the primary multicast routing support application for the *Multicast Backbone (MBONE)* project. Cisco routers can understand routing information from and provide routing information to DVMRP routers but do not use DVMRP for forwarding multicast packets. DVMRP uses a source-based routing tree with all packets being initially flooded down the tree until prune messages are received.

Although Cisco routers will automatically discover DVMRP sources on any attached network, the most common source of DVMRP information is via a DVMRP tunnel to attach to the MBONE. This is shown in Figure 14.3. A DVMRP tunnel is set up with a remote DVMRP participant as shown in the following example:

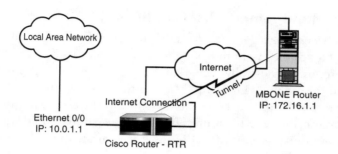

Figure 14.3
An example of a DVMRP implementation.

```
RTR (config)# interface tunnel 1
   tunnel source ethernet 0/0
   tunnel destination 172.16.1.1
   tunnel mode dvmrp
   ip unnumbered ethernet 0/0
   ip pim dense-mode

RTR (config)# interface Ethernet 0/0
RTR (config-if)# ip address 10.1.1.1 255.255.255.0
RTR (config-if)# ip pim dense-mode
```

This example shows the DVMRP tunnel configured in PIM dense mode using the
IP address of interface Ethernet 0/0. The tunnel destination is the actual IP address of
the source DVMRP router. PIM sparse or sparse-dense mode could have been enabled
in lieu of dense mode with the caveats related to RP configuration discussed previously.

 Key Concept

Cisco routers can participate in the MBONE and other multicast networks using
DVMRP but cannot use DVMRP to forward multicast packets in lieu of PIM.

The Cisco implementation of DVMRP is also capable of providing default routing information into the DVMRP tunnel. The following command accomplishes this:

```
RTR (config)# interface tunnel 1
   ...(other tunnel configuration commands)
   ip dvmrp default-information [ originate | only ]
```

If the originate keyword is present, the 0.0.0.0 route is advertised in addition to any
other multicast routes that are available. If the only keyword is used, only the 0.0.0.0
route is advertised. This command should never be used when connecting the MBONE.

Internet Group Management Protocol (IGMP)

The *Internet Group Management Protocol (IGMP)* is the protocol used by hosts to control which IP multicast groups they want to belong to. This is done via the use of several pre-defined multicast groups. All hosts, by definition, belong to the group 224.0.0.1, whereas all routers belong to the group 224.0.0.2. IGMP uses these definitions to communicate multicast-related information among connected systems. In the case of multicast sources, they announce their availability to the routers on the subnet so that multicast receivers can find them. For multicast receivers, IGMP is used to indicate to the routers on the subnet that a specific multicast group is required.

In a Cisco router, IGMP has a minimal number of features that might be configured. Of most importance is the definition of the IGMP version in use on a particular subnet. For proper operation, all hosts and routers on a subnet must operate with the same version of IGMP. By default the router treats all interfaces as supporting IGMP version 2. To force an interface to operate as an IGMP version 1 interface, you must use the `interface` command:

```
RTR (config)# ip igmp version 1
```

IGMP version 2 is normally preferred over version 1 because version 2 allows certain IGMP timeouts to be tuned for better performance.

As a troubleshooting tool, you can also force the router itself to issue IGMP join commands for a specific multicast group. This allows you to determine whether a specific group is reachable from the router. The interface command to initiate the join request is

```
RTR (config-if)# ip igmp join-group {group-address}
```

Finally, if you want to cache and potentially view session directory protocol records (commonly referred to as SDR) via the command line interface with the `show ip sdr` command, the following command is required:

```
RTR (config-if)# ip sdr listen
```

This enables the router to cache SDR version 2 announcements locally. SDR is a standard directory service available using a well-known multicast address that describes what data or programming is available on a specific multicast address.

Key Concept

All hosts and routers on a given subnet must be using the same version of IGMP for proper operation of multicast services.

Cisco Group Management Protocol (CGMP)

Cisco Group Management Protocol (CGMP) functions similarly to IGMP when a Catalyst switch is used in a multicast environment. CGMP was initially required by Catalyst switches because they could not tell the difference between an IGMP join request and a normal multicast data packet. To enable CGMP on a router interface, the following interface command is issued:

```
RTR (config-if)# ip cgmp [proxy]
```

The optional [proxy] keyword allows the Catalyst switch to interact with non-CGMP enabled routers on the same subnet. In this mode, the Cisco router with the CGMP proxy enabled sends join requests to the Catalyst with the non-CGMP router's MAC address.

Native IGMP support is now available in the latest releases of Catalyst hardware and software.

Key Concept

For Catalyst switches to use CGMP, a Cisco router running CGMP must be connected to the switch for each subnet or VLAN on which CGMP is to be run.

Summary

In this chapter, you have studied route redistribution, route management, and multicast management. These three routing protocol–independent topics have built on the material presented earlier in each of the chapters on specific IP routing protocols.

Route redistribution between routing processes involves choosing what metric translations are required and understanding how summarization can affect the actual routes that are redistributed and choosing which tag translations or assignments need to be made. Metrics are preserved when redistributing among IGRP and EIGRP processes. For all other scenarios, you must use a route-map to define the metric translation, a routing process default metric, or a generic default metric. Summarization issues between VLSM-aware protocols are minimal. However, when redistributing into a classful protocol, certain summarizations or expansions may result in loss of routing information. Tags applied to routes can be useful when working with OSPF to convey source information through the OSPF cloud. This is especially true of routes redistributed into OSPF from a BGP source.

Route management involved deciding what routes and what interfaces on a router would participate in any particular routing process along with selecting what routes

PART

IV

CH

14

are ultimately used to forward any given packet. Passive interfaces can be defined to allow a routing process to receive updates via an interface but not source any routing updates through the identified interface. Distribute lists can be applied to both incoming and outgoing updates to control what routes are received and forwarded by the routing process. These distribute lists can be applied globally to the routing process or on an interface-specific basis. Policy routing is used to alter the next-hop IP address of a packet based on information other than destination address. Possible inputs to the policy-routing process are source IP address, inbound interface, transport protocol, packet length, or application type. Route selection, when more than one routing process has information about a specific destination, can be controlled through the use of administrative distance. Administrative distance can be set per routing process, per neighbor, or per route, depending on the need.

The last part of the chapter covered multicast routing issues related to PIM, DVMRP, IGMP, and CGMP. Interfaces on a Cisco router can operate in three PIM modes: dense, sparse, and sparse-dense. The easiest to configure is dense mode where no further information is required. Sparse and sparse-dense modes require the existence of an RP to determine the source of a multicast group. In sparse-dense mode, the Auto-RP feature is available allowing multiple redundant and load-sharing RPs to exist within a single administrative zone. DVMRP is used to pass multicast routing information to and receive information from non-PIM devices. The most common use of DVMRP is to communicate with the MBONE. Although Cisco routers can exchange DVMRP information with others, DVMRP cannot be used to forward multicast traffic in a Cisco router. IGMP is the core IP protocol that allows both multicast sources and receivers to indicate what multicast groups they would like to participate in. IGMP has two versions and all IGMP devices on a given subnet must use the same version of IGMP. Finally, CGMP is used to communicate group membership information between Cisco routers and Catalyst switches. Cisco routers can also be configured to proxy CGMP for non-CGMP-enabled routers on the same subnet when required.

QUESTIONS AND ANSWERS

1. How do you prevent an interface from sending routing updates?

   A. Using the `passive-interface` command prevents routing updates from being provided via that interface. For OSPF, the interface will be seen as a stub network.

2. Can policy routing be fast switched?

   A. Policy routing can be fast switched with the caveat that no set ip default statements exist in the policy and that any set interface statements are assumed to be reasonable under all conditions.

3. Can you redistribute a VLSM-aware routing protocol into a classful routing protocol?

    A. Yes. The result is that all routing redistributed into the classful protocol will be forced into the subnet mask defined for the classful routing protocol on that network. As a result, any routes with masks that do not agree with the classful routing protocol mask for that network will be dropped.

4. How do you set the administrative distance for routes determined by a specific IP routing protocol?

    A. You would use the command `weight {number}`, where `{number}` is the administrative distance you would like to assign to all routes learned via that routing process.

5. How do you set the administrative distance for a specific route learned via a specific routing protocol?

    A. You would use an extension of the `weight` command of the form `weight {number} {ip-address} {mask} {access-list}`, where `{ip-address}` and `{mask}` define what routers the updates are sourced from, and `{access-list}` defines the specific routes that will be affected.

6. How do sparse-mode PIM and dense-mode PIM differ from each other?

    A. PIM sparse mode requires that a rendezvous point be configured to which all join requests are forwarded. PIM dense mode uses a source-based distribution tree that floods all traffic until a prune command is received.

7. What is a rendezvous point?

    A. An RP is a designated router within a PIM sparse-mode network to which all group join requests are forwarded. This allows the RP to act as a clearinghouse for requests from both senders and receivers. This is in contrast to a dense mode situation where all routers must know about all available groups at all times for join requests to succeed.

8. What is CGMP and what hardware components are required when implementing this protocol?

    A. CGMP is Cisco's group management protocol used between Cisco routers and Catalyst switches to convey group membership information to the switches. This runs in addition to IGMP which is required by the hosts and the routers. CGMP requires that at least one router on each VLAN participating in multicast activity be enabled for CGMP support.

PRACTICE TEST

1. Static routes pointing to an interface are automatically redistributed into an EIGRP routing process if that interface is up and would otherwise be participating in the routing process.

    A. True
    B. False

Answer A (True) is correct. Static routes pointing to an interface are treated as connected and are therefore always redistributed without need of a specific redistribute static command as long as the interface is up. This is true not only for EIGRP, but for any IGP running on a Cisco router.

2. There is an automatic mapping of metrics between the following protocols when redistributing (choose all that apply):

    A. IGRP to EIGRP, same AS
    B. RIP to IGRP
    C. OSPF to EIGRP
    D. EIGRP to IGRP, different AS
    E. IGRP to RIP

Answers A and D are correct because IGRP and EIGRP are the only protocols where metrics are preserved when doing route redistribution. Answers B, C, and E are incorrect because all other translations require a specific definition of metric value for the routes to actually be advertised.

3. Of the following routing protocols, which are VLSM aware? (Select all that apply.)

    A. OSPF
    B. RIP
    C. IGRP
    D. EIGRP
    E. IS-IS

Answers A, D, and E are correct. Answers B and C are incorrect because the subnet mask is not present in the routing protocol packet, making them unable to operate with VLSMs.

4. Route tags are forwarded by EIGRP for external routes.

    A. True
    B. False

Answer B (False) is correct. EIGRP has the concept of external routes but does not allow them to be tagged.

5. The following router rip command is used to prevent interface Ethernet 0/0 from sending RIP routing updates:

A. `no routing updates ethernet 0/0`

B. `distribute-list out passive ethernet 0/0`

C. `passive interface ethernet 0/0`

D. `access-group noupdate ethernet 0/0`

Answers A, B, and D are incorrect or invalid IOS configuration commands. **Answer C is correct because passive interfaces do not send routing updates.**

6. Based on the following EIGRP configuration, what routes received for the following networks will be eligible to be installed in the routing table (select all that apply):

```
RTR (config)# router eigrp 200
RTR (config-router)# network 10.0.0.0
RTR (config-router)# distribute-list in 99

RTR (config)# access-list 99 permit 10.1.0.0 0.0.255.255
RTR (config)# access-list 99 permit 172.16.0.0 0.0.255.255
RTR (config)# access-list 99 deny any
```

A. 172.16.0.0/16

B. 10.1.0.0/16

C. 172.16.7.0/24

D. 10.0.1.0/24

E. 10.0.0.0/8

Answer A is correct because the route is permitted by the Access List, and even though the network itself might not be directly connected to the router, a routing update might still contain a record for this network. Answer B is correct because the route shown is permitted by the Access List. Answer C is correct because the route shown is allowed by the Access List. It would be strange but not impossible for a subnet of the 172.16.0.0/16 network to be advertised directly to this router. Answers D and E are incorrect because these networks are not listed in the Access List and will not pass the Access List. They do not fall under the 10.1.0.0 0.0.255.255 network due to their subnet masks.

7. What route management tool can be used to change the default route taken by a packet based on source IP address?

A. Policy routing with fast switching enabled

B. Policy routing

C. Redistribution

D. DVMRP

PART
IV

CH
14

Answer A is incorrect because fast-switched policy routing does not allow the default destination to be altered. **Answer B is correct because policy routing enables you to set a next-hop IP address based on parameters other than destination address.** Answer C is incorrect because redistribution has to do with sending routing updates from one protocol into another protocol. Answer D is incorrect because DVMRP has to do with multicast management.

8. Up to eight equal-cost paths can be installed into the routing table for a given destination.

   A. True
   B. False

Answer B (False) is correct because, by default, the maximum number of paths is set to 4 but can be increased to a maximum of 6.

9. The following are true statements concerning CGMP (choose all that apply):

   A. All routers on a subnet with a Catalyst switch must have CGMP enabled.
   B. CGMP requires that a Cisco router with CGMP enabled be located on every VLAN in a Catalyst that has multicast traffic enabled on it.
   C. CGMP can be used in place of IGMP when using non-Catalyst switches.
   D. CGMP is a protocol that exchanges information between the router and the multicast host.

Answer A is incorrect because a single Cisco router can proxy for non-CGMP-enabled routers on the same subnet. **Answer B is correct.** Answer C is incorrect because CGMP is a Cisco-specific protocol for exchanging group information between Cisco routers and Catalyst switches. Answer D is incorrect because CGMP packets are not processed by the multicast host.

10. What is a rendezvous point?

    A. A router in the network that initiates all multicast traffic
    B. A router in the network that processes group join requests in a PIM sparse-mode network
    C. A core router that has a default route to the Internet
    D. Used in a PIM dense-mode network as the root for all multicast traffic
    E. Not required for PIM sparse-mode or sparse-dense mode operations

Answer A is incorrect because no router performs this task. **Answer B is correct because an RP (rendezvous point) is required for any PIM sparse-mode operations.** Answer C is incorrect because it has nothing to do with PIM. Answer D is incorrect because it is not the root of all multicast traffic, only to its PIM neighbors. Answer E is incorrect because it is used in sparse mode.

Other Network Protocols

15 IPX: Internet Packet Exchange

16 AppleTalk

17 Other LAN Protocols

CHAPTER PREREQUISITE

Chapter 1, "General Network Overview," Chapter 2, "General Topic Overview," and Chapter 3, "Ethernet." A basic understanding of how to identify a WAN link on a Cisco router and what it is used for.

IPX: Internet Packet Exchange

WHILE YOU READ

1. What is a SAP?

2. Where does IPX derive the Host portion of the IPX Network node address?

3. What is the default IPX encapsulation type on an Ethernet interface?

4. What is the only Link-State routing protocol available for IPX?

5. What is the routing metric used in IPX RIP?

6. What is a hop?

7. What is a tick?

8. How many hops indicate an unreachable network?

SEE
APPENDIX **F**

Novell NetWare is a *Network Operating System (NOS). Internet Packet Exchange (IPX)* is Novell's layer-3 routing protocol. Newer versions of Novell NetWare support the use of TCP/IP in most client/server environments. However, IPX is still the most prominent method of communicating in Novell client/server architectures. IPX operates at the Network layer of the OSI model and its purpose is to allow clients to find and use particular services offered by different servers anywhere on the network. One big difference from IP is the role the router plays. It not only keeps track of where particular networks are located, it also provides, on demand to clients, a list of servers, their location, and the services they provide. There are other protocols related to IPX that will be discussed here as well.

Frame Format

Figure 15.1 is the frame format of an IPX packet header. Note the fields and the difference between it and an IP packet header (shown in Chapter 8, "TCP/IP"). By understanding the frame, you will understand the features and function of IPX much better.

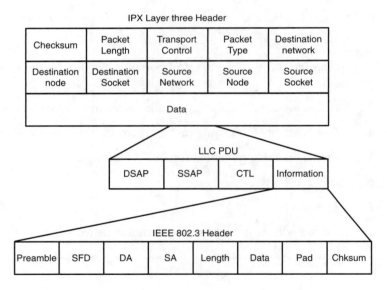

Figure 15.1
IPX header format.

IPX Addressing

An IPX address consists of two parts. The first part is the IPX network number. This can be any eight-character hexadecimal value (32 bits long). It is unnecessary to express any leading zeros in the network number. The network number is configured on the router port to identify the specific network.

The second part of the IPX address is the same as the local MAC address of the individual end device, referred to as the *Host*.

A workstation with the MAC address of "0123.4456.0123" (*Host* address) on its Network Interface Card (NIC) on the same backplane, ring, or VLAN as an interface on a Cisco router that has been assigned an IPX network "fad" (*Network* address) will have the IPX node address of "fad.0123.4456.0123".

Key Concept

There are two parts to an IPX node address:

- Network number used for routing, which points to the specific LAN
- MAC (host) address of the end station, client, or server

Encapsulation Types

An encapsulation type must be used for IPX to transmit across different physical media types. The encapsulation type must match on all stations that you want to communicate.

Ethernet

Actually, four different types of encapsulation can be used on Ethernet media:

- Novell-Ether—The default, this is a Novell specific variation of IEEE 802.2
- Ethernet-II (ARPA)
- 802.2 (SAP)
- Ethernet_snap (SNAP)—Specific only to IPX

These can be configured on individual Ethernet interfaces with the following respective commands:

```
RTR (config-if)# ipx encapsulation novell-ether = IEEE 802.3

RTR (config-if)# ipx encapsulation arpa = for Ethernet-II

RTR (config-if)# ipx encapsulation sap = IEEE 802.2

RTR (config-if)# ipx encapsulation snap = Ethernet_snap
```

Any of these can be configured on an Ethernet interface.

Token-Ring

Two different types of encapsulation can be used on Token-Ring media:

- Token_Ring_Snap (SNAP)
- Token_Ring (SAP)—default

Some end systems might require SNAP. The encapsulation type can be configured on an individual interface and is specific only to the IPX protocol. Use the following commands to change the encapsulation type:

```
RTR (config-if)# ipx encapsulation snap
RTR (config-if)# ipx encapsulation sap
```

FDDI

Three different types of encapsulation can be used on FDDI media:

- Fddi_Snap (*SNAP)*—default
- Fddi_802.2 (*SAP)*
- Fddi_raw (*Novell-fddi*)

Some end systems might require SAP or novell-fddi. The encapsulation type can be configured on an individual interface base and is specific only to the IPX protocol. Use the following commands to change the encapsulation types:

```
RTR (config-if)# ipx encapsulation sap

RTR (config-if)# ipx encapsulation novell-fddi
```

Serial

The default encapsulation type for a Serial interface is HDLC.

Key Concept

The encapsulation type for interfaces can be changed if needed. The default encapsulation type for Cisco interfaces is as follows:

- Ethernet—Novell-Ether
- Token-Ring—SAP
- FDDI—SNAP
- Serial—HDLC

Service Advertisement Protocol (SAP)

When a server wants to advertise a service it has available, it generates a SAP and broadcasts it onto the network. The packet is read by the router; the SAP information within the packet is then collected and put into a database on the router. It is then periodically forwarded to all other routers that it is connected to, and those routers will do the same. The information continues to be forwarded until it has saturated the network. IPX RIP/SAP uses split horizons to prevent a routing loop.

End stations (or *clients*) then get the service information from the router. In this way, they find out what services are available on the network and where the services are located.

The most common (and important to know for the CCIE exam) SAP types are

- File server—SAP type 4
- Print server—SAP type 7

Controlling the amount and frequency of the SAP advertisements is one of the most important aspects of managing a Novell network. This can be accomplished in a variety of ways, which will be explained later in IPX filtering.

Key Concept

Service Advertisement Protocol (SAP) is the primary way that clients find servers. SAP divines what services are available. Routers are key in distributing this information.

Get Nearest Server

A Get Nearest Server request is an initial broadcast by a workstation to locate the nearest Novell server. The router will respond to this broadcast. You can alter how the router responds to these requests.

IPX Configuration Fundamentals

Two steps are required to get basic IPX functionality throughout an IPX network on Cisco routers:

- Enable IPX routing.
- Assign IPX network numbers to interfaces.

IPX must be turned on in all applicable routers, and it will automatically include all IPX networks active on the router. The words *Novell* and *IPX* are interchangeable at the command prompt on Cisco routers; either can be used in any context. Use the following command to enable IPX routing:

```
RTR (config)# ipx routing
```

This command will show up in the configuration with a router-assigned MAC address after it. For example,

```
ipx routing 0123.4561.0101
```

Assign a network number to all IPX network interfaces using the following syntax:

```
RTR (config-if)# ipx network FAD
```

FAD is our selected IPX network for this example.

ipxwan

ipxwan enables you to assign a single IPX network to all WAN interfaces and can be used with IPX networks routed with RIP or EIGRP, but not NLSP. Using ipxwan is slightly more efficient in the way it handles IPX traffic. The main difference from the previous example is that with ipxwan you don't assign ipx network numbers to WAN interfaces; instead, you assign a single ipx network number to the router (ipx internal-network) and just define the WAN interfaces that will use it.

```
RTR (config)# ipx internal-network AAA
RTR (config-if)# ipx ipxwan
```

In this example, the interface has been configured to use ipxwan network "AAA".

Key Concept

There are two steps to enabling IPX routing on a Cisco router:

1. Turn on IPX routing.
2. Assign IPX network numbers to interfaces.

IPX Routing

IPX can be routed like any other layer-3 protocol. Most of the concepts of routing IP or AppleTalk are identical within IPX.

IPX RIP

IPX RIP is the simplest way to route IPX traffic. It is also the least efficient. The previous example shows how to enable IPX RIP. You can also enable IPX RIP using the command `ipx router rip` in the same manner as explained in the following EIGRP example (minus the AS number). This will allow you to choose individual networks to be routed.

IPX EIGRP

IPX EIGRP is a hybrid for the Advanced Distance Vector routing protocol. Enabling IPX EIGRP requires the assignment of an autonomous system number for the EIGRP process. The identification of the networks will need to be identified within the process. A single router can have multiple IPX EIGRP autonomous systems.

Use the following commands to enable IPX EIGRP routing:

```
RTR (config)# ipx router eigrp 100

RTR (config-ipx-router)# network fad

RTR (config-ipx-router)# network bad
```

Or you can specify all IPX networks connected to the router with the following syntax:

```
RTR (config-ipx-router)# network all
```

IPX NLSP

Novell Link Services Protocol (NLSP) is a link-state protocol, which means it keeps track of all other links within its area. NLSP has the advantages (highly efficient) and disadvantages (laborious design and configuration) of other link-state protocols such as OSPF. NLSP requires the definition of specific IPX network number ranges. These ranges specify an area. This allows other area routers to only have to keep track of the range, not all the individual IPX networks within the range.

There are three types of NLSP routers:

- Level 1—Connected to only one area.
- Level 2—Connected to at least two areas, with a maximum of four areas within the same domain. These are considered intradomain routers.
- Level 3—Connected to at least one area from two autonomous domains. These are considered interdomain routers.

Basic IPX Configuration Example

I will use Figure 15.2 for my example. After the figure are configuration excerpts from the routers in the figure. Only the information relevant to IPX is displayed.

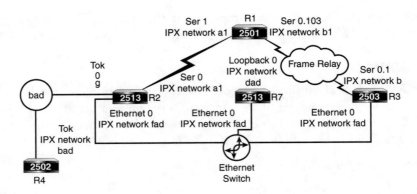

Figure 15.2
A basic IPX network.

This figure will be used in the following configuration examples, which are abbreviated outputs for the routers depicted in Figure 15.2. Only IPX-relevant text is being displayed. All outputs are directly explained earlier in this chapter. Figure 15.2 and the following output should be used as a reference for future output examples in this chapter.

R1

```
R1 (config)# ipx routing
R1 (config)# ipx maximum-paths 3

R1 (config)# interface ethernet0
R1 (config-if)# ipx network DAB

R1 (config)# interface Serial0.103 point-to-point
R1 (config-if)# ipx network B1

R1 (config)# interface Serial0
R1 (config-if)# ipx network A1
```

R2

```
R2 (config)# ipx routing
R2 (config)# ipx maximum-paths 3

R2 (config)# interface Serial1
R2 (config-if)# ipx network A1

R2 (config)# interface Ethernet0
R2 (config-if)#  ipx network FAD

R2 (config)# interface TokenRing0
R2 (config-if)#  ipx network BAD
```

R3

```
R3 (config)# ipx routing
R3 (config)# ipx maximum-paths 3

R3 (config)# interface Ethernet0
R3 (config-if)#  ipx network FAD

R3 (config)# interface Serial0.1 point-to-point
R3 (config-if)#  ipx network B1
```

R4

```
R4 (config)# ipx routing
R4 (config)# ipx maximum-paths 3

R4 (config)# interface Loopback0
R4 (config-if)# ipx network CAD

R4 (config)# interface TokenRing0
R4 (config-if)# ipx network BAD
```

R7

```
R7 (config)# ipx routing 0010.7b38.6725
R7 (config)# ipx maximum-paths 3
R7 (config)# interface Loopback0
R7 (config-if)# ipx network DAD
R7 (config)# interface Ethernet0
R7 (config-if)# ipx network FAD
```

Identifying Routes

The following is an output from R1. This output results from the show ipx route command. This shows the IPX RIP table. IPX uses split horizon to prevent routing loops.

```
R1#show ipx route
Codes: C - Connected primary network,    c - Connected secondary network
       S - Static, F - Floating static, L - Local (internal), W - IPXWAN
       R - RIP, E - EIGRP, N - NLSP, X - External, A - Aggregate
       s - seconds, u - uses, U - Per-user static

6 Total IPX routes. Up to 3 parallel paths and 16 hops allowed.

No default route known.

C         A1 (HDLC),          Se1
C         B1 (FRAME-RELAY),   Se0.103
C       DAB (NOVELL-ETHER),   Eth0
```

```
R          BAD [07/01]   via       A1.0010.7b80.c665,    24s,  Se1
R          CAD [08/02]   via       A1.0010.7b80.c665,    24s,  Se1
R          DAD [08/02]   via       A1.0010.7b80.c665,    24s,  Se1
                         via       B1.0010.7b80.5fe0,    42s,  Se0.103
R          FAD [07/01]   via       A1.0010.7b80.c665,    24s,  Se1
                         via       B1.0010.7b80.5fe0,    42s,  Se0.103
```

The first column is the way in which the router discovered the IPX network. The first three of the previous IPX networks are connected. All the others were learned via RIP. The second column is the name of the IPX network. The third column lists the encapsulation type for directly connected networks and the tick/hop count for remote networks.

The first number in brackets is the tick count. The router makes routing decisions based on this number. A tick is 1/18 of a second. The router estimates it based on expected delay through a particular type of media. The tick count can be altered on individual interfaces using the ipx delay command. The tick count is the first metric the router uses in making routing decisions. The second number in brackets is the hop count. It is simply the number of routers that have to be traversed to get to the desired network. There is a maximum of 15 hops; therefore, a count of 16 hops is considered unreachable. Hop count is the second metric used in choosing a route. It will only be used if the tick count is the same on two separate routes to the same IPX network.

IPX RIP is a Distance-Vector routing protocol, which means you need to know how far (distance) and which way (vector) a network is. The tick/hop count represents the distance. The next paragraph covers the vector. This information is shown next and represented in the IPX address and other information.

In the previous example, the route to get to IPX network BAD would be A1.0010.7b80.c665. The Network number "A1" is always an IPX network to which this router is directly connected. The MAC or Host "0010.7b80.c665" is a router that is also attached to that network "A1". Together, these represent the Vector for IPX RIP. Look at the configurations for router R2. Notice it is also attached to IPX network A1. If you were to view the running configuration, the MAC address after the ipx routing configuration command would be 0010.7b80.c665.

The next column shows the time it has been since its last RIP update with this particular route. IPX RIP sends updates every 60 seconds, so you should never see this number above 59s unless the network is no longer available or the RIP broadcast interval has been altered.

The final column indicates from which interface the route was learned. This is the vector. In the previous example, networks DAD and FAD both have dual routes (paths). One route was learned from A1.0010.7b80.c665; the other was learned from B1.0010.7b80.5fe0. You will need to have the configuration command ipx maximum-paths # in the router, where # is greater than 1 to get duplicate routes to the same network. Maximum-paths default is 1.

Key Concept

A Cisco router keeps track of all IPX networks it can reach. This information can be displayed with the show ipx route command. The command also shows the next hop, the tick/hop count, how the route was learned, when the route was last updated, and which outgoing interface to use to send traffic to that IPX network.

Identifying Servers

The following is the output from a show ipx server command in router R1 in Figure 15.2. This shows the IPX SAP table. This example shows that we have access to both a file server and printer server on IPX network FAD.

```
R1#sho ipx server
Codes: S - Static, P - Periodic, E - EIGRP, N - NLSP,
H - Holddown, + = detail
U - Per-user static
2 Total IPX Servers
```

Table ordering is based on routing and server info:

	Type	Name	Net	Address	Port	Route	Hops	Itf
P	4	Corp_Serv1	FAD.0101.1121.1122:0452			7/01	1	Se1
P	7	Corp_Serv1	FAD.0101.1121.1122:0454			7/01	1	Se1

The P in the first column indicates it is a periodic or RIP-derived SAP.

The Type code indicates the particular service that is being offered. This example shows two different services, 4 for file server and 7 for print server. All available services have their own type code.

The Name column has the name of the server. Here we notice that both of these SAPs originated at the same server.

The Net and Address fields indicate the Network and Host that are offering the service. Both of the previous SAP entries originated at same server.

In the previous example, the server is seven ticks and one hop away and the interface to be used is Serial 1 (Distance and Vector).

 Key Concept

Cisco routers keep track of all IPX servers and services (SAPs) they provide. They share this information with other devices on the network.

Filtering IPX Network Traffic

IPX is generally a chatty protocol. When you design or work with an IPX network, controlling unnecessary traffic is of critical importance.

Access Lists

Three different types of Access Lists are specific to IPX. The first is the Standard IPX Access List (800–899), which allows for filtering based on source and destination address only. The second is the Extended IPX Access List (900–999), which allows filtering on source and destination address as well as specific IPX protocol or SAP. The third is a SAP Access List (1000–1099), which allows the filtering of specific services, such as printing or file services. These were briefly discussed in Chapter 2, "General Topic Overview." They are discussed here in more detail, as needed for the CCIE Written Exam.

The best way to stop the traffic is before it leaves the first router it is connected to. Therefore, when setting up filtering by use of Access Lists, routing update filters, or SAP filters, it is best to plan to stop the traffic or advertisement of services (SAPs) as close to the source as possible.

Standard Access Lists

The Standard Access List (800–899) allows the filtering of Network addresses only.

The following example uses R1 in the same network shown in Figure 15.2:

```
R1(config)#access-list 800 deny 1.0000.0001.1212
R1(config)#access-list 800 deny -1 DAB
R1(config)#access-list 800 permit  -1 -1
R1(config)#interface serial 0.103
R1(config-sub-if)#ipx access-group 800
R1(config-sub-if)#inter serial 1
R1(config-if)#ipx access-group 800
```

This Access List will

- Deny any traffic from the specific address fad.0000.0001.1212 from coming into R1.
- Deny all traffic destined to network DAB (–1 = all networks in IPX Access Lists)
- Permit all other traffic

Extended Access Lists

The extended Access List (900–999) allows the specification of both Network nodes and SAPs.

Again, this example uses R1 from our Figure 15.2:

```
R1(config)#access-list 900 deny fad.0000.0001.1212 0000.0000.0000 7
R1(config)#access-list 900 deny  -1 4
R1(config)#access-list 900 permit -1 0
R1(config)#interface serial 0.103
R1(config-sub-if)#ipx access-group 900
R1(config-sub-if)#inter serial 1
R1(config-if)#ipx access-group 900
```

This Access List will

- Deny all (−1) print traffic (SAP 7) from node fad.0000.0001.1212 from entering R1
- Deny all (−1) file server traffic (SAP 4) from entering R1.
- Permit all other services (0)

SAP Filters

The SAP filters (1000–1099) allow filtering by SAP only.

This is an example of a simple SAP filter:

```
RTR (config)# access-list 1000 deny -1 7
RTR (config)# access-list 1000 permit -1
```

This list will deny all print services and allow all other services. There are different ways in which to apply this filter.

You can apply this to outgoing interfaces so that the Access List is applied to outgoing traffic. To do this, apply the Access List to an interface:

```
RTR (config-if)# ipx output-sap-filter 1000
```

This applies the previous Access List to outgoing traffic on the interface. So, all print service advertisements will be denied from going out that particular interface.

You can apply this to incoming interfaces so that the Access List is applied to incoming traffic. To do this, apply the Access List to an interface:

```
RTR (config-if)# ipx input-sap-filter 1000
```

This applies the previous Access List to incoming traffic on the interface. So, all print service advertisements will be denied from coming in that particular interface.

You can also use a router-sap-filter to apply the Access List to incoming RIP SAP updates which in this case would not allow anything advertising SAP 7 from becoming part of the ipx server list. You can also use this method to block the entire SAP table based on the router where the individual SAPs came from.

Key Concept

There are many different ways of controlling IPX network traffic. Filtering can occur on specific IPX traffic as well as the advertisement of specific services. It can be placed on any interface for traffic that is incoming, outgoing, or both. It can also be applied to filter-specific routers, specific nodes, specific SAPs, or specific servers.

Summary

This chapter provided the first step in the understanding of Novell's IPX protocol and how to configure it within a Cisco environment. You should have learned to create and apply IPX network numbers to interfaces within a Cisco router, as well as how to enable IPX RIP routing. You should have also learned to read a router's internal RIP table and to derive from that how the network was learned (RIP/NLSP/connected), how far away it is in ticks and hops, and what router is the next hop to get there. You should understand the origination and propagation of SAPs as well as the method of that propagation.

You should also understand the basics of filtering IPX SAPs as well as the actual IPX-directed traffic. You should also be able to read a router's internal SAP table and identify what services are available and from which servers.

QUESTIONS AND ANSWERS

1. What is a SAP?

    A: A Service Advertising Protocol is the method used by an IPX client to find a particular server offering a particular service. The SAP is generated by the server, collected and forwarded by the router, and provided to the client by both.

2. Where does IPX derive the Host portion of the IPX Network node address?

    A: The Host portion of the IPX node address is the MAC address of the node, workstation, server, or router.

3. What is the default IPX encapsulation type on an Ethernet interface?

    A: The default encapsulation of an Ethernet interface is Novell-Ether.

4. What is the only Link-State routing protocol available for IPX?

    A: NetWare Link Services Protocol (NLSP)

5. What is the routing metric used in IPX RIP?

A: IPX RIP uses ticks and then hops in determining the distance (metric) to a network.

6. What is a hop?

A: A hop is equal to the number of routers between networks.

7. What is a tick?

A: A tick is 1/18 of a second. It is estimated (by the router) based on expected delay through a particular type of media.

8. How many hops indicate an unreachable network?

A: Sixteen hops is regarded as infinity and therefore unreachable.

PRACTICE TEST

1. What is the default encapsulation type on a Token-Ring interface on a Cisco router?

A. SNAP
B. SAP
C. ARPA
D. Novell-Ether

Answer A is incorrect; although SNAP encapsulation can be used, it isn't the default. **Answer B is correct because SAP is the default encapsulation type on a Token-Ring interface**. Answers C and D are incorrect because ARPA and Novell-Ether are valid encapsulation types for Ethernet, not Token-Ring.

2. What is the numeric range for a Standard IPX Access List?

A. 100–199
B. 900–999
C. 1000–1099
D. 800–899

Answer A is incorrect; 100–199 is for extended IP Access Lists. Answer B is incorrect because 900–999 is for an extended IPX Access List. Answer C is incorrect because 1000–1099 is the numeric range for SAP Access Lists. **Answer D is correct; 800–899 is the numeric range for Standard Access Lists.**

   3. What is the numeric range for an extended IPX Access List?

   A. 100–199

   B. 900–999

   C. 1000–1099

   D. 800–899

Answer A is incorrect because 100–199 is the range for extended IP Access Lists. **Answer B is correct because 900–999 is the numeric range for extended Access Lists.** Answer C is incorrect because 1000–1099 is the numeric range for SAP Access Lists. Answer D is incorrect; 800–899 is the numeric range for Standard Access Lists.

   4. What is the numeric range for a SAP Access List?

   A. 100–199

   B. 900–999

   C. 1000–1099

   D. 800–899

Answer A is incorrect because 100–199 is for extended IP Access Lists. Answer B is incorrect because 900–999 is the numeric range for Extended Access Lists. **Answer C is correct because 1000–1099 is the numeric range for SAP Access Lists.** Answer D is incorrect; 800–899 is the numeric range for Standard Access Lists.

   5. Which of the following is the default IPX RIP update interval?

   A. 60ms

   B. 60s

   C. 59s

   D. 30s

Answer A is incorrect because the default IPX Rip update interval is not 60ms. **Answer B is correct because the default IPX RIP update interval is 60 seconds.** Answer C is incorrect because the default IPX Rip update interval is not 59s. Answer D is incorrect because the default IPX Rip update interval is not 30s.

   6. What is the SAP type code for print server?

   A. 4

   B. −1

   C. 7

   D. 5

Answer A is incorrect because SAP code 4 is for the file server. Answer B is incorrect because −1 is not a valid SAP code. **Answer C is correct because 7 is the SAP code for print server**. Answer D is incorrect because SAP code 5 is for job server.

7. What is the SAP type code for file server?

   A. 4

   B. −1

   C. 7

   D. 5

Answer A is correct because SAP code 4 is for the file server. Answer B is incorrect because −1 is not a valid SAP code. Answer C is incorrect because 7 is the SAP code for print server. Answer D is incorrect because SAP code 5 is for job server.

8. Which of the following commands will turn on IPX RIP?

   A. `Router(config)#ipx router rip`

   B. `Router(config)#novell router rip`

   C. `Router(config)#ipx routing`

   D. `Router(config)#novell routing`

   E. All of the above

Answer E is correct. All of the above commands can be used to initiate IPX RIP.

9. Which of the following commands will allow IPX RIP to keep two routes to the same network in the routing table?

   A. `ipx maximum-hops 2`

   B. `ipx paths 2`

   C. `ipx multi-route 2`

   D. `ipx maximum-paths 2`

Answer A is incorrect because `ipx maximum-hops #` sets the maximum number of hops for which the router keeps routes. Answers B and C incorrect because they are not valid commands. **Answer D is correct because `ipx maximum-paths #` is the command used to set the maximum number of routes to the same IPX network.**

10. What is used to specify all IPX networks within an IPX Access List?

   A. 0

   B. all

   C. −1

   D. mut-any

Answer A is incorrect because 0 is used to specify the internal or local network in IPX Access Lists. **Answer C is correct because −1 is used in IPX Access List to specify all networks.** Answers B and D are incorrect because they are not valid command syntax.

AppleTalk

WHILE YOU READ

1. What is the difference between an extended and a nonextended AppleTalk network?

2. What is the structure of an AppleTalk Address?

3. What is a zone?

4. What are the three types of AARP packets?

5. How does PAP differ from ASP?

6. What type of routing protocol is RTMP?

7. What is a seed router?

The AppleTalk protocol stack is a proprietary protocol stack developed by Apple specifically for use with Apple computers. It was originally designed for ease-of-use in small workgroups and peer-to-peer networks. It was also designed to provide seamless integration between the end-user desktop and the network.

This chapter outlines the technical details of the AppleTalk protocol suite as well as how its various components fit into the OSI network model. You will also become familiar with the various services and routing protocols that are used in an AppleTalk network.

AppleTalk Protocol Suite

The AppleTalk protocol suite roughly operates at all layers of the OSI model. Each layer and its associated AppleTalk protocols are outlined later in the chapter. Most protocols are discussed in further detail later in this chapter, as necessary. A graphical representation appears in Figure 16.1.

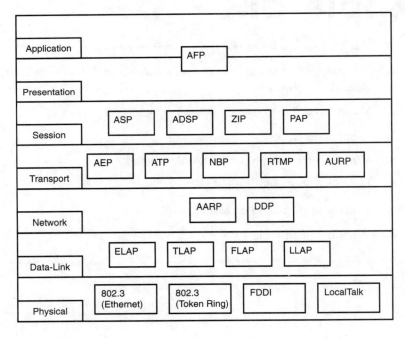

Figure 16.1
The AppleTalk suite and how it relates to the layers of the OSI model.

At the Physical layer of the OSI model, AppleTalk can ride over several media types: Ethernet (802.3), Token-Ring (802.5), FDDI, and Apple's proprietary *LocalTalk*. They are named appropriately:

- EtherTalk—AppleTalk running over Ethernet
- TokenTalk—AppleTalk over Token-Ring
- FDDITalk—AppleTalk over FDDI

PART

V

CH

16

Although Ethernet, Token-Ring, and FDDI are covered in other chapters of this book, LocalTalk is not. For purposes of the CCIE exam, all you need to know about LocalTalk is that it employs a bus topology similar to Ethernet and that Cisco routers and internet-working equipment do not support LocalTalk interfaces.

At the Data Link layer, each of these physical media technologies has its own corresponding Link Access Protocol (LAP):

- EtherTalk Link Access Protocol (ELAP)
- TokenTalk Link Access Protocol (TLAP)
- FDDITalk Link Access Protocol (FLAP)
- LocalTalk Link Access Protocol (LLAP)

Because each physical media type has its own form of hardware addressing, the various LAPs isolate the data-link addressing from the higher-level protocols. In EtherTalk, TokenTalk, and FDDITalk, this isolation is done in conjunction with the AppleTalk Address Resolution Protocol (AARP) in the Network layer of the OSI model.

At the Network layer of the OSI model reside *AppleTalk Address Resolution Protocol (AARP)* and *Datagram Delivery Protocol (DDP)*. For the time being, you can think of AARP as being roughly analogous to Address Resolution Protocol (ARP) and DDP as being roughly analogous to Internet Protocol (IP) in the TCP/IP realm.

The Transport layer of the OSI model consists of several protocols that work together to ensure reliable network connectivity between network devices. These protocols are as follows:

- AppleTalk Echo Protocol (AEP)
- AppleTalk Transaction Protocol (ATP)
- Name Binding Protocol (NBP)
- AppleTalk Update-Based Routing Protocol (AURP)
- Router Table Maintenance Protocol (RTMP)

The Session layer of the OSI model comprises the following protocols:

- AppleTalk Session Protocol (ASP)
- AppleTalk Data Stream Protocol (ADSP)
- Zone Information Protocol (ZIP)
- Printer Access Protocol (PAP)

As you know from Chapter 1, "General Network Overview," the Session layer is responsible for initiating, establishing, and managing data connections between devices.

The Presentation layer is composed of the *Apple Filing Protocol (AFP)*. To some extent, AFP applies to the Application layer of the OSI model, as well. It is responsible for managing network access to shared file services and file transfer, as well as seeing to it that shared network volumes appear transparently on the end-user desktop.

Addressing

As part of AppleTalk's original Plug-and-Play design goal, AppleTalk addresses are assigned dynamically without end-user intervention. A complete AppleTalk network address consists of a 16-bit network number, an 8-bit dynamically assigned node number, and an 8-bit socket number. Socket numbers are roughly analogous to TCP service ports in a TCP/IP environment. An AppleTalk address is commonly written in dotted-decimal format. For example, the AppleTalk address of 1556.200.157 refers to socket 157 on node 200, which belongs to network 1556. Occasionally you will find AppleTalk addresses expressed in hexadecimal format, especially the network portion of the address.

Key Concept

AppleTalk addresses consist of a 16-bit network number, an 8-bit node number, and an 8-bit socket number written in dotted-decimal notation:
`network.node.socket`.

Addressing Structure

The original incarnation, *AppleTalk Phase 1*, had a limit of 254 nodes on a network (nodes 0 and 255 are reserved). Phase-1 networks are also commonly referred to as nonextended networks. Node ID 0 specifies any router on the destination network. Node ID 255 is used for broadcast purposes.

In 1989, *AppleTalk Phase 2* was added to overcome this 254-node limitation, so Phase-2 networks commonly referred to as *extended networks*. Phase-2 AppleTalk added the concept of a *cable range* to the network numbering scheme. Instead of a network having a single network number (as in Phase 1), a network could now have a range of sequential network numbers behave as a single network. For each network number in a cable range, the network can have 253 nodes (0, 254, and 255 are reserved node numbers in an extended AppleTalk network). A cable range is expressed as a pair of hyphen-separated network numbers. For example, the cable range of 6053-6056 encompasses network numbers 6053, 6054, 6055, and 6056. You should note that a cable range can encompass just a single network number (6057-6057).

Valid numbers for a network number are 1 through 65279. Network number 0 is reserved for the unknown or local network. Network numbers 65280 through 65534 (hexadecimal FF00 through FFFE) are reserved for the startup process, which is described later in this chapter, or when no router is present.

A *socket* is a software entity that exists within a node for providing service to another node or for using the services published by other nodes. A socket is generally owned by a process or service, and that process or service can send only datagrams over the sockets that it owns. Socket addresses are 8-bit numbers, so a maximum of 254 sockets can exist within a node (0 and 255 are reserved). Sockets 1 through 63 are statically assigned and reserved specifically for use by other protocols within the AppleTalk stack, such as Zone Information Protocol (ZIP) and Router Table Maintenance Protocol (RTMP). Sockets 64 through 127 are statically assigned as well, but reserved for experimental use. Sockets 128 through 254 are available for dynamic assignment on an as-needed basis.

Address Assignment

In an AppleTalk internetwork, the network number is assigned to the node by the routers located on that network. When a node starts up, it selects an arbitrary network number from the startup range (network numbers 65280 through 65534) and an arbitrary node ID. It then uses this temporary network address to send a Zone Information Protocol (ZIP) GetNetInfo request to the nearest router. The router replies with the valid network number or cable range for that network. The node then selects an arbitrary node ID on that network number and sends an AppleTalk Address Resolution Protocol (AARP) probe to see whether any other node on the network is using that address. If no response is received to that probe, the node keeps the newly selected address. If another device is already using that network address, it sends a reply to the startup node, which in turn selects a new node ID and repeats the process. Many AppleTalk devices store the last-used network address in nonvolatile memory and attempt to reuse that address on next startup. If that is the case, the address-acquisition process begins with the startup node sending out the AARP probe.

Key Concept

AppleTalk addresses are chosen dynamically by each node at startup.

Zones

A *zone* is a logical grouping of network devices. Zone names are arbitrarily assigned by the network administrator, and are usually defined along geographic or organizational boundaries. Zones were implemented to enable end users to locate network services more easily. A single node can belong only to one zone, and all the services published by that node appear native to the zone in which that node resides. Due to their arbitrary nature, a single zone can span one or more networks or cable ranges, and multiple zones can exist on a single network or cable range. The available zone or zones for a given network is assigned by the routers on that network via Zone Information Protocol (ZIP) as described later in the chapter.

Key Concept

A zone is a logical, arbitrary grouping of nodes created to simplify the process of locating network services.

Services

The AppleTalk protocol stack includes a variety of services or protocols that work together. Each protocol provides a distinct function within the AppleTalk stack.

DDP

The Datagram Delivery Protocol (DDP) resides at the Network layer and is responsible for several functions within the AppleTalk stack. DDP's primary function is the sending and receiving of packets. In a node's startup process, DDP is responsible for acquiring the node's protocol address in conjunction with AARP. After the address-acquisition phase is complete, DDP is responsible for socket-to-socket connectivity between two nodes. DDP works on a best-effort basis and contains no error correction or mechanism, much the same as Internet Protocol (IP). Error correction and retransmission are handled by higher-level protocols. The routing of packets to other networks is also handled by DDP.

Key Concept

DDP provides an uncorrected, best-effort method for end-to-end, socket-to-socket connectivity.

A datagram consists of a DDP header followed by a data portion. A DDP packet can have either a long header (for extended networks) or a short header (for nonextended networks). A short header includes only the 8-bit node and 8-bit socket addresses of the source and destination sockets. A long header also includes the network numbers of the source and destination socket addresses. It begins with two bits set to 0 to indicate the start of the datagram. The two 0s are followed by a 4-bit hop count and a 10-bit datagram length specifier. A 2-byte optional DDP checksum follows the length specifier. The destination network number, source network number, destination node number, source node number, destination socket number, and the source socket number follow the optional DDP checksum. Finally, an 8-bit DDP type specifier is placed immediately before the data portion of the datagram. The data portion of a datagram can be no longer than 586 bytes.

AARP

The AppleTalk Address Resolution Protocol (AARP) sits in the Network layer of the OSI model and serves three main functions:

- Protocol-to-hardware address mapping
- Filtering incoming packets
- Assigning protocol addresses

For outbound packets, AARP maps AppleTalk protocol addresses (such as 3003.215.129) to the hardware address of the destination machine before passing the outbound packet down to the Data Link layer. For inbound packets, AARP examines each incoming packet to see whether the destination address of the packet matches the node's address or the broadcast address. If neither condition is true, AARP discards the packet. Lastly, AARP is used during the address-assignment process to verify whether a desired node address has already been used on the network.

Key Concept

AARP maps AppleTalk network addresses to hardware addresses.

AARP maintains an Address Mapping Table (AMT) to cache known protocol-to-hardware address mappings. Entries are timed out when a specified amount of time has passed since the mapping was added to the AMT or when an AARP Probe packet is received for that address.

There are three types of AARP packets:

- AARP Requests
- AARP Responses
- AARP Probes

An AARP Request is sent out when a node seeks to discover the hardware address of another node with which it wants to communicate. AARP Requests are sent out only when the node cannot find a valid entry in the AMT that matches the destination's protocol address. It requests that any node using a specified protocol address reply with its hardware address. An AARP Response packet is a reply to either an AARP Request or an AARP probe. It contains the hardware address requested by the Request packet. An AARP Probe packet is similar to a Request packet, except that it requests to know whether any other nodes are using the tentative address chosen by the node in the startup processes. AARP Probes are used primarily in the address-acquisition process described earlier in the chapter.

AEP

The AppleTalk Echo Protocol (AEP) operates at the Transport layer and determines whether another node is accessible over the internetwork. It also determines the approximate round-trip travel time to a particular node. The Echoer process within each node resides on statically assigned socket number 4, commonly referred to as the *Echoer socket*. AEP adds a 1-byte header to the beginning of the DDP data portion of a datagram, immediately following the end of the DDP header. This header determines the Echo function of that particular datagram: 1 for AEP Request or 2 for AEP Response. Additionally, AEP packets have the DDP type field and the destination socket both set equal to 4.

ATP

The AppleTalk Transaction Protocol (ATP) operates at the Transport layer and is responsible for ensuring that communications from source-socket to destination-socket occur without any losses. A transaction is initiated when a socket client on one node sends a service request to the socket-client on the other node. The servicing (destination) node is expected to service that request (such as "read this disk block"), and respond to the requesting node with the results of the requested action. This interaction between the requesting node and the responding node is referred to as a *transaction*.

Each transaction is given a unique *transaction identifier (TID)* by the requestor to enable the requestor to have several simultaneous transactions open at any time. Each transaction response must refer to the requestor-assigned TID so that the requestor knows that the requested transaction has been completed. If the responder's acknowledgment is not received within a specified timeout period, the transaction is assumed to have failed, and the requestor goes into an error-recovery process that involves reinitiating the transaction.

NBP

Name Binding Protocol (NBP) also sits at the Transport layer. It provides a name-to-address mapping for network entities, allowing the end user to refer to network entities via a user-friendly name instead of a numeric network address. NBP is responsible for registering, deleting, looking up, and confirming names of *Network Visible Entities (NVE)*. NVEs are typically socket clients within a node, not the entire node. Therefore, a single node can publish several NVEs. NVE names are of the format `Object:Type@Zone`. For example, `5thfloorprinter:LaserWriter@Sales` refers to the LaserWriter print service named `5thfloorprinter` that is located in the `Sales` zone. The Object, Type, and Zone name must all be 32 characters or fewer. When doing NBP lookups, an equal sign (=) can be used as a wildcard for either the Object or Type fields, and an asterisk (*) can be used as a wildcard for the zone name. For example, `=:AFPServer@Sales` returns the names of all AFP file servers located in the `Sales` zone.

Key Concept

NBP provides name-to-address mappings. NBP names are in the format of `Object:Type@Zone`.

Unlike Domain Name Service (DNS) in the TCP/IP realm, NBP does not use a centralized name server. Each node only has information about the NVEs that it serves. If a node wants to access services on another node, it broadcasts an NBP lookup request to the Names Information Socket (NIS; statically assigned socket 2). If the NBP process on the receiving node has an NVE that matches the lookup request, a reply containing the name and network address pair (a names tuple) is sent back to the requestor. If there is no match, the lookup is ignored.

ZIP

Zone Information Protocol (ZIP) operates at the Session layer. It is responsible for providing the mapping of networks to zone names throughout the internetwork. ZIP also assists nodes in the startup process by providing a list of available zone names on the startup node's network. Each router on the network maintains a Zone Information Table (ZIT) that contains a single entry for each network on the internetwork, coupled with the zones that are available on that network. The ZIT's maintenance is closely tied to RTMP. When a router learns of a new network number, it adds an entry for that network to the ZIT. The ZIP process then sends a ZIP query to neighboring routers, requesting the names of any zones that are valid on that network. Any routers that have that information will send a ZIP reply to the requestor listing the valid zones on that network.

ASP

The AppleTalk Session Protocol (ASP) is responsible for setting up and tearing down logical connections between workstations and servers. Each connection, or session, is given a unique session identifier. After this connection is established, the workstation client is free to send a sequence of commands to the server, and the server sends back the responses to those commands. However, the server cannot send commands to the workstation within that same session: ASP sessions are asymmetrical in that sense.

ADSP

The Apple Data Stream Protocol (ADSP) is a Session-layer protocol. It is responsible for the reliable transmission of data after the session is established between two nodes. It provides a reliable full-duplex byte stream between the logically connected nodes. Within this data stream, bytes are delivered in the order in which they were sent. Flow control is used to regulate the rate at which data flows over the connection.

PAP

The Printer Access Protocol (PAP) is another Session-layer protocol and is used for setting up and tearing down logical connections between workstations and servers (usually print servers). PAP is a client of ATP in that it uses a series of transactions over this logical connection to complete the requested job. PAP also uses NBP for name resolution. Although originally designed for use in print clients and print servers, PAP is not limited to use only for printing.

Before a PAP session can be started, the PAP server must open a Session Listening Socket (SLS) and register its socket address using NBP. This is done via an SLInit call and allows the service being provided by the PAP server to be visible to other nodes on the network. A PAP session is initiated by a workstation node's PAP client process issuing a PAPOpen call to the PAP server. After this connection is established, either PAP client (workstation or server) can read or write from the other PAP client via PAPRead and PAPWrite calls. While the connection is open, data is transferred using ATP. After data transfer is complete, either the workstation or the server can close the connection using a PAPClose call.

AFP

Apple Filing Protocol (AFP) is the facility by which files and directories are shared over a network. It sits straddling the Presentation and Application layers. AFP consists of a filesystem structure, a series of AFP system calls, and a number of algorithms associated with those system calls. These system calls handle such features as user-authentication, file and directory access, and file and directory manipulation. The bulk of AFP is beyond the scope of what you will need to take the CCIE exam. However, you will need to know that AFP is a Presentation-layer protocol that relies on the sessions established by ASP to transfer data requests.

AppleTalk Routing

AppleTalk routing occurs in the Network layer of the OSI model, as you would expect. The actual routing of packets is handled within the Datagram Delivery Protocol (DDP). Prior to sending an outbound packet down to the Data Link layer, DDP examines the source and destination network addresses. If the destination is found to be on the local network, DDP encapsulates the data in a DDP header and sends it directly to the destination. If the destination is found to be on another network, DDP encapsulates the data in a DDP header and sends it to a router attached to the local network. Unlike TCP/IP networks, AppleTalk does not have the concept of a default route or a default router.

Routing decisions are made within the router by examining a routing table. An AppleTalk routing table consists of a network number, the distance (in hops) to that network, the router port through which it would need to send that packet, the network address of the next router on the path (if any), and the state of that entry in the routing table (good, bad, or suspect). A routing table can have only one entry for each network number or cable range. If a router receives a route with a shorter distance, the route with the longer distance is discarded. If a new route has a longer distance than the route that already exists in the routing table, the new route is ignored. If a router receives two routes with the same distance, the one that is received last (the newest route) is the one that is kept.

Unlike many other protocols, AppleTalk does not require that every router on a network be configured with the appropriate zone names and cable ranges for that network. AppleTalk only requires that a single router on each network be configured with this information. This router is referred to as the *seed router*. The other routers on the network learn the information that they need from the seed router. Other routers on the network *can* be configured with the cable range and zone information, but all routers on the network must agree with one another with regard to cable range and zone name for a given network.

 Key Concept

A seed router provides cable-range and zone information to unconfigured routers on the network.

RTMP

The Routing Table Maintenance Protocol (RTMP) is the process through which routers on an AppleTalk internetwork exchange information about their routing tables. RTMP is similar to RIP in the IP realm in that both routing protocols use hops as the metric by which routing decisions are made. The maximum hop count allowed on an AppleTalk internetwork is 15 hops. If the destination is more than 15 hops away, it is deemed unreachable. A distance, or hop count, equal to 0 indicates a network to which the router is directly connected.

RTMP is a distance-vector routing protocol. Each router on the network constructs its own routing table based on the information that it receives from its neighboring routers. Each router communicates only with its immediate neighbors. It relies on its neighbors to give correct information about the networks located beyond each neighbor. RTMP updates are sent and received on statically assigned socket 1, which is commonly referred to as the RTMP socket. Periodically (usually every 10 seconds), each router broadcasts its known routes out each of its ports that are configured for AppleTalk. However, the entire routing table is not broadcast out each port. To reduce traffic associated with these broadcasts, RTMP uses the Split Horizon technique discussed in Chapter 9, "Routing Concept Overview." Using Split Horizon techniques, a router will not send routing data back out the port through which it was received.

Key Concept

RTMP is a split-horizon, distance-vector routing protocol.

Routing updates include the cable range of a network and distance to the network. This information is commonly referred to as a routing *tuple*. On receiving a routing tuple for an unknown network, a router constructs an entry in its routing table for that cable range. It combines the received cable range and distance (adding one hop to the distance) with the port on which the RTMP update was received and the address of the router from which the RTMP update was received, and then sets the entry state to good.

AURP

AppleTalk Update-Based Routing Protocol (AURP) is an extension of RTMP that allows the connection of noncontiguous AppleTalk networks via tunneling. This tunneling is accomplished by encapsulating the AppleTalk packets in UDP headers. After they're encapsulated in UDP headers, these AppleTalk packets can traverse a TCP/IP network transparently. AURP is similar to RTMP in that it is based on distance-vector and split-horizon principles, and it shares a maximum hop count of 15. After an AURP network has stabilized, AURP reduces bandwidth further by only sending updates when a change in link state or distance occurs.

Key Concept

AURP allows the tunneling of AppleTalk packets over TCP/IP networks.

The tunneling of AppleTalk via TCP/IP and AURP is accomplished by installing exterior routers to perform the encapsulation and unencapsulation of packets. These exterior routers also convert RTMP updates into AURP updates (when necessary) and send them over the TCP/IP backbone. You should note that a tunnel is a logical connection between two routers, not a physical connection. A logical tunnel can encompass many physical nodes or hops, but each tunnel counts only as a single RTMP or AURP hop.

AppleTalk EIGRP

Cisco routers are capable of using EIGRP, as discussed in Chapter 11, "IGRP and EIGRP," to distribute AppleTalk routes. EIGRP and RTMP routes are automatically redistributed between each other. Please refer to that chapter for an explanation of how EIGRP works. The commands used to configure EIGRP are listed in the following "Configuration Commands" section.

Configuration Commands

The following is a list of commands that are useful when configuring AppleTalk routing on Cisco routers. The entries listed in parentheses are the modes that the router must be in when entering that command.

```
RTR (config)# appletalk routing
RTR (config)# appletalk routing eigrp router-number
RTR (config)# appletalk eigrp-timers hello-interval hold-time
RTR (config-if)# appletalk address address
(used for nonextended networks)
RTR (config-if)# appletalk cable-range cable-range[network.node]
        (used for extended networks)
RTR (config-if)# appletalk zone zonename
RTR (config-if)# appletalk protocol eigrp
RTR (config-if)# appletalk discovery
RTR> ping appletalk-node-address
RTR# show appletalk interface interface-name
RTR# show appletalk route
RTR# show appletalk globals
RTR# debug appletalk routing
```

Summary

AppleTalk is a proprietary protocol developed by Apple Computers, Inc. for use in connecting Apple computers over a network. AppleTalk can ride over a variety of media types. Packets in an AppleTalk network are transported between sockets on nodes using DDP. The reliability of that transport is handled by higher-level protocols such as ATP.

AppleTalk entities are denoted using numeric, dynamically assigned AppleTalk addresses. These addresses take the form `network.node.socket`. To make AppleTalk more user-friendly, these numeric addresses are mapped to named entities using NBP. These named entities are then grouped into logical zones via ZIP.

The actual routing of packets is handled in DDP. Routing decisions are made via routing tables constructed by each router. Routing tables are computed from RTMP updates received by neighboring routers. RTMP is a split-horizon, distance-vector routing protocol. AppleTalk packets can be tunneled through TCP/IP networks using AURP.

QUESTIONS AND ANSWERS

1. What is the difference between an extended and a nonextended AppleTalk network?

   A: A nonextended network can have up to 254 nodes, whereas an extended network can have more than 254 nodes.

2. What is the structure of an AppleTalk Address?

   A: A 16-bit network number, an 8-bit node number, and an 8-bit socket number, written as `network.node.socket`

3. What is a zone?

   A: A zone is a logical grouping of nodes.

4. What are the three types of AARP packets?

   A: Request, Response, and Probe

5. How does PAP differ from ASP?

   A: PAP allows the workstation and server to issue commands to each other, whereas ASP allows only the workstation to issue commands to the server.

6. What type of routing protocol is RTMP?

   A: RTMP is a split-horizon, distance-vector routing protocol.

7. What is a seed router?

   A: A seed router is a router configured with the cable range and zone information for a network. Other routers on the network receive this information from the seed router.

PRACTICE TEST

1. Which of the following terms describe RTMP?

   A. Link-state

   B. Distance-vector

   C. Split-horizon

   D. Poison-reverse

   E. Broadcast-based

   F. Periodic

   G. Update-based

PART
V
CH
16

Answers A and G are incorrect because RTMP does not send out link status updates. **Answers B, C, E, and F are correct because RTMP is described as a distance-vector, split-horizon protocol. An RTMP router shares its routing tables with its neighbors via periodic broadcasts.** Answer D is incorrect because RTMP does not use a poison-reverse methodology to prevent routing loops.

2. Which of the following AppleTalk addresses would be valid for a socket on an active node residing on an extended AppleTalk network?

   A. 10003.254.9

   B. 65493.101.25

   C. 65278.207.1

   D. 1.1.0

   E. 1.1.1

   F. 10.100.256

Answer A is incorrect because the node number 254 is invalid on an extended network; however, it would be valid on a nonextended network. Answer B is incorrect because the network number is valid only during the address-acquisition process, so it would not be valid on an active node. **Answers C and E are correct because they consist of a 16-bit network number, an 8-bit host number, and an 8-bit socket number, and their network numbers are not in the startup range reserved for the address-acquisition process.** Answers D and F are both incorrect because the socket ID is not in the range of 1 through 254.

3. Which of the following commands would you execute to assign a node ID of 22 to an interface of a Cisco router residing on extended network number 26?

   A. `appletalk address 26.22`

   B. `appletalk cable-range 26-26 26.22`

   C. `appletalk address 22.26`

   D. `appletalk network 26 node 22`

   E. `appletalk route 26 ethernet 0`

Answer A would be correct if this were a nonextended network, but the question specifies an extended network. **Answer B is correct because the AppleTalk cable-range command is used for extended networks.** Answer C is incorrect because it specifies a nonextended network, and the node ID and network number are swapped. Answers D and E are both nonsense answers.

4. Which of the following shows the correct order in which protocols in the AppleTalk stack are encountered when traveling from the Application layer to the Physical layer of the OSI model?
   A. ATP, ASP, DDP, ELAP, PAP
   B. PAP, ASP, ATP, DDP, ELAP
   C. ELAP, PAP, ATP, ASP, DDP
   D. DDP, ASP, PAP, ELAP, ATP

Answer B is correct because PAP and ASP are Session-layer protocols (layer 5). ATP resides in the Transport layer (layer 4). DDP resides in the Network layer (layer 3). ELAP resides in the Data Link layer (layer 2).

5. Which of the following would be valid NBP lookup queries?
   A. `*:*@Engineering`
   B. `=:AFPServer@Sales`
   C. `bob:=@*`
   D. `printer_at_the_end_of_the_hall:LaserWriter@HumanResources`
   E. `really_really_really_really_big_file_server:AFPServer@Marketing`

Answer A is incorrect because the wildcard for object name and type is an equal sign (=), not an asterisk (*). **Answers B, C, and D are correct; answer B returns the name of all AFP servers in the Sales zone; answer C returns any type of device named bob located in any zone; answer D is valid because the object name is still fewer than 32 characters.** Answer E is incorrect because the object name is greater than 32 characters.

6. What would happen within a nonrouter node if that node receives a nonbroadcast AppleTalk packet destined for another node on the network?
   A. DDP would discard the packet.
   B. AARP would discard the packet.
   C. AARP would resolve the hardware address of source node.
   D. RTMP would pass the packet to the nearest router on the network.
   E. DDP would pass the packet on to its correct destination.

Answer A is incorrect because AARP, not DDP, is responsible for filtering incoming packets based on hardware address. **Answer B is correct because AARP is responsible for filtering incoming packets based on hardware addresses, not DDP.** Answer C is incorrect because AARP would pay no attention to the source address of an incoming packet;

it would examine only if the destination hardware address matched the node's hardware address. Answers D and E are incorrect because this is a nonrouter node.

7. Which of the following does *not* occur during the AppleTalk address-acquisition process?

   A. The node chooses an arbitrary network number from the startup range.
   B. The node chooses an arbitrary node ID.
   C. The node sends a ZIP `GetNetInfo` request to the nearest router.
   D. The router informs the node of the correct cable range for the node's network.
   E. The router assigns the node a new node ID from the correct cable range.
   F. The node performs an AARP probe to see whether any other devices are using the same address.

Answer E is correct because after the router informs the node of the correct cable range, the node chooses its own node ID on that cable range. Answers A, B, C, D, and F are incorrect because they all occur during the address-acquisition process.

8. How often are RTMP update packets typically sent out?

   A. Every 5 seconds
   B. Every 10 seconds
   C. Every 30 seconds
   D. Only when the network topology changes
   E. None of the above

Answers A and C are incorrect because RTMP update packets are sent out every 10 seconds. **Answer B is correct; RTMP update packets are sent out every 10 seconds.** Answer D is incorrect because RTMP is not a link-state routing protocol.

9. How many routers, or hops, can an AppleTalk packet pass through before its destination is considered unreachable?

   A. 5
   B. 10
   C. 15
   D. 20
   E. There is no limit.

Answers A and B are incorrect because a packet can pass through 15 hops. **Answer C is correct; destinations more than 15 hops away are considered unreachable.** Answers D and E are incorrect because if the destination is more than 15 hops away, the packet can be encapsulated in UDP headers via an AURP tunnel to reduce the logical hop count.

PART

V

CH

16

10. Which of the following statements are *not* true?

   A. ADSP provides a full-duplex byte stream between two logically connected nodes.

   B. ATP is responsible for establishing a logical connection between a workstation and a node.

   C. DDP relies on ATP to detect and correct the loss of datagrams.

   D. AEP packets can be used to ping other devices on the network.

   E. PAP is used primarily for sharing files between workstations and servers.

Answer A is incorrect because the statement is true. **Answer B is not true because ASP, not ATP, is responsible for establishing logical connections (sessions) between a workstation and a server.** Answers C and D are incorrect because the statements are true. **Answer E is not true because AFP, not PAP, is primarily used for sharing files between workstations and servers. PAP is used primarily to handle communications between print clients and print servers.**

Other LAN Protocols

WHILE YOU READ

1. What is the most current version of DECnet?

2. How many layers does DNA Phase IV have?

3. Which version of DNA supports TCP/IP?

4. How many nodes can a DECnet network support?

5. How many levels of routers are there in a DECnet network?

6. True or False? NetBIOS is routable.

SEE
APPENDIX **F**

DECnet

In 1975 *Digital Equipment Corporation (DEC)* introduced DECnet, a protocol used for communication of LAN devices. The first release of DECnet was used for communications between two directly attached PDP-11 minicomputers. Since that time DEC has released several more versions with a great deal more functionality. The most recent and widely used versions are DECnet Phase IV and DECnet/OSI, the latter being the more recent. Both are backward compatible with the preceding versions.

Key Concept

There are currently two versions of DECnet: DECnet Phase IV and DECnet/OSI.

DECnet Phase IV is based on Phase IV *Digital Network Architecture (DNA)*. DECnet/OSI is based on DECnet/OSI DNA. Both versions support proprietary and standard protocols but DECnet/OSI also supports subsets of the OSI protocols.

DNA is a multilayered network architecture similar to the OSI reference model. DNA Phase IV has eight layers:

- User—With the network-management layer, corresponds to the OSI Application layer
- Network management—With the user layer, corresponds to the OSI Application layer
- Network application—Corresponds to the OSI Presentation layer
- Session control—Corresponds to the OSI Session layer
- End communications—Corresponds to the OSI Transport layer
- Routing—Corresponds to the OSI Network layer
- Data Link—Corresponds to the OSI Data Link layer
- Physical—Corresponds to the OSI Physical layer

DECnet/OSI DNA differs from DNA Phase IV in that it implements three protocol suites: OSI, DECnet, and TCP/IP. The implementation of TCP/IP allows transmission of DECnet traffic over TCP transport protocols.

Key Concept

Phase IV DNA architecture is similar to the OSI model; the main difference is an eighth layer.

DECnet/OSI DNA supports three protocol suites: OSI, DECnet, and TCP/IP.

Addressing

A DECnet Phase IV address is 16 bits long. The addressing scheme used by DECnet Phase IV incorporates area/node address pairs. An area can be numbered from 1 through 63 (using 6 bits) and nodes can be addressed from 1 through 1,023 (using 10 bits). Therefore, a total of 64,449 (63×1,023) nodes is possible for each DECnet network.

The Media Access Control (MAC) layer address of the DECnet node is not used in DECnet. Instead, the network address is converted to form a MAC-layer address. DECnet uses an algorithm to convert the area/node pair at the network level into the MAC layer address. First, the area number is multiplied by 1,024. Then, the node number is added to this product. The result is a 16-bit value. The resulting value is then converted to hexadecimal, byte-swapped, and appended to DECnet's standard MAC prefix of AA00.0400.

For example, the DECnet area/node pair 3.58 would be converted like this:

3 (area number) × 1024 =	3072	
Add the node number	+ 58	
Result	3130	
Convert to binary	0011000000111010	
Convert to hex*	30	3A
Byte swap	3A	30
Add to standard prefix	AA00.0040.3A30	

*Each hex character represents 4 bits, in order:

0011 = 3

0000 = 0

0011 = 3

1010 = A

The resulting MAC layer address for 3.58 would be AA00.0400.3A30.

For more information about converting to hex, see Chapter 2, "General Topic Overview."

Routing

Routing in DECnet Phase IV is implemented by the *DECnet Routing Protocol (DRP)*, which is part of the DNA routing layer. In addition to DRP, DECnet/OSI uses standard OSI routing protocols, such as ISO 8473, ISO 9542, and ISO 10589.

Routing decisions in DECnet Phase IV are based on a *cost metric*. The network administrator assigns arbitrary *costs* to each path in the network. Hop counts or link bandwidths are frequently used for costs.

In a DECnet network there are two types of routers: level 1 and level 2. Level-1 routers exchange only packets with end nodes and other level-1 routers within the same area. Level-1 routers ignore level-2 packets. A level-1 router is known as an *intra-area router*. Conversely, level-2 routers exchange packets with routers in other areas; they are known as *interarea routers*.

Key Concept

There are two levels of routers in a DECnet network: level 1 (intra-area) and level 2 (interarea).

Cisco routers support DECnet Phase IV local-area and wide-area routing over Token-Ring, Ethernet, FDDI, and serial lines. Cisco routers and DECnet routers are interoperable and DECnet hosts cannot tell the difference between the two.

The following list outlines Cisco's support of DECnet:

- Cisco routers use HDLC framing for point-to-point lines.
- Point-to-point lines must have the same type of equipment on each end of the line—that is, either Cisco equipment or Digital equipment.
- Cisco routers support Address Translation Gateway (ATG).
- Cisco routers support DECnet Phase IV-to-Phase V conversion.
- Cisco routers and DECnet Phase IV routers have incompatible X.25 support.

Key Concept

Cisco routers and DECnet routers are interoperable.

Configuration

A host in a DECnet network is a node in an area. An area can contain many routers and the interface on a router can be connected to many areas. A router with multiple interfaces in an area uses a single node/area address. See Figure 17.1.

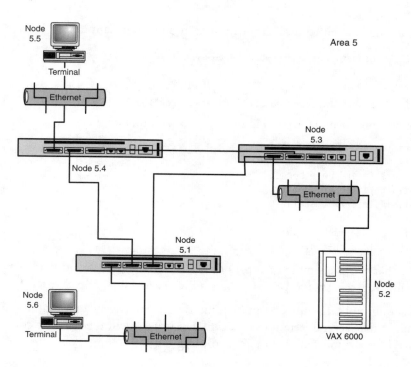

Figure 17.1
Notice that all interfaces on a router use the same DECnet address.

Use the following three steps to enable DECnet routing on a Cisco router:

1. Enable DECnet Phase IV routing or enable DECnet Phase IV Prime routing.
2. Add a cost to each interface.
3. Name the node type.

The following is a simple DECnet configuration.

To enable DECnet Phase IV or DECnet Phase IV Prime routing,

```
RTR (config)# decnet [network-number] routing decnet-address
```
or

```
RTR (config)# decnet [network-number] routing iv-prime  decnet-address
```
To assign a cost to an interface,

```
RTR (config-if)# decnet cost cost-value
```

PART

V

CH

17

Designate the node as either an interarea router or an intra-area router,

```
RTR (config)# decnet [network-number] node-type area
```

or

```
RTR (config)# decnet [network-number] node-type routing-iv
```

The configuration for node 5.1 in Figure 17.1 would look like this:

```
RTR (config)# decnet routing 5.1
RTR (config)# decnet node-type area
RTR (config)# interface ethernet o
RTR (config-if)# decnet cost 5
RTR (config)# interface serial 0
RTR (config-if)# decnet cost 5
RTR (config)# interface serial 1
RTR (config-if)# decnet cost 4
```

Please note that this is a simple example of DECnet configuration and that many more options exist. But, this should be more than sufficient for the CCIE Written Exam.

Also, you should note that the cost in each interface is effectively altering the routing table. It might take several iterations of a DECnet infrastructure before the costs are set appropriately for the most efficient packet routing.

NetBIOS

IBM created the *Network Basic Input/Output System (NetBIOS)* to allow applications on computers to communicate over a LAN using a generic set of Application Programming Interfaces (APIs). Since then it has become a de facto standard.

NetBIOS has two modes of operation. They differ primarily in how they deal with error detection and recovery:

- Session mode allows sessions to be established between computers and also provides error detection and recovery.
- Datagram mode leaves error detection and recovery up to the applications.

Key Concept

NetBIOS operates in either session mode or datagram mode; session mode provides error detection and recovery.

NetBIOS can run over most LAN media including Ethernet and Token-Ring. If NetBIOS is to be transported across networks, it must be bridged. It cannot be routed because it does not provide a standard frame or data format for transmission, even though it provides the session and transport services described in the Open Systems Interconnection (OSI) model. A standard frame format is provided in the *NetBIOS Extended User Interface (NetBEUI)*.

Other than transparent bridging (or source route bridging for Token-Ring), Cisco routers can transport NetBIOS using Data-Link Switching (DLSw). Also, if IPX NetBIOS needs to be transported, this can be accomplished by simply enabling ipx type 20 propagation on each appropriate interface.

Key Concept

NetBIOS cannot be routed; it must be bridged. Cisco routers can transport NetBIOS using Data-Link Switching (DLSw), bridging, or route-source bridging.

PART

V

CH

17

Summary

DECnet was introduced in 1975. Currently two versions are being used: DECnet Phase IV and DECnet/OSI. Both versions support proprietary and standard protocols but DECnet/OSI also supports subsets of the OSI protocols. DNA/OSI is the basis for DECnet/OSI, and DNA Phase IV is the basis for DECnet Phase IV. The main difference between the two is that DNA/OSI allows transport of DECnet over TCP/IP.

DECnet uses a 16-bit combination of area and node for addressing. A DECnet network can have up to 64,449 nodes. This address is converted to create the MAC layer address. The manufacturer-assigned hardware (MAC) address is not used. DECnet routing uses a cost metric, which is manually assigned by a network administrator. Hop count or bandwidth is frequently used for costs.

DECnet routers are either level 1 or level 2: Level 1 is an intra-area router, whereas level 2 is an interarea router. Cisco routers and DECnet routers are interoperable to the point that DECnet nodes cannot tell the difference.

There are three steps to enable DECnet routing:

1. Enable DECnet Phase IV routing or enable DECnet Phase IV Prime routing.
2. Add a cost to each interface.
3. Name the node type.

IBM created NetBIOS to allow applications in different computers on a LAN to communicate. NetBIOS operates in either session mode or datagram mode; only session mode provides error detection and recovery. NetBIOS is not routable, but NetBEUI is. Cisco routers can transport NetBIOS through bridging, source-route bridging, or DLSw.

QUESTIONS AND ANSWERS

1. What is the most current version of DECnet?

   A: DECnet/OSI

2. How many layers does DNA Phase IV have?

   A: Eight layers

3. Which version of DNA supports TCP/IP?

   A: DECnet DNA/OSI

4. How many nodes can a DECnet network support?

   A: 64,449 nodes.

5. How many levels of routers are there in a DECnet network?

   A: Two levels

6. True or False? NetBIOS is routable.

   A: False

PRACTICE TEST

1. Which of the following is the most recent version of DECnet?
   - **A.** DECnet/OSI
   - **B.** DECnet Phase IV
   - **C.** DECnet Type II
   - **D.** DECnet DNA Phase IV

Answer A is correct because the most recent and widely used versions are DECnet Phase IV and DECnet/OSI, the latter being the more recent. Both are backward compatible with the preceding versions.

2. Which of the following choices best describes DNA?
   - **A.** The molecular basis of heredity
   - **B.** A multilayered network architecture similar to the OSI reference model
   - **C.** The addressing scheme used by DECnet
   - **D.** Digital Network Architecture

Answer A would be correct in the context of biology. **Answer B is correct because DNA is Digital's network architecture.** Answer C is incorrect. Answer D is incorrect because it is what the abbreviation *DNA* stands for.

   3. The DNA Phase IV *network application layer* corresponds to which of the following OSI layers?

   A. The Presentation layer
   B. The Network layer
   C. The Physical layer
   D. The Application layer

Answer A is correct. Answer B is incorrect because OSI's Network layer corresponds to DNA Phase IV's routing layer. Answer C is incorrect because OSI's Physical layer corresponds to DNA Phase IV's Physical layer. Answer D is incorrect because the DNA Phase IV Network management, with the user layer, corresponds to the OSI Application layer.

   4. How many nodes can a DECnet network support?

   A. 32,000
   B. 64,449
   C. 63
   D. 1,023

Answer A is incorrect because it is an arbitrary number. **Answer B is correct because a DECnet network can support 64,449 nodes. This number is derived by multiplying the number of possible areas (63) by the number of possible nodes per area (1,023).** Answer C is incorrect because 63 is the number of possible areas in a DECnet network. Answer D is incorrect because 1,023 is the number of possible nodes in a DECnet area.

   5. Which of the following choices *best* describes DRP?

   A. Data Resource Pool
   B. DECnet Routing Protocol
   C. The routing protocol implemented by DECnet Phase IV
   D. The routing protocol implemented by DECnet/OSI

Answer A is incorrect. Answer B is incorrect because it's what the abbreviation *DRP* stands for. **Answer C is correct.** Answer D is incorrect because routing in DECnet/OSI is accomplished by standard OSI routing protocols, not by the DECnet Routing Protocol.

   6. Which of the following choices *best* describes the DECnet Phase IV routing metric?

   A. Hop count
   B. Bandwidth
   C. Lowest MAC address
   D. An arbitrary number set by the network administrator

Answers A and B are incorrect because hop count and bandwidth are numbers frequently used by network administrators. Answer C is incorrect because MAC addresses are not considered metrics. **Answer D is correct because the DECnet Phase IV metric is an arbitrary number set by the network administrator.**

7. A DECnet level-2 router performs which of the following procedures?

  A. DHCP

  B. Level-2 routers exchange packets with routers in other areas.

  C. Level-2 routers exchange packets only with end nodes and other level-2 routers within the same area.

  D. None of the above

Answer A is incorrect. **Answer B is correct because level-2 routers exchange packets with routers in other areas, making them** *interarea* **routers**. Answer C is incorrect because it's *level-1 routers* that exchange packets only with end nodes and other level-1 routers within the same area, making them *intra-area* routers.

8. Which of the following describe Cisco's support of DECnet routing?

  A. Cisco routers use HDLC framing for point-to-point lines.

  B. Cisco routers and DECnet Phase IV routers have incompatible X.25 support.

  C. Point-to-point lines must have the same type of equipment on each end of the line—that is, either Cisco equipment or Digital equipment.

  D. All of the above

  E. None of the above

Answer D is correct because all three choices describe Cisco's support of DECnet routing.

9. How many steps are there to enable DECnet routing on a Cisco router?

  A. Five

  B. Three

  C. Four

  D. One

Answer B is correct; there are three steps to enable DECnet routing on a Cisco router.

10. NetBIOS operates in either one of two modes. Which modes are they?

  A. Level 1 and level 2

  B. Session and datagram

  C. Fast packet and base packet

  D. Binary and hexadecimal

Answer A is incorrect because level 1 and level 2 are types of routers, not modes. **Answer B is correct; NetBIOS operates in either session mode or datagram mode. The session mode provides error detection and recovery; the datagram mode leaves error detection and recovery to the application.** Answer C is incorrect because fast packet could be any of the packet technologies and base packet does not exist. Answer D is incorrect because binary and hexadecimal are counting systems.

11. Which of the following statements are true regarding NetBIOS?

   A. IBM created NetBIOS.

   B. NetBIOS can run over most LAN media.

   C. NetBIOS must be bridged; it cannot be routed.

   D. Cisco routers can transport NetBIOS using Data-Link Switching (DLSw).

   E. All of the above

Answer E is correct because all four statements are true.

The WAN

18 ISDN and DDR

19 X.25

20 Frame Relay

21 ATM: Asynchronous Transfer Mode

CHAPTER PREREQUISITE

You should be familiar with the OSI model discussed in Chapter 1, "General Network Overview," Access Lists, which are discussed in Chapter 2, "General Topic Overview," and route selection, which is discussed in Chapter 9, "Routing Concept Overview."

ISDN and DDR

WHILE YOU READ

1. What is ISDN?

2. What is DDR?

3. What is the difference between POTS and ISDN?

4. What is the difference between the ISDN B and D channels?

5. What is interesting traffic?

6. What protocol sets up and tears down layer-2 connections on ISDN B channels?

7. What do HDLC and LAPD have in common?

8. What is the key difference between CHAP and PAP?

9. What are the advantages of the PPP Callback feature?

10. What is LCP?

ISDN

Entire books are devoted to the subject of ISDN, so the purpose of this chapter is to summarize some of the basic concepts of ISDN and DDR as they relate to the CCIE Routing and Switching written test. It is important to remember that Cisco also offers an ISP Dial CCIE track, and although the two tests overlap concerning ISDN, the primary focus for ISP Dial is remote access, whereas the primary focus for Routing and Switching is Dial-on-Demand Routing, including dial backup. Therefore, Dial-on-Demand Routing and dial backup occupy the primary focus of this chapter.

Integrated Service Digital Network (ISDN) offers a digital connection to the *PSTN (Public Switched Telephone Network)* at much higher bandwidths than standard dialup connections using analog modems. ISDN offers two types of connection services: BRI and PRI.

- Basic Rate Interface (BRI) provides two 64Kbps B (*Bearer*) channels and one 16Kbps D (*Delta*) channel. This is called 2B+D. BRIs are used at smaller, remote sites for temporary network connections that do not require the higher bandwidth of a PRI.
- Primary Rate Interface (PRI) provides 23 B (Bearer) channels of 64Kbps each, and one 64Kbps D (Delta) channel on a traditional T-1 leased line. This is called 23B+D. A slightly larger E-1 Leased line is used in Europe, so the PRI would be 30B+D. The B channels are used to carry data, voice or video, whereas the D channel is primarily used for out-of-band call setup and teardown (signaling) of the B channel connections. This signaling takes place between the customer's equipment and the provider's switch. PRI service is typically used at large, central sites such as Internet service providers (ISPs).

This chapter focuses on BRI.

Key Concept

ISDN BRI is called 2B+D. ISDN PRI is called 23B+D.

ISDN Function Groups and Reference Points

ISDN service is physically organized into several function groups separated by reference points, as shown in Figure 18.1.

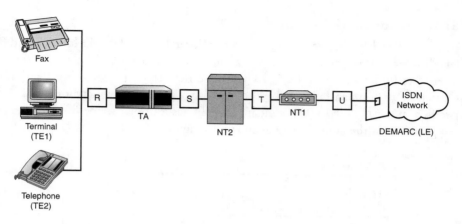

Figure 18.1
ISDN function groups.

The function groups are divided as follows:

- TE1 (Terminal Equipment 1)—A digital telephone or a router with an ISDN interface (BRI port).
- TE2 (Terminal Equipment 2)—An analog telephone or a router with a normal serial interface (V.35, and so on). These devices require a Terminal Adapter (TA).
- TA (Terminal Adapter)—A device for converting a non-ISDN signal to ISDN.
- NT1 (Network Termination 1)—A modem and a 2-wire to 4-wire converter.
- NT2 (Network Termination 2)—A device that manages switching between multiple ISDN channels, usually part of a private branch exchange (PBX).
- LE (Local Exchange)—The ISDN service provider's equipment.

ISDN Reference Points are broken out as follows:

- U (User)—Between the NT1 and LE.
- T (Terminal)—Between the NT2 and the NT1 (if applicable).
- S (System)—Between the TE1 or TA and the NT2.
- R (Rate)—Between the TE2 and the TA.

It is important to note that because the NT2 is often not applicable, S and T are often referred to together as the *S/T reference point.*

The U reference point is the DEMARC (the boundary between the customer's network and the Local Exchange Carrier; LEC). In the U.S., NT1 equipment is provided by the customer. The S or T reference point is the DEMARC in Europe, so NT1 equipment is provided by the LEC.

ISDN Protocols (HDLC and LAPD)

Although B and D channels share a common layer 1, they differ in layers 2 and 3. The default layer 2 protocol for ISDN B channels is the same Cisco implementation of High-Level Data Link Control (HDLC). This is also the default for serial links, although PPP is much more popular. Layer 2 for D channels is Link Access Procedure D (LAPD), as specified in the ITU-T Q.921 standard. LAPD has a similar frame format as HDLC, differing mainly in the address field as shown in Figure 18.2.

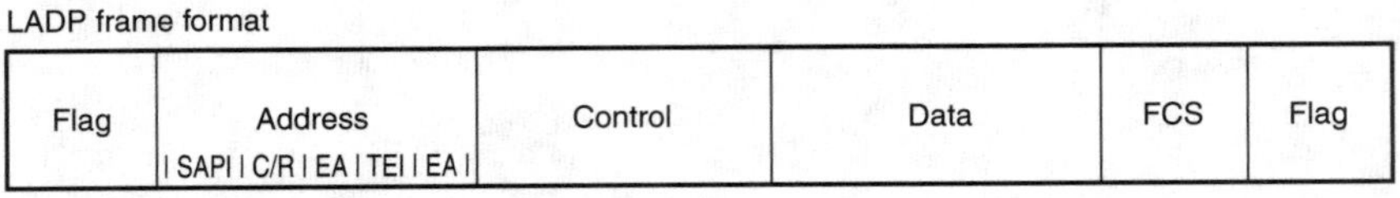

LADP frame format

Flag	Address	Control	Data	FCS	Flag
	I SAPI I C/R I EA I TEI I EA I				

Figure 18.2
LAPD frame format.

Field lengths in bits:

Flag	8
Address	16
Control	8
Data	Varies
Frame Control Sequence	8
Flag	8

Address subfields length in bits:

SAPI—Service Access Point Identifier	6
C/R—Command and Response	1
EA—Extended Addressing	1
TEI—Terminal Endpoint Identifier	7
EA—Extended Addressing	1

Key Concept

To carry data, ISDN B channels use HDLC or PPP for layer 2 and IP, IPX, AppleTalk, DECnet, and so on for layer 3.

ISDN D channel uses Q.921 for layer 2 and Q.931 for layer 3 to set up, maintain, and tear down connections between the ISDN device (TE) and the local ISDN switch (LE).

Q.921 is used on the D channel to set up, maintain, and terminate the layer-2 link between the S/T reference point (BRI interface) and the LE (Local ISDN switch). Q.931 provides the same function for layer 3. The status of these links can be checked with the show isdn status or the debug isdn q921 and debug isdn q931 commands. Cisco tests usually include several questions about what information is available using these commands. It is important to remember that show isdn status will give layer 1, 2, and 3 states. Layers 1 and 2 should normally be up, whereas layer 3 will be up only when there is an active network connection to another router. debug isdn q921 is used to check the layer-2 connection to the ISDN switch, and debug isdn q931 is used to check layer-3 connections to another router. The following are some examples of these commands on a Cisco 2503 connected to an NI-1 (National ISDN-1) switch.

Here, OSI layers 1 and 2 (Physical and Data Link layers) are up and there is no active call:

```
Router1#show isdn status
The current ISDN Switchtype = basic-ni1
ISDN BRI0 interface
    Layer 1 Status:
        ACTIVE
    Layer 2 Status:
        TEI = 71, State = MULTIPLE_FRAME_ESTABLISHED
        TEI = 72, State = MULTIPLE_FRAME_ESTABLISHED
    Spid Status:
        TEI 71, ces = 1, state = 5(init)
            spid1 configured, no LDN, spid1 sent, spid1 valid
            Endpoint ID Info: epsf = 0, usid = 1, tid = 1
        TEI 72, ces = 2, state = 5(init)
            spid2 configured, no LDN, spid2 sent, spid2 valid
            Endpoint ID Info: epsf = 0, usid = 3, tid = 1
    Layer 3 Status:
        0 Active Layer 3 Call(s)
    Activated dsl 0 CCBs = 1
        CCB:callid=0, callref=0, sapi=0, ces=1, B-chan=0
    Number of active calls = 0
    Number of available B-channels = 2
    Total Allocated ISDN CCBs = 1

Here is an uput with an active call (Layer 1, 2 and 3 up):
Router1#show isdn status
The current ISDN Switchtype = basic-ni1
ISDN BRI0 interface
    Layer 1 Status:
        ACTIVE
```

```
Layer 2 Status:
    TEI = 75, State = MULTIPLE_FRAME_ESTABLISHED
    TEI = 76, State = MULTIPLE_FRAME_ESTABLISHED
Spid Status:
    TEI 75, ces = 1, state = 5(init)
        spid1 configured, no LDN, spid1 sent, spid1 valid
        Endpoint ID Info: epsf = 0, usid = 1, tid = 1
    TEI 76, ces = 2, state = 5(init)
        spid2 configured, no LDN, spid2 sent, spid2 valid
        Endpoint ID Info: epsf = 0, usid = 3, tid = 1
Layer 3 Status:
    1 Active Layer 3 Call(s)
Activated dsl 0 CCBs = 1
    CCB:callid=800A, callref=0, sapi=0, ces=1, B-chan=1
Number of active calls = 1
Number of available B-channels = 1
Total Allocated ISDN CCBs = 1
```

Note that the Layer 1 Status: "ACTIVE" and Layer 2 Status: "MULTIPLE_FRAME_ ESTABLISHED" would be missing if the ISDN switch were down or the BRI were disconnected.

Here is a typical q921 debug trace where the BRI is connected to a switch, with no layer-3 connection:

```
RTR#debug isdn q921
ISDN Q921 packets debugging is on
ISDN BR0: TX -> RRp sapi = 0  tei = 76 nr = 1
ISDN BR0: RX <- RRf sapi = 0  tei = 76  nr = 1
ISDN BR0: TX -> RRp sapi = 0  tei = 75 nr = 23
ISDN BR0: RX <- RRf sapi = 0  tei = 75  nr = 26
ISDN BR0: TX -> RRp sapi = 0  tei = 76 nr = 1
ISDN BR0: RX <- RRf sapi = 0  tei = 76  nr = 1
ISDN BR0: TX -> RRp sapi = 0  tei = 75 nr = 23
ISDN BR0: RX <- RRf sapi = 0  tei = 75  nr = 26
```

Here is a typical q921 debug trace where the BRI is connected to a switch, with a layer-3 connection:

```
ISDN BR0: TX -> RRp sapi = 0  tei = 76 nr = 1
ISDN BR0: RX <- RRf sapi = 0  tei = 76  nr = 1
ISDN BR0: RX <- INFOc sapi = 0  tei = 75  ns = 26  nr = 29  i = 0x08018975
ISDN BR0: TX -> RRr sapi = 0  tei = 75  nr = 27
ISDN BR0: TX -> INFOc sapi = 0  tei = 75  ns = 29  nr = 27  i = 0x0801097D
ISDN BR0: RX <- RRr sapi = 0  tei = 75  nr = 30
ISDN BR0: TX -> RRp sapi = 0  tei = 76 nr = 1
ISDN BR0: RX <- RRf sapi = 0  tei = 76  nr = 1
```

Here is a q931 debug trace of a ping request causing a DDR connection to Router 2 (note the use of the dialer string 5551211). Because ISDN works so fast, the ping results are returned before the debug trace and the interface change of state are displayed.

```
Router1#debug isdn q931
ISDN Q931 packets debugging is on
Router1#ping 10.1.1.2
Sending 5, 100-byte ICMP Echos to 10.1.1.2, timeout is 2 seconds:
!!!!!
Success rate is 100 percent (5/5), round-trip min/avg/max = 32/156/644 ms
Router1#
ISDN BR0: TX ->  SETUP pd = 8  callref = 0x0A
        Bearer Capability i = 0x8890
        Channel ID i = 0x83
        Keypad Facility i = '5551211'
ISDN BR0: RX <-  CALL_PROC pd = 8  callref = 0x8A
        Channel ID i = 0x89
        Locking Shift to Codeset 5
        Codeset 5 IE 0x2A  i = 0x809402, '`=', 0x8307, '5551211',
        ➥0x8E0B, ' TERMINAL2 '
ISDN BR0: RX <-  CONNECT pd = 8  callref = 0x8A
%LINK-3-UPDOWN: Interfa ce BRI0:1, changed state to up
ISDN BR0: TX ->  CONNECT_ACK pd = 8  callref = 0x0A
%LINEPROTO-5-UPDOWN: Line protocol on Interface BRI0:1, changed state to up
%ISDN-6-CONNECT: Interface BRI0:1 is now connected to 5551211 Router2
```

Although not widely used, the ISDN D channel can be configured to transport X.25 data traffic.

PPP

Although the default layer 2 encapsulation for ISDN B channels is HDLC, Point-to-Point Protocol (PPP) is usually the preferred encapsulation because of the useful features available. PPP is implemented with the following command:

```
RTR(config-if)# encapsulation ppp
```

PPP Features

PPP is a versatile protocol. It has many features that make it ideal for use over leased or toll-based telephone company connections. The following list shows the more-common PPP features and in some cases, the Cisco commands that enable them:

- Multiprotocol support—PPP can be used with all Cisco IOS supported network protocols (IP, IPX, AppleTalk, and so on).
- PAP or CHAP Authentication—Call authentication using Password Authentication Protocol (PAP) or the more popular Challenge Authentication

Protocol (CHAP) prevents unauthorized hosts or routers from connecting to the network. CHAP is more secure and therefore more popular because it does not send the authentication password as clear text (which could be "sniffed") as does PAP. As described in RFC 1994, CHAP uses a two-way challenge-response dialogue to authenticate a call. For example, Router 1 calls Router 2, and Router 2 answers and issues a "challenge" to Router 1 containing a username and a hashed version of a password (not the password itself). If Router 1 has a match for this username and password, it issues a response containing its username and a hashed password. Router 2 will also have to have a match for this username/password; if it does, the connection is allowed. This dialogue can be monitored with the debug ppp authentication command. Authentication is enabled with the commands ppp authentication chap or ppp authentication pap.

- PPP Multilink—This protocol, described in RFC 1717, allows two or more different physical links to bond and act like one logical link. This is particularly important in ISDN where several B channels might be needed to provide the necessary bandwidth to link two networks. Multilink ensures that bandwidth across multiple paths will be properly reassembled at the remote end. Related Cisco command: ppp multilink.

- Link Quality Monitoring (LQM)—PPP can be configured to monitor a link for a minimum quality and close the link if the quality drops below the configured minimum (expressed as a percentage of 100). Related Cisco command: ppp quality 70.

- Automatic Detection of Encapsulation Type—PPP can also be configured to dynamically change an interface's encapsulation to match the calling router's encapsulation. The command is autodetect encapsulation ppp.

- Compression of PPP Data—Assuming that the majority of the traffic is not already compressed (it only helps once), PPP can be configured to compress the PPP frames using the Stacker (LZS), Predictor, or MPPC compression algorithms. Because this feature is CPU intensive, Cisco does not recommend its use if CPU utilization exceeds 65%. Related Cisco command: compress stac.

- IP Address Pooling—In a situation in which a remote PPP interface must be able to dynamically obtain its IP address through DHCP, TACACS, or a locally administered pool, PPP has individual commands to implement those solutions. Related Cisco commands: ip address-pool, dhcp-proxy-client, and ip address-pool local.

- PPP Callback—This feature creates a client/server relationship between the router placing a call (the callback client) and the router receiving it (the callback server). After the client is authenticated, the server will disconnect and call the client back.

Configuring the Callback feature will be covered at the end of the following section.

■ PPP Reliable Link—This feature is available on ISDN and synchronous links, but not asynchronous links. Basically, reliable link uses Numbered Mode LAPB provided for the retransmission of "errored" packets, as described in RFC 1663. This feature does not work with PPP Multilink. The command is `ppp reliable-link`.

■ Virtual Private Dial-up Networks (VPDNs)—This feature can be used on PPP dial-up networks only. VPDNs use *Level 2 Forwarding (L2F)* protocol tunneling to separate and protect private traffic traveling across public domains (such as the Internet), or other less-trusted private domains. With this feature, remote users access a private corporate network using an Internet dialup, saving the company the expense of a maintaining a dial-up network. The following partial configurations list relevant VPDN commands allowing a remote Router 1 a secure connection to Router 2 via an Internet cloud:

```
Router 1:
  hostname Router1
  !
  !
  username Router2 password cisco
  username george@internet_cloud.com password cisco2
  vpdn enable
  vpdn incoming Router2 Router1 virtual-template 1
  !
  !
  interface Ethernet0
   ip address 10.3.1.2 255.255.255.0
  !
  interface Virtual-Template1
   ip unnumbered Ethernet0
   ppp authentication chap

Router 2:
  hostname Router2
  !
  username Router1 password cisco1
  vpdn enable
  vpdn outgoing internet_cloud.com Router2 ip 10.3.1.2
  !
```

PPP Frame Format

Figure 18.3 shows the format of a PPP frame. Note the difference between PPP and the previously mentioned LAPD.

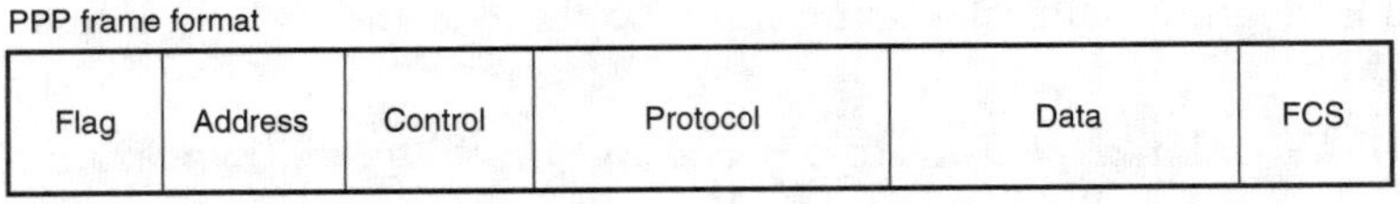

PPP frame format

Flag	Address	Control	Protocol	Data	FCS

Figure 18.3
PPP frame format.

PPP frame field lengths in bits are

Flag	8
Address	8
Control	8
Protocol	16
Data	Varies
Frame Control Sequence	16 or 32

PPP Protocols

Link Control Layer Protocol (LCP) is a layer-2 protocol responsible for building, maintaining, and tearing down a PPP connection. As described in RFC 1661, LCP goes through the following phases:

- Link Dead (Physical layer not ready)—The beginning and end of any connection.
- Link Establishment Phase—A series of configuration requests and acknowledgments are made.
- Authentication Phase (optional)—CHAP or PAP requests and responses might be exchanged.
- Network Layer Protocol Phase—The layer-3 protocols using protocol specific NCPs.
- Link Termination Phase—LCP exchanges a termination request/response when it ends a connection. Reasons a connection might be ended would be that there is no more interesting traffic and the idle-timeout has expired, authentication has failed, or there is a loss of carrier.

Network Control Protocol (NCP) actually describes a group of protocols for establishing specific layer-3 connections. Examples of NCPs include IPCP (IP Control Protocol) as described in RFC 1332, IPXCP (IPX Control Protocol), and ATCP (AppleTalk Control Protocol).

ISDN and DDR

Dial-on-Demand Routing (DDR) is used for temporary connections between routers where there is not enough traffic to justify the expense of a leased line. A DDR connection is merely a temporary Point-to-Point serial connection. DDR can be implemented over Plain Old Telephone Service (POTS) lines, using standard analog modems, but the maximum bandwidth is 56Kbps and is often quite a bit less. So, ISDN is generally used. The general configuration tasks, along with the majority of the commands are the same for both asynchronous and synchronous (ISDN) DDR. Figure 18.4 shows a basic DDR network. Networks 10.1.3.0 and 10.1.4.0 are connected to each other via an ISDN cloud between Router 1 and Router 2.

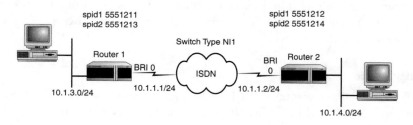

Figure 18.4
A basic ISDN network.

Two important configuration steps are unique to ISDN:

1. The first specifies the switch type. In North America, there are three main types: 5ESS (AT&T), DMS-100 (Northern Telecom), and NI-1 (National ISDN-1). Starting in IOS release 12.0, the switch type can be assigned per interface so multiple providers can be used. The global command for configuring a router with a BRI interface for an NI-1 switch would be

```
RTR(config)# isdn switch-type basic-ni1
```

2. The second step, configuring the Service Profile Identifiers (SPIDs), might not be required depending on the switch type. SPIDs are similar to phone numbers except they usually have four extra digits (1s or 0s) at the end. They are used by the TE1/TA (router) to connect to the ISDN switch. But when dialing an ISDN line, just the phone number is used (without the extra 1s or 0s). So, to call a router with a SPID of 61255512110101, you would dial 612-555-1211. SPIDs are used only between the TE1/TA and the ISDN switch. SPID numbers must be

configured on DMS-100 and National ISDN-1 switches, but not on the 5ESS. Examples of configuring SPIDs:

```
RTR(config-if)# isdn spid1 61255512110101
RTR(config-if)# isdn spid2 61255512130101
```

Two other important steps are involved in making a DDR connection:

1. First, specify what type of traffic is "interesting." Traffic defined as interesting is traffic that will initiate a DDR connection.

2. Second, specify what techniques will be used to make the connection. A basic scenario would be Router 1 calling Router 2 using a `dialer map` command. A more complex scenario might be Router 1 calling Router 2, and Router 2 disconnecting the call and then calling Router 1 back. These features are discussed in the following sections of the chapter.

Interesting Traffic

The global command `dialer-list` is used to specify what constitutes the "interesting traffic" that will trigger a DDR call. This can be a broad category of traffic if desired, such as specifying that IP traffic be deemed "interesting traffic." Type the command

```
Router1(config)# dialer-list 1 protocol ip permit
```

To specify a more narrow category, such as using an Access List where only traffic from a single subnet can trigger a call, type

```
Router1(config)# dialer-list 1 protocol ip list 10
Router1(config)# access-list 10 permit 10.1.2.0 0.0.0.255
```

Then, the interface command `dialer-group` is used to associate a dialer interface with the `dialer-list`. The number that follows the `dialer-group` command *must* match the number in the `dialer-list` command. Only one `dialer-group` statement and the `dialer-list` it is mapped to can be used on an interface. A single `dialer-list` can service several dialer interfaces. For example,

```
Router1(config-if)# dialer-group 1
```

It is important to understand exactly what a particular `dialer-list` does and does not allow! Poorly designed filters will prevent DDR from coming up when needed or can allow DDR to stay up indefinitely. Imagine the network administrator who didn't filter RIP updates (every 60 seconds) and finds that his ISDN DDR link to Tokyo has stayed up for a week!

Key Concept

> After a DDR connection is up, both "interesting" and "uninteresting" traffic will flow. The `dialer-list` command filters what type of traffic will trigger and maintain a DDR call, not what type of traffic will cross the link after it's up. If you do not want a particular type of traffic to use the dial-up connection, you must add separate Access Lists to filter that traffic.

If interesting traffic stops reaching the dialer interface, an `idle-timeout` timer begins to count down and will disconnect the call when it reaches 0. This timer is reset when the interface receives additional interesting traffic. The default `idle-timeout` is 120 seconds. This could be set to 300 seconds with the command

```
RTR# (config-if) dialer idle-timeout 300
```

The Dialer `idle-timeout` setting and status can be viewed with the `show dialer` command.

Dialer Maps

As with X.25 and Frame Relay, DDR can use the interface command `dialer map` to associate protocol next-hop addresses to the dial string (telephone number) of the remote router. Dialer `map` statements are very flexible because they give the router the ability to connect to different remote routers depending on the traffic. A frequently used option of the `Dialer map` command is the name parameter, which can be used with PPP CHAP/PAP to transport usernames for authentication. Other command options include the ability to accept broadcast packets and set the speed to 56Kbps for providers that do not support the default 64Kbps. Following is an example of the `dialer map` command:

```
RTR(config-if)#dialer map ip 10.1.1.2 name Router2 speed 56 broadcast 5551212
```

Another method to make a remote connection is with the `dialer-string` command. A dialer interface can have either a `dialer map` statement or a `dialer-string` statement, but not both. `dialer map` statements are more flexible and scalable than dialer strings. Here is an example of the command

```
RTR(config-if)# dialer string 5551212
```

Other interface configuration requirements include a network address. Because it is common in DDR designs to have multiple routers needing to connect with one another, the obvious networking conflicts are solved by the addressing feature `ip unnumbered`, where the dialer interface assumes the IP address of another interface, usually the Loopback.

```
RTR(config-if)# ip unnumbered Loopback 0
```

For asynchronous and synchronous connection (but not ISDN BRI), it is necessary to use the `dialer in-band` command to configure the interface to do call setup and teardown, such as modem chat scripts. Remember that ISDN uses the D channel for out-of-band call setup and teardown.

```
Router1(config-if)# dialer in-band
```

ISDN Callback

This PPP feature can increase security and control costs on DDR calls between routers by creating a client/server relationship between the router placing a call (the callback client) and the router receiving it (the callback server). After the client is authenticated, the server will disconnect and call the client back. In this scenario, the server initiates the bulk of the dialup time, so billing is consolidated and can usually be discounted. Security is inherently enhanced because the server can only call preconfigured clients. Even if a hacker has a valid username and password, the server will hang up and call the real client. Following is a sample configuration with Callback-specific commands in bold.

Callback Server (Router1):

```
interface BRI0
  ip address 10.1.1.1 255.255.255.0
  encapsulation ppp
  dialer callback-secure
  dialer enable-timeout 2
  dialer map ip 10.1.1.2 name Router2 class call_back_1 5551211
  dialer-group 1
  ppp callback accept
  ppp authentication chap
!
map-class dialer call_back_1
  dialer callback-server Router1
```

Callback Client (Router2):

```
interface BRI0
  ip address 10.1.1.2 255.255.255.0
  encapsulation ppp
  dialer map ip 10.1.1.1 name Router1 5551212
  dialer-group 1
  ppp callback request
  ppp authentication chap
```

ISDN and Dial Backup

Another subcategory of DDR is Dial Backup. Dial Backup, as the name implies, is a DDR link that stays idle as long as the primary link (Frame Relay, dedicated lease-line, and so on) is up, but comes up and takes over if the primary link fails or if this link becomes overloaded. (Dial Backup is sometimes called Bandwidth-on-Demand.) The basic command is backup interface with the optional backup delay and backup load commands. Figure 18.5 illustrates a basic Dial Backup connection. The router connections to the ISDN cloud are used in addition to, not instead of, the lease line. The "lease line" can be any type of permanent connection (Frame Relay, X.25, ATM, and so on).

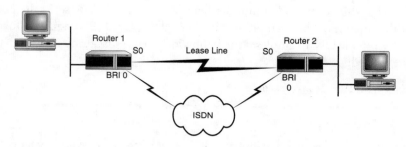

Figure 18.5
Basic Dial Backup.

In the following example, the backup interface is BRI 0, backup delay is set to bring up BRI 0 five seconds after Serial 0 goes down (or its load exceeded), and it won't disconnect BRI 0 until Serial 0 has stayed up for 15 seconds. Backup load is set to bring up BRI 0 if the traffic load on Serial 0 goes above 50% (based on a five-minute moving average) and won't bring BRI 0 down until the traffic load on Serial 0 drops to 10%:

```
RTR (config)# interface serial 0
RTR (config-if)# backup delay 5 15
RTR (config-if)# backup load 50 10
RTR (config-if)# backup interface bri 0
```

One disadvantage of using this method is that the dial-up line cannot be tested without taking the primary line down.

Another way of triggering a Dial Backup connection is by using a floating static route. A floating static route is created by adding a default route pointing toward the dialer interface and assigning it an administrative distance greater than the normal routing protocols. As long as the primary interface is up and passing routing updates, it will be the preferred path. If the primary interface fails, routing table entries referencing that interface will be dropped, and the static route will point traffic to the dialer interface:

```
RTR (config)# ip route 0.0.0.0 0.0.0.0 BRI 0 150
```

One advantage of this method is that a static host route can be added for the purposes of periodically testing the dialup line (the route is to Null0 so the packets are dropped if they can't use BRI 0):

```
RTR (config)# ip route 10.3.1.5 255.255.255.255 BRI 0
RTR (config)# ip route 10.3.1.5 255.255.255.255 Null0 100
```

Another way of implementing bandwidth-on-demand is with the `dialer load-threshold` command. Using this command, a number between 1 and 255 represents the percentage of bandwidth which must be used before another call is placed (255 equals 100%). In the example shown in "ISDN Examples," the bandwidth load must reach about 50% before another line is used:

```
RTR(config-if)#dialer load-threshold 127
```

Key Concept

It is important to know that with Cisco IOS, there are often several methods of accomplishing the same objective. It is also important to know the strengths and weaknesses of each method.

More Examples

Because knowing the `debug`, `show`, and `configuration` commands is so important, this section provides additional examples. It is important to study complete and correct configurations, so an incomplete or incorrect configuration can be easily recognized. It is also important to compare and contrast `show` and `debug` commands under different circumstances.

Example 1

Here is the minimum configuration necessary for communications between two routers (good to use for testing)—anything less and the two routers cannot communicate. Notice that PPP encapsulation is not a requirement.

Router 1:

```
version 12.0

!
hostname Router1
!
!
isdn switch-type basic-ni
!
```

```
interface BRI0
 ip address 10.1.1.1 255.255.255.0
 dialer string 555361093801
 dialer-group 1
 isdn switch-type basic-ni
 isdn spid1 55536109420101
 isdn spid2 55536109430101
!
!
dialer-list 1 protocol ip permit
```

Router 2:

```
version 12.0

!
hostname Router2
!
!
interface BRI0
 ip address 10.1.1.2 255.255.255.0
 dialer string 555361094201
 dialer-group 1
 isdn switch-type basic-ni
 isdn spid1 55536109380101
 isdn spid2 55536109390101
!
!
dialer-list 1 protocol ip permit
```

Example 2

Here is a more typical configuration using the `dialer map` command, PPP encapsulation, and CHAP authentication. Router 1 must have a username of Router 2 and vice versa; the username passwords must also match on both routers for authentication to be successful.

Router 1:

```
hostname Router1
!
username Router2 password 0 cisco
!

!
isdn switch-type basic-ni
!
```

```
interface BRI0
  ip address 10.1.1.1 255.255.255.0

  encapsulation ppp
  dialer map ip 10.1.1.2 name Router2 55536109380
  dialer-group 1
  isdn switch-type basic-ni
  isdn spid1 55536109420101
  isdn spid2 55536109430101
  ppp authentication chap

dialer-list 1 protocol ip permit
```

Router 2:

```
hostname Router2
!
username Router1 password 0 cisco
!
isdn switch-type basic-ni
!
interface BRI0
  ip address 10.1.1.2 255.255.255.0

  encapsulation ppp
  dialer map ip 10.1.1.1 name Router1 555361094201
  dialer-group 1
  isdn switch-type basic-ni
  isdn spid1 55536109380101
  isdn spid2 55536109390101
  ppp authentication chap
!
dialer-list 1 protocol ip permit
```

Example 3

Here is a debug ppp authentication trace of a successful CHAP authentication:

```
Router1#debug ppp authentication      (ppp authentication debugging is turned on)
PPP authentication debugging is on
Router1#ping 10.1.1.2              (generates interesting
                                  ➥traffic to initiate session)

Type escape sequence to abort.
Sending 5 100-byte ICMP Echoes to 10.1.1.2, timeout is 2 seconds:
1d11h: %LINK-3-UPDOWN: Interface BRI0:1, changed state to up
1d11h: %ISDN-6-CONNECT: Interface BRI0:1 is now connected to 555361093801 .!!!!
Success rate is 80 percent (4/5), round-trip min/avg/max = 44/60/108 ms
```

```
Router1#
1d11h: BR0:1 PPP: Treating connection as a callout
1d11h: BR0:1 PPP: Phase is AUTHENTICATING, by both
1d11h: BR0:1 CHAP: O CHALLENGE id 2 len 28 from "Router1"
1d11h: BR0:1 CHAP: I CHALLENGE id 2 len 28 from "Router2"
1d11h: BR0:1 CHAP: O RESPONSE id 2 len 28 from "Router1"
1d11h: BR0:1 CHAP: I SUCCESS id 2 len 4
1d11h: BR0:1 CHAP: I RESPONSE id 2 len 28 from "Router2"
1d11h: BR0:1 CHAP: O SUCCESS id 2 len 4
1d11h: %LINEPROTO-5-UPDOWN: Line protocol on Interface BRI0:1,
➥changed state to up
1d11h: %ISDN-6-CONNECT: Interface BRI0:1 is now connected to
➥555361093801 Router2
Router1#
```

Example 4

Here is a debug ppp authentication trace of an unsuccessful CHAP authentication (the password is incorrect). Notice how this trace differs from the previous one:

```
Router1#debug ppp authentication
PPP authentication debugging is on
Router1#ping 10.1.1.2

Type escape sequence to abort.
Sending 5, 100-byte ICMP Echoes to 10.1.1.2, timeout is 2 seconds:

1d11h: %LINK-3-UPDOWN: Interface BRI0:1, changed state to up
1d11h: %ISDN-6-CONNECT: Interface BRI0:1 is now connected to 555361093801
1d11h: BR0:1 PPP: Treating connection as a callout
1d11h: BR0:1 PPP: Phase is AUTHENTICATING, by both
1d11h: BR0:1 CHAP: O CHALLENGE id 3 len 28 from "Router1"
1d11h: BR0:1 CHAP: I CHALLENGE id 3 len 28 from "Router2"
1d11h: BR0:1 CHAP: O RESPONSE id 3 len 28 from "Router1"
1d11h: BR0:1 CHAP: I FAILURE id 3 len 25 msg is "MD/DES compare failed".
1d11h: %LINK-3-UPDOWN: Interface BRI0:1, changed state to down
```

Example 5

Here is a show dialer command output on an idle ISDN line, note the Dialer state is idle statements:

```
Router1#show dialer
BRI0 - dialer type = ISDN
Dial String      Successes    Failures    Last DNIS   Last status
713361093801             2           0     00:12:58       successful   Default
0 incoming call(s) have been screened.
0 incoming call(s) rejected for callback.
```

```
BRI0:1 - dialer type = ISDN
Idle timer (120 secs), Fast idle timer (20 secs)
Wait for carrier (30 secs), Re-enable (15 secs)
Dialer state is idle

BRI0:2 - dialer type = ISDN
Idle timer (120 secs), Fast idle timer (20 secs)
Wait for carrier (30 secs), Re-enable (15 secs)
Dialer state is idle
Router1#
```

Example 6

Here is another show dialer command output, this time with BRI channel 1 in use. Notice the differences compared to the previous example:

```
Router1#show dialer

BRI0 - dialer type = ISDN

Dial String      Successes  Failures  Last DNIS  Last status
713361093801             5         0   00:00:15  successful   Default
0 incoming call(s) have been screened.
0 incoming call(s) rejected for callback.

BRI0:1 - dialer type = ISDN
Idle timer (120 secs), Fast idle timer (20 secs)
Wait for carrier (30 secs), Re-enable (15 secs)
Dialer state is data link layer up
Dial reason: ip (s=10.1.1.1, d=10.1.1.2)
Time until disconnect 116 secs
Current call connected 00:00:16
Connected to 555361093801

BRI0:2 - dialer type = ISDN
Idle timer (120 secs), Fast idle timer (20 secs)
Wait for carrier (30 secs), Re-enable (15 secs)
Dialer state is idle
Router1#
```

Example 7

Here is a trace of a ping triggering Router 1 to make a call with debug dialer on. Note how the trace records each step the router goes through to make a connection:

```
Router1#debug dialer
Router1#ping 10.1.1.2
```

```
Type escape sequence to abort.
Sending 5, 100-byte ICMP Echos to 10.1.1.2, timeout is 2 seconds:

1d10h: BRI0 DDR: Dialing cause ip (s=10.1.1.1, d=10.1.1.2)
1d10h: BRI0 DDR: Attempting to dial 555361093801
1d10h: %LINK-3-UPDOWN: Interface BRI0:1, changed state to up
1d10h: %ISDN-6-CONNECT: Interface BRI0:1 is now connected to 555361093801 .!!!!
Success rate is 80 percent (4/5), round-trip min/avg/max = 44/51/68 ms
Router1#
1d10h: isdn_call_connect: Calling lineaction of BRI0:1
1d10h: BR0:1 DDR: Dialer protocol up
1d10h: BRI0:1 DDR: dialer protocol up
1d10h: BRI0: dialer_ckt_swt_client_connect: incoming circuit switched call
1d10h: %LINEPROTO-5-UPDOWN: Line protocol on Interface
➥BRI0:1, changed state to up
1d10h: %ISDN-6-CONNECT: Interface BRI0:1 is now connected to 555361093801
Router1#
```

Summary

The goal in Dial-on-Demand Routing is for two routers to create a connection between two networks only when needed. This connection can be used to handle occasional traffic, as a Dial Backup to a lease line, or to provide extra Bandwidth-on-Demand. Several implementation and configuration choices in DDR affect the usefulness of the network. ISDN BRI service is a popular choice for DDR because it has greater bandwidth. Not only does BRI service provide two 64Kbps B channels for data, but call setup and teardown are done out of band on the 16Kbps D channel. PPP is the encapsulation of choice for DDR because it has many useful features such as CHAP authentication, Compression, and Callback.

The most important concept in DDR is "interesting traffic." The `dialer-list`, `dialer group`, and `access-list` commands are used together to determine what traffic is "interesting" and therefore allowed to trigger a DDR call to a remote network. It is also important to remember that `dialer-list` only determines what traffic can trigger or maintain a DDR connection. After a DDR link is up, any traffic that is compatible with the dialer interface protocols will go across the link, unless filtered by a separate Access List. It is also important to remember that with Cisco IOS, there are often several different ways to do something (dialer map versus dial string) and the trick is to know which one is best under what circumstances.

PART
VI

CH
18

QUESTIONS AND ANSWERS

1. What is ISDN?

   A: Integrated Service Digital Network (ISDN) offers a digital connection to the Public Switched Telephone Network (PSTN) at much higher bandwidths than standard dialup connections using analog modems.

2. What is DDR?

   A: Dial-on-Demand Routing (DDR) is used for temporary connections between routers where there is not enough traffic to justify the expense of a lease line.

3. What is the difference between POTS and ISDN?

   A: POTS (Plain Old Telephone Service) is an analog service with a smaller bandwidth capability (56Kbps or less), whereas ISDN is a digital service commonly offering two 64Kbps channels.

4. What is the difference between the ISDN B and D channels?

   A: The B channels are used to carry data, voice, or video, whereas the D channel is primarily used for out-of-band call setup and teardown (signaling) of the B channel connections between the customer's equipment and the provider's switch.

5. What is interesting traffic?

   A: Traffic which causes the router to make a DDR connection.

6. What protocol sets up and tears down layer-2 connections on ISDN B channels?

   A: Q.921

7. What do HDLC and LAPD have in common?

   A: They are the default layer-2 protocols for ISDN. HDLC works on the B channel, whereas LAPD works on the D channel.

8. What is the key difference between CHAP and PAP?

   A: CHAP is a more-secure authentication protocol than PAP because it does not send the password as clear text.

9. What are the advantages of the PPP Callback feature?

   A: It can help control dial-up costs (by centralizing them) and increase security (by limiting who gets a connection).

10. What is LCP?

    A: Link Control Layer Protocol (LCP) is a layer-2 protocol responsible for building, maintaining, and tearing down a PPP connection.

PRACTICE TEST

1. Which of the following characteristics are associated with BRIs?
   - **A.** 16Kbps D channel
   - **B.** 64Kbps D channel
   - **C.** Two 64Kbps B channels
   - **D.** 23 64Kbps B channels

Answers A and C are correct because BRI service consists of two 64Kbps B channels and one 16Kbps D channel. Answers B and C are incorrect because 23 64Kbps B channels and one 64Kbps D channel refer to PRI service.

2. Which two compression methods are used on Cisco routers?
   - **A.** `enable lzs`
   - **B.** `predictor`
   - **C.** `stacker`
   - **D.** `compress`

Answers B and C are correct because `predictor` and `stacker` are valid compression methods. Answers A and D are incorrect because they are made-up answers.

3. What is the purpose of the L2F protocol in virtual private dial-up networks?
   - **A.** User authentication
   - **B.** Network authentication
   - **C.** Tunneling link level protocols across untrusted networks
   - **D.** Establishing multiple virtual paths to a remote destination

Answers A and B are incorrect because, although user and network authentication are used in VPDN, they have nothing to do with the specifics of L2F. **Answer C is correct because L2F is a protocol that is used for tunneling across untrusted networks.** Answer D is also incorrect. Again, although the statement "Establishing multiple virtual paths to a remote destination" applies to VPDN, it has nothing to do with L2F.

4. You are configuring dial backup on BRI 0 for a primary link. Which command do you use to indicate the backup?
   - **A.** `backup ip bri 0`
   - **B.** `backup dial bri 0`
   - **C.** `backup interface bri 0`
   - **D.** `backup dial interface bri 0`

Answer C is correct because the command is `backup interface interfacename`. Answers A, B, and D are incorrect because they are made-up answers.

5. What is the key advantage of CHAP over PAP?

   A. CHAP does not send a visible password

   B. CHAP authentication takes fewer steps

   C. CHAP has a lower overhead

   D. If authentication fails, CHAP retries

Answer A is correct because PAP sends a plain-text password that can be seen on a sniffer. Answers B, C, and D are incorrect because CHAP actually takes more steps, has more overhead, and does not retry.

6. Which ISDN encapsulation is preferred because it has low overhead, available compression, multiple protocol support, and good security options?

   A. PPP

   B. HDLC

   C. LAPD

   D. LCP

Answer A is correct because its large set of useful features makes PPP unique. Answers B and C are incorrect because HDLC and LAPD do not support compression and security options. Answer D is incorrect because it is not an encapsulation type; instead, it is the layer-2 protocol in PPP.

7. What command associates access-list 101 with a dialer-group 1?

   A. `dialer-list 101`

   B. `dialer-group list 101`

   C. `dialer-list 1 protocol ip list 101`

   D. `dialer-group protocol 1 list 101`

   E. `access-list 101 dialer-group 1`

Answer C is correct because remembering what things go in what order is very important. Answers A, B, D, and E are incorrect because they are made-up answers.

8. Why would the statement `deny rip any any` save money when used as part of access-list 101 and linked to the `dialer-list` for the DDR interface?

   A. All routing updates will initiate a call.

   B. No routing updates will initiate a call.

   C. All traffic except RIP will initiate a call.

   D. No traffic will initiate a call.

Answers A, B, and D are incorrect because `deny rip any any` targets RIP updates for filtering only, not anything else. **Answer C is correct because RIP updates are sent every 30 seconds, so if they are not filtered, the line will stay up indefinitely.**

9. Which of the following are ISDN reference points?

    A. User reference

    B. Router reference

    C. Terminal reference

    D. Telco reference

Answers A and C are correct because User and Terminal are both ISDN reference points. Answers B and D are incorrect because they are made-up answers.

10. Which of the following characteristics are associated with PRIs?

    A. 16kbps D channel

    B. 64kbps D channel

    C. Two 64Kbps B channels

    D. 23 64Kbps B channels

Answers B and D are correct because PRI service consists of 23 64Kbps B channels and one 64Kbps D channel. Answers A and C are incorrect because BRI service consists of two 64Kbps B channels and one 16Kbps D channel.

PART
VI

CH
18

CHAPTER PREREQUISITE

You should read and fully understand all the concepts included in Chapter 1, "General Network Overview." Also, you should be well versed in the ISDN concepts of Chapter 18, "ISDN and DDR," especially how to configure ISDN calling and the HDLC and LAPD protocols.

CHAPTER

19

X.25

— WHILE YOU READ —

1. What layers of the OSI model does X.25 packet switching operate?

2. What are X.121 addresses used for?

3. What is the basic function of X.25 routing?

4. What are the three types of LAPB frames?

5. Which LAPB frame provides "error detection and recovery"?

6. What three flow-control methods are used to handle network congestion?

7. Which CCITT recommendations does X.25 support for their Physical-layer signaling?

8. What two types of encapsulation methods are used in an X.25 mapping configuration?

9. What are the two types of X.25 virtual circuits?

10. What two types of translation methods are used in an X.25 protocol translation configuration?

SEE
APPENDIX **F**

This chapter reviews a few of the basics related to X.25 packet switching and discusses different features and technologies that are used to enhance an X.25 packet-switched network design. In general, all the features discussed will help in the configuration and troubleshooting of an X.25 packet-switched network.

Packet-switching technology was first developed by Paul Baran and his research team for the RAND Corporation in the early 1960s and published in 1964 as a secure method of transmitting military voice communications. The next step in packet-switching history was taken when the *Advanced Research Projects Agency (ARPA)* of the United States Department of Defense (DoD), implemented packet switching to handle computer communications requirements, thus forming the basis of the *ARPAnet.* Soon after ARPAnet, many commercial companies also developed packet-based networks.

X.25 packet switching evolved from the growing demand to connect highly distributed computer sites, assure interoperability among diverse vendor products, and maximize the sharing of network resources. X.25 is often viewed as virtually identical with packet switching. The goal of X.25 packet switching is to provide a limited set of interface conventions to a data communications packet network. X.25 packet switching has simplified the task of joining dissimilar vendor products with each other and with packet networks.

The X.25 standard is an *International Telecommunication Union—Telecommunication Standardization Sector (ITU-T)* protocol standard for WAN communications that defines how connections between user devices and network devices are established and maintained. X.25 packet switching is a packet transmission protocol, which defines the procedures for exchanging data between DTE and DCE devices (not end-to-end). In 1976, the X.25 standard was recommended as the desired protocol by the *International Consultative Committee for Telegraphy and Telephony (CCITT)*, called the *International Telecommunication Union (ITU)* since 1993. As a result, X.25 packet switching is truly a global standard.

Features

X.25 packet switching is designed to operate effectively regardless of the type of computer systems connected to the network. X.25 handles bursty, terminal-to-host data traffic, over noisy analog telephone network facilities. X.25 packet switching provides a connection-oriented technology for transmission over highly error-prone facilities.

Error checking is performed at each node, which can slow overall throughput and renders X.25 incapable of handling real-time voice and video.

The X.25 packet-switching technology was designed to become a worldwide public data network (PDN), similar to the global telephone system for voice, but it never came to be. X.25 has been used primarily outside the U.S. for low-speed applications (up to 56Kbps) such as credit card verifications, automatic teller machines (ATMs), and other financial transactions. With the arrival of fiber-optic technology, and with the emergence of new bandwidth-hungry applications such as imaging and multimedia, applications will require a tremendous amount of bandwidth, which makes transmission over X.25 packet-switching networks impractical. As a result, newer and faster technologies will assume X.25's place as the most widely used data communications transport method.

X.25 and the OSI Model

X.25 packet switching comes with three levels, as shown in Figure 19.1. The X.25 layers are based on the first three layers of the *Open Systems Interconnect (OSI)* model. The X.25 standard defines the following three layers, which are used to interface DTEs with DCEs:

- Physical layer: level 1—Describes the interface with the physical environment. It is similar to the Physical layer in the OSI model.

- Data Link Control layer: level 2—Responsible for the reliable communication between the DTE and the DCE. It is similar to the Data Link layer in the OSI model.

- Packet-Switched Network layer: level 3—Describes the data-transfer protocol in the packet switched network. It is similar to the Network layer in the OSI model.

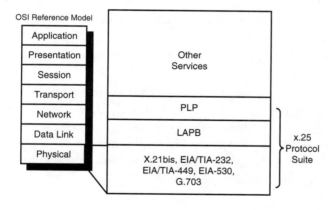

PART
VI

CH
19

Figure 19.1
X.25 and the OSI Reference Model.

Key Concept

The X.25 protocol suite maps to the lowest three layers of the OSI reference model: the Network, Data Link, and Physical layers.

Addressing

The ITU-T X.121 standard defines the design, characteristics, and application of the Numbering Plan for *Public Data Networks (PDNs)*. The International Numbering Plan allows for the identification of a country as well as a specific public data network in that country by means of Data Country Codes and *Data Network Identification Codes (DNIC)*.

X.25 uses the X.121 protocol for addressing of destinations. The X.25 call-setup procedure identifies both the calling (source) and the called (destination) X.121 addresses. When an interface is the source of a call, it encodes the interface X.121 address as the source address. An interface determines that it is the destination of a received call if the destination address matches the interface's address. A null X.121 address (the X.121 address that has zero digits) is a special case. In this case, the router acts as the destination host for any call it receives that has the null destination address.

The X.25 Packet-Layer Protocol (PLP) uses an X.121 address in call-setup mode to establish switched virtual circuits (SVCs). The X.121 Address field includes the *International Data Number (IDN)*, which consists of two fields: the Data Network Identification Code (DNIC) and the National Terminal Number (NTN). The *National Terminal Number (NTN)* identifies the exact DTE device in the PSN for which a packet is destined. This field varies in length.

The DNIC has two subfields:

- Country—The Country subfield specifies the country in which the destination *Packet-Switched Network (PSN)* is located.
- PSN—The PSN field specifies the exact PSN in which the destination DTE device is located.

A router can be configured to just participate in X.25 switching but cannot originate or terminate calls. However, if the router is attached to a public data network (PDN), you must use the interface X.121 address assigned by the X.25 network service provider. When you are connecting to a PDN, the PDN administrator will assign the X.121 address to be used. X.25 interfaces that engage in X.25 switching only (not call origination or termination) do not need to assign an X.121 address.

Key Concept

Within the X.25 protocol suite, the X.121 protocol covers the international numbering plan for public data networks (PDNs). The network portion of the address specifies three or four decimal digits as the Data Network Identification Code (DNIC). This DNIC includes a Data Country Code (DCC). An example is 310 for the United States, followed by the network number 6 for TYMNET—one of the major PDNs. The node address portion is called the NTN. X.25 users usually obtain these NTNs from an authority within the X.25 data network service provider.

To enable and address an X.25 interface, use the following commands:

```
RTR (config)# interface serial number
RTR (config-if)# encapsulation x25 [dte | dce] [ddn | bfe] | [ietf]
RTR (config-if)# x25 address x121-address
```

X.25 Routing

X.25 packet switching can also route (place and accept) X.25 calls, but the router is neither the source nor the destination for these calls. Routing X.25 does not modify the source or destination addresses, thus preserving the addresses specified by the source host. Routed (switched) X.25 simply connects two logical X.25 channels to complete an X.25 virtual circuit. An X.25 virtual circuit, then, is a connection between two hosts (the source host and the destination host) that is switched between routed X.25 links.

The X.25 routing implementation allows virtual circuits to be routed from one X.25 interface to another and from one router to another. The routing behavior can be controlled with switching and *X.25-over-TCP (XOT)* configuration commands, based on a locally built table.

Encapsulation

X.25 encapsulation can share an X.25 serial interface with the X.25 switching support. Switching or forwarding of X.25 virtual circuits can be done two ways:

- Incoming calls received from a local serial interface running X.25 can be forwarded to another local serial interface running X.25. This is known as *local X.25 switching* because the router handles the complete path. It does not matter whether the interfaces are configured as DTE or DCE devices, because the software takes the appropriate actions.

- An incoming call can also be forwarded using the *XOT* service (previously *remote switching* or *tunneling*). On receipt of an incoming X.25 call, a TCP connection is established to the destination XOT host (for example, another Cisco router) that will, in turn, handle the call using its own criteria. All X.25 packets are sent and received over the reliable TCP data stream. Flow control is maintained end-to-end. It does not matter whether the interface is configured for DTE or DCE, because the software takes the appropriate actions.

Key Concept

X.25 virtual circuits can be switched or forwarded two ways: local X.25 switching and XOT service.

X.25 Over TCP/IP (XOT)

Running *X.25 Over TCP/IP (XOT)* provides a number of benefits:

- Other routers can switch the datagram containing the X.25 packet by using their high-speed switching abilities.

- X.25 connections can be sent over networks running only the TCP/IP protocols.

- X.25 data can now be forwarded over almost any medium to another router.

When a connection is made locally, the switching configuration is used. When a connection is across a LAN, the XOT configuration is used. Also, *Connection-Mode Network Service (CMNS)* provides a mechanism through which X.25 services can be extended to nonserial media through the use of packet-level X.25 over frame-level LLC2.

The basic function is the same for both types of connections, but different configuration commands are required for each type of connection. The X.25 switching subsystem supports the following facilities and parameters:

- D-bit negotiation (data packets with the D-bit set are passed through transparently)

- Variable-length interrupt data (if not operating as a DDN or BFE interface)

- Flow-control parameter negotiation:

Window size up to 7, or 127 for modulo 128 operation

Packet size up to 4096 (default is 128 bytes, if the LAPB layers used are capable of handling the requested size)

- Basic closed user group selection

- Throughput class negotiation

- Reverse charging and fast select

Key Concept

The X.25 routing command enables X.25 switching between the X.25 services (X.25, CMNS, and XOT). X.25 calls will not be forwarded until this command is issued. Normally, calls received over a TCP connection (remote routing reception) will have the window sizes and maximum packet sizes indicated, because proper operation of routed X.25 requires that these values match at both ends of the connection.

Route Tables

An X.25 route table permits you to control which destination is selected for several applications. When an X.25 service receives a call that must be forwarded, the X.25 route table determines which X.25 service (X.25, CMNS, or XOT) and destination should be used. When a PAD call is originated by the router, either from a user request or a protocol translation event, the route table similarly determines what X.25 service and destination should be used.

You manually create the X.25 route table and add route entries to it. You can optionally specify the entry's order in the table, the criteria to match against the virtual circuit information, and whether to modify the destination or source addresses. Each entry must specify the disposition of the virtual circuit (that is, what is done with the virtual circuit). Each route can also specify XOT keepalive options.

The route table is used as follows:

- Virtual circuit information is matched against selection criteria specified for each route.
- The table is scanned sequentially from the top.
- The first matching route determines how the virtual circuit is handled.
- After a matching entry is found, the call addresses can be modified and the call is disposed of (forwarded or cleared) as instructed by the entry.

Each application can define special conditions if a route will not be used or what occurs if no route matches. For instance, switched X.25 will skip a route if the disposition interface is down and clear a call if no route matches.

PART

VI

CH

19

Key Concept

An X.25 route table determines which X.25 service (X.25, CMNS, or XOT) and destination should be used.

X.25 Routing Related Commands:

To enable X.25 routing, perform the following task in global configuration mode:

```
RTR (config)# x25 routing [tcp-use-if-defs]
```

To configure an X.25 route (thus adding the route to the X.25 routing table), perform the following task in global configuration mode:

```
RTR (config)# x25 route [#position] [selection] [modification]
    ➥disposition [xot-keepalive]
```

You can configure an X.25 PVC in the X.25 switching software. As a result, DTEs that require permanent virtual circuits (PVCs) can be connected to a router acting as an X.25 switch and have a properly functioning connection. Both interfaces must define complementary locally switched PVCs. If the connection between two PVCs is across a LAN, the XOT service is used. To configure a locally switched PVC, perform the following tasks in interface configuration mode:

```
RTR (config)# interface serial number
RTR (config-if)# x25 pvc number1 xot address interface serial
⮞string pvc number2 [option]
```

Link Access Procedure Balanced (LAPB)

X.25's packet-switching Data Link layer corresponds to the second layer of the OSI model. At this layer, *Link Access Procedure Balanced (LAPB)* is used to provide efficient and timely data transfer, synchronize the data link signals between the transmitter and receiver (flow control), perform error-checking and error-recovery, and identify and report procedural errors to higher levels of the system architecture. LAPB ensures the accurate transmission of packets delivered by the Packet-Switched Network Layer and contained in High-Level Data Link Control (HDLC) information frames between the DTE and the network. This layer also defines the unit of data transfer (see Figure 19.2). Frames consist of three major elements: a header, body, and trailer. The specific data-link protocol determines the organization and interpretation of each field.

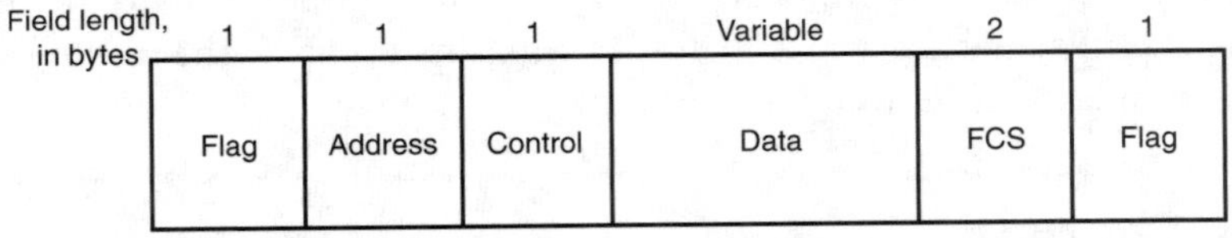

Field length, in bytes	1	1	1	Variable	2	1
	Flag	Address	Control	Data	FCS	Flag

Figure 19.2
The LAPB frame.

The general definitions of each field of the LAPB frame are as follows:

- Flag—Delimits the beginning and the end of the LAPB frame. Bit stuffing is used to ensure that the flag pattern does not occur within the body of the frame.
- Address—Indicates whether the frame carries a command or a response. This field contains the address of the DTE/DCE.
- Control—Qualifies command and response frames and indicates whether the frame is an I-frame, an S-frame, or a U-frame. In addition, this field contains the

frame's sequence number and its function (for example, whether receiver-ready or disconnect). Control frames vary in length depending on the frame type.

- Data—Contains upper-layer data in the form of an encapsulated Packet-Layer Protocol (PLP) packet.

- Frame Check Sequence (FCS)—Handles error checking and ensures the integrity of the transmitted data. Transmitted after the data bits are sent, provides error checking using the cyclic redundancy check (CRC). Frames that are received with errors are retransmitted.

Key Concept

The LAPB frame consists of three major elements: a header, body, and trailer. Within these elements, there are five LAPB frame fields: Flag, Address, Control, Data, and FCS.

Three types of LAPB frames exist: information, supervisory, and unnumbered. The general definitions of each field are as follows:

- Information Frame—The information frame (I-frame) carries upper-layer information and some control information. I-frame functions include sequencing, flow control, and error detection and recovery. I-frames carry send and receive sequence numbers.

- Supervisory Frame—The supervisory frame (S-frame) carries control information. S-frame functions include requesting and suspending transmissions, reporting on status, and acknowledging the receipt of I-frames. S-frames carry only receive sequence numbers.

- Unnumbered Frame—The unnumbered frame (U-frame) carries control information. U-frame functions include link setup and disconnection, as well as error reporting. U-frames carry no sequence numbers.

You can use only LAPB as a serial encapsulation method if you have a private serial line. You must use one of the X.25 packet-level encapsulations when attaching to an X.25 network. The LAPB standards distinguish between two types of hosts: data terminal equipment (DTE) and data circuit-terminating equipment (DCE). At level 2, or the Data Link layer in the OSI model, LAPB allows for orderly and reliable exchange of data between a DTE and a DCE. A router using LAPB encapsulation can act as a DTE or DCE device at the protocol level, which is distinct from the hardware DTE or DCE identity.

Key Concept

There are three types of LAPB frames: Information Frame, Supervisory Frame, and Unnumbered Frame.

Link Access Procedure Balanced (LAPB) Related Commands:

To set the appropriate LAPB encapsulation to run datagrams over a serial interface (one end of the link must be DTE, and the other must be DCE), perform the following tasks in global configuration mode:

```
RTR (config)# interface serial number
RTR (config-if)# encapsulation lapb [dte | dce] [multi | protocol]
```

Several protocol parameters can be modified to change LAPB protocol performance on a particular link. Because X.25 operates the Packet-Level Protocol (PLP) on top of the LAPB protocol, these tasks apply to both X.25 links and LAPB links. The following is an example of modifying an LAPB protocol parameter (LAPB T1: The retransmission timer; T1):

```
RTR (config-if)# lapb t1 milliseconds
```

Error Control/Recovery

A typical data communications network performs error detection and recovery on various levels, some of which overlap:

- X.25 specifies several error-checking levels.
- The network might provide some level of error control.
- The DTE/DCE software might contain error-control mechanisms.

X.25 provides the following guidelines for handling packet-level errors:

- Procedural errors that occur during call establishment and clearing are reported to the calling DTE with a diagnostic packet that clears the call.
- Procedural errors that occur during the data transfer phase (such as loss of synchronization) are reported to the sending DTE with a diagnostic packet that resets the sequence counters of both the DTE and DCE.
- A diagnostic field, included in the packet, provides additional information to the DTE and to the network.
- Timeouts that resolve some deadlock conditions are defined for two major areas: the length of time the DTE has to respond to an incoming call (the minimum is typically three minutes), and the amount of time the DCE has to wait for confirmation

of a reset, clear, or restart packet. To avoid looping conditions, the DCE takes an appropriate action for the indication packet and continues operation.

- Misalignments of subscription options between the DTE and the DCE can cause DTE procedural errors.

- Error tables, which define the actions to be taken by the DCE on receipt of various packet types in various stages of the interface and the state to which the DCE enters, define the diagnostic code generated for each error condition.

X.25 also identifies a number of special error cases, such as a packet received on an unassigned logical channel, that cause a diagnostic packet to be sent to the DTE rather than resetting or clearing the logical channel. A diagnostic packet includes the logical channel number on which the error occurred and a diagnostic code. There are diagnostic codes for reset, clear, and restart packets. Because the diagnostic packet is nonprocedural, it does not affect the normal meanings of call progress signals, nor is a DTE required to take action on receipt of a diagnostic packet. The DTE logs diagnostic packets for troubleshooting information.

The transmitting DTE, the receiving DTE, and the network can detect errors in transferred data packets. If an error is detected by a DTE, it informs the other DTE and requests that the affected packets be resent. If the network detects an error, it informs both DTEs by sending a reset call-progress signal. These signals include remote DTE out-of-order (permanent virtual circuit only), procedural error at the remote DTE/network boundary, network congestion, or the inability of the remote DTE to support a particular function.

Data generated before and after an error-caused reset occurs is handled in one of two ways. If a reset occurs before data reaches its destination, that data either continues to its destination or, more likely, is discarded by the network. Data generated after both local and remote ends recover from the reset continues to its destination. Data generated by a remote DTE before it receives the error indication from the local DTE either continues to its destination or, again more likely, the network discards it. In this case, the appropriate DTE resends discarded packets. The assigned resources for a given virtual circuit and the network end-to-end transmission delay and throughput characteristics determine the maximum number of packets that might be discarded.

Key Concept

X.25 packet-switching networks perform error detection and recovery at various levels. X.25 packet-switching networks are able to detect packet errors, lost packets, and duplicate packets, and can route around X.25 network failures.

PART

VI

CH

19

Flow Control/Windowing

In X.25 packet switching, the send and receive sequence numbers in the X.25 packet layer are also used to provide flow control between the packet layer DTE and DCE devices. The send sequence number is a sequential number for the current packet. Numbers are incremented modulo the maximum window size.

This means that with a modulo of 8, the sequence numbers are incremented in the order of 0, 1, 2, 3, 4, 5, 6, 7, 0, 1, 2, 3, 4, 5, 6, 7, 0, and so on. The receive sequence number in the acknowledgment indicates the next send sequence number expected in the next packet from the other end for that virtual circuit.

Therefore, the receive sequence number acts as an acknowledgment for all packets up to one less than the receive sequence number. The modulo parameter determines which of LAPB's two modes is to be used (Basic or Extended). The modulo values derive from the fact that basic mode numbers information frames between 0 and 7 (modulo 8), whereas extended mode numbers them between 0 and 127 (modulo 128). Basic mode is widely available and is sufficient for most links. Extended mode is an optional LAPB feature that can achieve greater throughput on high-speed links that have a low error rate.

Sliding Window Flow Control

The transmitter can send no more packets than the modulo minus 1 without acknowledgment; otherwise, the sender could become confused as to which packets the receiver was acknowledging. The sender transmits up to the configured modulo number and then waits for the acknowledgment before sending any additional packets. This is called a *sliding window flow control* protocol. This process allows the receiver to control the maximum rate of transmission over a virtual circuit and is therefore a form of traffic control. This is still an essential function for a slow receiver (such as a printer) to control a fast transmitter (a computer) in many data communications applications today. The receive sequence number acknowledgment can be *"piggybacked"* in the packet header for a packet headed in the opposite direction on a virtual circuit or might be sent in a separate acknowledgment packet.

Window size is directly proportional to traffic load on the logical channel, so resources should be used wisely, balancing the cost of providing more logical channels and bandwidth against maintaining performance. The default window setting is 2. While this method operates at both the data-link and network levels, it allows the network to throttle individual logical channels rather than an entire physical circuit. Some protocols, such as TCP/IP, have the intelligence to reduce the window size during network congestion and increase the window size after the congestion has been relieved.

Buffering Flow Control

Network devices use *buffering* to temporarily store bursts of excess data in memory until they can be processed. Occasional data bursts are easily handled by buffering. Excess data bursts can exhaust memory, however, forcing the device to discard any additional datagrams that arrive.

Source-Quench Messages

Receiving devices use *source-quench messages* to help prevent their buffers from overflowing. The receiving devices send source-quench messages to request that the source reduce its current rate of data transmission. First, the receiving device begins discarding received data due to overflowing buffers. Second, the receiving device begins sending source-quench messages to the transmitting device at the rate of one message for each packet dropped. The source device receives the source-quench messages and lowers the data rate until it stops receiving the messages. Finally, the source device then gradually increases the data rate as long as no further source-quench requests are received.

The control packet forms the basis of the *flow control* element of X.25. These packets operate between DTE and DCE devices and limit the rate of packet acceptance by updating the packet data's receive sequence number. This flow control is negotiated separately in each direction, in the form of opening and closing windows. Receive Ready (RR) and Receive Not Ready (RNR) play an important role in postponing or closing and opening the DTE window during problem DCE conditions. Out-of-Band interrupt packets can also be used to control transmissions.

If the window size is changed while the X.25 protocol is up, the new value takes effect only when the protocol is reset. You will be informed that the new value will not take effect immediately. When using the LAPB modulo 128 mode (extended mode), you must increase the window parameter setting to send a larger number of frames before acknowledgment is required. This increase is the basis for the router's ability to achieve greater throughput on high-speed links that have a low error rate. This configured value must match the value configured in the peer X.25 switch. Nonmatching values will cause repeated LAPB reject (REJ) frames.

Signaling

The Physical-layer protocol (level 1) signaling deals with the electrical, mechanical, procedural, and functional interfaces between the DTE and the DCE. The physical level also handles the activation and deactivation of the physical medium connecting DTE and DCE devices. The physical level is specified by the X.21, X.21-bis, and the V.24 recommendation for modems and interchange circuits.

PART

VI

CH

19

- X.21 is a CCITT recommendation for operation of digital circuits. The X.21 interface operates over eight interchange circuits (that is, signal ground, DTE common return, transmit, receive, control, indication, signal element timing, and byte timing). Their functions are defined in recommendation X.24, and their electrical characteristics in recommendation X.27. This standard is mainly implemented in Europe and Japan.

- X.21-bis is a CCITT recommendation that defines the analog interface to allow access to the digital circuit-switched network using an analog circuit. X.21-bis provides procedures for sending and receiving addressing information which enable a DTE to establish switched circuits with other DTEs that have access to the digital network. This standard is equivalent to the EIA/TIA-232 standard.

- V.24 is also a CCITT recommendation; it provides procedures that enable the DTE to operate over a leased analog circuit connecting it to a packet-switching node or concentrator.

Even though the X.25 Physical layer defines X.21 and X.21-bis as the standard, other Physical-layer serial interfaces such as EIA/TIA-449, EIA-530, G.703, and so on can be used for Physical-layer signaling.

Key Concept

The Physical layer (level 1) of X.25 uses the X.21-bis Physical-layer protocol, which is roughly equivalent to EIA/TIA-232 (formerly RS-232-C). X.21-bis was derived from ITU-T Recommendations V.24 and V.28, which identify the interchange circuits and electrical characteristics, respectively, of a DTE-to-DCE interface. X.21-bis supports point-to-point connections, speeds up to 19.2Kbps, and synchronous, full-duplex transmission over four-wire media. The maximum distance between DTE and DCE is 15 meters.

Mapping

X.25 support is most commonly configured as a transport for datagrams across an X.25 network. Datagram transport (or encapsulation) is a cooperative effort between two hosts communicating across an X.25 network. You configure datagram transport by establishing a mapping on the encapsulating interface between the far host's protocol address (for example, IP or DECnet) and its X.121 address. Because the call identifies the protocol that the virtual circuit will carry (by encoding a Protocol Identifier, or PID, in the first few bytes of the CUD field), the terminating host can accept the call if it is configured to exchange the identified traffic with the source host. X.25 mapping allows you to establish a static map between a Network-layer protocol and the X.121 address used within the X.25 network.

The X.25 single-protocol and multiprotocol encapsulation options that are available describe how to map protocol addresses to an X.121 address for a remote host. Because no defined protocol can dynamically determine LAN protocol-to-remote host mappings, you must enter all the information for each host with which the router can exchange X.25 encapsulation traffic. Two methods are available to encapsulate traffic:

- Cisco's long-available encapsulation method
- Internet Engineering Task Force's (IETF) standard method (defined in RFC 1356)

Cisco's encapsulation method is the default (for backward compatibility) unless the interface configuration command specifies IETF encapsulation. The latter allows hosts to exchange several protocols over a single virtual circuit. When you configure multiprotocol maps, you can specify a maximum of nine protocol and address pairs for X.25 mapping. However, you can specify a protocol only once. Bridging over X.25 is supported only if you are using Cisco's traditional encapsulation method. For correct operation, bridging maps must specify the broadcast option.

Because most datagram routing protocols rely on broadcasts or multicasts to send routing information to their neighbors, the broadcast keyword is needed to run such routing protocols over X.25. Encapsulation maps might also specify that traffic between the two hosts should be compressed, thus increasing the effective bandwidth between them at the expense of memory and computation time. Because each compression virtual circuit requires memory and computation resources, compression must be used with care and monitored to maintain acceptable resource usage and overall performance.

You can modify the options for an X.25 mapping configuration by restating the complete set of protocols and addresses specified for the map, followed by the desired options. To delete a map command, you must also specify the complete set of protocols and addresses; the options can be omitted when deleting a map.

After defined, a map's protocols and addresses cannot be changed. This requirement exists because the Cisco IOS software cannot determine whether you want to add to, delete from, or modify an existing map's protocol and address specification, or whether you simply mistyped the command. To change a map's protocol and address specification, you must delete it and create a new map. A given protocol-address pair cannot be used in more than one map on the same interface.

Key Concept

The X.25 map command provides a static conversion of higher-level addresses to X.25 addresses. The command correlates the network layer addresses of the peer host to the peer host's X.121 address. The protocol address and the X.121 addresses are both required in order to specify the complete network protocol-to-X.121 mapping. You can specify how multiple protocols reach a specified destination using a single virtual circuit (IETF RFC 1356: Multi-protocol encapsulations).

X.25 Mapping Related Commands:

To establish an X.25 encapsulation map, perform the following tasks in interface configuration mode:

```
RTR (config)# interface serial number
or
RTR (config)# interface serial number.subinterface-number
➥[point-to-point | multipoint]


RTR (config-if)# x25 map protocol address [protocol2 address2[
    [protocol9 address9]]] x121-address [option]
```

To establish an encapsulation PVC, perform the following task in interface configuration mode:

```
RTR (config-if)# x25 pvc circuit protocol address [protocol2 address2]
   [protocol9 address9]]] x121-address [option]
```

Switched Virtual Circuit (SVC)/Permanent Virtual Circuit (PVC)

A *virtual circuit* is a logical connection created to ensure reliable communication between two network devices. A virtual circuit denotes the existence of a logical, bidirectional path from one DTE device to another across an X.25 packet-switched network. Physically, the connection can pass through any number of intermediate nodes, such as DCE devices and packet-switching exchanges (PSEs). Multiple virtual circuits (logical connections) can be multiplexed onto a single physical circuit (a physical connection). Virtual circuits are demultiplexed at the remote end, and data is sent to the appropriate destinations.

There are two types of X.25 virtual circuits, *switched* and *permanent*:

- *Switched virtual circuits (SVCs)* are temporary connections used for sporadic data transfers. They require that two DTE devices establish, maintain, and terminate a session each time the devices need to communicate.

■ *Permanent virtual circuits (PVCs)* are permanently established connections used for frequent and consistent data transfers. PVCs do not require that sessions be established and terminated. Therefore, DTEs can begin transferring data whenever necessary, because the session is always active.

The X.25 Packet-Layer Protocol (PLP) operates in five distinct modes when managing packet exchanges between DTE devices:

■ Call Setup—Call setup mode is used to establish SVCs between DTE devices. PLP uses the X.121 addressing scheme to set up an SVC. Call setup mode is executed on a per-virtual-circuit basis.

■ Data Transfer—Data transfer mode is used for transferring data between two DTE devices across a virtual circuit. In this mode, PLP breaks up and reassembles user messages if they are too long for the maximum packet size of the circuit. Each data packet is given a sequence number, so error and flow control can occur across the DTE/DCE interface. Data transfer mode is executed on a per-virtual-circuit basis.

■ Idle—Idle mode is used when an SVC is established, but data transfer is not occurring. Idle mode is executed on a per-virtual-circuit basis.

■ Call Clearing—Call clearing mode is used to end communication sessions between DTE devices and to terminate SVCs. It is executed on a per-virtual-circuit basis.

■ Restarting—Restarting mode is used to synchronize transmission between a DTE device and a locally connected DCE device. This mode is not executed on a per-virtual-circuit basis. It affects all the DTE device's established virtual circuits.

SVCs use all five modes. PVCs are always in data transfer mode because these circuits have been permanently established.

The basic operation of an X.25 virtual circuit begins when the source DTE device specifies the virtual circuit to be used (in the packet headers) and then sends the packets to a locally connected DCE device. At this point, the local DCE device examines the packet headers to determine which virtual circuit to use and then sends the packets to the closest PSE in the path of that virtual circuit. PSEs (switches) pass the traffic to the next intermediate node in the path, which might be another switch or the remote DCE device.

When the traffic arrives at the remote DCE device, the packet headers are examined and the destination address is determined. The packets are then sent to the destination DTE device. If communication occurs over an SVC and neither device has additional data to transfer, the virtual circuit is terminated.

The X.25 protocol maintains multiple connections over one physical link between a DTE and a DCE. These connections are called virtual circuits (VCs) or logical channels (LCs).

Logical Channel Numbers (LCNs) are assigned to each of the incoming and outgoing virtual calls for each DTE and DCE, respectively, as well as to all PVCs. X.25 can maintain up to 4095 virtual circuits numbered 1 through 4095. You identify an individual virtual circuit by giving its logical channel identifier (LCI) or virtual circuit number (VCN). Many documents use the terms virtual circuit and LC, VCN, LCN, and LCI interchangeably. Each of these terms refers to the virtual circuit number.

An important part of X.25 operation is the range of virtual circuit numbers. Virtual circuit numbers are broken into four ranges (listed here in numerically increasing order):

- Permanent virtual circuits (PVCs)
- Incoming-only circuits
- Two-way circuits
- Outgoing-only circuits

The incoming-only, two-way, and outgoing-only ranges define the virtual circuit numbers over which an SVC can be established by the placement of an X.25 call, much like a telephone network establishes a switched voice circuit when a call is placed.

SVCs can add even more delay than when using a PVC. SVCs, in addition to encountering connection blocking and connection delay, can encounter queuing and retransmission delays. These delay factors must be taken into account during the X.25 network design.

There is no difference in the operation of the SVCs in the different ranges except the restrictions on which device can initiate a call. These ranges can be used to prevent one side from monopolizing the virtual circuits, which can be useful for X.25 interfaces with a small total number of SVCs available.

Six X.25 parameters define the upper and lower limit of each of the three SVC ranges. A PVC must be assigned a number less than the numbers assigned to the SVC ranges. An SVC range is not allowed to overlap another range.

The rules about DCE and DTE devices initiating calls are as follows:

- Only the DCE device can initiate a call in the incoming-only range.
- Only the DTE device can initiate a call in the outgoing-only range.
- Both the DCE device and the DTE device can initiate a call in the two-way range.

The ITU-T Recommendation X.25 defines "incoming" and "outgoing" in relation to the DTE or DCE interface role; Cisco's documentation uses the more intuitive sense. Unless the ITU-T sense is explicitly referenced, a call received from the interface is an incoming call and a call sent out the interface is an outgoing call.

Key Concept

There are two types of virtual circuits used in X.25 network implementations; switched virtual circuits (SVCs) and permanent virtual circuits (PVCs). SVCs are temporary connections that are used when there is only sporadic data transfer between DTE devices across the X.25 packet-switched network. PVCs are permanently established connections that are used when there is frequent and consistent data transfer between DTE devices across the X.25 packet-switched network. Communication across a PVC does not require the call setup and termination states that are used with SVCs.

Protocol Translation

When receiving an X.25 connection request to a particular destination address, the Cisco router can automatically translate the request to another outgoing protocol connection type. *Protocol Translation* provides transparent translation between systems running different protocols. The Cisco IOS software supports two-way virtual terminal protocol translation between nodes running X.25, LAT, and Telnet.

The protocol translation feature provides transparent protocol translation between systems running different protocols. It enables terminal users on one network to access hosts on another network, despite differences in the native protocol stacks associated with the originating device and the targeted host. Protocol translation is a resourceful facility for many business applications.

The Cisco IOS software supports virtual terminal connections in both directions between the protocols in the following list. You can configure the router to translate automatically between them. This is called one-step translation, which is the most popular translation method:

- X.25 and local-area transport (LAT)
- X.25 and Telnet sessions using the Transmission Control Protocol (TCP)
- LAT and TCP/Telnet

When you make a one-step connection to the router, the Cisco IOS software determines which host the connection is for and which protocol that host is using. It then establishes a new network connection using the protocol required by that host.

Use the one-step protocol-translation method when network users repeatedly log on to the same remote network hosts through a router. This connection is more efficient and enables the device to have more knowledge of the protocols in use because the router acts as a network connection rather than as a terminal. The one-step method provides transparent protocol conversion. When connecting to the remote network host, the user enters the connection command to the remote network host but does not need to specify protocol translation. The network administrator has already created a configuration that defines a connection and the protocols to be translated. The user performs only one step to connect with the host.

Unlike other protocols, such as LAT, X.25, and TCP, which are actually translated when you use one-step protocol translation, SLIP, PPP, and AppleTalk Remote Access (ARA) are not translated to the destination protocol. Instead, they are carried inside a LAT, X.25, or TCP tunnel specific to the device on the remote network. However, the protocol translation facility is used to enable tunneling of SLIP, PPP, or ARA. On outgoing connections, you can also use the one-step protocol translation facility to tunnel SLIP or PPP to IP and IPX networks or ARA to AppleTalk networks across X.25, LAT, or IP (on outgoing connections only).

Key Concept

One-step translation is the most popular protocol translation method, which allows terminal users on one network to access hosts on another network, despite both hosts running different protocols. It supports virtual terminal connections between nodes running X.25, LAT, and Telnet (TCP). You can use the protocol-translation facility to tunnel SLIP or PPP to IP and IPX networks. Also, you can tunnel ARA to AppleTalk networks across X.25, LAT, or IP (on outgoing connections only).

Cisco IOS software supports limited connections in both directions between the following protocols. Connecting between these protocols requires that you first connect to a router and then to the host to which you want to connect. This is called two-step translation, which is the least popular translation method:

- XRemote to SLIP/PPP and X.25 PAD environments (XRemote must use the two-step method).
- LAT, X.25, SLIP/PPP, and TCP (Telnet) to TN3270 (TN3270 must use the two-step method).

A disadvantage of the one-step protocol-translation method is that the initiating computer or user does not know that two networking protocols are being used. This means that parameters of the foreign network protocols cannot be changed after connections are established. The exception to this limitation is any set of parameters common to both networking protocols. Any parameter common to both can be changed from the first host to the final destination.

With the two-step connection process, you can modify the parameters of either network connection, even while a session is in process. This process is similar to connecting a group of terminal lines from a PAD to a group of terminal lines from a TCP server. The difference is that you do not encounter the wiring complexity, unreliability, management problems, and performance bottlenecks that occur when two devices are connected via asynchronous serial lines.

As with the one-step method, Cisco recommends that you configure virtual templates for this feature.

Key Concept

Two-step translation is the least-popular protocol-translation method that supports limited connections in both directions between protocols XRemote to SLIP/PPP and X.25 PAD environments, and LAT, X.25, SLIP/PPP, and TCP (Telnet) to TN3270. Use two-step protocol translation for one-time connections or when you use the router as a general-purpose gateway between two types of networks (for example, X.25 PDN and TCP/IP).

The Cisco IOS software simplifies the process of configuring protocol translation to tunnel PPP or SLIP across X.25, TCP, and LAT networks. It does so by providing *virtual-interface templates* that you can configure independently and apply to any protocol-translation session. You can configure virtual-interface templates for one-step and two-step protocol translation.

A virtual-interface template is an interface that exists just inside the router (it is not a physical interface). You can configure virtual-interface templates just as you do regular asynchronous serial interfaces. You then apply these virtual-interface templates for one-step and two-step protocol translation. Virtual-access interfaces replace virtual-asynchronous interfaces for both one-step and two-step translation. You can configure up to 25 virtual-interface templates and have up to 300 virtual-access interfaces per router.

Key Concept

You can configure virtual-interface templates for both one-step and two-step protocol translations.

Protocol Translation Related Commands:

When receiving an X.25 connection request to a particular destination address, the Cisco router can automatically translate the request to another outgoing protocol connection type. To set this up, use the X.25 translate global configuration command:

```
RTR (config)# translate protocol incoming-address [in-options] protocol
    outgoing-address [out-options] [global-options]
```

To configure a one-step protocol translation virtual-interface template to enable tunneling of PPP or SLIP across an X.25 WAN, first create and configure a virtual-interface template, and then apply it as the single outgoing option to the translate command. This will assign an IP address to a device connecting to the virtual access interface. Complete the following tasks beginning in global configuration mode:

```
RTR (config)# interface virtual-template number
RTR (config-if)# ip unnumbered type number
RTR (config-if)# encapsulation {ppp | slip}
RTR (config-if)# peer default ip address {dhcp | pool [pool-name]}
RTR (config-if)# exit
RTR (config)# translate {lat | tcp | x25} incoming-address [in-options]
    virtual-template number [global-options]
```

Configuration Example

The following is an X.25 mapping configuration example. Figure 19.3 illustrates two routers sending datagrams across an X.25 public data network (PDN).

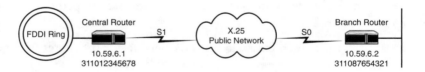

Figure 19.3
Map protocol addresses to X.121 addresses.

Configuration of the Central Router:

```
Central (config)# interface serial1
Central (config-if)# encapsulation x25
Central (config-if)# x25 address 311012345678
Central (config-if)# ip address 10.59.6.1 255.255.248.0
Central (config-if)# x25 map ip 10.59.6.2 311087654321 broadcast
```

Branch Router:

```
Branch (config)# interface serial0
Branch (config-if)# encapsulation x25
Branch (config-if)# x25 address 311087654321
Branch (config-if)# ip address 10.59.6.2 255.255.248.0
Branch (config-if)# x25 map ip 10.59.6.1 311012345678 broadcast
```

Summary

The X.25 protocol defines how connections between user devices and network devices are established and maintained across public data networks (PDNs). It is typically used in the packet-switched networks (PSNs) of common carriers. The X.25 specification defines a point-to-point interaction between data terminal equipment (DTE) and data circuit–terminating equipment (DCE). The X.25 protocol suite maps to the lowest three layers of the OSI reference model. The format of X.25 addresses is defined by the International Telecommunication Union—Telecommunication Standardization Sector (ITU-T) X.121 standard. X.121 addresses are used by the Packet-Layer Protocol (PLP) to establish switched virtual circuits (SVCs).

In an X.25 packet-switched environment, the Link Access Procedure Balanced (LAPB) is the Data Link layer protocol that manages communication and packet framing between DTE and DCE devices. An X.25 frame is made up of a series of layer-3 and layer-2 fields. Layer 3 X.25, or PLP fields, make up an X.25 packet and include a header and user data. Layer-2, or LAPB, frames include a header, encapsulated data, and a trailer. There are three types of LAPB frames: Information Frame (I-Frame), Supervisory Frame (S-Frame), and Unnumbered Frame (U-Frame).

You must set interface parameters such as X.25 encapsulation, X.121 address, and X.25 mapping for correct X.25 behavior. Additional configuration tasks can be performed so that a router works correctly with the service provider network. The X.25 software implementation allows virtual circuits to be routed from one X.25 interface to another and from one router to another. Switching or forwarding of X.25 virtual circuits can be done in two ways: Local X.25 Switching and XOT Switching. You set basic X.25 configuration parameters, and then you set additional parameters, such as layer-3 and flow-control parameters. You use the Show Interface command to display monitoring information about an interface. Sliding window flow control is a method of flow control in which a receiver gives a transmitter permission to transmit data until a window is full. When the window is full, the transmitter must stop transmitting until the receiver advertises a larger window. X.25 layers 2 and 3 were designed with strong flow-control and error-checking capabilities. The three commonly used methods for handling network congestion are windowing, buffering, and transmitting source-quench messages. X.21-bis is a physical, layer-1 protocol, used in X.25 networks, that defines the electrical and mechanical procedures for using the physical medium.

PART

VI

CH

19

The X.25 Map command provides a static conversion of higher-level addresses to X.25 addresses. Both the protocol address and the X.121 addresses are required to specify the complete network protocol-to-X.121 mapping. There are two types of X.25 encapsulation methods: Cisco's Encapsulation Method, and the Internet Engineering Task Force's (IETF) standard method (defined in RFC 1356: Multi-protocol encapsulations). A virtual circuit indicates the existence of a logical, bidirectional path from one DTE to another across an X.25 network. There are two types of X.25 virtual circuits: switched virtual circuits (SVCs) and permanent virtual circuits (PVCs). The protocol translation feature provides transparent protocol translation between systems running different protocols. There are two types of protocol translation methods: one-step translation (virtual terminal connections), and two-step translation (connect to the router first and then to host).

QUESTIONS AND ANSWERS

1. What layers of the OSI model does X.25 packet switching operate?

   A: The X.25 protocol suite maps to the lowest three layers of the OSI reference model: Physical layer, Data Link layer, and the Network layer.

2. What are X.121 addresses used for?

   A: X.121 addresses are used by the X.25 Packet-Layer Protocol (PLP) in call-setup mode to establish switched virtual circuits (SVCs).

3. What is the basic function of X.25 routing?

   A: X.25 routing simply connects two logical X.25 channels to complete an X.25 virtual circuit.

4. What are the three types of LAPB frames?

   A: The three types of LAPB frames are Information Frame, Supervisory Frame, and Unnumbered Frame.

5. Which LAPB frame provides "error detection and recovery"?

   A: The Information Frame (I-Frame) provides error detection and recovery.

6. What three flow-control methods are used to handle network congestion?

   A: The three commonly used methods for handling network congestion are windowing, buffering, and transmitting source-quench messages.

7. Which CCITT recommendations does X.25 support for their Physical-layer signaling?

   A: The X.25 Physical layer defines X.21 and X.21-bis as the standard, but other Physical-layer serial interfaces such as EIA/TIA-449, EIA-530, G.703, and so on can be used for Physical-layer signaling.

8. What two types of encapsulation methods are used in an X.25 mapping configuration?

A: The two types of encapsulation methods used in an X.25 mapping configuration are Cisco's long-available encapsulation method and the Internet Engineering Task Force's (IETF) standard method (defined in RFC 1356).

9. What are the two types of X.25 virtual circuits?

A: The two types of X.25 virtual circuits are switched virtual circuits (SVCs) and permanent virtual circuits (PVCs).

10. What two types of translation methods are used in an X.25 protocol translation configuration?

A: The two types of translation methods used in an X.25 protocol translation configurations are one-step translation (virtual terminal connections) and two-step translation (connect to the router first and then to the host).

PRACTICE TEST

1. Which of the following statements is true regarding the CCITT X.21-bis standard?
   - **A.** X.21-bis defines the packet-switching procedures.
   - **B.** X.21-bis does not support connecting DTE and DCE devices.
   - **C.** X.21-bis defines the electrical and mechanical procedures for using the physical medium.
   - **D.** X.21-bis is a Data Link layer (layer-2) protocol.

Answer A is incorrect because X.21-bis does not define the packet-switching procedures. Answer B is incorrect because X.21-bis handles the activation and deactivation of the physical medium connecting DTE and DCE devices. **Answer C is correct because X.21-bis defines the electrical and mechanical procedures for using the physical medium.** Answer D is incorrect because X.21-bis is a Physical-layer (layer 1) protocol.

2. What is the purpose of permanent virtual circuits (PVCs)?
   - **A.** Infrequent data transfer between DTEs
   - **B.** Frequent and consistent data transfer between DCEs
   - **C.** Infrequent data transfer between DCEs
   - **D.** Frequent and consistent data transfer between DTEs

Answer A is incorrect because this is the definition for switched virtual circuits (SVCs). Answer B is incorrect because it references DCE instead of DTE. Answer C is totally incorrect, again because of reference to DCE, and because of sporadic data transfer. **Answer D is correct because permanent virtual circuits (PVCs) are used for frequent and consistent data transfer between DTEs.**

3. What form of upper-level data is contained in the "Data Field" of the LAPB frame?

    A. X.21-bis Frame

    B. Encapsulated Packet-Layer Protocol (PLP) packet

    C. X.121 Address

    D. Delimits the beginning and the end of the LAPB frame

    E. Indicates whether the frame carries a command or a response

Answer A is incorrect because X.21-bis is a Physical-layer (level-1) protocol. **Answer B is correct because the data field of the LAPB frame contains upper-layer data in the form of an encapsulated PLP packet.** Answers C and E are both incorrect because they are contained in the address field of an LAPB frame. Answer D is incorrect because this is contained in the flag field of an LAPB frame.

4. True or False: The Sliding Window Flow Control protocol is a method of flow control in which a receiver gives a transmitter permission to transmit data until a window is full.

    A. True

    B. False

Answer A (True) is correct because the Sliding Window Flow Control protocol is a method of flow control in which a receiver gives a transmitter permission to transmit data until a window is full. When the window is full, the transmitter must stop transmitting until the receiver advertises a larger window.

5. Which parameters are essential for correct X.25 behavior? (Choose all that apply.)

    A. Selecting the X.25 encapsulation style

    B. Assigning the X.121 address

    C. Defining the map statements to associate X.121 addresses with higher-level protocol addresses

    D. Defining which router will be involved in placing and accepting virtual calls

    E. Defining the router's packet window size

Answers A, B, and C are correct. Certain parameters are essential for correct X.25 behavior, such as selecting the X.25 encapsulation style, assigning the X.121 address, and defining map statements to associate X.121 addresses with higher-level protocol addresses. Answer D is a fictitious answer. Answer E is incorrect because the packet size will default to 128 bytes, which is used by most X.25 networks.

6. In anticipation of connecting other sites to the network, the leased serial line between Router A and Router B is replaced by an X.25 network. The X.121 address assigned to Router A is 31373105551212 and the X.121 address assigned to Router B is 3137408767399. What configuration changes need to be made to Router A and Router B?

A. Their serial interface needs to be changed to "encapsulation x25."

B. The X.121 address needs to be configured.

C. The correct packet size, window size, and timers need to be set to match the X.25 network.

D. The X.25 map commands must be configured for each protocol being sent through the X.25 network.

E. All of the above

Answer E is correct. All the above changes are required to complete the X.25 configurations on both Router A and B.

7. San Francisco's router will forward datagrams destined for Sydney's router. San Francisco's serial0 interface has an X.121 address of 311082194567 and an IP address of 172.16.8.1. Sydney's serial0 interface has an X.121 address of 311082191234 and an IP address of 172.16.8.2. Identify the correct X.25 map statement configurations for San Francisco's and Sydney's routers?

A. `x25 map ip 172.16.8.1 311082194567`

B. `ip address 172.16.8.1 255.255.248.0`

C. `x25 map ip 172.16.8.1 311082191234`

D. `x25 map ip 172.16.8.2 311082194567`

E. `x25 map ip 172.16.8.2 311082191234`

Answer A is correct because the x25 map statement configuration is for the Sydney router. Answer B is incorrect because it just defines an IP address for a serial interface. Answers C and D are both incorrect because the x25 map statement configurations have the X.121 and IP addresses reversed. **Answer E is correct because the x25 map statement configuration is for the San Francisco router.**

8. Which command is issued to specify X.25 encapsulation on a DCE?

A. `encapsulation x25`

B. `x25 win 7`

C. `x25 address 311082198756`

D. `encapsulation x25 DCE`

E. `encapsulation x25 DTE`

PART

VI

CH

19

Answers A and E are both incorrect because these commands will assign the default encapsulation of DTE. Answer B is incorrect because this defines the X.25 window size. Answer C is incorrect because this defines an X.121 address on a serial interface. **Answer D is the correct answer, and this will assign X.25 encapsulation of DCE.**

9. Which command is issued to enable X.25 routing?

    A. `encapsulation x25`

    B. `x25 route 1012 interface serial0`

    C. `x25 routing`

    D. `encapsulation x25 routing`

    E. `encapsulation lapb DTE`

Answer A is incorrect because this will assign the X.25 encapsulation of DTE on a serial interface. Answer B is incorrect because this is an X.25 route statement, which will define a static route for local switching. **Answer C is correct because this defines the global configuration command for X.25 routing.** Answer D is a fictitious answer. Answer E is incorrect because this will assign the LAPB encapsulation of DTE on a serial interface.

10. Which of the following statements are true about X.25 error control and recovery? (Choose all that apply.)

    A. X.25 specifies several error-checking levels.

    B. The DTE device, DCE device, and the network can detect errors in transferred data packets.

    C. X.25 layers 2 and 3 were designed with strong flow control and error checking.

    D. LAPB ensures frames are correctly ordered and error-free.

    E. X.25 packet-switching networks are able to detect packet errors, lost packets, and duplicate packets, and can route around X.25 network failures.

    F. All of the above

Answer F is correct. All the statements are true about X.25 error control and recovery.

Frame Relay

WHILE YOU READ

1. How does frame relay relate to the OSI model?

2. What are PVCs and DLCIs?

3. How important is LMI to router configurations?

4. Can a frame relay circuit provide multiple connections?

5. What are the differences between Cisco and ANSI LMI standards?

6. How is Frame Relay Traffic Management defined in Cisco routers?

7. What is the basic method of mapping DLCI layer-2 addresses to IP addresses in layer 3?

8. What are frame relay subinterfaces?

9. How is frame relay link status maintained?

10. What is Cisco frame relay traffic shaping?

Frame relay is one of the most popular WAN technologies in use today. Virtually all moderate-to-large networks make at least some use of frame relay, which is a packet-switching technology that bears a topological resemblance to X.25. In fact, frame relay is often thought of as a stripped-down, more-efficient version of X.25. The original frame relay specifications were derived from ISDN. The frame relay specifications are governed and published by the Frame Relay Forum.

This section reviews the major elements of frame relay and how Cisco routers implement it.

Frame Relay Overview

Figure 20.1 shows a simple frame relay network implementation. Router A has a digital serial line connection to a frame relay switch that is the ingress switch to the network. Router A is defined to be the DTE interface; the frame relay switch connected to the router is the DCE. This circuit between the router DTE and the switch DCE is called the *User-to-Network Interface (UNI)* and is the heart of the frame relay protocol discussed here. UNI circuits are defined from DS-0 (56Kbps) to DS-3 (44.736Mbps) in speed. The other major defined interface is the *Network-to-Network Interface (NNI)*, which connects different frame relay networks. It is not discussed further here, because it is out of the scope of the CCIE Written Exam.

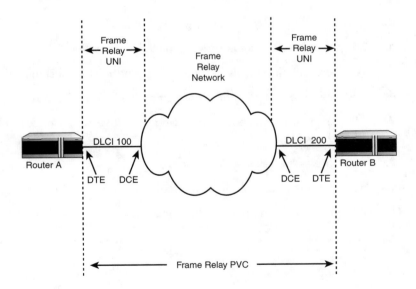

Figure 20.1
A frame relay network and its major components.

Frame relay operates at layer 2 of the OSI model, the Data Link layer. Frame relay exchanges frames between the DTE and DCE using HDLC frame type *LAPF (Link Access Protocol for Frame bearer services)*. The frame relay frame follows the generic HDLC format of flag, address, control, data, frame check sequence, and flag described in Chapter 19, "X.25." In frame relay, the address and control fields are condensed into one field, the address field, and are described in subsequent sections. The key distinction concerning the use of the frame check sequence field is essential to understanding frame relay operations.

Key Concept

The frame relay protocol provides error checking, but no error correction. It is left to upper-layer protocols to guarantee delivery of data.

Data-link protocols prior to the development of frame relay made extensive use of error checking and correction at each data-link connection in a particular data packet's route. X.25 and SDLC, for example, have provisions for data-link ACKs between DTEs and DCEs. Frame relay has no method of ACKing defined. If a frame arrives with a bad FCS field, the frame is merely discarded. It is left to upper-layer protocols, such as TCP, to provide end-to-end reliable data delivery. In this way frame relay is more efficient and stripped down than other data-link protocols. Frame relay was originally intended to be a "best-effort" type of service. The network would make its best effort to deliver a packet but would not guarantee it.

Permanent Virtual Circuits and DLCIs

Referring again to Figure 20.1, Router B communicates with the frame relay network using the same UNI interface and protocol as Router A. Routers A and B communicate with each other over the frame relay network via a *Permanent Virtual Circuit (PVC)*. PVCs are provisioned and maintained by the frame relay provider. Like X.25, the circuit is considered "virtual" because the path between the network switches is unknown and out of the control of the administrator of Routers A and B. The routing inside the network is dynamic, and can change without interference to, or knowledge of, the end users.

A UNI circuit can carry multiple PVCs for different destinations simultaneously. Each PVC is denoted by the *Data Link Connection Identifier (DLCI)* field in the frame relay header. The DLCI field comprises the address field in the HDLC LAPF frame. The DLCI field is 10 bits long, yielding 1,024 possible PVC designations per UNI circuit. DLCI designations for particular PVCs are defined and configured by the service provider. However, the provider can implement DLCI numbering systems designed by the end user. Table 20.1 shows the valid DLCI usage.

PART
VI

CH
20

Table 20.1 Valid DLCI Usage	
DLCI	*Usage*
0	Link Management
1–15	Reserved
16–1007	Available for PVC Designation
1008–1022	Reserved
1023	Link Management

DLCIs are *locally significant*, which means that DLCIs are local to UNI circuits only. For example, when Router A sends a packet to Router B, it inserts DLCI 100 into the frame header. The frame relay switch uses DLCI 100 to send the frame on its way toward Router B. When the frame arrives at the service provider's switch connected to Router B, the switch builds a frame relay header with DLCI 200. Router B sees DLCI 200 and interprets the frame as having arrived from Router A. A later section discusses how DLCIs are mapped to higher-level addresses.

Key Concept

DLCIs are local to UNI circuits only. This means they are *locally significant*.

Link Management Interface (LMI)

The *Link Management Interface (LMI)* protocol of frame relay defines the control messages exchanged between the frame relay switch and user. There are five LMI messages:

- Status Enquiry—By default sent by the user to the switch
- Status Response—Response of enquiry to user
- Full Status Enquiry—The user requests PVC status from the switch
- Full Status Response—The switch informs the user of PVC status
- Asynchronous Status—From switch to user with specific PVC status

By default, the user sends a Status Enquiry message every 10 seconds and a Full Status Enquiry every sixth Status Enquiry message. If the switch does not respond to an enquiry within 15 seconds, the enquiry is in error. If three out of four messages fail, the *link protocol* on the link is declared down. The router show interface command output will show the information link protocol up/down. This is specifically referring to the exchange of these LMI status enquiry/response messages.

There are three LMI message types defined, as shown in Table 20.2.

Table 20.2   LMI Message Types

LMI Type	Definition	DLCI Used
Cisco	Developed by "Group of Four" Vendors	1023
ANSI	Defined by specification ANSI Annex D	0
Q933a	Defined by ITU-T Q.933 Annex A	0

The LMI type can be specified on the frame relay interface with the `frame-relay lmi-type [cisco/ansi/q933]` command. Cisco LMI type uses DLCI 1023, whereas ANSI and q933a messages use DLCI 0.

A basic frame relay interface configuration example is shown.

```
interface serial 0
encapsulation frame-relay
frame-relay lmi-type ansi
```

The encapsulation frame-relay command turns on frame relay protocol on this interface. In this case, ANSI Annex-D is selected as the LMI type. The LMI type configured on the router must match the LMI type configured on the service provider's switch; otherwise, the frame relay protocol will fail and the interface status will be link protocol down.

By default, if `frame-relay lmi-type` is not specifically coded on an interface, LMI *autosense* will be used. Autosense will cause the router to attempt establishing the link protocol with the switch by attempting each LMI type until the switch responds positively. If the router receives all positive responses from the switch, it will use the last one received for the LMI type.

The output of a show interface command for a frame relay link is shown.

```
routera#show interface s 2/0
Serial2/0 is up, line protocol is up
  Hardware is M4T
  Description: ==> Frame Relay Access Link <==
  MTU 1500 bytes, BW 2048 Kbit, DLY 20000 usec,
 ➥rely 255/255, load 96/255
  Encapsulation FRAME-RELAY, crc 16, loopback not set,
 ➥keepalive set (10 sec)
  LMI enq sent  89077, LMI stat recvd 89077, LMI upd
 ➥recvd 0, DTE LMI up
  LMI enq recvd 0, LMI stat sent  0, LMI upd sent  0
  LMI DLCI 0  LMI type is ANSI Annex D  frame relay DTE
  FR SVC disabled, LAPF state down
```

PART

VI

CH

20

```
Broadcast queue 7/64, broadcasts sent/dropped 7105135/970,
  interface broadcasts 6959025
    Last input 00:00:00, output 00:00:00, output hang never
    Last clearing of "show interface" counters 1w3d
    Queueing strategy: fifo
    Output queue 0/40, 5312 drops; input queue 0/75, 0 drops
    5 minute input rate 440000 bits/sec, 191 packets/sec
    5 minute output rate 776000 bits/sec, 212 packets/sec
        146170080 packets input, 2332197079 bytes, 0 no buffer
        Received 0 broadcasts, 0 runts, 0 giants, 0 throttles
        0 input errors, 0 CRC, 0 frame, 0 overrun, 0 ignored, 0 abort
        149988876 packets output, 532361220 bytes, 0 underruns
        0 output errors, 0 collisions, 0 interface resets
        0 output buffer failures, 0 output buffers swapped out
        0 carrier transitions     DCD=up  DSR=up  DTR=up  RTS=up  CTS=up
```

Ouput of show interface command for a frame relay interface

The status of this interface (shown in line 2 of the command output) is Serial 2/0 is up, line protocol is up. The first up status informs that there is a good carrier signal on the circuit. The link protocol up indicates that the router and the frame relay switch are exchanging LMI messages according to the protocol. The output that 89077 LMI status enquiry messages have been sent by the router to the network and the router has received 89077 responses. The LMI type is ANSI Annex D, and LMI messages are traveling on DLCI 0. The interface is configured as a DTE, the default.

Key Concept

The router learns of PVC status from the network via Full Status Response messages. PVC Status can be displayed with the show frame-relay pvc command.

The Full Status Enquiry and Full Status Response messages request and provide status information about PVCs. By default, the Full Status Enquiry is sent to the switch every sixth Status Enquiry message, or by default every 60 seconds. The PVC is not active, and in fact does not exist until the network has the PVC provisioned and it is up and active across the network.

Frame Relay and Layer 3 Addressing

Thus far, the discussion of frame relay has centered around it as a layer-2 protocol. A layer-2 protocol only exists to connect upper-layer protocols. A method must exist to hand data between layers 3 and 2. Specifically, how can the DLCI layer 2 address be mapped to an IP address at layer 3? This section will describe the several methods available in Cisco routers to relate DLCIs to IP addresses.

Inverse ARP

The most basic method for DLCI to higher-level address resolution is *Inverse ARP*. Figure 20.2 and the following sample configuration show an architecture that would use Inverse ARP. Router 1 receives a Full Status Response from the frame relay network informing it that the PVCs with DLCIs 100 and 400 are active. Router 1 sends out Inverse ARP requests on both PVCs. Routers 2 and 3 receive their Inverse ARP message and respond with their respective IP addresses. Router 1 then maps IP address 192.168.1.20 to DLCI 100 and 192.168.1.30 to DLCI 400.

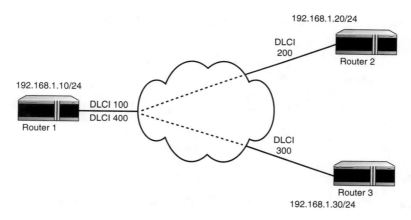

Figure 20.2
Mapping IP addresses to DLCIs.

Inverse ARP is used in the following sample configuration:

```
Router 1 Configuration
interface serial 0
encapsulation frame-relay
ip address 192.168.1.10  255.255.255.0


Router 2 Configuration
interface serial 0
encapsulation frame-relay
ip address 192.168.1.20 255.255.255.0

Router 3 Configuration
interface serial 0
encapsulation frame-relay
ip address 192.168.1.30 255.255.255.0
```

Inverse ARP is on by default for multipoint interfaces. A table showing the result of the mapping procedure can be displayed with the show frame-relay map command. Note that Inverse ARP will work with other layer-3 protocols such as AppleTalk and IPX provided they are configured on the interface.

Frame Relay Maps

Another method for address mapping is to explicitly define a DLCI-Layer 3 address map in the configuration. This is done with the frame-relay map interface command. The full command is

```
frame-relay map protocol address dlci [broadcast] [ietf/cisco]

protocol = ip, decnet, ipx, xns, appletalk, vines, or clns
address = protocol address of interface on opposite side of the PVC
dlci = DLCI of this side of PVC
broadcast = enables broadcast messages on this PVC Optional,
       but may be required for routing updated on this PVC.

ietf/cisco = encapsulation method.  Either ietf or cisco.  Cisco is
    the default and is used when two Cisco routers are communicating
    across the same PVC.
  Use IETF when connecting a Cisco to a non-Cisco router.
```

The same physical configuration shown in Figure 20.2, configured with frame relay maps, becomes

```
Router 1 Configuration
interface serial 0
encapsulation frame-relay
ip address 192.168.1.10  255.255.255.0
frame-relay map ip 192.168.1.20 100
frame-relay map ip 192.168.1.30 400



Router 2 Configuration
interface serial 0
encapsulation frame-relay
ip address 192.168.1.20 255.255.255.0
frame-relay map ip 192.168.1.10 200

Router 3 Configuration
interface serial 0
encapsulation frame-relay
ip address 192.168.1.30 255.255.255.0
frame-relay map 192.168.1.10 300
```

Subinterfaces

Another method to map layer-3 addresses to PVCs is to use frame relay *subinterfaces* on the physical frame relay serial interface. Subinterfaces allow the creation of multiple virtual interfaces on one physical interface.

One limitation of map statements and inverse ARP is the issue of split horizon. When a routing update arrives on a PVC defined with a frame-relay map statement, routing information will not be propagated out the other PVCs on that serial interface. Subinterfaces allow the distribution of routing updates received on a PVC out to other PVCs on the same serial interface.

Many network managers also prefer subinterfaces because they provide slightly more granular information for troubleshooting and documentation. With subinterfaces, it is advisable to use a description command for documentation. In addition, subinterface change status gets logged in the system log.

The method for creating a frame relay subinterface follows:

1. Specify the physical interface with this command:

```
interface serial x
```

2. Enable frame relay protocol on the interface with this command:

```
encapsulation frame-relay
```

3. Create the subinterface for one or more PVCs with this command:

```
interface serial x.subinterface number [point-to-point| multipoint]
```

A subinterface can be either *multipoint* (using frame relay maps) or *point-to-point* (using one PVC per subinterface). If a subinterface is defined as either multipoint or point-to-point, it cannot be changed to the other without a router reload. In earlier IOS releases, subinterfaces defaulted to multipoint, requiring a reload if a point-to-point was really desired. Current releases require an explicit coding of the multipoint or point-to-point option.

The next step is to provide a layer-3 address for the subinterface, and define the DLCI number.

4. Define a layer-3 address using this command:

```
ipx network 100
```

or

```
ip address  192.168.1.5  255.255.255.252
```

The allowed layer-3 addresses include all the usual layer-3 protocols, such as IPX, IP, or AppleTalk.

5. Define the DLCI number using this command:

```
frame-relay interface-dlci number  [ietf|cisco]
```

or

```
frame-relay map  protocol address  dlci
```

The `frame-relay map` command is configured as described earlier in this chapter. The `frame-relay interface-dlci` command assigns a local DLCI number to this subinterface. As described before, the DLCI numbers for a PVC are provisioned by the frame relay provider. So if a DLCI number is defined for a PVC but no such DLCI is used by the provider, the PVC will be unusable. This might seem obvious, but it is a possible source of configuration mismatch and error.

Again referring to the physical setup shown in Figure 20.2, the configurations are

```
Router 1:
interface serial 0
description == > frame relay access link  < ==
encapsulation frame-relay
no ip-address

interface serial 0.200 point-to-point
description == > PVC to router 2 < ==
ip address 192.168.1.5 255.255.255.252
frame-relay inteface-dlci 200

interface serial 0.400 point-to-point
description == > PVC to router 3 < ==
ip address 192.168.1.9 255.255.255.252
frame-relay interface-dlci 400


Router 2:
interface serial 0
description == > frame relay access link < ==
encapsulation frame-relay
no ip-address

interface serial 0.200 point-to-point
description == > PVC to router 1 < ==
ip address 192.168.2.6 255.255.255.252
frame-relay interface-dlci 200
```

```
Router 3:
interface serial 0
description == > frame relay access link  < ==
encapsulation frame-relay
no ip-address

interface serial 0.300 point-to-point
description == > PVC to router 1 < ==
ip address 192.168.1.10 255.255.255.252
frame-relay interface-dlci 300
```

Frame Relay Traffic Management

Another way that frame relay is more efficient and simpler than X.25 is that frame relay provides no method for traffic windowing. Traffic windowing is again left to upper-layer protocols. However, traffic management must still be considered in frame relay.

There are three major sources of congestion associated with frame relay:

- Multiple virtual circuits can coexist on a single physical access link.
- The access links on either end of a virtual circuit might not have equal port speeds. One end might be a full T1, whereas the other is only 56Kbps. If the T1 circuit were to send more than 56,000 bits of data in a second, the other end would be flooded.
- The frame relay internal network resources are shared among many users. It is necessary to throttle individual virtual circuit usage so one user does not crowd out other users.

As the building block for dealing with these issues, frame relay defines the following traffic parameters for each PVC:

- Committed Information Rate (CIR)—This is the logical bandwidth of any particular PVC.

  The maximum CIR for a PVC is the physical bandwidth of the lower bandwidth access link, of the two access links that comprise the PVC. CIR is measured in bits per second.

- Committed Burst Size (B_c)—The number of bits the network guarantees to transport, in time period T_c, under normal circumstances. The Network always has the option of discarding any traffic it deems necessary, but this value specifies the amount of data that will receive the network's best effort.

- Excess Burst Size (B_e)—The number of bits, in time period T_c, by which the user can exceed B_c. The network will still accept, and attempt to transport, this data, but this is the most likely data to be discarded in the event of congestion.

The policies, guidelines, and defaults for determining these values for a given virtual circuit will vary by network provider. In fact, the overall issue of CIR policies is one of the most controversial and problematic a network manager might encounter.

Frame relay also provides three notification methods of traffic congestion. All three are bits in the frame relay header of normal data frames.

- Discard Eligible (DE)—The DE bit is set when the B_c is exceeded. It is set in all frames thereafter until $B_c + B_e$ is reached. Frames with DE set will be discarded first in the event of network congestion. End-user equipment might also set DE in frames to indicate traffic of lower priority.

- Forward Explicit Congestion Notification (FECN)—Notifies the receiver that congestion was encountered inside the network along this frame's path.

- Backward Explicit Congestion Notification (BECN)—Notifies the receiver that congestion exists in the direction opposite from which this frame traveled. The receiver is informed that subsequent frames sent out on this PVC might encounter congestion.

Note that DE is normally set at ingress to the network to indicate CIR overruns, whereas FECN and BECN indicate congestion inside the network "cloud." There is another congestion notification called *implicit congestion notification*, which basically states that upper-layer protocols detect congestion due to packet loss. Implicit congestion notification is not covered here.

Figure 20.3 shows a PVC between two routers where one access link is a T1 and the other is a 56Kbps circuit. In this case, the provider sets a default CIR of one-half the minimum physical port speed on the PVC—in this case, the 56Kbps link. Therefore, the CIR on this PVC is 28Kbps. Assuming the time increment for measurement is one second (T_c = 1 sec.), B_c is 28,000 bits.

This means that the first 28,000 bits that arrive in the network in each second will be accepted without being marked discard eligible. Let's say for discussion's sake that the first frame in a second arrives and it is 28,001 bits long. That frame would be marked DE because it exceeded the committed burst size.

In this case, the provider's policy is that no single PVC should use more then 7/8 of a port's bandwidth. Therefore, $B_c + B_e \leq 7/8(56Kbps)$, or $B_c + B_e \leq 48Kbps$. So B_e for this PVC would be 20,000 bits. After B_c is exceeded another 20,000 bits will be accepted. After both the committed and excess burst levels are exceeded, frames are discarded on ingress to the network. After the measurement period T_c expires, the entire cycle repeats.

Figure 20.3
Simple traffic-shaping example.

Cisco's Implementation of Traffic Shaping

The preceding section described the methods a frame relay network can detect traffic condition and inform end-user equipment of congestion situations. In the first years of frame relay deployment, most end-user access equipment implemented no methods of handling the concept of CIR or reacted to receipt of BECN bits in frames. With IOS release 11.2, Cisco introduced its traffic-shaping configuration command suite.

Cisco frame relay traffic shaping provides the following major options:

- Configure the router to match the CIR, B_c, and B_e parameters of the provider network
- Allow the router to throttle traffic rates based on the receipt of BECNs
- Assign queuing lists on a PVC basis

The three major steps for configuring traffic shaping are

- Enable traffic shaping on the serial interface of the frame relay access link with the `frame-relay traffic-shaping` interface command
- Define one or more lists of traffic-shaping parameters with the `map-class frame-relay` command.
- Apply these map-class lists to either the serial interface or to individual subinterfaces for each PVC with the `frame-relay class` command.

In Cisco routers, the default T_c interval is 125ms. So if a provider's parameters are in terms of a one-second T_c, care must be taken to divide the provider's figures by 8. Cisco traffic shaping provides many permutations and options in its command suite. How to apply these commands might vary by provider requirements, also.

Key Concept

Although frame relay provides methods to inform users of congestion situations, user equipment is under no obligation to act on these notifications. Cisco *traffic shaping* implements frame relay congestion management in the router.

Using the example from Figure 20.3, the following is a configuration example:

```
Router A
interface serial 0
encapsulation frame-relay
frame-relay traffic-shaping
no ip address

interface s0.1 point-to-point
description == > PVC to Router B < ==
ip address 192.168.1.5 255.255.255.252
frame-relay interface-dlci 16
frame-relay class 28kb

map-class frame-relay 28kb
 frame-relay CIR 28000
 frame-relay bc 7000
 frame-relay be 2500
 frame-relay mincir 14000
```

The following is an explanation of the configuration statements:

- The `frame-relay traffic-shaping` command on serial interface 0 enables traffic shaping for the interface.

- The `frame-relay class 28kb` applies the traffic-shaping list named 28kb to subinterface 0.1. It is also possible to apply the map class to the major interface, and that map class will default for all subsequent PVCs. A default map class can be overridden on a subinterface with the `class [map-class name]` command.

- The `map-class frame-relay 28kb` command creates a map class named 28kb.

- `Frame-relay CIR`—The normal rate for sending data. Measured in bits per second. This might be the same value as set by the provider. In this example, it is.

- `Frame-relay bc`—The number of bits to send in time period T_c. Because T_c on Cisco routers defaults to 125 ms, this is normally 1/8 of CIR.

- `Frame-relay be`—The number of excess bits permitted to transmit during interval T_c. In this case, it is 1/8 of the B_e value of 20,000 bits.

■ `Frame-relay mincir`—The minimum rate the router will transmit during periods of congestion. When the router receives a BECN bit during the interval T_c, it will decrease its transmit rate by 25%. This is the minimum transmit rate that the router will step down to. The default is one-half *frame-relay CIR*.

Another method for configuring traffic shaping in this example is to use the `frame-relay traffic-rate` command, as shown here:

```
map-class 28kb
 frame-relay traffic rate 28000 48000
```

`frame-relay traffic-rate average [peak]` is where the average and peak are in bits per second. The average is normally CIR and peak is $B_c + B_e$. Peak is an optional parameter and will default to the bandwidth of the interface in use. In this case, omitting the peak parameter on router 1 will result in a peak rate of 1.544Mbps.

One last item to mention in traffic shaping is that it is possible to apply either priority or custom queuing to a map class using either the `frame-relay priority-group` or `frame-relay custom-queue-list` commands, respectively. The following is the `frame-relay priority` command:

```
map-class 28kb
 frame-relay traffic rate 28000 48000
 frame-relay priority-group 1
```

The `show frame-relay pvc` command provides detailed information on DE, FECN, and BECN packets received and sent, as shown:

```
routera#show frame-relay pvc

PVC Statistics for interface Serial2/0 (Frame Relay DTE)

DLCI = 16, DLCI USAGE = LOCAL, PVC STATUS = ACTIVE, INTERFACE = Serial2/0.16

  input pkts 37572410       output pkts 37539065      in bytes 504050898
  out bytes 1637116272      dropped pkts 9717         in FECN pkts 30660
  in BECN pkts 865350       out FECN pkts 0           out BECN pkts 0
  in DE pkts 2278860        out DE pkts 0
  out bcast pkts 1257552     out bcast bytes 807770800
  Shaping adapts to BECN
  pvc create time 4w3d, last time pvc status changed 4w3d

Show Frame Relay PVC Output
```

The `show traffic-shape` and `show traffic-shape statistics` commands provide traffic-shaping status.

Summary

Frame relay is a virtual circuit–based, data-link protocol that operates at layer 2 of the OSI model. The frame relay layer-2 address is the DLCI, and control messages are quite basic. Frame relay link status is maintained by LMI messages. The router is responsible for initiating the keep-alive process by sending Status Enquiry messages to the frame relay switch. There are three possible LMI message types: Cisco, ANSI Annex D, and Q933a.

The network informs the router of PVC status with Full Status Enquiry Responses, as requested by the router. Frame relay relies on upper-layer protocols for error recovery. There are no data-link ACKs in frame relay.

There are three methods for linking PVCs to layer-3 addresses: Inverse ARP, the `frame-relay map` command, and subinterfaces with the `frame-relay interface-dlci` command.

Logical bandwidth is defined for each PVC via the Committed Information Rate. Frame relay does not provide for traffic windowing, but congestion is indicated to user equipment with the BECN, FECN, and DE bits. DE is set when CIR is overrun, whereas BECN and FECN are set when congestion is encountered inside the frame relay network.

Traffic shaping is the router method for throttling traffic to the CIR limits. With traffic shaping enabled, the router can step down the rate at which it sends data based on receipt of BECN bits.

QUESTIONS AND ANSWERS

1. How does frame relay relate to the OSI model?

   A: Frame relay operates at layer 2 of the OSI model, the Data Link layer.

2. What are PVCs and DLCIs?

   A: PVCs, or *Permanent Virtual Circuits*, are provisioned and maintained by the frame relay provider. Each PVC is denoted by the *Data Link Connection Identifier (DLCI)*, which are defined and configured by the service provider.

3. How important is LMI to router configurations?

   A: The LMI protocol defines the control messages that are exchanged between the frame relay switch and the user. The LMI definitions must be part of the Cisco router definitions so the link is properly defined so that the router can interface properly to the frame relay circuit.

4. Can a frame relay circuit provide multiple connections?

A: Yes, provided that there is adequate bandwidth in the frame relay circuit to support multiple PVCs over that circuit.

5. What are the differences between Cisco and ANSI LMI standards?

A: Cisco uses a DLCI definition of 1023, whereas the ANSI standard uses 0.

6. How is Frame Relay Traffic Management defined in Cisco routers?

A: With IOS release 11.2, Cisco introduced traffic-shaping configuration command suite. The three major options are to configure the router to match the CIR B_c and B_e parameters of the provider network, allow the router to throttle traffic rates based on the receipt of BECNs, and assign queuing lists on a PVC basis.

7. What is the basic method of mapping DLCI layer-2 addresses to IP addresses in layer 3?

A: The basic method for DLCI to upper-layer address resolution is *inverse ARP.* The router receives PVC and DLCI information on the interface. The router then sends out inverse ARP requests using the DLCI information and responses are received, mapping IP addresses to DLCI definitions.

8. What are frame relay subinterfaces?

A: A subinterface can be either multipoint or point-to-point (using one PVC per subinterface). If a subinterface is defined as either multipoint or point-to-point, it cannot be changed to the other without a router reload. In earlier IOS releases, subinterfaces defaulted to multipoint, requiring a reload if a point-to-point were really desired. Current releases require an explicit coding of the multipoint/point-to-point option.

9. How is frame relay link status maintained?

A: Frame relay link status is maintained by LMI messages.

10. What is Cisco frame relay traffic shaping?

A: Cisco traffic shaping implements frame relay congestion management in the router.

PRACTICE TEST

1. Which of the following are UNI-defined circuit speeds?
   A. 28.8Kbps
   B. 14.4Kbps
   C. 56Kbps
   D. 1.44Mbps
   E. 44.736Mbps

Answers A and B are incorrect because they are not provided for in the frame relay specification. **Answers C, D, and E are correct because UNI circuit speeds are defined from DS0 (56Kbps) to DS-3 (44.736Mbps).**

2. Which of the following PVC parameters is most likely to discard data in the event of congestion?
   A. Committed Information Rate
   B. Excess Burst Size
   C. Committed Burst Size
   D. Output Buffer Failure
   E. Excessive Collision Overrun

Answers A, B, and C are correct because they all describe parameters that can determine whether a frame is discarded. Answers D and E are incorrect because they are fictitious terms.

3. Which of the following are notification methods of traffic congestion?
   A. Backward Explicit Congestion Notification
   B. CIR Override
   C. Forward Explicit Congestion Notification
   D. Discard Eligible
   E. Buffer overflows statistic

Answers A, C, and D are correct because they are bits in the frame relay header that indicate that congestion has been encountered. Answers B and E are incorrect because they are fictitious.

4. The Discard Eligible bit is set in which of the following conditions?
   A. Severe congestion occurs.
   B. The link is down.
   C. CIR is overrun.
   D. Committed Burst Size is exceeded.

Answer A is incorrect because there is no special condition known as "severe" congestion. Answer B is incorrect because no traffic will flow when the link is down. **Answers C and D are correct because discard eligible will be set under these conditions.**

    5. In Cisco routers, which of the following values is the default T_c?

        A. 100ms

        B. 200ms

        C. 120ms

        D. 125ms

Answers A, B, and C are incorrect because they give incorrect T_c values. **Answer D is correct.**

    6. The `show frame-relay pvc` command provides detailed information on which of the following?

        A. FECN

        B. UNI

        C. DLCI

        D. DE

Answers A, C, and D are correct because the `show frame-relay PVC` output displays FECN, DE and DLCI information. Answer B is incorrect because UNI is a type of frame relay access link and has nothing to do with PVC information.

    7. By default, the user sends a Status Enquiry message every 10 seconds. A Full Status Enquiry is sent every _____ Status Enquiry Message.

        A. fourth

        B. fifth

        C. sixth

        D. eighth

Answers A, B, and D are incorrect because they provide incorrect timing for Full Status Enquiries. **Answer C is correct because, according to both Cisco default and the Frame Relay specifications, Full Status is requested every sixth status request.**

    8. Which of the following valid DLCI usage numbers are used for Link Management:

        A. 0

        B. 1–15

        C. 16–1007

        D. 1023

Answers A and D are correct because DLCI 0 is used for Annex D and Q.933a LMI, and DLCI 1023 is used for Cisco LMI. Answers B and C are incorrect because DLCIs 1–15 are reserved, and DLCIs 16–1007 are available for user PVCs.

PART VI

CH 20

9. Creating a frame relay subinterface requires which of the following?

 A. interface serial x

 B. frame-relay map

 C. encapsulation frame-relay

 D. interface serial x.subinterface number

 E. map-class frame-relay

Answers A, C, and D are correct because these show configuration statements that are required at a minimum to make a subinterface functional. Answers B and E are incorrect because they are valid subinterface options but are not required.

10. Which IOS release introduced the traffic-shaping configuration command suite?

 A. 10.16.2

 B. 10.19.4

 C. 11.2

 D. 11.2.A

Answers A, B, and D are incorrect because they list incorrect IOS releases. **Answer C is correct because it lists the correct IOS release containing the traffic-shaping configuration command.**

CHAPTER PREREQUISITE

Chapter 1, "General Network Overview," and Chapter 20, "Frame Relay." A complete understanding of general internetworking, the layers of the OSI model, and frame relay are important.

ATM: Asynchronous Transfer Mode

WHILE YOU READ

1. What is the size of an ATM cell's payload?

2. What is the size of an ATM NSAP address?

3. What ATM address is used for private networks?

4. What type of routing protocol does PNNI resemble?

5. Which part of the ATM Model handles PNNI?

6. Does ATM in cell-switching technology fragment frames as they transverse through an ATM circuit?

7. Which signaling protocol is used for interchangeable vendor ATM switches?

8. SSCOP is at what layer of the OSI model?

9. Which layer of the OSI model is similar to the higher layers of the ATM Protocol model?

10. Name the signaling protocol that can be defined for parallel links.

ATM is an ITU-T standard for high-speed multimedia communications over a cell-switched network. The ATM cell is the most significant difference between ATM and any other switched network. Most other networks switch packets or frames.

Key Concept

An ATM cell is a fixed-sized, 53-byte cell composed of a 5-byte header with a 48-byte payload. ATM is connection-oriented, so it requires end-to-end virtual connections to be established before data transfer.

ATM PVCs are similar to Frame Relay DLCIs. To accomplish this, ATM uses two types of Virtual Circuits: PVCs and SVCs.

PVCs and SVCs

Permanent Virtual Circuits (PVCs) are, as the name implies, connections that are always established and active. They are manually configured on Cisco routers. Network statistics can be gathered for monitoring of continuous utilization of the circuits.

Key Concept

Permanent Virtual Circuits (PVCs) are connections that are always established and active. *Switched Virtual Circuits (SVC)* are on-demand circuits and are active only when traffic is destined for a specific remote end.

If no traffic exists, SVCs become idle and drop the connection. SVCs create a problem when attempting to gather network statistics on the circuits with network management protocols. Since SVCs are temporary, continuous utilization can't be obtained on ATM SVCs.

ATM Interfaces

In an ATM network, there are two types of interfaces: UNI and NNI. Within each interface type, there are two classes: public and private.

The UNI (User-to-Network) interface defines the connection between an endpoint into the ATM network (Private UNI) or between two distinct ATM networks (Public UNI). UNI connections are established dynamically and continuously. UNI is supported for PVCs and SVCs, which means that UNI connections are set up for PVCs and are on-demand for SVCs.

The NNI (Network-to-Network) interface defines a connection between two ATM devices in the same public or private ATM network or organization. Figure 21.1 shows the interfaces being used in an ATM network.

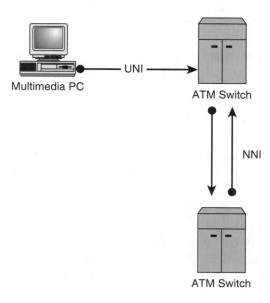

Figure 21.1
Interfaces in an ATM network.

PNNI

Public or Private Network-to-Network Interface (PNNI) is a deceiving term. It actually defines a protocol. It is also sometimes called Private Network-Node Interface. Private NNI is used for ATM switch-to-switch for local ATM network interfaces. Public NNI defines the routing protocol for the connection between ATM switches.

Key Concept

Private NNI is used for ATM switch-to-switch for local ATM network interfaces. Public NNI defines the routing protocol for the connection between ATM switches.

PNNI uses an link-state architecture and has QOS features such as available cell rate, maximum cell transfer delay, maximum cell loss ratio, and maximum cell rate.

When a node comes up, PNNI sends hello packets and database synchronization messages to the receiving node and develops a route in the table for this node. PNNI sends updates when changes occur for synchronization. PNNI can be defined for redundant links. This is the ability to do parallel links with configuration additional parameters. If a specific route failed, PNNI will adjust to the failure and dynamically select a new path.

ATM Cell Header Format

Following is a description of the fields in an ATM cell header. A cell header can be a UNI or an NNI cell header.

- GFC—The Generic Flow Control field is only used by the device that originates the cell.

- VCI—The Virtual Channel Identifier identifies the virtual circuit that has been established to carry traffic to the destination. The VCI is a local definition so it is only significant to the UNI. The ATM switch will map the VCIs together throughout the switching process.

- VPI—The Virtual Path Identifier is a part of the connection required for an ATM definition. The VPI configuration must be the same on both ends. The name describes it well with the path keyword. Remember ATM is connection oriented, so a defined path must be established. The path must be the same to complete the ATM connection.

- PT—The Payload Type is used to identify the type of data transported.

- CLP—The Cell Loss Priority has a value of 0 or 1 and indicates the possibility of cells being dropped. The ATM cell or the client can set this value.

- HEC—The Header Error Check is a value that is calculated based on the first four bytes.

ATM Protocol Reference Model

Figure 21.2 shows the ATM reference model. It has four major layers, which are listed here with the characteristics of each:

- Physical layer—Defines the Physical network media and framing
- ATM layer—Defines ATM cell relaying and Multiplexing (Asynchronous TDM)
- ATM Adaptation layer—Performs conversion from higher layer to ATM cell. There are three versions:
  - AAL1 (ATM Adaptation Layer 1) which is how ATM works with Time Division Multiplexing (TDM)

- AAL3/AAL4: For SMDS
- AAL5: Defined as the Simple Effective Adaptation Layer (SEAL) that is mostly used today. AAL5 has better bandwidth utilization. This layer doesn't have error recovery so the ATM higher layer handles the error-recovery process.

■ Higher layers—Define ATM signaling, addressing, and routing

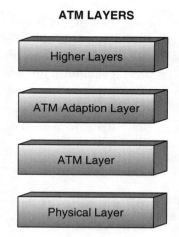

Figure 21.2
The four major layers in the ATM Reference model.

 Key Concept

The ATM reference model has four layers: Physical, ATM, AAL, and Higher layers.

ATM Addressing

A network uses ATM addresses to identify devices and end stations. Normal ATM communications are used during call setup. When the call setup is complete, the remaining operations are performed by the VPI/VCI for the remainder of the connection.

ATM uses two forms of addresses:

■ E.164—Used for public ATM networks.
■ Network Service Access Point (NSAPA)—Used for private networks. The NSAP address is 20 bytes long, and the ATM address of the interface must be unique across the network.

PART
VI

CH
21

Key Concept

ATM uses two forms of addresses: E.164, used for public ATM networks, and Network Service Access Point (NSAPA), used for private networks.

The private network address (NSAPA) uses a 20-byte format. The private address is broken into two parts:

- Initial Domain Part (IDP)—First 13 bytes. An Initial Domain Part (IDP) consists of two elements: an authority and format identifier (AFI) that identifies the type and format of the second element, the initial domain identifier (IDI). The IDI identifies the address allocation and administration authority.

- Domain Specific Part (DSP)—Remaining 7 bytes. A Domain Specific Part (DSP) contains the actual routing information in three elements: a high-order domain specific part (HO-DSP), an end system identifier (ESI), which is the MAC address, and NSAP selector (SEL) field.

Figure 21.3 illustrates the NSAPA ATM address format.

AFI 1 byte	LCD or DCC 2 bytes	user hierarchy 10 bytes	ESI 6 bytes	SEL 1 byte

Figure 21.3
NSAPA format ATM address.

ATM Signaling

ATM requires signaling and addressing. A virtual connection must be established for the transmission of traffic across the ATM network. The ATM end points will originate the ATM call.

The Q.2931 signaling protocol operates over the SSCOP (Service Specific Convergence Protocol). SSCOP is a Data Link layer protocol that ensures the reliable transport of signaling requests.

Key Concept

Q.2931 operates over the SSCOP (Service Specific Convergence Protocol). SSCOP is a reliable Data Link layer protocol for signaling requests.

ATM Features and Terminology

The following key features of ATM are important concepts of ATM technology: SSCOP, PNNI, and Quality of Service.

Service Specific Convergence Protocol (SSCOP)

As mentioned earlier, Service Specific Convergence Protocol (SSCOP) is an OSI Data Link layer protocol that ensures the reliable transport of signaling requests. Q.2931 signaling protocol operates over SSCOP. Signaling requests are encapsulated into the SSCOP frame. SSCOP frames are carried across the ATM network in AAL5 encapsulation.

Key Concept

SSCOP frames are carried across the ATM network in AAL5 encapsulation.

Interim-Interswitch Signaling Protocol (IISP)

IISP is Interim-Interswitch Signaling Protocol and it is basically static ATM routing. IISP protocol is interchangeable between ATM networks. Static routing tables must be set up in each switch while UNI is used between switches. IISP allows multivendor switch connections. IISP can be defined for redundancy, but doesn't adjust to route failures without manual configuration.

Key Concept

IISP is Interim-Interswitch Signaling Protocol, and it is basically static ATM routing.

Quality of Service (QoS)

ATM has the capability to provide guaranteed Quality of Service (QoS). This allows the prevention of congestion issues caused by events such as traffic bursts during periods of high utilization. When traffic such as video requires constant connection without delay to avoid disruption, ATM QOS is beneficial.

Quality of Service (QOS) is negotiated when initial connection is made. QOS defines how the source will send traffic over an ATM cloud. Usually the default settings are fine for ATM to work properly, but there might be times when QOS features are necessary. The fixed-size cells are sent at different rates to support different application bandwidth

PART

VI

CH

21

requirements. ATM QOS is a method used for congestion management when a network experiences bandwidth issues. This is when high rates of traffic exceed the amount of available bandwidth. When this occurs, the traffic is normally dropped or delayed with other transport mechanisms (such as a leased line). Some types of traffic such as video can't be delayed or it will not work effectively. This is a case where an increased amount of bandwidth becomes necessary. ATM QOS fills this need.

Key Concept

ATM QOS is used for congestion management when high rates of traffic exceed the amount of available bandwidth.

The following are examples of ATM QOS features:

- CBR—Constant Bit Rate
- VBR—Variable Bit Rate
- UBR—Unspecified Bit Rate

Configuration Examples

The following section explains the requirements and various techniques for the configuration of ATM PVCs and SVCs. This will include configuration examples of both.

ATM Permanent Virtual Circuit (PVC) Configuration Examples Using AAL5snap and AAL5mux Encapsulations

The following PVX examples describe AAL5snap and AAL5mux encapsulations. I focus on these because they are the more commonly used ATM encapsulations. In the following example, PVCs are statically configured on an ATM interface of two routers to bind traffic between PVC-ROUTER-A and PVC-ROUTER-B. Notice that signaling (QSAAL) and ILMI is not defined for Permanent Virtual Circuits (PVCs) because static mappings are required for direct mappings from end to end. In this case, a map-list called `cisco` defines a mapping of IP and IPX addresses from the remote end's ATM interface, and the `map-group cisco` command binds this map to the local ATM interface.

Notice that IP and IPX are defined on separate PVCs using AALMUX encapsulation. This creates separate PVC paths for each type of traffic. This is the difference and advantage over using AALSNAP. The advantage of AALSNAP is that it allows the use of Inverse ARP, which doesn't require static configuration maps from the remote to the local ATM interface. The local end will send an ARP request to resolve the IP address of the remote end. This works only for IP, so static maps are still required for other protocols. In the following example, the PVC configuration is defined without Inverse ARP between Routers A and B, so you will need to obtain the IPX address of the remote router's interface to bind this to the local interfaces. To obtain this information, issue the command show ipx interface atm0/0.1 on the remote ends. Routers A and C have users that require IP services only from one another and are configured for Inverse ARP between them.

PVC-ROUTER-A#:

```
interface ATM0/0
 no ip address

interface ATM0/0.1 multipoint
 ip address 10.5.99.2 255.255.255.0
 map-group cisco                    (binds the map list below to this interface)
 atm pvc 3 0 132 aalmux ip
(creates a PVC for IP on this interface to the remote end)
 atm pvc 5 0 133 aal5mux novell
    (creates a PVC for IPX to the remote end)
 atm pvc 4 0 134 aal5snap ip  inarp
(creates a PVC for IP on this interface to the remote end using inverse arp)

 map-list cisco
 (creating a mapping of the remote ATM device for IP and IPX)
 ipx C0016044.0000.30c8.74da atm-vc 5 broadcast
 ip 10.5.99.1 atm-vc 3 broadcast
```

PVC-ROUTER-B#:

```
interface ATM0/0
 no ip address

interface ATM0/0.1 multipoint
 ip address 10.5.99.1 255.255.255.0
 map-group cisco                    (binds the map list below to this interface)
 atm pvc 3 0 132 aal5mux ip
(creates a PVC for IP on this interface to the remote end)
 atm pvc 5 0 133 aal5mux novell
    (creates a PVC for IPX to the remote end)
 map-list cisco
 (creating a mapping of the remote ATM device for IP and IPX)
 ipx C0016044.0000.30c8.1292 atm-vc 5 broadcast
 ip 10.5.99.2 atm-vc 3 broadcast
```

PVC-ROUTER-C#:

```
interface ATM0/0
 no ip address
```

```
interface ATM0/0.1 multipoint
 ip address 10.5.99.3 255.255.255.0
atm pvc 4 0 134 aal5snap ip  inarp
(creates a PVC for IP on this interface to the
 remote end using Inverse ARP)
```

The following are all the encapsulations used for ATM PVCs:

- Qsaal—Signaling PVC.

- Ilmi—PVC for status and enquiry information.

- Nlpid—When a High Speed Serial Interface (HSSI) is connected to an ATM network and is configured for ATM-DXI or when an ATM interface connects to an HSSI interface across an ATM network.

- aal45smds—PVCs for SMDS.

- aal5snap—The only PVC encapsulation that supports Inverse ARP. This is used for transport of multiple network layer protocols over a single PVC.

- aal5mux—This PVC encapsulation is used to transport multiple network layer protocols over multiple PVCs.

ATM Switched Virtual Circuit (SVC) Configuration Example

The following SVC configuration provides information necessary for ATM ARP and mappings from the clients to the ATM ARP server for requests from ATM to IP. You should notice in SVC-Router-A that it is defined as the ATM ARP server with the command ATM ARP server self within the configuration. All other SVC connections to Router A must establish an NSAP address connection to this router because it is the ARP Server for the ATM network. Notice in SVC-Router-B that the ATM ARP server is configured with the NSAP address of Router A. This provides the NSAP address connection from Router B to Router A. The IP connection is configured for Inverse ARP between both routers. Remember the difference between Inverse ARP and ATM ARP. Inverse ARP is used for PVCs to determine the IP address of the remote end. ATM ARP is used to establish and maintain a connection to the ATM ARP Server for ATM to IP maps.

SVC-ROUTER-A:

```
interface ATM0/0
 no ip address
 atm pvc 1 0 5 qsaal
(signaling for connections to remote ATM addresses)

 atm pvc 3 0 3 aal5snap inarp (Inverse Arp for remote
IP Address)
```

```
interface ATM0/0.1 multipoint
 ip address 10.5.99.2 255.255.255.0
atm nsap-address
47.0091810000000010000030000.00100758C800.ca
(defines the ATM NSAPA address for this interface)
 map-group cisco
Atm arp-server self
```

SVC-ROUTER-B:

```
interface ATM0/0
 no ip address
 atm pvc 1 0 5 qsaal
 (signaling for connections to remote ATM addresses)
 atm pvc 3 0 3 aal5snap inarp (inverse arp for
 remote IP Address)

interface ATM0/0.1 multipoint
 ip address 10.5.99.3 255.255.255.0
atm nsap-address 47.0091810000000010000030000.00100758C800.C8
(defines the ATM NSAPA address for this interface)
Atm arp-server 47.0091810000000010000030000.00100758C800.ca
```

Summary

ATM is a connection-oriented cell-switching protocol that requires end-to-end circuits connectivity to be established before traffic is forwarded. ATM is a 53-byte cell composed of a 5-byte header and a 48-byte payload. ATM uses Quality of Service (QoS) features for congestion control and traffic management. ATM uses the 20-byte NSAPA address scheme for private networks and E.164 for public networks.

In ATM, there are two types of circuits: Permanent Virtual Circuits (PVCs) and Switched Virtual Circuits (SVCs). There are two ATM interfaces: User to Network Interface (UNI) and Network or Node to Network Interface (NNI).

ATM is divided into layers within the ATM Reference model. Following are the layers from highest to lowest:

- Higher layers
- ATM Adaptation layer
- ATM layer
- Physical

PART
VI

CH
21

QUESTIONS AND ANSWERS

1.   What is the size of an ATM cell's payload?

     A. 48 bytes

2.   What is the size of an ATM NSAP address?

     A. 20 bytes

3.   What ATM address is used for private networks?

     A. NSAPA

4.   What type of routing protocol does PNNI resemble?

     A. Link-state protocols

5.   Which part of the ATM Model handles PNNI?

     A. Higher layers

6.   Does ATM in cell-switching technology fragment frames as they transverse through an ATM circuit?

     A. No

7.   Which signaling protocol is used for interchangeable vendor ATM switches?

     A. IISP

8.   SSCOP is at what layer of the OSI model?

     A. Data Link layer

9.   Which layer of the OSI model is similar to the higher layers of the ATM Protocol model?

     A. Network layer

10. Name the signaling protocol that can be defined for parallel links.

     A. PNNI

PRACTICE TEST

1. What is the size of an ATM cell's payload?

   A. 53 bytes

   B. 5 bytes

   C. 48 bytes

Answer A is incorrect because the entire ATM cell is 53 bytes and is composed of the header and the payload. Answer B is incorrect because the header is 5 bytes. **Answer C is correct because an ATM cell's payload is 48 bytes and the header is 5 bytes.**

2. ATM PVCs are temporary connections and tear down a call when traffic rates end.

   A. True

   B. False

Answer A is incorrect because PVCs are permanent connections and don't terminate when traffic ends. **Answer B (False) is correct because an ATM PVC is a permanent virtual circuit. It is connection oriented and does not terminate when the traffic ends.**

3. Which field in the header only originates in the local cell?

   A. HEC

   B. GFC

   C. PT

Answer A is incorrect because the Header Error Check (HEC) is a value that is calculated based on the first four bytes of the cell. **Answer B is correct because the Generic Flow Control field is used only by the device that originates the cell.** Answer C is incorrect because the Payload Type (PT) is used to identify the type of data transported.

4. What is the size of an ATM NSAP address?

   A. 48 bytes

   B. 53 bytes

   C. 20 bytes

Answer A is incorrect because the ATM cell header, not the NSAP address, is 48 bytes. Answer B is incorrect because the ATM cell is 53 bytes, not the ATM NSAP address. **Answer C is correct. An ATM NSAPA is 20 bytes.**

5. What ATM address is used for private networks?

   A. q2931

   B. NSAPA

   C. Private NNI

PART

VI

CH

21

Answer A is incorrect because the Q.2931 is a signaling protocol that operates over the SSCOP (Service Specific Convergence Protocol). **Answer B is correct because NSAPA is the address format used for private networks.** Answer C is incorrect because Private NNI is the protocol used between interfaces to define the connection between an endpoint into the ATM network private networks.

6. What type of routing protocol does PNNI resemble?

   A. Distance vector

   B. Link-state

   C. EIGRP

Answer A is incorrect because PNNI updates only when changes occur, unlike distance vector, which updates its routing table at a specific set of intervals. **Answer B is correct. PNNI resembles link-state protocols, such as OSPF. PNNI sends hello packets to establish neighbors and updates when changes occur for synchronization.** Answer C is incorrect because EIGRP is not a link-state protocol; it is a hybrid protocol that updates routing tables instead of link-state information, which is similar to PNNI operation.

7. Which layer of the ATM model handles PNNI?

   A. Layer 2

   B. ATM Adaptation layer

   C. ATM higher layers

Answer A is incorrect because layer 2 is part of the OSI Protocol Reference Model, not the ATM model. Answer B is incorrect because the ATM Adaptation layer performs conversion from higher layer to ATM cell. **Answer C is correct. The ATM higher layers handles PNNI signaling and routing.**

8. ATM is cell-switching technology that fragments frames as it transverses through an ATM circuit.

   A. True

   B. False

Answer A is incorrect because ATM has no concept of frames being fragmented. **Answer B (False) is correct because ATM has no concept of frames. ATM is a cell-switching technology.**

9. Which signaling protocol is used for interchangeable vendor ATM switches?

   A. Public NNI

   B. Private NNI

   C. IISP

Answer A is incorrect because Public NNI is the ATM routing protocol used between ATM switches. Answer B is incorrect because Private NNI is the protocol used between end stations and the local ATM switch. **Answer C is correct because IISP is the signaling protocol used for signaling between multivendor ATM switches.**

10. SSCOP is at what layer of the OSI model?

A. Physical layer

B. Data Link layer

C. Network layer

D. ATM layer

Answer A is incorrect because the Physical layer refers to the physical devices and the media for transporting information. SSCOP is a Data Link layer protocol. **Answer B is correct because SSCOP is a Data Link layer protocol.** Answer C is incorrect because SSCOP is a layer 2 protocol. Answer D is incorrect because SSCOP is layer 2 protocol that ensures the reliable transport of signaling requests.

11. Which layer of the OSI model is similar to the higher layers of the ATM Protocol model?

A. Network

B. Transport

C. Data Link

D. Physical

Answer A is correct. The ATM higher layer is similar to the Network OSI layer because this is the layer where routing occurs. Answer B is incorrect because the Transport layer doesn't provide routing, unlike the Network layer. Answer C is incorrect because the Data Link layer doesn't provide routing similar to the ATM higher layers. Answer D is incorrect because the Physical layer has no concept of any features above layer 1. The Physical layer is associated with the media that transport information and network devices.

12. Which signaling protocol doesn't support ILMI?

A. IISP

B. PNNI

C. Neither A nor B

Answer A is correct. IISP doesn't support ILMI for obtaining configuration information for the remote end because this only supports static routes and connections between ATM switches. Answer B is incorrect because PNNI supports ILMI for route discovery. Answer C is incorrect because PNNI does support ILMI for router discovery.

PART

VI

CH

21

13. Name the signaling protocol that can be defined for parallel links and automatic redundancy.

    A. PNNI

    B. IISP

    C. Q.2931

Answer A is correct because PNNI is used for parallel routes. If a route fails, PNNI will adjust to the failure and dynamically select a new path. Answer B is incorrect because IISP is used to define static routes and doesn't provide a concept for automatic discovery. Answer C is incorrect because the Q.2931 is a signaling protocol that operates over the SSCOP (Service Specific Convergence Protocol).

14. What is the size of an ATM cell header?

    A. 20 bytes

    B. 5 bytes

    C. 48 bytes

Answer A is incorrect because 20 bytes is the size of an ATM NSAP address, not the ATM cell header. **Answer B is correct. An ATM cell is 53 bytes and composed of a header that is 5 bytes and the payload, which is 48 bytes.** Answer C is incorrect because 48 bytes defines the size of the ATM payload.

Appendixes

A Objectives Index

B Glossary

C CCIE Certification Process and Testing Tips

D Alternative Resources

E Using the CD-ROM

F Lab Exercises

Objectives Index

Objective	Subobjective	Topic	Chapter(s)	Section	Page(s)
1) Cisco Device Operation	Commands	2, 5–21	Throughout Each Chapter		
	Infrastructure	NVRAM	2	Router Infrastructure Review	42
		Flash Memory and CPU	2	Router Infrastructure Review	42
		File system	2	Router Infrastructure Review	43
		Configuration	2	Router Management	43
		Register	2	Router Management	43
	Operations	File transfers	2	Router Management	44
		Password recovery	2	Router Management	44
		SNMP	2	SNMP	47
		Accessing devices	2	Router Management	43
		Security and passwords	2	Router Management	46

...continues

...continued

Objective	Subobjective	Topic	Chapter(s)	Section	Page(s)
2) General Networking Theory	OSI Model	Layer comparisons	1	OSI Model	10
		Functions	1	OSI Model	10
	General Routing Concepts	Split Horizon	9	Split Horizon	180
		Poison Reverse	9	Poison Reverse	181
		Switching versus Routing	1	Switching Versus Routing	13
		Summarization	14	Summarization Issues	264
		Link State versus Distance Vector	9	Link State Versus Distance Vector	183
		Routing loops	9	Loop Prevention Distance Techniques	180
		Tunneling	1	Tunneling	13
	Protocol Comparisons	IP versus IPX	8, 15	Entire Chapters	
		TCP versus UDP	8	TCP & UDP Sections	160, 163
	Protocol standards and limitations	802.x	1	Layer 2 Standards	14
		Other Layer 2 Protocols	1, 7	Layer 2 Standards, Entire Chapter	14, 123
	Protocol Mechanics	Windowing/ACKs	1, 8	Windowing, ACKs, TCP	18, 160
		MTU	1	MTU	19
		Handshaking	1	Handshaking	17
		Termination	1	Termination	19
3) Bridging and LAN Switching	Transparent Bridging	IEEE/DEC Spanning Tree	6	STP	108
		Translational Bridging	7	SR/TLB	136
		Bridge Protocol Data Unit (BPDU)	6	BPDU	108

Objective	Subobjective	Topic	Chapter(s)	Section	Page(s)
		Integrated Routing and Bridging (IRB)	7	IRB	126
		Concurrent Routing and Bridging (CRB)	7	CRB	124
		Access Lists	2	Access Lists	27
		Configuration (STP)	6	STP	107
		Configuration (Translational Bridging)	7	SR/TLB	137
	Source Route Bridging	Source-Route Translational Bridging (SR/TLB)	7	SR/TLB	136
		Source-Route Transparent Bridging (SRT)	7	SRT	135
		Data-Link Switching (DLSw)	7	DLSw	139
		Remote Source-Route Bridging (RSRB)	7	RSRB	134
		Access Lists	2	Access Lists	27
		Configuration	7		Throughout entire chapter
	LAN Switching	Trunking	6	Trunking	111
		VLAN Trunk Protocol (VTP)	6	VTP	114
		Inter-Switch Link (ISL)	6	Trunking	111
		Virtual LAN's (VLANs)	6	Trunking	111
		FastEther Channel (FEC)	6	EtherChannel	113
		Cisco Discovery Protocol (CDP)	2	CDP	46
		Cisco Group Management Protocol (CGMP)	6, 14	CGMP	117, 281

...continues

...continued

Objective	Subobjective	Topic	Chapter(s)	Section	Page(s)
	LANE	LAN Emulation Client (LEC)	5	LANE Components	86
		LAN Emulation Server (LES)	5	LANE Components	86
		Broadcast and Unknown Server (BUS)	5	LANE Components	86
		LAN Emulation Configuration Server (LECS)	5	LANE Components	86
		Simple Server Replication Server (SSRP)	5	SSRP	95
4) IP	Addressing				
		Address Resolution Protocol (ARP)	8	ARP	158
		Network Address Translation (NAT)	8	NAT	169
		Hot Standby Router Protocol (HSRP)	8	HSRP	167
	Services	Domain Name System (DNS)	8	DNS	165
		Bootstrap Protocol (BOOTP)	8	Well-Known TCP/ UDP Ports	164
		Dynamic Host Configuration Protocol (DHCP)	8	DHCP	168
		Internet Control Message Protocol (ICMP)	8	ICMP	166
	Applications	Telnet	8	Well-Known TCP/ UDP Ports	164
		File Transfer Protocol (FTP)	8	Well-Known TCP/ UDP Ports	164
		Trivial File Transfer Protocol (TFTP)	8	Well-Known TCP/ UDP Ports	165
	Transport	IP Fragmentation	8	IP	152
		Sockets	9	IPX	183
		Ports	8	Well-Known TCP/ UDP Ports	164

Objective	Subobjective	Topic	Chapter(s)	Section	Page(s)
	Access Lists	IP Standard and Extended	2	Access Lists	29
5) IP Routing Protocols	Open Shortest Path First (OSPF)	Areas	12	Entire Chapter	
		Virtual Links	12	Virtual Links	236
		Router Types	12	Router Types	234
		Redistribution	14	Route Redistribution	262
		Media Dependencies	12	OSPF Features	228
		External versus Internal	12	Area Types	233
		Summarization	14	Summarization Issues	264
		Link State Advertisements (LSAs)	12	Route Discovery	232
		Link-State Database	12	Route Discovery	232
		SPF Algorithm	12	Features	228
		Authentication	12	Authentication	228
	Border Gateway Protocol (BGP)	Peer Groups	13	Neighbors/Peers	250
		Filters	13	Filters	248
		Confederations	13	Confederation	256
		Clusters	13	Terms and Commands	246
		Attributes	13	Terms and Commands	246
		Autonomous System (AS)	13	BGP	246
		Route Maps	13	Route Maps	247
		Neighbors	13	Neighbors/Peers	250
		Decision Algorithm	13	Decision Algorithm	250
		Interior BGP	13	IBGP	252
		Exterior BGP	13	EBGP	252

...continues

...continued

Objective	Subobjective	Topic	Chapter(s)	Section	Page(s)
	Enhanced Interior Gateway Routing Protocol (EIGRP)	Metrics	11	Decision Algorithm	217
		Mechanism	11	Terms and Commands	217
		Configuration	11	Entire Chapter	
	Intermediate System to Intermediate System (IS-IS)	Metrics	9	Link State Versus Distance Vector	183
	Multicast	Protocol Independent Multicast (PIM)	14	PIM	275
		Distance Vector Multicast Routing Protocol (DVMRP)	14	DVMRP	278
		Internet Group Management Protocol (IGMP)	6, 14	IGMP	116, 280
6) Desktop Protocols	Internetwork Packet Exchange (IPX)	NetWare Link Services (NLSP)	15	IPX NLSP	295
		IPX-RIP	15	IPX RIP	294
		IPX-EIGRP	11	IPX EIGRP	219
		IPX-SAP	15	SAP	293
		Sequenced Packet Exchange (SPX)	1	OSI Protocol Map	12
		Network Control Protocol (NCP)	1	OSI Protocol Map	12
		ipxwan	15	ipxwan	294
		Addressing	15	IPX Addressing	290
		Get Nearest Server (GNS)	15	Get Nearest Server	293
		Access Lists	2	Access Lists	27

Objective	Subobjective	Topic	Chapter(s)	Section	Page(s)
	AppleTalk	Routing Table Maintenance Protocol (RTMP)	16	RTMP	318
		AppleTalk Update-based Routing (AURP)	16	AURP	318
		AppleTalk EIGRP	11	EIGRP	219
		Datagram Delivery Protocol (DDP)	16	DDP	312
		Zone Information Protocol (ZIP)	16	ZIP	315
		Name Binding Protocol (NBP)	16	NBP	315
		Addressing	16	Addressing	310
		Access Lists	2	Access Lists	27
	DECnet/OSI	Addressing	17	DECnet	327
		Access Lists	2	Access Lists	27
	NetBIOS	Overview	17	NetBIOS	330
7) Performance Management	Traffic Management	Resource Reservation Protocol (RSVP)	2	RSVP	36
		Traffic Shaping	20	Traffic Shaping	405
		Load Balancing	2	Load Balancing	37
	Queuing	Weighted Fair Queuing (WFQ)	2	Queuing	34
		Priority Queuing	2	Queuing	35
		Custom Queuing	2	Queuing	35
8) WAN	ISDN	LAPD	18	ISDN Protocols	342
		BRI versus PRI	18	ISDN	340
		Framing and Signaling	18	ISDN Protocols	342
		Configuration	18	Examples	354
		Interface Types	18	Reference Points	340
		Channel Bonding	18	PPP	345
	Frame Relay	Link Management Interface (LMI)	20	LMI	396
		Data Link Connection Identifier (DLCI)	20	Permanent Virtual Circuits and DLCIs	395

…continues

PART
VII

APP
A

...continued

Objective	Subobjective	Topic	Chapter(s)	Section	Page(s)
		Framing	20	LMI	396
		Traffic Shaping	20	Traffic Shaping	
		Forward Explicit Congestion Notification (FECN)	20	Frame Relay Traffic Management	403
		Backward Explicit Congestion Notification (BECN)	20	Frame Relay Traffic Management	403
		CIR	20	Frame Relay Traffic Management	403
		Discard Eligible (DE)	20	Frame Relay Traffic Management	404
	X.25	Addressing	19	Addressing	368
		Routing	19	X.25 Routing	369
		LAPB	19	LAPB	372
		Error Control and Recovery	19	Error Control/Recovery	374
		Windowing	19	Flow Control/Windowing	376
		Signaling	19	Signaling	377
		Mapping	19	Mapping	378
		PVC versus SVC	19	SVC/PVC	380
		Protocol Translation	19	Protocol Translation	383
	ATM	PVC versus SVC	21	PVCs and SVCs	414
		ATM Adaptation Layer (AAL)	21	ATM Protocol Reference Model	416
		Service Specific Convergence Protocol (SSCOP)	21	SSCOP	419
		User-Network Interface (UNI) and Network-Network Interface (NNI)	21	ATM Interfaces	414
		Cell Format	21	ATM Cell Header Format	416

Objective	Subobjective	Topic	Chapter(s)	Section	Page(s)
		Quality of Service (QoS)	21	QoS	419
		Private Network-Network Interface (PNNI)	21	PNNI	415
		Interim-Interswitch Signaling Protocol (IISP)	21	IISP	419
	Physical Layer	Synchronization	18-21	Protocol Overview Sections	339-428
		SONET	1	OSI Protocol Map	13
		T1 and E1	1	WAN Interfaces	20
	Leased Line Protocols	High-Level Data Link Control (HDLC)	18	ISDN Protocols	342
		Point to Point Protocol (PPP)	18	PPP	345
		Compression	2	Compression	36
	Dial on Demand Routing (DDR)	Dial Backup	18	ISDN and DDR	349
9) LAN	Data Link Layer	Addressing	1	Layer 2 Standards	14
		802.2 (LLC)	1	802.2 (LLC)	15
	Ethernet, FastEthernet, and Gigabit Ethernet	Encapsulation	3	Ethernet II Versus IEEE 802.3	64
		CSMA/CD	3	Carrier Sense and Collision Detection	60
		Topology	3	Definition and Architecture	58
		Speed	3	Definition and Architecture	59
		Controller Errors	3	IEEE 802.3 MAC Frame and Address Format	62
		Limitations	3	Limitations and Troubleshooting	65
		802.3	3	Ethernet II Versus IEEE 802.3	63

...continues

PART

VII

APP

A

...continued

Objective	Subobjective	Topic	Chapter(s)	Section	Page(s)
	Token-Ring	Token Passing	4	Token-Ring Operation	73
		Beaconing	4	Token-Ring Fault-Management Mechanisms	75
		Active Monitor	4	Token-Ring Fault-Management Mechanisms	75
		Ring Insertion	4	Token-Ring Operation	73
		Topology	4	Token-Ring	72
	FDDI	Dual Ring (Topology)	4	FDDI	76
	CDDI	Class Redundancy	4	Physical Features	76
		Dual Homing	4	Physical Features	76
		Physical Medium	4	FDDI	77
		Station Management (SMT)	4	Fault-Management Features	77
10) Security	Authentication, Authorization, and Accounting (AAA)	General Concepts	2	AAA	37
		Usage	2	AAA	37
	TACACS	Features	2	TACACS	38
		Usage	2	TACACS	38
	RADIUS	Features	2	RADIUS	38
		Usage	2	RADIUS	38
		Comparison	2	TACACS, RADIUS	38
	Firewalls	PIX	2	Firewalls	39
		Access lists	2	Access Lists	27
	Encryption	Public/Private Key	2	Encryption Keys and DES	40
		Data Encryption	2	Encryption Keys and DES	40

Objective	Subobjective	Topic	Chapter(s)	Section	Page(s)
11) Multiservice		Voice/Video, H.323	2	H.323	41
		Codecs	2	Codecs	41
		Signaling System 7 (SS7)	2	SS7	41
		Real-Time Transport Protocol (RTP)	2	RTP	42
		Quality of Service (QoS)	2	QoS	36

Glossary

5ESS   One of three main telco switch (including ISDN) types in North America.

10BASE-2   10Mbps baseband Ethernet specification using 50-ohm thin coaxial cable. 10BASE-2, which is part of the IEEE 802.3 specification, has a distance limit of 606.8 feet (185 meters) per segment.

10BASE-T   10Mbps baseband Ethernet specification using two pairs of twisted-pair cabling (Category 3, 4, or 5): one pair for transmitting data and the other for receiving data. 10BASE-T is part of the IEEE 802.3 specification.

100BASE-FX   100Mbps baseband Fast Ethernet specification using two strands of multimode fiber-optic cable per link. To guarantee proper signal timing, a 100BASE-FX link cannot exceed 1,312 feet (400 meters) in length.

100BASE-T   100Mbps baseband Fast Ethernet specification using UTP wiring. Like the 10BASE-T technology on which it is based, 100BASE-T sends link pulses over the network segment when no traffic is present.

1000BASE-CX   Full duplex over copper wire.

1000BASE-LX   Full duplex long-wavelength (1300-nm) devices over multimode or single-mode optical fiber.

1000BASE-SX   Full duplex short-wavelength (850-nm) devices over multimode optical fiber

1000BASE-T   Uses Unshielded Twisted Pair.

AAA   Authentication, Authorization, and Accounting, Referred to as *Triple A*. It is a model for security software.

AAL1   ATM Adaptation Layer 1. This is how ATM interacts with TDM (Time Division Multiplexing).

AAL3   ATM Adaptation Layer 3. Supports connectionless and connection-oriented links. Primarily used in conjunction with SMDS (Switched Multimegabit Data Service).

AAL5   ATM Adaptation Layer 5. Supports better bandwidth utilization with low overhead but does not provide error recovery.

AARP   AppleTalk Address Resolution Protocol. AppleTalk's proprietary method for a node to dynamically acquire a network address.

ABR   Area Border Router. A type of OSPF router that has interfaces in more than one OSPF area.

Access List   A configurable list on a Cisco router used to filter incoming or outgoing packets of a particular type or types.

Access-Class   The command access-class defines an access list (from 1 through 99) that filters access to the virtual terminal (telnet) lines on a Cisco router. It is used with an Access List to define the filter parameters.

ACK   Acknowledgment Packet. In TCP, an ACK packet is sent in response to the receiving the SYN packet. See *SYN*.

acknowledgment   See *ACK*.

acknowledgment number   In the TCP header, it contains the next ACK sequence number of the next packet the sending device expects to receive.

active monitor   The management node on a Token-Ring. It is selected on the basis of the highest MAC address on the ring. The active monitor is responsible for ensuring that a token is always in circulation and that frames do not circulate indefinitely.

active router   In HSRP, the router with the highest priority configured is the active router in the standby group. See *HSRP*.

adjacency   A distinction of OSPF routers. An adjacency is formed between two connected routers via the hello protocol. An Adjacencies Database is then formed.

adjacent   Routers that share a common network segment.

administrative distance   A metric used to determine the reliability of the source of routing information. The lower the administrative distance value, the more trustworthy the information. Administrative distances range from 0 to 255.

ADSP   AppleTalk Data Stream Protocol. A reliable protocol that is responsible for transmission of data after the session is established between two nodes.

AEP   AppleTalk Echo Protocol. A Transport layer AppleTalk suite protocol that is similar to ICMP in the TCP/IP suite.

AFP   AppleTalk Filing Protocol. Responsible for managing network access to shared file services and file transfer, as well as seeing to it that shared network volumes appear transparently on the end-user desktop

AMT   Address Mapping Table. In AppleTalk, AARP caches known protocol-to-hardware address mappings in the AMT.

AppleTalk Phase 1   First version of AppleTalk that only supported 254 nodes on a "nonextended" network.

AppleTalk Phase 2   Second version of AppleTalk that supports cable ranges to form "extended" networks of thousands of nodes.

AppleTalk socket   A software entity that exists within an AppleTalk node to provide information about what application is working between the nodes.

Area 0   Always the OSPF backbone area. All areas must be attached to Area 0, either directly or via a Virtual Link. See *Virtual Link*.

ARP   Address Resolution Protocol. Provides dynamic address resolution by mapping MAC addresses to IP address.

ARP cache   Table of MAC address to IP address mappings, so they can be used in the future without sending out ARP messages.

ARPA   Advanced Research Projects Agency. Part of the U.S. Department of Defense that is responsible for creation of the earliest form of what is now the Internet.

ARPAnet   The network developed in the 1970s by the ARPA.

ASBR   Autonomous System Border Router. An OSPF router with one interface connected to one Autonomous System and another interface connected to another Autonomous System.

ASP   AppleTalk Session Protocol. Responsible for setting up and tearing down logical connections between AppleTalk workstations and servers.

ATM   Asynchronous Transfer Mode. ITU-T standard for high-speed multimedia communications over a cell-switched network.

ATM Adaptation layer   Performs conversion from higher layers to ATM cells.

ATP   AppleTalk Transaction Protocol. Responsible for ensuring that communications from source-socket to destination-socket occur without any losses.

AUI   Attachment Unit Interface. Where a MAU attaches to a piece of hardware. See *MAU*.

AURP   AppleTalk Update-based Routing Protocol. Allows the connection of noncontiguous AppleTalk networks via tunneling, typically via TCP/IP.

authoritative   In DNS, it is a server database containing data for a requested domain name. The server will respond directly to the client with the IP address associated to the domain name.

Autonomous System   A group of networks using the same routing protocol and under the same administrative control.

Autonomous System (AS) numbers   In IGRP and EIGRP, all routers must use the same Autonomous System number to exchange routing updates. OSPF does not use AS numbers.

autoreconfiguration   Process performed by nodes in a Token-Ring network. Nodes automatically perform diagnostics in an attempt to work around failed areas.

backbone area   OSPF area in which all traffic must flow between areas. It always is Area 0.

backbone router   An OSPF router with any one of its interfaces connected to Area 0.

B_c   Committed burst size. The number of bits the network guarantees to transport, in time period T_c, under normal circumstances.

B_e   Excess burst size. The number of bits, in time period T_c, by which the user can exceed the B_c. See *B_c*.

BDR   Backup Designated Router. In OSPF, the router that is elected to become the Designated Router (DR) if the DR fails. See *DR*.

beacon   A special frame from a Token-Ring or FDDI device indicating a serious problem with the ring. A beacon frame contains the address of the station assumed to be down.

BECN   Backward Explicit Congestion Notification. The receiver is notified that congestion exists in the opposite direction the frame has traveled.

Bellman-Ford algorithm   The mathematical formula (algorithm) used in Distance Vector Routing to determine the best path.

BGP   Border Gateway Protocol. A loop-free interdomain routing protocol between Autonomous Systems.

BGP next hop   The next-hop IP address that BGP will use to reach a certain destination.

binary   Numbering system characterized by ones and zeros (1 = on, 0 = off).

Blocking Bridge State   A port is listening to BPDUs and sending no user data.

BPDU   Bridge Protocol Data Unit. Spanning-Tree Protocol hello packet that is sent out at configurable intervals to exchange information among bridges in a network.

BRI   Basic Rate Interface. ISDN interface composed of two 64kpbs B (Bearer) channels and one 16kbps D (Delta) channel, typically noted as 2B+D.

bridge ID   Part of a BPDU, the Bridge ID has two parts: a 2-byte Bridge Priority value (0–65,535) and the MAC address of the switch.

broadcast   A data packet that is sent to all nodes on the network.

broadcast storm   An event in which many broadcasts are sent simultaneously across all network segments. Indicates a serious problem in the network configuration.

buffer   A storage area used for temporarily storing data in memory until it can be processed.

BUS   Broadcast and Unknown Server. Multicast server used in LANE ELANs that is used when a LEC wants to send a broadcast or multicast to an unknown ATM address. The BUS handles sending data to multiple locations, thus emulating the effect of broadcasts and multicasts.

BVI   Bridge Virtual Interface. Used in Integrated Routing and Bridging (IRB). Represents the bridging interfaces to the routing process. See *IRB*.

canonical   Within each byte, bits are read from left to right.

canureach Cs   canureach circuit setup message. After an icanreach frame is sent from a DLSw peer router, a canureach Cs triggers the peering routers to establish a circuit.

canureach Ex   canureach explorer message. In DLSw, after an icanreach frame is sent from a peer router, a canureach Ex is sent to find the resource.

canureach frame   When a DLSw router receives an explorer frame, the router sends a canureach frame to each of its DLSw peers. If one of these partners can reach the specified MAC address, it replies with an icanreach frame.

CCITT   Consultative Committee for Telegraphy and Telephony. An international organization responsible for the development of communication standards. Now called ITU-T.

CDDI   Copper Distributed Data Interface. Implementation of FDDI protocols over STP and UTP cabling at data rates of 100Mbps using a dual-ring architecture.

CDP   Cisco Discovery Protocol. Proprietary Data Link protocol used to exchange information about other Cisco devices.

CGMP   Cisco Group Management Protocol. Works with IGMP to control unwanted multicast flooding.

CHAP   Challenge Handshake Authentication Protocol. Security protocol supported by PPP.

CIR   Committed Information Rate. In Frame Relay, it is a data rate transfer that is guaranteed by the service provider.

Classful Routing   A routing protocol that abides to the bit boundaries of public IP address classes. Variable length subnet masks (VLSMs) are not supported because the subnet mask is not included in the classful routing updates.

Classless Routing   A routing protocol that does not abide by the bit boundaries of the IP address classes. Subnet masks are advertised in classless routing updates.

CLNP   Connectionless Network Protocol. OSI Network layer protocol.

CMNS   Connection-Mode Network Service. X.25 services can be extended to nonserial media through the use of packet level X.25 over frame-level LLC2.

codec   Coder-Decoder. Device which sends a signal that represents the actual data. Typically uses Pulse Code Modulation (PCM).

configuration register   In Cisco routers, a 16-bit, user-configurable value that instructs the router how to boot itself.

CONP   Connection-Oriented Network Protocol. OSI protocol providing connection-oriented operation to upper-layer protocols.

convergence   The process of all routers "agreeing" on the network routing topology.

cost   IGRP and EIGRP use a number of metrics to calculate the cost of a route to a destination network. The lower the cost, the better the route.

Count to Infinity   When a maximum hop count value is reached a network is considered to be infinitely far away, and, therefore, unreachable.

CRB   Concurrent Routing and Bridging. Employing a single router to bridge a routable protocol on one group of interfaces and concurrently to route that protocol on another group of interfaces.

CRC   Cyclic Redundancy Check. Error-checking method performed by calculating the CRC value of a frame with a known value to determine whether any transmission errors occurred.

CSMA/CD   Carrier Sense Multiple Access Collision Detect. Media-access mechanism whereby devices that have data to transmit first check the media for activity. If no activity is sensed, a device can transmit. The device will then monitor and detect any collisions and then wait a random period of time before retransmitting.

custom queuing   Reserves an amount of bandwidth you would like a particular type of traffic to use.

DA   Destination Address. The 32-bit MAC address in the IP header that defines the packet's destination.

DAS   Dual Attachment Station. Device attached to both the primary and secondary FDDI rings. Also called a *Class A station*.

Data Link layer   Layer 2 of the OSI reference model. Provides reliable transit of data across a physical link. The Data Link layer handles physical addressing (MAC addresses), line discipline, error notification, delivery of frames, and flow control.

DCE   Data Circuit-terminating Equipment. Provides a physical connection to the network for a WAN link.

DDP   Datagram Delivery Protocol. Provides a connectionless datagram service at layer 3 of the OSI model.

DDR   Dial-on-Demand Routing. Typically implemented with ISDN, it enables a router to initiate and terminate connections to other routers whenever needed. The link is not used when no "interesting traffic" requires transmission.

DE   Discard Eligible. In Frame Relay, any frames with the DE set can be discarded in the event of network congestion.

DEC   Digital Equipment Corporation. A company (now owned by Compaq) that served businesses with a computer platform that accommodates mainframe and PC environments.

DEC LAT   DEC Local Area Transport. A virtual terminal protocol developed by Digital Equipment Corporation.

DEC MOP   DEC Maintenance Operation Protocol. Provides minimal maintenance operations of DECnet networks.

DECnet   A proprietary LAN protocol developed by Digital Equipment Corporation.

DECnet Phase IV   Most recent and widely used version of DECnet protocol in conjunction with DECnet/OSI.

DECnet/OSI   Most recent and widely used version of DECnet protocol in conjunction with DECnet Phase IV.

default route   A routing table entry that provides a route for packets for which the router has no other route in its table.

DEMARC   Demarcation Point between the telephone carrier's equipment and the customer premise equipment (CPE).

Designated Port   Switches need to delegate one oncoming port for each LAN segment it services. The switch uses path costs to select the Designated Port.

destination unreachable   An ICMP message sent when a route to a network destination is not in the routing table.

DHCP   Dynamic Host Configuration Protocol. A protocol that enables the automation of IP addresses assignments within a network.

DHCP discover   A UDP broadcast message sent by a client workstation when it needs to find a DHCP server.

dial backup   A DDR link that stays idle as long as the primary link fails or is overloaded, at which point the dial backup link is used.

Dijkstra algorithm   A routing algorithm that uses the length of the path to determine its route. See *SPF*.

Disabled Bridge State   A bridge port is manually shut down by the administrator.

Distance Vector Protocol   A type of routing protocol in which each router is required to send its entire routing table to its neighbors. The routing algorithm uses the number of hops to determine the best route to a destination network. Uses the Bellman-Ford algorithm.

DIX   The collaborative group—including Digital Equipment Corporation, Intel, and Xerox—that originally developed Ethernet. The standard is now known as Ethernet II.

DLC   Data Link Connections. This is a standard method for sending data over a single communications link.

DLCI   Data Link Connection Identifier. Specifies an SVC or a PVC in Frame Relay networks.

DLSw   Data-Link Switching. Provides a method for forwarding SNA and NetBIOS traffic over TCP/IP networks using Data Link layer encapsulation and switching. See *DLSw circuits*.

DLSw circuits   Data Link Switching Circuits. The process of creating a Data Link connection between an SNA device and a router, followed by a TCP connection to another router, and the Data Link connection between that router and the destination SNA device.

DLSw peer   A router that maintains a connection between other DLSw routers, or peers.

DMS-100   One of three main switch types for ISDN in North America.

DNA   Digital Network Architecture. Multilayered network architecture, similar to the OSI reference model, designed by Digital Equipment Corporation.

DNIC   Data Network Identification Codes. Part of the International Data Number (IDN) which is part of the X.121 address in an X.25 network. The DNIC is divided into two parts: The first part specifies the country, and the second part specifies the packet-switched network itself.

DNS   Domain Name Service. Maps and resolves IP addresses to hostnames. DNS is hierarchical in nature and is used by the Internet and many corporate intranets.

DoD   Department of Defense. A government agency that has frequently funded communication protocol development, including the ARPAnet project.

dotted decimal notation   Representation of a 32-bit integer consisting of four 8-bit numbers with periods (dots) separating them. Used to represent IP addresses in the Internet, as in 192.67.67.20. Also called *dotted quad notation*.

downstream neighbor   The next station that will receive packets in a Token-Ring environment. Each station is responsible for transmitting frames to its downstream neighbor.

DQDB   Distributed Queue Dual Bus. MAN specification that allows multiple nodes to access two unidirectional buses.

DR   Designated Router. An OSPF router that is elected to represent all other routers in the same LAN.

DRP   DECnet Routing Protocol. A routing protocol used to determine optimal paths in a DECnet Phase IV network.

DTE   Data Terminal Equipment. Device at the user end of the network that includes devices such as terminals and computers. Connects to the data network though a DCE device.

DUAL   Diffusing Update Algorithm. A Cisco proprietary protocol used by EIGRP that is designed to be a hybrid between Distance Vector protocols and Link-State protocols. It calculates routes in a way similar to Distance Vector Protocols but advertises them like Link State Protocols.

DVMRP   Distance Vector Multicast Routing Protocol. Used to forward multicast traffic by multicast routers.

E1   WAN digital service (used predominantly in Europe) that carries data at a rate of 2.048Mbps over 30 channels.

early release   In Token-Ring networks, it allows a token to be released by the sending workstation as soon as it has sent its data frame, rather than waiting for the frame to return from the destination.

EBGP   External Border Gateway Protocol. An external routing protocol that exchanges routing information with external BGP neighbors.

EBGP Multihop   A neighbor connection to be established between two indirectly connected external peers.

EEPROM   Electronic Erasable Programmable Read-Only Memory. Also known as *flash memory*. Where the Cisco IOS is stored.

EIGRP   Enhanced Interior Gateway Routing Protocol. A Cisco proprietary protocol that is a hybrid of link-state and distance-vector protocols. Uses the DUAL algorithm.

ELAN   Emulated LAN. ATM network in which an Ethernet or Token-Ring LAN is emulated using a client/server model. ELANs are composed of devices called LEC, LES, BUS, and LECS.

ELAP   EtherTalk Link Access Protocol. Link-access protocol built on top of the standard Ethernet Data Link layer protocol.

encapsulation   The "wrapping" of data in another protocol's header.

EtherChannel   Allows combining two or more physical links between the two devices into a single logical link.

Ethernet   Baseband LAN specification invented by Xerox Corporation and developed jointly by Xerox, Intel, and Digital Equipment Corporation. Ethernet is similar to the IEEE 802.3 series of standards.

EtherTalk   AppleTalk running over Ethernet.

expiration timer   One of two timers used in RIP to ensure invalid routes are removed from the routing table. Also known as *timeout* or *invalid timer.*

exterior route   A type of IGRP route that defines a route to a network outside the Autonomous System.

Fast Ethernet   Any of a number of 100Mbps Ethernet specifications. Fast Ethernet preserves normal Ethernet frame formats, MAC mechanisms, and MTUs.

FCS   Frame Check Sequence. Frame that enables error checking and ensures the integrity of transmitted data.

FDDI   Fiber Distributed Data Interface. LAN standard defined by ANSI X3T9.5, specifying a 100Mbps token-passing network using fiber-optic cable.

FDDI encapsulation types   There are three types of FDDI encapsulation types in Cisco routers: Fddi_Snap (SNAP), the default; Fddi-802.2 (SAP), and Fddi_raw (Novell-FDDI).

FDDITalk   AppleTalk over FDDI.

FECN   Forward Explicit Congestion Notification. The receiver is notified that congestion was encountered along the frame's path in a Frame Relay network.

firewall   Devices designated as a security shield between untrusted networks.

FLAP   FDDITalk Link Access Protocol. Link-access protocol built on top of the standard FDDI Data Link layer protocol.

flapping   A link going up and down frequently and repeatedly.

flash memory   Nonvolatile storage that can be electrically erased and reprogrammed so that software images can be stored, booted, and rewritten as necessary. Also known as *EEPROM.*

floating static route   A default route with an administrative distance greater than the administrative distance of the routing protocol being used.

flow control   A method of ensuring that a sender does not overflow the receiver with data the receiver cannot transmit or buffer.

flush timer   One of two timers used in RIP to ensure invalid routes are removed from the table. Also known as *garbage collection timer*.

forwarding bridge state   A designated or root port starts forwarding user data.

Frame Relay   An industry standard switched Data Link layer protocol using HDLC encapsulation between network devices.

Frame Status Field   In Token-Ring, the destination host sets the A and C bits of the Frame Status Field to 1 before sending the frame to its downstream neighbor.

FTP   File Transfer Protocol. Application-layer protocol, part of the TCP/IP protocol stack, used for transferring files between network nodes.

full duplex   Capability for simultaneous data transmission and reception between a sending node and a receiving node.

garbage collection timer   One of two timers used in RIP to ensure invalid routes are removed from the table. Also known as *flush timer*.

GBIC   Gigabit Ethernet Interface Carrier. Gigabit Ethernet allows you to choose on a port-by-port basis what physical media type you will use by using GBIC.

GetNetInfo request   In AppleTalk it is a request to get a valid network number or cable range for that network.

Gigabit Ethernet   An extension of the IEEE 802.3 Ethernet standard. Gigabit Ethernet builds on the Ethernet protocol but increases speed tenfold over Fast Ethernet, to 1000Mbps, or 1Gbps.

global address   IP address space that is recognizable to the Internet.

GNS   Get Nearest Server. This is an IPX broadcast by a node to locate the nearest Novell server.

GWINFO   One of the earliest versions of the RIP protocol.

H.323   Extension of ITU-T standard H.320 that enables videoconferencing over LANs and other packet-switched networks, as well as video over the Internet.

half duplex   Capability for data transmission in only one direction at a time between two nodes.

handshake   Sequence of messages exchanged between two or more nodes to synchronize transmissions.

HDLC   High-level Data Link Control. A default data-encapsulation method on synchronous serial links.

header checksum   Provides error control for the integrity of the IP header only.

Hello packet   Nodes exchange these packets (via the Hello Protocol) to discover and maintain status of each other.

Hello protocol   Protocol that helps network nodes discover and maintain status of each other.

hexadecimal   Describes a base-16 numbering system. The hexadecimal numbers are 0–9 and letters A–F; a total of 16 characters each representing a number between 0 and 15.

Holddown Timer   A route is not advertised to other routers as a bad route for this time period. Prevents routes being prematurely advertised as down.

HSRP   Hot Standby Routing Protocol. A Cisco proprietary protocol that creates "backup" router group.

IBGP   Interior Border Gateway Protocol. BGP updates are exchanged within one Autonomous System. One Autonomous System can act as a transit system to other Autonomous Systems.

icanreach frame   Response to a DLSw canureach frame, if a DLSw peer router can reach the specified MAC address.

ICMP   Internet Control Message Protocol. A Network-layer protocol within IP that provides an error-reporting mechanism.

IDN   International Data Number. X.121 addresses are sometimes called IDNs. It is made of the DNIC and the NTN.

IEEE   Institute of Electrical and Electronics Engineers. A professional organization whose activities include the development of communications and network standards.

IEEE 802.2   IEEE LAN protocol that specifies an implementation of the LLC sublayer of the Data Link layer. IEEE 802.2 handles errors, framing, and flow control.

IEEE 802.3   IEEE LAN protocol that uses CSMA/CD at a variety of speeds over a variety of physical media.

IEEE 802.5   Uses token-passing access at 4- or 16Mbps over STP cabling. Commonly referred to as Token-Ring, which is an IBM topology.

IEEE 802.6   IEEE MAN specification based on DQDB. IEEE 802.6 supports data rates of 1.5–155Mbps.

IETF Internet Engineering Task Force. A multinational volunteer task force responsible for developing Internet standards.

IGMP Internet Group Management Protocol. A method for routers to track which hosts are interested in receiving traffic for a multicast group.

IGP Interior Gateway Protocol. Routing protocols that operate within a single Autonomous System. Examples are RIP, IGRP, EIGRP, and OSPF.

IGRP Interior Gateway Routing Protocol. A distance-vector routing protocol developed to overcome the inflexibility of RIP. Not limited to the 16 hop-count limitation.

IISP Interim-Interswitch Signaling Protocol. A manually configured ATM signaling protocol for interswitch communication.

information frame If a Token-Ring station does have information to transmit, it seizes the token and appends the information it wants to transmit. It then becomes an information frame.

interactive query A request asking a DNS server to respond with the best information it has about a requested domain name.

interior routes In IGRP, routes are advertised between subnets.

internal router An OSPF router that has all its interfaces within a single area.

invalid timer One of two timers used in RIP to ensure invalid routes are removed from the table. Also known as *timeout* and *expiration timer*. Cisco IOS uses the term *invalid timer*.

Inverse ARP Inverse Address Resolution Protocol. A method for an access server to build dynamic address mappings of the devices associated with the virtual circuit.

IOS Internetworking Operating System. Cisco's proprietary code used to operate many of its networking devices.

IP helper address The address to which a communication server will forward UDP broadcasts.

IPX Internetwork Packet Exchange. Novell's proprietary protocol used to transfer information from servers to workstations.

IPX EIGRP A routing protocol that can be used to route IPX traffic. A variation of EIGRP.

IPX encapsulation types   Four types of encapsulation can be used on Ethernet media for IPX to transmit across different physical media: Novell-Ether, the default Novell-specific variation of IEEE 802.2; Ethernet II (ARPA); 802.2-(SAP); and Ethernet-snap, specific only to IPX.

IPX RIP   Routing protocol to route IPX traffic. Enabled by default when IPX routing is turned on.

IPX socket   The IPX equivalent of IP port numbers. A socket advertises the upper-layer process in IPX.

IPXwan   Feature that allows a single IPX network to be assigned to all WAN interfaces.

IRB   Integrated Routing and Bridging. Configuring a single router to integrate its routing and bridging process on the same interfaces.

ISDN   Integrated Service Digital Network. This is a public digital communication protocol that operates at higher bandwidth than standard dialup connections.

ISDN Callback   Allows a router to return a call to the originating node after that node is authenticated.

ISL   Inter-Switch Link. Cisco-proprietary protocol that allows inter-VLAN trunking.

ISP   Internet service provider. A company that can provide Internet access to other companies and individuals.

ITU-T   International Telecommunication Union-Telecommunication Standardization Sector.

Kerberos   An emerging standard method for network authentication.

L2F   Level 2 Forwarding Protocol. Creates a secure Virtual Private Dial-up Network over the Internet. Used in VPDNs.

LAN   Local area network. Network covering a relatively small geographic area and not involving telecommunication links (via a telecom service provider). LAN standards include Ethernet, FDDI, and Token-Ring.

LANE   LAN Emulation. Layer 2 (Data Link) technology that allows an ATM network to function as a LAN backbone.

LAPB   Link Access Procedure, Balanced. A protocol derived from HDLC.

LAPD   Link Access Procedure D. A protocol derived from LAPB used for ISDN signaling.

PART

VII

APP

B

LAPF Link Access Protocol for Frame Bearer Services. A protocol that follows the generic HDLC format of flag, address, control, data, frame check sequence, and flag.

LCP Link Control Layer Protocol. Layer 2 protocol that is responsible for building, maintaining, and tearing down a PPP connection.

LE Local Exchange. The ISDN service provider's equipment.

Learning Bridge State A port is building bridge tables and not sending user data.

LE_ARP LAN Emulation Address Resolution Protocol. Protocol that provides the ATM address that corresponds to a MAC address.

LEC LAN Emulation Client. An end system that performs data forwarding, address resolution, and other control functions for a single ES in an ELAN.

LEC Local Exchange Carrier. Local telephone company that owns and operates the telephone network a customer connects to.

LECS LAN Emulation Configuration Server. Device that assigns individual LANE clients to particular ELANs. There is logically one LECS per domain, and this serves all ELANs within that domain.

LES LAN Emulation Server. Device that implements the control function for a particular ELAN. There is only one logical LES per ELAN.

link-state A status of a link between two routers.

link-state database Also known as *Topological Database*. It is a list of link-state entries of all routers in the internetwork.

Link-State Protocol A protocol that sends partial routing tables to everyone and then sends updates when necessary. Link-state protocols use more complex metrics to determine the best route to a destination, such as SPF.

Listening Bridge State Sending and receiving BPDUs. Convergence process is taking place.

LLAP LocalTalk Link Access Protocol. A Data Link layer using AppleTalk LocalTalk protocol.

LLC Logical Link Control. Sublayer that handles error control, flow control, framing, and MAC-sublayer addressing.

LMI Local Management Interface. A Frame Relay keepalive that defines control messages between the Frame Relay switch and transmission device (router).

LNNI   LAN Emulation Network-to-Network Interface. The LANE protocol used for ATM switch-to-switch communication.

load balancing   The ability of a router to distribute traffic over multiple network ports.

LocalTalk   Apple Computer Corporation's proprietary baseband protocol that operates at the Data Link and Physical layers of the OSI model.

loopback interface   A virtual interface on a router that remains in the up state.

LQM   Link Quality Monitoring. In PPP, it monitors and manages the quality of a link.

LSA   Link-State Advertisement. An advertisement packet that describes the state of all links, or networks, that each router knows about.

LSU   Link-State Update. Link-state information exchanged between routers.

LUNI   LAN Emulation User-to-Network Interface. Defines the communication between an end station and an ATM switch.

MAC   Media Access Control. Lower of the two sublayers of the Data Link layer defined by the IEEE. The MAC sublayer handles access to shared media.

MAC address   Media Access Control address. The 32-byte address of a node. Also referred to as the physical address, even though it is managed by the MAC sublayer of Layer 2.

MAN   Metropolitan-Area Network. Network that spans a metropolitan area. Too big to be called a LAN, but too small to be called a WAN.

MAU   Media Attachment Unit. Provides the interface between the AUI port of a station and an Ethernet cable. In Token-Ring, a MAU is known as a *Multistation Access Unit* and is usually abbreviated *MSAU* to avoid confusion. See *MSAU*.

MBONE   Multicast Backbone. A virtual multicast network made up of connected multicast LANs via the point-to-point tunnels.

MD5   Message Digest 5. Encryption algorithm used for message authentication. It is used in various protocols such as SNMP v.2, BGP, OSPF, and others.

MED   Multi-Exit Discriminator. Used to influence traffic preference to Autonomous Systems. Lower values are preferred.

metrics   Information used by a routing protocol to determine the best route to a destination. Different routing protocols use different metrics.

MIB   Management Information Base. Database that allows NMS stations to communicate with SNMP agents on network devices.

PART

VII

APP

B

MSAU   Multistation Access Unit. The Token-Ring version of a MAU. See *MAU*.

MTU   Maximum Transmission Unit. Maximum packet size, in bytes, that a particular interface can handle.

multicast   A message sent to a group of addresses.

multiplexing   Allows multiple logical signals to be transmitted over the same physical link.

multipoint   A network connection of multiple points of service.

NAT   Network Address Translation. A mechanism for converting addresses on one network to new addresses that are usable in another network. Most commonly used to convert private addresses into addresses that are usable on the Internet.

NAUN   Nearest Active Upstream Neighbor. In Token-Ring or IEEE 802.5 networks, the NAUN is the closest upstream network device that is still active.

NBP   Name Binding Protocol. Associates AppleTalk names with addresses.

NCP   Network Control Protocol. Describes a group of protocols for establishing specific layer 3 connections over ISDN.

neighbor   Another network device that shares a common network.

NetBEUI   NetBIOS Extended User Interface. Enhanced version of NetBIOS. NetBEUI is used by network operating systems such as LAN Manager, LAN Server, Windows for Workgroups, and Windows NT.

NetBIOS   Network Basic Input/Output System. API used by applications on an IBM LAN to request services from lower-level network processes.

Network layer   Layer 3 of the OSI reference model. Routing occurs at this layer. This layer provides connectivity and path selection between two end systems.

network mask   A 32-bit number used in conjunction with an IP address to delineate the network portion of an IP address from the host portion. Also known as *subnet mask*.

Network Unreachable   An ICMP protocol message indicating that a route is available but there is come kind of routing failure rendering it unreachable.

NI-1   One of three main switch types for ISDN in North America (National ISDN-1).

NLSP   Novell Link Service Protocol. A link-state protocol that can be used to route IPX traffic.

NMS   Network Management System. A computer system responsible for proactively gathering information about the status of a network.

NNI   Network-to-Network Interface. An interface that defines a connection between two ATM devices in the same public or private ATM network or organization, or that connects different Frame Relay networks.

nonauthoritative   A type of query when the DNS server sends out an interactive query to all DNS servers that it knows about.

noncanonical   Within each byte, bits are read from right to left.

NOS   Network Operating System. A term used for the software that runs servers. Examples include NT, LAN Manager, and NetWare.

not-so-stubby area   An OSPF area type that accepts some types of LSAs from external Autonomous Systems.

NSAP   Network Service Access Point. ISO network addresses.

NT1   Network Termination 1. In ISDN, a device that includes an ISDN modem and a 2-to-4 wire converter.

NT2   Network Termination 2. A device that manages switching between multiple ISDN channels. Usually part of a private branch exchange (PBX).

NTN   National Terminal Number. Part of the IDN which is part of the X.121 address in X.25 networks.

NVE   Network Visible Entities. In AppleTalk they are socket clients within a node, not the entire node.

NVRAM   Nonvolatile RAM. RAM that does not erase when power is lost. Where the Cisco router configuration file is saved.

OC   Optical Carrier. Physical protocols for high-speed fiber-optic networks (OC-1, OC-2, OC-3, and so on).

octet   8 bits. A byte is almost always 8 bits, or 1 octet, long.

one-step translation   Seamless conversion technique. When a connection is made to a router, the router determines what host that connection is destined for and which protocol that host is using. It then establishes a new network connection using the protocol required by that (destination) host.

optical bypass switch   Optical switch that permits a signal to pass directly through it, thereby bypassing the unavailable station on a FDDI ring, thereby avoiding segmentation.

OSI   Open Systems Interconnect. An architectural model that describes functional aspects of data communications. This model is composed of seven layers.

OSPF   Open Shortest Path First. A Link-State Routing Protocol designed to overcome the earlier limitations of RIP. OSPF is an open standard. It uses the Dijkstra algorithm or Shortest Path First algorithm to determine its routing table.

OUI   Organizational Unique Identifier. The first 3 octets of a MAC address that are assigned to vendors. The last 24 bits then define the unique address.

packet   An organized set of data, typically defined at the Network layer.

PAD   Packet Assembler/Disassembler. Device that assembles and disassembles packets in an X.25 implementation.

PAP   Password Authentication Protocol. An authentication mechanism over PPP that sends password information in unencrypted form.

PAP   Printer Access Protocol. AppleTalk's connection-oriented protocol that establishes and maintains connections between clients and servers.

PAPClose   In AppleTalk, after data transfer is complete, a workstation or server can use this to close communication.

PAPOpen   In AppleTalk, a PAP session is initiated by a workstation to a PAP server.

PAPRead   In AppleTalk, after a connection is established, a PAP client (server or workstation) can read from the other PAP client.

PAPWrite   In AppleTalk, after a connection is established, a PAP client (server or workstation) can write from the other PAP client.

passive interface   A passive interface on a router does not send routing updates on that particular interface. A passive interface will still receive routing updates.

path cost   A value (usually manually configured) that helps a routing protocol determine the best path to a destination network. Lowest path cost is the best path. Also known as *cost*.

PDN   Public Data Network. A network operated by an organization that is available for the public to use on a fee-for-services basis.

PDU   Protocol Data Unit. Also known as *packet*.

PHY   Physical sublayer. One of the sublayers of the Physical layer in a FDDI network. Specifies framing, data coding and decoding, and timing.

Physical layer   Layer 1 of the OSI reference model. The Physical layer defines the parameters necessary to build, maintain, and break the physical link connections. It defines the characteristics of the connectors, data transmission rates and distances, and the interface voltages.

PIM   Protocol Independent Multicast. A routing protocol routers use to determine which multicast groups need to be forwarded. Operates independent of unicast protocols.

PLP   Packet-Layer Protocol. Level 3 or Network-layer protocol in the X.25 protocol stack.

PMD   Physical Medium Dependent. Layer that specifies the characteristics of the cable, including connectors, power levels, bit error rates, and all optical components.

PNNI   Public or Private Network-to-Network Interface. Private NNI is used for ATM switch to switch for local ATM network interfaces. Public NNI defines the routing protocol for the connection between ATM switches.

Point-to-Point   A network connection of only two points of service.

Poison Reverse   A routing protocol loop-prevention technique in which a router will advertise a route as unreachable out the interface in which it was learned.

port number   A value that indicates an upper-layer process in the IP protocol stack.

POTS   Plain Old Telephone Service. Standard two-wire telephone service.

PPP   Point-to-Point Protocol. Provides a router-to-router or host-to-network connection over synchronous or asynchronous private or public networks.

PPP callback   Creates a client/server relationship between the router placing a call and the router receiving it.

PPP multilink   Allows two or more different physical links to bond together and act like one logical link using PPP.

PPP reliable link   Uses the Numbered Mode LAPB provided for the retransmission of packets with errors.

Presentation layer   Layer 6 of the OSI reference model. It is responsible for encoding and decoding data that is passed from the Application layer. Typical coding schemes include ASCII, EBCDIC, MPEG, GIF, and JPEG.

PRI   Primary Rate Interface. ISDN interface over a channelized T1 line. It is composed of 23 64kbps B (Bearer) channels and one 64kpbs D (Delta) channel. Referred to as 23B+D.

primary ring   The main FDDI or CDDI ring (out of the two) which is used as the primary ring data.

priority field   One of two fields that control a Token-Ring frame's priority. Only stations with a priority equal to or higher than the priority field shown in the token are able to acquire the token and send data.

priority queuing   Queuing technique in which traffic is allocated to one of four priority levels (high, medium, normal, and low).

private address   IP addresses that are reserved for use in private networks and not usable on the Internet. Private addresses are

- Class A—10.0.0.0 to 10.255.255.255
- Class B—172.16.0.0 to 172.31.255.255
- Class C—192.168.0.0 to 192.168.255.255

protocol translation   Translation of different protocols between systems that allows them to communicate.

Protocol Unreachable   An ICMP message that means a receiving host does not support the upper-layer protocol specified in the Protocol field of the IP header.

pseudo-ring   The ring number that represents the transparent domain to a source-route bridged (SRB) domain.

PSN   Packet-Switched Network. A network that transmits packets (as opposed to frames or cells).

PSTN   Public-Switched Telephone Network. Term used to refer to the worldwide public telephone network.

PVC   Permanent Virtual Circuit. Permanently established connections used for frequent and consistent data transfers.

Q.921   The ITU-T standard LAPD standard used on the ISDN D channels. Operates at layer 2.

Q.931   Layer 3 protocol for ISDN D channels between the CO and the TE.

QoS   Quality of Service. The capability to provide guaranteed data transmission for a particular type of traffic. More commonly found in an ATM network.

R   Rate. ISDN access point between the TE2 and the TA.

RADIUS   Remote Authentication Dial-In User Service. AAA protocol (RFC 2058). Uses a database that holds a list of conditions that must be met for a user to be positively authenticated (username, password, port number, and so on).

RAM   Random access memory. Memory that a processor can use as needed. It is a volatile (data is lost when powered off) form of memory.

recursive query   Instructs a DNS server that the client is requesting one of three responses:

- The IP address associated with the domain name
- An error stating that the DNS server can't respond to the request
- A message stating the domain name doesn't exist

redistribution   Route redistribution is the method by which routes learned using one protocol are advertised to routers via a different routing protocol.

request messages   In RIP, a router that has joined the network will send out a request for route updates to all adjacent routers.

Reservation field   One of two fields that control priority in a Token-Ring network. When a token is seized, only stations with a priority value higher than that of the transmitting station can reserve the token for the next pass around the network.

response messages   In RIP, the message type that is a response to a request message. This message will include the responding router's entire routing table.

reverse route   In RIP, this is a condition caused when routing updates are sent out the same interface in which they are learned. Can cause routing loops.

RIF   Route Information Field. A header in Token-Ring used in source-route bridging to which segments a packet must travel.

RII   Ring Information Indicator. When set to 1, indicates the frame will have a RIF and is destined for another ring.

RIP   Routing Information Protocol. A Distance-Vector Algorithm using hop count as the metric. There are two versions of RIP: version 1 and version 2. See *RIPv1* and *RIPv2*.

RIP_JITTER   Variance in time between the RIP updates.

RIPv1   Routing Information Protocol version 1. RIPv1 is a classful routing protocol that does not support Variable-Length Subnet Masks (VLSMs).

RIPv2   Routing Information Protocol version 2. RIPv2 is a classless routing protocol that supports Variable-Length Subnet Masks (VLSMs).

ROM   Read only memory. Memory that cannot be written by a processor. It is a non-volatile type of memory (data is saved when power is lost). In a Cisco router, the ROM assists the router during bootup and stores a basic version of IOS.

root bridge   A root bridge is the logical center of the bridged network. All distances are calculated from the root bridge.

root port   The port with the lowest Root Path cost on a switch.

Route Control field   A field used in source-route bridging that specifies the route type, length, direction, and MTU of a frame.

route descriptor   A field used in source-route bridging necessary to specify the route to the destination host. Composed of Ring number and Bridge number.

route summarization   Advertises a range of networks via a single network address. Consolidates multiple networks to simplify routing tables and preserve bandwidth consumed by router advertisements.

route tagging   Communicates information about a route within the normal information passed along by a routing protocol.

router   A device that switches (forwards) packets from one network to another based on network layer addressing information.

router ID   In OSPF, it is the value used to select the DR and BDRs in case of ties of router priority. In case of ties, it uses the highest IP address, which can be controlled by configuring a high IP on a loopback interface.

router priority   In OSPF, a router with highest priority will become the DR. Router priority is determined by the router with the highest Router ID. The router priority can be manually configured.

routing tuple   An AppleTalk routing update that includes the cable-range and distance to an unknown network.

RSVP   Resource Reservation Protocol. A protocol that works in conjunction with IGMP. It enables end stations to acquire a QoS for certain applications.

RTMP   Router Table Maintenance Protocol. A protocol that establishes and maintains AppleTalk routing tables.

RTP   Real-Time Transport Protocol. A Transport-layer protocol designed to guarantee fast delivery of time-sensitive data (such as video or voice). An IPv6 protocol.

RTP   Reliable Transport Protocol. EIGRP feature that is responsible for guaranteed, ordered delivery of EIGRP packets to all neighbors.

S   System. ISDN device between the TE1 or TA and the NT2.

SA   Source Address. A 32-bit address defining the originating node. It is contained in the IP header.

SAP   Service Access Point. 802.2 (LLC) field that identifies the upper-layer protocol that will receive or send the packet. There is a source and destination SAP (SSAP and DSAP) field in each packet and each field is one byte long.

SAP   Service Advertisement Protocol. Protocol by which IPX servers advertise their services to the network.

SAPI   Service Access Point Identifier. Identifies the portal at which LAPD services are communicated to layer 3 in ISDN.

SAS   Single Attachment Station. Class B or single-attachment stations (SAS) have a single connection to the FDDI ring, typically via a concentrator (which itself is a DAS).

secondary ring   The backup ring in a FDDI or CDDI network.

seed router   AppleTalk only requires one router to be configured with the appropriate zone names and cable ranges. This router helps configure other routers as they enter the network.

sequence number   In TCP, specifies the number assigned to the first byte following the TCP header.

Session layer   Layer 5 of the OSI reference model. The Session layer is responsible for creating, managing, and terminating sessions that are used by entities at the Presentation layer.

sliding window   Allows the receiver to control the maximum rate of transmission over a virtual circuit. This is a form of flow control.

SLInit   An AppleTalk message where the PAP server registers its socket address using NBP.

SMDS   Switched Multimegabit Data Service. A switched WAN service that is capable of high speeds, typically using ATM via AAL3.

SMT   Station Management. ANSI FDDI for station configuration, including station initialization, insertion, and removal; ring control and configuration; error detection and recovery; and statistics gathering.

SMTP   Simple Mail Transfer Protocol. The Internet standard protocol for email transmission.

SNA   Systems Network Architecture. Architecture developed by IBM for transmitting data to and from a mainframe.

SNAP   Sub-Network Access Protocol. Encapsulation method for IP over IEEE networks.

SNMP   Simple Network Management Protocol. SNMP is a protocol that operates over UDP (ports 161 and 162). It is used by one or more Network Monitoring Stations (NMS) to monitor and control network devices such as routers, switches, servers, and other equipment.

socket   See *AppleTalk socket* and *IPX socket*.

SOF   Start of Frame. Set to a bit pattern of 10101011 to delimit the start of IEEE 802.3 frame.

source quench   An ICMP message type indicating that a neighboring router does not have the buffer space required to queue the packet for output to the next network.

Spanning-Tree protocol   Bridge protocol that uses the spanning-tree algorithm to prevent loops in a switched (bridged) network topology.

SPF   Shortest Path First. A routing algorithm that relies on the length of the path to determine a packet's best route. Used in link-state protocols and sometimes referred to as the Dijkstra algorithm.

SPID   Service Profile Identifier. Like an ISDN phone number. An ISDN device uses a SPID when connecting to the service provider's switch (at the CO).

Split Horizon   A loop-prevention technique that prevents a router from advertising a route out the same interface in which it is learned.

SR/TLB   Source-Route Translational Bridging. Allows source-route bridging and transparent bridging process to exchange frames.

SRT   Source-Route Transparent Bridging. Allows source-route bridging and transparent bridging to happen within the same router.

SS7   Signaling System 7. SS7 is responsible for routing, link status, and connection-control information in the public telephone network.

SSCOP   Service Specific Convergence Protocol. OSI Data Link protocol that ensures the reliable transport of signaling requests in an ATM network.

SSP   Switch-to-Switch Protocol. Protocol that provides a method for forwarding SNA and NetBIOS traffic over TCP/IP networks using Data Link layer encapsulation and switching.

SSRP   Simple Server Replication Protocol. It enables the existence of multiple LECSs on a LANE network. SSRP is enabled by creating a list of LECSs in each LEC.

standby group   An HSRP standby group is made up of all active routers and standby routers.

standby router   In HSRP, the router with the second highest configured priority is the standby router. It becomes the active router when the active router does not respond to a hello message in the configured amount of time.

start-of-frame delimiter   The start delimiter serves to alert each station to the arrival of a token (or data/command frame). To send data, a workstation must seize or acquire the token and flip one bit in the header, transforming it into a start-of-frame delimiter.

static routes   Routes that are administratively configured in routers. They are never dynamically learned.

stub area   OSPF area that does not accept routing updates from external Autonomous Systems.

subnet mask   A 32-bit number used in conjunction with an IP address to delineate the network portion of an IP address from the host portion.

subnetwork   A network that is segmented by a network administrator to provide multilevel, hierarchical routing while shielding network complexity from the attached networks.

SVC   Switched Virtual Circuit. A virtual circuit that is used for inconsistent data transmission. They are dynamically established and terminated.

switch   Network layer-2 network device that forwards packets based on their destination MAC addresses.

switch filtering   If more than one MAC address is learned for a single segment (port), packets between devices on that segment will be seen and then dropped by the switch.

switch forwarding   Sending a packet to the appropriate outgoing port or, if no outgoing port is known for the destination MAC address, broadcasting the packet out all ports (except the incoming port).

switch learning   Passively entering the MAC addresses of all nodes on each segment (port) into its forwarding table.

SYN   In TCP, a SYN bit is set to indicate a connection request. The bit can be X. See *ACK*.

system routes   A type of IGRP route that advertises routes to networks within an Autonomous System.

T   Terminal. ISDN device between the NT2 and the NT1 (if applicable).

T1   1.544Mbps WAN service through the public telco network.

TA   Terminal Adapter. A device to convert non-ISDN signal to ISDN.

TACACS   Terminal Access Controller Access Control System. Authentication protocol that provides remote access authentication and related services, such as event logging.

TACACS+   Cisco proprietary version of TACACS that provides additional support for authentication, authorization, and accounting.

TCP   Provides applications with reliable, connection-oriented (end-to-end) data delivery service at layer 4 of the OSI model.

TDM   Time Division Multiplexing. Allocates time slots to each input channel for carrying data over a single circuit.

TE1   Terminal Equipment 1. A digital telephone or router with an ISDN interface.

TE2   Terminal Equipment 2. Analog telephone or a router with a normal serial interface. These devices require a TA.

TEI   Terminal End Identifier. A field that indicates a single terminal or multiple terminals on an ISDN network.

TID   Transaction Identifier. In AppleTalk, a transaction is given to the requester to enable the requester to have several transactions open at any time.

Time To Live   See *TTL*.

timed updates   When a routing protocol sends out updates on a scheduled basis (for example, every 60 seconds).

timeout   One of two timers used in RIP to ensure invalid routes are removed from the table. Also known as *expiration timer* and *invalid timer*.

TLAP   Token Talk Link Access Protocol. Link-access protocol built on top of the standard Token-Ring Data Link layer protocol. Used in Apple TokenTalk networks.

token   The Token-Ring frame that allows a node to transmit (access the media) when it is in possession of it.

Token-Ring Encapsulation Types   Two types of encapsulation are used on Token-Ring media: Token_Ring_Snap (SNAP) and Token_Ring (SAP), which is the default.

TokenTalk   AppleTalk running over Token-Ring.

Topological database   Also known as *Link-State database*. List of link-state entries of all routers in a network.

totally stubby area   An OSPF area that does not accept routing updates from external areas.

traffic shaping   A means of managing how traffic is sent over a network. More common in Frame Relay networks.

transparent bridging   Transparent bridges forward frames based on a table of MAC addresses and outgoing ports on the device.

Transport layer   Layer 4 of the OSI reference model. The Transport layer implements reliable internetwork data transport services that are transparent to upper-layer protocols. The services include flow control, multiplexing, and error checking and recovery.

Triggered Update   A routing protocol will send out updates due to a change in network topology information.

TTL   Time To Live. The maximum time that a packet can be on the network in the IP header fields.

tunneling   The technique of transmitting one Network-layer protocol via another Network-layer protocol.

two-step translation   Method of protocol translation that requires a node to first connect to a router and then to the destination host to which you want to connect. Each connection uses a different protocol. This is the least-common method of protocol translation.

type of service   Assigned by upper-layer protocols that instruct IP how they want the data within the packet handled, in the IP header fields.

U   User. ISDN interface between the NT1 and LE.

U/L address bit   The MAC address bit that determines whether the address is universally or locally administered.

UDP   User Datagram Protocol. A connectionless layer-4 protocol in the TCP/IP suite.

UDP port numbers   Like TCP, UDP has different port numbers for higher-layer applications.

UNI   The UNI defines the connection between an endpoint into a network or between two distinct networks.

unicast   A data message transmitted to a specific destination (Data Link or Network layer) address.

update synchronization   When RIP updates are sent at the exact same time. This can cause the updates to collide.

VCC   Virtual Channel Connection. Logical circuits that provide communication paths from LEC to LEC and between LANE servers in a LANE network.

PART

VII

APP

B

virtual circuit   A logical circuit between nodes that is used only when needed.

virtual link   A "tunnel" created to virtually connect an OSPF area to the backbone area (Area 0).

virtual ring   Used in source-route bridging that will logically connect two or more physical rings together to overcome some of the limitations of pure SRB.

VLAN   Virtual LAN. The logical grouping of nodes into their own broadcast domain, regardless of their physical location in a network.

VLSM   Variable-Length Subnet Mask. A network mask that does not comply with the default mask of a network. Enables a network to be divided into further subnets.

VPDN   Virtual Private Dial-up Networks. A type of VPN over a dial-up network that uses L2F protocol tunneling to separate and protect private traffic traveling across public domains.

VTP   Virtual Trunking Protocol. A Cisco proprietary layer-2 multicast protocol designed to manage VLANs in a switched environment. The purpose of VTP is to automate the administration of VLANs.

VTP messages   Messages that carry VTP information. The four types are Summary Advertisements, Subset Advertisements, Advertisement Requests, and VTP Join Messages.

VTP client mode   A switch in VTP client mode can be configured using VTP messages and can forward VTP messages, but cannot create domains, does not generate VTP messages, and will not remember its VTP configuration when rebooted.

VTP pruning   A VTP feature that prevents frames from being flooded to a VLAN other than the source port's VLAN.

VTP server mode   A switch in VTP server mode can create and delete VLANs, generate and send new VTP messages, act on and forward VTP messages, and remember its own VTP information when rebooted.

VTP transparent mode   A switch in VTP transparent mode does not generate and send or act on VTP messages. The switch does not advertise or learn VLAN configurations from the network.

WAN   Wide area network. Network covering a relatively large geographic area and involving telecommunication links (via a telecom service provider). Examples of WAN protocols are Carrier Services (T1 and so on), Frame Relay, ATM, SMDS, ISDN, and X.25.

WFQ   Weighted Fair queuing. Default queuing technique on Cisco routers that operates by assigning a high priority to traffic "conversations" that are low volume in nature.

window   The number of octets that can be transmitted before it has to stop for an Acknowledgment.

windowing   A technique used to improve the throughput of a connection-oriented protocol. It defines the number of packets that can be sent at a time.

X.21   A Physical-layer protocol dealing with the electrical, mechanical, procedural, and functional interfaces between the DTE and the DCE.

X.25   Type of packet switching that defines procedures for exchanging data between DTE and DCE devices. X.25 is a global standard defined by ITU-T.

X.121   The ITU-T standard that defines the design, characteristics, and application of the Numbering Plan for Public Data Networks (PDNs) in an X.25 network.

XID frame   Exchange Identification Frame. An explorer frame is sent prior to a session between a router and a Token-Ring host. These are request and response packets.

XOT   X.25 Over TCP. X.25 packets are sent over a reliable TCP data stream.

ZIP   Zone Information Protocol. AppleTalk Session-layer protocol that is responsible for providing the mapping of networks to zone names throughout the network.

zone   A logical grouping of AppleTalk network devices.

CCIE Certification Process and Testing Tips

CCIE Certification Process

The CCIE Certification process is relatively straightforward. Basically, it is a two-step process:

1. Take and pass the written exam.
2. Take and pass the lab exam.

Certification Information

Cisco does an excellent job of keeping its Web site up to date with changes in all its certification programs. A couple of good Web sites to know about are

- Main CCIE page—http://www.cisco.com/warp/public/625/ccie/
- CCIE program overview—
  http://www.cisco.com/warp/public/625/ccie/certifications/routing.html
- Updates and changes to the CCIE program—
  http://www.cisco.com/warp/public/625/ccie/ccie_program/whatsnew.html

Note that URLs are as of date of publication and might change at any time at Cisco's discretion.

Scheduling

The written exam can be taken at any Sylvan Prometric testing location. There are hundreds, if not thousands, of these locations in the United States alone. Here are two ways to contact Sylvan to sign up for your test:

- Call 1-800-829-6387 (Option 2 and then 4)
- Go to https://www.2test.com/register/frameset.htm

As of this book's writing, the written exam costs $200. Many companies will reimburse you for this expense—especially if you pass. Check with the appropriate representative at your company for details before you register for your exam.

When you show up for your test, you must register at the receptionist's desk with two forms of identification. You will be shown the computer station on which your test will be administered. The exam is 100 questions long and you will have two hours to complete your test. For test-taking tips, see the section "Testing Tips" in this appendix.

The Test

One nice thing about the computer-based exam is that when you complete your exam, you get immediate results: Your score is displayed on your computer screen. Even though your results are automatically sent to Cisco, don't leave the testing center yet. Return to the front desk. You will receive a stamped certified printout of your results for your records. Even if you don't pass, this document is useful because it shows the general categories of the test and how you scored in each category. Obviously, this can be useful to guide your study for when you retake it.

Also, don't feel bad if you don't pass the first time. Many people need to take it a second time, especially if they have not taken many of the other Cisco certification exams (for CCNA and CCNP). The questions and test-taking style sometimes take some getting used to. Besides, you'd be surprised how much some people forget when under pressure of the actual exam! We have tried to alleviate this as much as possible with the elements of each chapter and the Mastery Test on the CD-ROM.

Testing Tips

If you are like many people in the networking field, it has probably been a while since you've taken a test. And when you did, it was after taking a semester-long class to prepare you for it. This appendix provides you some of our best tips on how to successfully prepare for and take your CCIE Written Exam.

More than likely, the last time you were taking tests on a regular basis, all you had to do was listen to the teacher or professor closely enough and you had a pretty good idea of what would be on the exam. This is not so with the CCIE Written Exam. All you get from Cisco is an Exam Blueprint: a list of general topics you need to know. The Blueprint is available at `http://www.cisco.com/warp/public/625/ccie/rsblueprint.html`.

Of course, that is where this book comes in. We have taken the topics from the Blueprint and combined them with our test-taking experiences to frame the Blueprint topics for your preparation. As you would expect, some topics will be weighted more heavily on exam than others. However, we are not at liberty to be more specific than our descriptions in this book. We'd love to be able to poll all our people who have passed the CCIE Written Exam and compile their experiences in order to provide you an insight into how important each topic is on a typical CCIE exam. Of course, we can't (and wouldn't) because ethics and legality prevent it.

What we *can* do is provide some insight for you on how to prepare for and take an exam such as the CCIE Written Exam. That is the purpose of this appendix. Some of our tips are (hopefully) obvious, and others probably aren't. Regardless, it is easy to forget when under pressure, so we have written them down for you. Here are some of our tips:

- Take as many practice tests as possible—When you can score near perfection on practice tests, you are probably ready for the real thing.

- Feel overprepared—Your confidence will carry you far and prevent second-guessing yourself out of right answers.

- Schedule your test at a time in the day when you are typically most awake and energetic—For most people, avoid midafternoon after a big lunch!

- Arrive at the test facility early with your notes—You are more than welcome to sit in the reception area, kitchen area, or other place to do some final review. This is a good time to double-check any tables or lists you have memorized.

- Try not to feel rushed when you take the exam—Even though you have an average of 72 seconds for each question, you should be able to answer some questions pretty easily (if you are prepared), and that "saved" time adds up.

- Do not dwell on questions you are unsure of—Mark them to return later. If you spend too much time, you will likely argue yourself into problems.

- Use your scratch paper to your advantage—Write out all math. Don't trust yourself under pressure. Also, use it for the questions that ask, "Which of the following answers is correct?" If you are given options A through G, write the letters A, B, C, D, E, F, G on your paper and start your process of elimination on your paper. It is much easier to keep track this way.

- If you need to get up and go to the bathroom in the middle of the test, do—It's time well spent.

Notes

Here is some space for other notes. Write down things you want to remember to do or bring with you, last-minute tips to yourself, or whatever!

-
-
-
-
-
-
-
-
-
-

Moving On to the Lab Exam

After you pass your written exam, it is time to start seriously working on preparing for your lab exam.

You can register for your lab exam by contacting Sylvan again (see the following section titled "Scheduling"). The lab exam will be at one of Cisco's lab-testing facilities, such as the one in San José, California. We have listed the sites in North America here.

The lab exam is a two-day, hands-on exam. During these two days, you will be asked to build, configure, and troubleshoot complex internetworking scenarios. The two days are broken into different sections. If you do not score well enough on any section, your test is done. An employee of Cisco Systems proctors the exam.

Locations

The lab exam can be taken at one of the following lab-testing centers in North America:

- Raleigh, North Carolina, USA
- San José, California, USA
- Halifax, Nova Scotia, Canada

Scheduling

There are two ways to contact Sylvan to sign up for your test:

- Call 1-800-829-6387 (Option 2 and then 2)
- Go to `https://www.2test.com/register/frameset.htm`

Practice Facilities

Some colleges, universities, and Cisco facilities have practice labs that you might be able to use to prepare for the lab exam. A list of them is on Cisco Connection Online (CCO) at `http://www.cisco.com/warp/public/625/ccie/exam_preparation/practice_labs.html`.

Another resource can be your Cisco sales representative or Systems Engineer (SE). Many local Cisco offices have lab equipment for employee use, but they can sponsor qualified CCIE candidates and potentially let you have access to their lab. In practice, this varies widely from office to office.

Lab Exam Preparation

Information on how to prepare for your lab exam is also available on CCO at `http://www.cisco.com/warp/public/625/ccie/exam_preparation/lab.html`.

Most candidates do not pass the lab exam on their first try. Do not be discouraged. Go back, practice some more, and try, try again. The effect on your career will be well worth it.

Alternative Resources

The following is a list of additional resources you may find helpful. Many of them are recommended on Cisco's Web site. Others are books that we have found useful in preparing for our CCIE Exams.

- *CCIE Fundamentals: Network Design and Case Studies, Second Edition,* 1999. Cisco Press; ISBN: 1578701678

- *Cisco CCIE Fundamentals: Network Design and Case Studies,* 1998, Cisco Press; ISBN: 1578700663

- Caslow, Andrew Bruce, *Cisco Certification: Bridges, Routers, and Switches for CCIEs,* 1998, Prentice Hall, ISBN: 0130825379

- *Cisco IOS 12.0 Configuration Fundamentals,* 1999, Cisco Press; ISBN: 1578701554

- Cisco's CCIE Certification Home Page— http://www.cisco.com/warp/public/625/ccie/

- Cisco's Documentation Home Page (also on CD-ROMs shipped with most Cisco products)—http://www.cisco.com/univercd/home/home.htm

- Clark, Kennedy and Kevin Hamilton, *CCIE Professional Development: Cisco LAN Switching* (The Cisco Press CCIE Professional Development Series), 1999, Cisco Press; ISBN: 1578700949

- Downes, Kevin ed., *Internetworking Technologies Handbook, Second Edition,* 1998, Cisco Press, ISBN: 1578701023

- Doyle, Jeff, *CCIE Professional Development: Routing TCP/IP,* 1998, Cisco Press; ISBN: 1578700418

■ Martinez, Anne, *Get Cisco Certified and Get Ahead*, 1999, Computing McGraw-Hill; ISBN: 0071352589

■ Paquet, Catherine, ed., *Building CISCO Remote Access Networks*, 1999 Cisco Press; ISBN: 1578700914

■ Retana, Alvaro et al., *CCIE Professional Development: Advanced IP Network Design* (Cisco CCIE Professional Development Series) 1999, Cisco Press; ISBN: 1578700973

■ Slattery, Terry et al., *Advanced IP Routing with Cisco Networks* (Cisco Technical Expert), McGraw-Hill Text; 1998 ISBN: 0070581444

■ Source of RFCs: `http://www.cis.ohio-state.edu/hypertext/information/rfc.html`

■ Velte, Toby and Tom Shaughnessy, *Cisco: A Beginner's Guide* (Network Professional's Library), 1999, Osborne McGraw-Hill; ISBN: 0072121157

Using the CD-ROM

Using the Test Pro Software

The test engine on the CD-ROM consists of three main test structures:

- Non-Randomized Test—This is useful when you first begin to study and want to run through sections that you have read to make sure you understand them thoroughly before continuing.

- Adaptive Test—This emulates an adaptive exam and randomly pulls questions from the database. You are asked 15 questions of varying difficulty. If you successfully answer a question, the next question you are asked is of higher difficulty; it tries to "adapt" to your skill level. If you miss a question, the next one you're asked is easier because again, the engine tries to "adapt" to your skill level. This tool is useful for getting used to the adaptive format, but not for actual study because the number of questions presented is so low.

- Random/Mastery Test—This is the big one. This test is different from the two others in the sense that questions are pulled from all objective areas. You are asked 50 questions, and it simulates the exam situation. At the conclusion of the exam, you will get your overall score and will be allowed to view all wrong answers. You will also be able to print a report card featuring your test results.

All test questions are of the type currently in use by Cisco on this exam. In some cases, that consists solely of multiple-choice type questions offering four possible answers. In other cases, there will be exhibits, scenarios, and other question types.

Equipment Requirements

To run the self-study test preparation software, you must have at least the following equipment:

- IBM-compatible Pentium
- Microsoft Windows 95, 98, or NT 4.0 (Workstation or Server)
- 16MB of RAM
- 256-color display adapter, configured as 800×600 display or larger
- Double-speed CD-ROM drive

Running the Test Pro Software

The Test Pro software installs on your hard drive from the CD-ROM and runs directly from there. Follow the simple installation steps. You will then find the software very intuitive and self-explanatory.

Lab Exercises

Reading this book will prepare you for your CCIE Written Exam by focusing you on applicable topics. Most people, however, find it nearly impossible to learn this incredibly wide body of knowledge just from reading a book. There is no substitute for hands-on experience. Most successful CCIE candidates have been actively working in Networking with Cisco routers and switches for at least two years. Many of them have much more experience.

If you have access to some routers and computers (preferably running multiple protocols), we recommend that you spend some time brushing up on some techniques and technologies that you might not use every day in your job. To this end, we have taken some of the configuration examples from certain chapters and created some hands-on exercises for you.

This appendix is not meant to be an exhaustive set of exercises after which you will know everything. That would require at least another book in itself. Instead, the exercises here are chosen for their relevance. Because there is much more OSPF in the world than BGP, we have an OSPF exercise. This does not imply that a typical CCIE exam will lack *any* BGP; it probably will contain something. We just feel that it's more important to know hands-on skills for OSPF. We have also included some ISDN work. For instance, we could have included X.25, but there is not as much of it out there in the real world. We have also not included exercises on topics that we have mentioned should be review for you. Such topics include, but are not limited to, the following:

- Access Lists
- IP addressing and subnetting

- VLSMs
- OSI model
- Router management (IOS image management, config file management, and so on)
- Binary
- Switching
- RIP
- IPX Routing
- AppleTalk Routing

We would have liked to include other exercises (DLSw, Trunking, X.25, LANE, ATM, Frame Relay, and others) but didn't due to the sheer equipment expense required to perform them. Nonetheless, the exercises presented here will help you brush up on some very important skills.

In each configuration exercise, configuration *tasks* are listed, not configuration *commands*. This is to force you to remember or figure out what the exact command is. Also, in each exercise, we reference the corresponding chapter. In each configuration exercise, a configuration example from the corresponding chapter for the technology can be referenced for help. Specific commands are shown there, but try to figure it out first. Also, router configuration commands are always listed but not numbered. This is because sometimes you will be unable to follow the steps in order. You will need to figure out why. Typically, you simply need to enable something listed later and return later to the command that didn't work. Also, you will need to do all your own IP address planning. Although this is relatively basic, it will help you.

Have fun!

Exercise 1: Configure IRB (from Chapter 7)

You will need

- At least two PCs
- A Cisco router with at least three Ethernet interfaces

1. Configure the router.
   - Configure IP addresses on interface Ethernet0.
   - Enable IRB.
   - Choose a bridge group number and assign interfaces Ethernet2 and Ethernet3 to it.

- Create the virtual interface for the bridge group to the routing process.
- Assign a bridge protocol for your bridge group.
- Specify what protocol you want to route into your bridge group.

2. Connect PCs to Ethernet0 and Ethernet2 or 3.

3. Assign an appropriate IP address to the PCs.

4. Confirm IP connectivity between your PCs.

Exercise 2: Analyze a RIF (from Chapter 7)

Analyze the following RIF, to the bit level by filling in the chart below.

0830.034B.0185.0350

Hex:	0	8	3	0	034	B	018	5	035	0
Binary:										
Bit Length:										
Field Name:										
Meaning:										

Practice with other RIFs. Either sample them from a live network, or make them up. Here are a few to start with:

0380.0343.019D.0350

08B0.034B.0185.0350

08B0.0343.019D.0350

Exercise 3: Configure CRB (from Chapter 7)

For this exercise, you will need

- A Cisco router with at least three Token-Ring interfaces
- At least two PCs (with Token-Ring NICs)

1. Configure the router for pure SRB:
- Configure interfaces TokenRing0 and TokenRing1 for SRB.

2. Connect PCs to Ethernet0 and Ethernet2 or 3.

3. Confirm IP connectivity between your PCs.

Hint: There might be other bridging commands you need to enter in the router.

4. Configure the router for multiport SRB:
   - Create the virtual ring.
   - Reconfigure SRB on TokenRing0 and TokenRing1 with the virtual ring number.
5. Reconfirm IP connectivity between your PCs.

Exercise 4: Configure RSRB (from Chapter 7)

For this exercise, you will need

- Two Cisco routers with at least one Token-Ring and one serial port each
- A serial cable appropriate for your serial interfaces
- At least two PCs (with Token-Ring NICs)

1. Configure both routers:
   - Create connectivity via the serial line.
   - Configure the virtual ring for the serial network.
   - Configure IP addresses on the serial ports.
   - Configure RSRB peers.
   - Point the traffic from the Token-Ring ports (on both routers) to use RSRB.
2. Attach the PCs to the configured Token-Ring ports:
3. Confirm connectivity between the PCs.

Exercise 5: Canonical/Noncanonical Addresses

If performing any type of translational bridging, you must know about canonical versus noncanonical MAC address formats, because the addresses appear one way on an Ethernet segment and a different way on a Token-Ring. This is covered in Chapter 7.

Convert the following MAC address from its present canonical to noncanonical form by filling in the chart below:

0000.0c13.d717

Practice with other MAC addresses. Either sample them from a live network, or make them up. Here are a few to start with:

0060.08f5.1f28

0600.f508.f281

0800.b643.d361

Ethernet	Hex	00	00	0C	13	D7	17
	Binary						
Token Ring	Binary						
	Hex						

Exercise 6: NAT (from Chapter 8)

For this exercise, you will need

- Two Cisco routers with at least one Ethernet and one serial port each
- A serial cable appropriate for your serial interfaces
- At least two PCs (with Ethernet NICs)

1. Configure both routers:
    - Name one router "RouterA" and the other "RouterB".
    - Create an NAT address pool in RouterA.
    - Enable static NAT mapping on RouterB.
    - Assign IP addresses to Serial0 and Ethernet0 interfaces on both routers.
    - Define the Serial0 and Ethernet0 interfaces as inside or outside ports.
2. Connect the PCs to both routers' Ethernet0 ports.
3. Confirm connectivity between the two PCs.

Exercise 7: Static Routing (from Chapter 9)

For this exercise, you will need

- Two Cisco routers with at least one Ethernet and one serial port each
- One Cisco router with at least two serial ports
- Two serial cables appropriate for your serial interfaces
- At least two PCs (with Ethernet NICs)

1. Configure the routers:
    - Connect Establish connectivity from one router to the other two routers.
    - Configure IP addresses on the Serial0 interfaces and the Ethernet0 interfaces on all the routers.
    - Configure static routes on all routers so there is complete connectivity to and from all Ethernet0 interfaces.

2. Connect the PCs to the Ethernet0 ports of both routers that only have one serial connection.

3. Confirm connectivity between the two PCs.

4. Change the static route statements in the router with both connections to a different style of static route statement.

Exercise 8: EIGRP (from Chapter 11)

For this exercise, you will need

- Three Cisco routers with at least two serial interfaces each and one Ethernet interface each
- Three serial cables appropriate for your serial interfaces

1. Configure the routers:
   - Achieve connectivity to all neighboring routers via the Serial ports.
   - Configure the Ethernet interfaces on all the routers with three distinctly different network addresses.
   - Configure IP addresses on each connected Serial port on all routers.
   - Enable EIGRP on all three routers.

2. Confirm that each router can see routes to all networks.

3. Change the route metrics:
   - Alter the bandwidth on one of the serial interfaces.

4. Observe how this changed the routing tables.

5. Change another route metric:
   - Alter the interface speed on one of the serial interfaces.

6. Observe and fix what happened, without undoing step 4.

7. After the problem in step 5 is resolved, observe how the speed change affected the routing tables.

8. Change the EIGRP configuration on one of the routers.
   - Remove the EIGRP process from one of the routers.
   - Enable EIGRP, using a different AS number from the other two routers.

9. Observe how this changes the routing tables of all routers.

Exercise 9: OSPF (from Chapter 12)

For this exercise, you will need

- Three Cisco routers with at least one serial and one Ethernet interface each
- One serial cable appropriate for your serial interfaces

1. Configure the routers:
   - Connect two routers via their Serial0 interfaces.
   - Achieve connectivity to the two routers connected via their Serial0 interfaces.
   - Connect the other router to one of the two via their Ethernet0 interfaces.
   - Configure IP addresses on all connected interfaces and at least one other interface on each router.
   - Enable OSPF on all the routers, assigning them all to the same area.

   As a reminder, the area number should not be arbitrary; instead, it should be something specific because it is the only area in the internetwork.

2. Confirm that each router can see routes to all networks.
3. Find out which router is the DR and the BDR.
4. Monitor the OSPF messages and determine what type of messages are being sent and received.
5. Configure multiarea OSPF on your internetwork:
   - Remove the network on the serial link from the OSPF network.
   - Create a new OSPF area for the serial link network.
   - Create a new OSPF area for the Ethernet0 interface on the router that has only the serial cable attached to it.

6. Observe how this changed the routing tables.
7. Observe how this changed the OSPF message types being sent and received.
8. Make the Serial network an OSPF stub area.
9. Observe how this changed the routing tables.
10. Observe how this changed the OSPF message types being sent and received.
11. Create a virtual link from the Ethernet0 interface that is its own OSPF area to the Ethernet link's OSPF network.
12. Observe how this changed the routing tables.
13. Observe how this changed the OSPF message types being sent and received.

PART
VII

APP
F

Exercise 10: ISDN DDR

Although most people do not have dual ISDN lines or an ISDN simulator available (due to their costs), ISDN is very important to know for the CCIE Written Exam, so we have included this exercise anyway. ISDN is covered in Chapter 18.

For this exercise, you will need

- Two Cisco routers with at least one ISDN BRI interface each
- Two ISDN BRI lines or an ISDN simulator

1. Connect the routers via the ISDN lines (or to the ISDN simulator).
2. Monitor the status of the ISDN BRI interfaces and the ISDN circuit throughout step 3.
3. Configure the routers:
   - Assign IP addresses to the ISDN BRI interfaces on both routers.
   - Define interesting traffic as all IP traffic.
   - Configure the Service Provider Identifiers on both routers' BRI interfaces.
   - Configure each router to call the other via their ISDN circuit.
   - Link the BRI interface with the definition of interesting traffic.

   Hint: There might (or might not) be at least one other command you need to enter.
4. Confirm connectivity between the two routers via the ISDN interfaces.
5. Configure the routers to use PPP.
6. Confirm connectivity between the two routers via the ISDN interfaces.
7. Configure the routers to authenticate each other via CHAP.
8. Monitor the CHAP authentication process while attempting to connect to another router.
9. Confirm connectivity between the two routers via the ISDN interfaces.
10. Remove the dial string and configure the routers to use dialer maps to call each other.
11. Confirm connectivity between the two routers via the ISDN interfaces.
12. Monitor DDR (dialer) while attempting to connect to another router.

Symbols-A

10BASE-2 Ethernet, 59
10BASE-5 Ethernet, 59
10BASE-T Ethernet, 59
100BASE-FX Ethernet, 59
100BASE-T Ethernet, 59

AAA (authentication, authorization and accounting), 37-38
AARP (AppleTalk Address Resolution Protocol), 309, 313-314
  Address Mapping Table (AMT), 313
  packets, 314
ABRs (Area Border Routers), 234
Access level (networks), 48
Access Lists. *See also* **filters**
  access-class, 34
  AppleTalk, 32-33
  Cisco Access List numbers, 28
  commands, 28-29
  configuring, 28-29
  deleting, 29
  distribute lists, 33
    distribute-list in command, 268-269
    distribute-list out command, 269-270
  exam questions, 27
  implicit deny feature, 29
  IP
    extended, 30-31
    standard, 29-30

  IPX
    extended, 32, 300-301
    NLSP filters, 32
    SAP filters, 32, 301
    standard, 31, 300
access-accept messages (RADIUS), 39
access-challenge messages (RADIUS), 39
access-class (Access Lists), 34
access-reject messages (RADIUS), 39
access-request messages (RADIUS), 39
accounting (AAA), 37
acknowledgments (protocols), 18
ACKs (protocols), 18
active monitors (Token-Ring), 75
Active routers (HSRP), 167
Adaptive Security Algorithm (ASA), 39
address field (LAPB), 372
Address Mapping Table (AMT), AARP, 313
Address Resolution Protocol. *See* **ARP**
address-recognized indicator bits (FDDI), 80
address-recognized indicator bits (Token-Ring), 75
addresses
  Address Mapping Table (AMT), AARP, 313
  AppleTalk
    assigning, 311-312
    cable ranges, 310

    format, 310
    sockets, 311
  ATM, 417-418
  DECnet, 327
  IP
    ARP, 158-160
    classes, 154-155
    determining network/broadcast addresses, 156-158
    DHCP, 168-169
    DNS, 165-166
    dotted-decimal format, 154
    frame-relay map commands, 400
    global address space, 169-171
    Inverse ARP, 399-400
    IP address pooling (PPP), 346
    masks, 156-158
    NAT, 169-171
    private address space, 155, 169-171
    public address space, 155
    reserved, 155
    router IDs (OSPF), 231
    subinterfaces, 401-403
    subnetting, 156
    VLSM, 156
    wildcard masks, 30
  IPX, 290-291
  LES NSAP address configuration, 95
  loopback addressing (BGP), 247
  MAC
    ARP, 158-160
    broadcast addresses, 60

Ethernet/Token-Ring MAC
address conversion, 136-137
functional addresses, 60
I/G address bit, 60
multicast bits, 128
OUIs, 60
U/L Address Bit, 60
unicast traffic, 60
addressing, X.25, 368
adjacencies. *See also* peers
EIGRP, 217, 220
OSPF, 230-231
administrative distances
default, 189
selecting routes, 189-190
ADSP (AppleTalk Data Stream
Protocol), 310, 316
*Advanced IP Routing with
Cisco Networks*, 482
Advanced Research Projects
Agency (ARPA), 366
Advertisement Requests
(VTP), 115
AEP (AppleTalk Echo
Protocol), 309, 314
AFP (Apple Filing Protocol),
310, 316
algorithms
DES, 40
Diffie-Hellman, 40
DUAL, 183, 217-218
AMT (Address Mapping
Table), AARP, 313
AppleTalk, 308
AARP, 309, 313-314
*Address Mapping Table
(AMT), 313*
packets, 314
Access Lists, 32-33
addresses
assigning, 311-312
cable ranges, 310
format, 310
sockets, 311
ADSP, 310, 316
AEP, 309, 314
AFP, 310, 316
Application layer (OSI model),
310

ASP, 310, 316
ATP, 309, 314-315
AURP, 309, 318-319
Data Link layer (OSI model),
309
DDP, 309, 312-313, 317
EIGRP, 219, 319
ELAP, 309
FLAP, 309
LAP, 309
LLAP, 309
LocalTalk, 309
NBP, 309, 315
Network layer (OSI model),
309
PAP, 310, 316
Phase 1, 310
Phase 2, 310
Physical layer (OSI model),
309
Presentation layer (OSI
model), 310
routers, seed, 317
routing, 317-319
configuring, 319
routing tables, 317
RTMP, 309, 318
Session layer (OSI model),
310
TLAP, 309
Transport layer (OSI model),
309
tunneling, 318-319
ZIP, 310, 315-316
assigning zones, 312
ZITs, 315
AppleTalk Address Resolution
Protocol. *See* AARP
AppleTalk Data Stream
Protocol (ADSP), 310, 316
AppleTalk Echo Protocol
(AEP), 309, 314
AppleTalk Session Protocol
(ASP), 310, 316
AppleTalk Transaction
Protocol (ATP), 309,
314-315
AppleTalk Update-based

Routing Protocol (AURP),
309, 318-319
Application layer (OSI
model), 12, 310
applications, mrouted program, 278
Area Border Routers (ABRs),
234
areas (OSPF), 230, 233-234
backbone, 233-234
NSSA, 234
stub, 234, 237-238
totally stubby, 234
ARP (Address Resolution
Protocol), 158-160
Inverse ARP, 399-400
proxy ARP, 159
ARPA (Advanced Research
Projects Agency), 366
AS (autonomous system)
numbers, 210, 216
ASA (Adaptive Security
Algorithm), 39
ASBR (Autonomous System
Boundary Router), 234
ASP (AppleTalk Session
Protocol), 310, 316
assigning
addresses (AppleTalk),
311-312
cost (DECnet), 329
zones (ZIP), 312
asynchronous traffic (FDDI),
79
Asynchronous Transfer Mode.
See ATM
ATM (Asynchronous Transfer
Mode), 16, 414
addresses, 417-418
cell header format, 416
IISP, 419
layers, 416-417
NNI, 415
PNNI, 415-416
PVCs
*configuration example,
420-422*
defined, 414
QoS, 419-420

signaling, 418
SMDS (Switched Multi-Megabit Data Service), 16
SSCOP, 418-419
SVCs
  configuration example, 422-423
  defined, 414
UNI, 414
ATP (AppleTalk Transaction Protocol), 309, 314-315
Attachment Unit Interface (AUI), 59
AUI (Attachment Unit Interface), 59
AURP (AppleTalk Update-based Routing Protocol), 309, 318-319
authentication
AAA, 37
CHAP
  debug ppp authentication command, 356-357
  PPP, 346, 355-356
OSPF, 230
PAP, 345
RIPv2, 200, 202
authentication, authorization and accounting (AAA), 37-38
authorization (AAA), 37
auto reconfiguration (Token-Ring), 75
Auto-RP feature (sparse-dense mode), 277
autodetect encapsulation ppp command, 346
autonomous system (AS) numbers, 210, 216
autonomous system (BGP), 254
Autonomous System Boundary Router (ASBR), 234
autosense (LMI), 397

B

backbone areas (OSPF), 233-234
Backbone Routers (OSPF), 234

backbones, MBONE project, 278-279
backdoor command (BGP), 255
Backup Designated Router election (BDR election), 231-232
backups, Dial Backup (DDR), 352
basic, 353
dialer load-threshold command, 354
floating static routes, 353-354
bandwidth
broadcast storms, 108
EIGRP, 220
FDDI, 79
full-duplex operation, 60-61
half-duplex operation, 60-61
OSPF, bandwidth conservation, 229
path cost, 108
Basic Rate Interface (BRI), 340
beaconing (Token-Ring), 75
BECN (Backward Explicit Congestion Notification), frame relay, 404
BGP (Border Gateway Protocol), 246
autonomous system, 254
backdoor command, 255
BGP next hop, 246
CIDR, 253-254
communities, 256
confederations, 256
EBGP, 252-253
EBGP multihop, 247
filters, 248
  filter by community example, 249-250
  filter by path example, 249
  filter by route example, 248
IBGP, 252
loopback addressing, 247
MED, 255
overlapping protocols, 247

peers
  defined, 250
  neighbor definition, 254
  validating peer connections, 254
redistribution, 247, 255
redistribution metric issues, 263
route flap dampening, 256
route maps, 247, 255
route reflectors, 257
route selection process, 250-252
TCP, 246
BID (Bridge ID), 108
binary values
bits, 26
bytes, 26
converting, 26-27
hex character table, 26-27
bit 6 (configuration registers), 44
bits
address-recognized indicator
  FDDI, 80
  Token-Ring, 75
binary values, 26
bit 6 (configuration registers), 44
canonical order, 136
decimal values, 26
frame-copied indicator
  FDDI, 80
  Token-Ring, 75
hex values, 26
I/G address bit (MAC addresses), 60
multicast, MAC addresses, 128
noncanonical order, 137
OUIs (MAC addresses), 60
U/L Address Bit (MAC addresses), 60
block ciphers, 40
Blocking mode (STP), 109
books
Advanced IP Routing with Cisco Networks, 482
Building CISCO Remote Access Networks, 482
CCIE Fundamentals: Network Design and Case Studies, 481

CCIE Fundamentals: Network Design and Case Studies, Second Edition, 481

CCIE Professional Development: Advanced IP Network Design, 482

CCIE Professional Development: Cisco LAN Switching, 481

CCIE Professional Development: Routing TCP/IP, 481

Cisco Certification: Bridges, Routers, and Switches for CCIEs, 481

Cisco IOS 12.0 Configuration Fundamentals, 481

Cisco: A Beginner's Guide, 482

Get Cisco Certified and Get Ahead, 482

Internetworking Technologies Handbook, Second Edition, 481

boot fields (configuration registers), 43-44

boot order lists (routers), 44-45

booting routers
boot order lists, 44-45
IOS, 42
ROM, 42

Border Gateway Protocol. *See* **BGP**

BPDUs (Bridge Protocol Data Units), 108-109

BRI (Basic Rate Interface), 340

Bridge ID (BID), 108

bridge ports. *See* **ports**

Bridge Protocol Data Units (BPDUs), 108-109

Bridge Virtual Interface (BVI), IRB, 126-127

bridges, root, 108

bridging. *See also* **routers; routing**
CRB, 124
configuration, 125-126
interfaces, 125
nonroutable protocols, 125

IRB, 126
Bridge Virtual Interface (BVI), 126-127
configuration, 127
nonroutable protocols, 126
NetBIOS, 331
routing comparison, 124
RSRB, 134-135
SR/TLB, 134
advantages, 136
configuration, 137-138
drawbacks, 136
transparent bridges, 137
SRB, 127
configuration, 132-134
process, 128-129
RIFs, 129-132
size limitations, 128
SRT, 134-136

broadcast addresses (MAC addresses), 60

broadcast storms, 108

buffering, X.25 flow control, 377

Building CISCO Remote Access Networks, **482**

building RIFs, 131-132

BUS (Broadcast and Unknown Server), 88, 94

BVI (Bridge Virtual Interface), IRB, 126-127

bytes
binary values, 26
canonical order, 136
decimal values, 26
hex values, 26
noncanonical order, 137

C

cable range filters, 33

cable ranges (AppleTalk), 310

cabling
10BASE-2 Ethernet, 59
10BASE-5 Ethernet, 59
10BASE-T Ethernet, 59
100BASE-FX Ethernet, 59

100BASE-T Ethernet, 59
Ethernet, 15
Token-Ring, 16
UTP, 64

callback (PPP), 347, 352

canonical order, 136

carrier sense (CSMA/CD), 60

Carrier Sense Multiple Access/Collision Detection. *See* **CSMA/CD**

CCIE Certification exam. *See* **exam**

CCIE Certification home page, 475, 481

CCIE Certification process, 475

CCIE Fundamentals: Network Design and Case Studies, **481**

CCIE Fundamentals: Network Design and Case Studies, Second Edition, **481**

CCIE Professional Development: Advanced IP Network Design, **482**

CCIE Professional Development: Cisco LAN Switching, **481**

CCIE Professional Development: Routing TCP/IP, **481**

CCIE program overview (Cisco Web site), 475

CCIE program updates (Cisco Web site), 475

CDDI (Copper Distributed Data Interface), 76

CDP (Cisco Discovery Protocol), 46-47

cell headers (ATM), 416

Cell Loss Priority (CLP), ATM cell header, 416

central processing units. *See* **CPUs**

CGMP
Cisco Group Management Protocol, 117, 281

CHAP (Challenge Authentication Protocol), 346
debug ppp authentication command, 356-357
PPP, 346, 355-356
Chapter 1 practice test, 22-23
Chapter 2 practice test, 51-53
Chapter 3 practice test, 67-70
Chapter 4 practice test, 81-84
Chapter 5 practice test, 99-101
Chapter 6 practice test, 119-121
Chapter 7 practice test, 144-147
Chapter 8 practice test, 173-177
Chapter 9 practice test, 191-194
Chapter 10 practice test, 206-208
Chapter 11 practice test, 224-226
Chapter 12 practice test, 241-244
Chapter 13 practice test, 258-260
Chapter 14 practice test, 284-286
Chapter 15 practice test, 303-305
Chapter 16 practice test, 321-323
Chapter 17 practice test, 332-334
Chapter 18 practice test, 361-362
Chapter 19 practice test, 388-392
Chapter 20 practice test, 410-412
Chapter 21 practice test, 425-427
checking errors
frame relay, 395
X.25, 366
checksums, 19
CIDR (Classless Inter-Domain Routing), 253-254
ciphers, 40

CIR (Committed Information Rate), frame relay, 403
circuits
DLSw, 139-140
virtual, 380-382
Cisco
Access level, 48
Cisco Connection Online Web site, 36
Cisco Web site
CCIE Certification home page, 475, 481
CCIE program overview, 475
CCIE program updates, 475
certification information, 2
documentation home page, 481
Exam Blueprint, 477
lab exam practice facilities list, 479
lab exam preparation information, 479
Core level, 48
Distribution level, 48
Cisco Certification: Bridges, Routers, and Switches for CCIEs, **481**
Cisco Discovery Protocol (CDP), 46-47
Cisco Group Management Protocol (CGMP), 117, 281
Cisco IOS 12.0 Configuration Fundamentals, **481**
Cisco: A Beginner's Guide, **482**
classful routing protocols, 184
Classless Inter-Domain Routing (CIDR), 253-254
classless routing protocols, 184
clear ip bgp command, 254
clients, LEC (LAN Emulation Client), 87
configuration, 94
LEC communication, 92-93
LEC setup, 90-91
CLP (Cell Loss Priority), ATM cell header, 416
CMNS (Connection-Mode Network Service), 370

codecs, 41
collisions
collision detection, 61
random backoff, 61
troubleshooting, 65
command lines, IPX command-line keywords, 294
commands
Access Lists, 28-29
autodetect encapsulation ppp, 346
backdoor (BGP), 255
clear ip bgp, 254
command conventions, 4-5
compress stac, 346
compressing traffic, 36
configuring AppleTalk routing, 319
Custom queuing, 35-36
debug dialer, ISDN example, 358-359
debug ip igrp (IGRP), 216
debug ip ospf, 239
debug isdn q921, 343-344
debug isdn q931, 343-345
debug ppp authentication, 346, 356-357
default routes, 187-188
default-metric, 255, 263
description, 401
dhcp-proxy-client, 346
dialer in-band (DDR), 352
dialer load-threshold, 354
dialer map (DDR), 351, 355-356
dialer-group, 350
dialer-list, 350-351
dialer-string (DDR), 351
distance, selecting routes, 273-274
distribute-list in command, 268-269
distribute-list out command, 269-270
frame-relay custom-queue-list, 407
frame-relay interface-dlci command, 402

frame-relay map commands, 400

frame-relay priority-group, 407

frame-relay traffic-rate, 407

interface (IGMP), 280

ip address-pool, 346

ip address-pool local, 346

ip unnumbered (DDR), 351

ipx delay, 298

ipx maximum-paths #, 298

LAPB, 374

mapping (X.25), 380

neighbor send-community, 249

no auto-summary, 202, 219

passive-interface, 268

ping (ICMP), 166-167

ppp authentication chap, 346

ppp authentication pap, 346

ppp multilink, 346

ppp quality 70, 346

ppp reliable-link, 347

Priority queuing, 35

protocol translation (X.25), 386

redistribute, 263

redistribute metric, 263

redistribute route-map, 263-264

redistribute static, 263

route redistribution issues, 263-264

route-map setcommunity, 249

set metric, 255, 263-264

show dialer (ISDN), 357-358

show frame-relay pvc, 398, 407

show interface, 213, 396

show ip bgp, 253

show ip eigrp neighbor, 220

show ip igrp (IGRP), 214

show ip interfaces (IGRP), 215

show ip ospf database, 239

show ip ospf neighbor detail, 239

show ip protocol (IGRP), 214-215

show ip sdr, 280

show ipbgp neighbor, 254

show ipx route, 297-298

show ipx server, 299

show isdn status, 343-344

static routes, 185

trace (IGRP), 216

version (RIPv2), 202

X.25 routing, 371

Committed Burst Size (frame relay), 403

Committed Information Rate (CIR), frame relay, 403

communities (BGP), 256

community strings, 47

compatibility, Cisco/DECnet router interoperability, 328

components (routers), 42

compress stac command, 346

compressing

data (PPP), 346

traffic, 36

Concurrent Routing and Bridging. *See* **CRB**

confederations (BGP), 256

configuration register (routers), 43

bit 6, 44

boot fields, 43-44

configuring

Access Lists, 28-29

addresses, LES NSAP address configuration, 95

ATM

PVC configuration example, 420-422

SVC configuration example, 422-423

BPDUs, 109

BUS (Broadcast and Unknown Server), 94

Cisco traffic shaping (frame relay), 406-407

CRB, 125-126

DDR

Dial Backup, 352-354

dialer in-band command, 352

dialer map command, 351, 355-356

dialer-string command, 351

interesting traffic, 350-351

ip unnumbered command, 351

ISDN, 349-350

SPIDs, 349

switch type, 349

DECnet, 328, 330

default routes, 186, 188

DLSw, 141-142

EIGRP, 221-222

EtherChannel, 113

frame relay (LMI), 397-398

HSRP, 167-168

IGRP, 216

IPX

configuration example, 295-297

configuration steps, 293-294

IRB, 127

ISDN, 354-355

LEC (LAN Emulation Client), 94

LECS (LAN Emulation Configuration Server), 94-95

LES (LAN Emulation Server), 94

OSPF

basic configuration, 236-237

stub area configuration, 237-238

virtual link configuration, 238-239

passive interfaces, 268

passwords (routers), 45-46

PPP callback feature, 352

RIP

RIPv1, 202-203

RIPv2, 203-205

routers

copying to/from TFTP servers, 45

loading, 45

NVRAM, 43

RAM, 43

RSRB, 134-135

SR/TLB, 137-138

SRB

multiport SRB, 133-134

pure SRB, 132

SRT, 136

static routes, 185-186

Token-Ring, auto reconfiguration, 75
transparent bridges, 107
trunks (VLANs), 112
VTP, 116
X.25, 386-387
Connection-Mode Network Service (CMNS), 370
connection-oriented protocols, 17, 160
connectionless protocols, 17
IP, 152
UDP, 163
connections
DLSw process, 140-142
handshakes (protocols), 17
ISDN
BRI, 340
checking, 343
PRI, 340
PSTN, 340
peer
BGP, 254
DLSw, 139-140
PVCs
configuration example, 420-422
defined, 414
SVCs
configuration example, 422-423
defined, 414
TCP, establishing, 163
termination, 19
control field (LAPB), 373
Control VCCs (LANE), 88
controlling
errors (X.25), 374-375
packet flow (X.25), 376-377
convergence
OSPF, 229
routes (EIGRP), 220
converting
binary values, 26-27
decimal values, 26-27
hex values, 26-27
voice/digital signal conversions (codecs), 41
Copper Distributed Data Interface (CDDI), 76

copying
configuration files (routers), TFTP servers, 45
IOS (TFTP servers), 44-45
Core level (networks), 48
cost
CCIE Certification exams, 476
DECnet, 328-329
OSPF, 228-229
Token-Ring, 16
Count to Infinity (routers), 182
counterrotating rings (FDDI), 78-79
Country subfield (DNIC), 368
CPUs (central processing units), 43
OSPF, 230
routers, 43
CRB (Concurrent Routing and Bridging), 124
configuration, 125-126
interfaces, 125
nonroutable protocols, 125
CRC (Cyclic Redundancy Check), 63
creating route tables (X.25), 371
CSMA/CD (Carrier Sense Multiple Access/Collision Detection), 58-60
carrier sense, 60
collision detection, 61
IEEE 802.3, 14-15
multiple access, 60
troubleshooting, 65
Custom queuing, 35-36
Cyclic Redundancy Check (CRC), 63

D

dampening flapping routes (BGP), 256
DAS (dual-attachment stations), FDDI, 77
Data Encryption Standard (DES), 40
data field (LAPB), 373

Data Link Connection Identifier fields (DLCI fields), 395-396, 402
Data Link layer (OSI model), 10
AppleTalk, 309
LLC, 11, 15
MAC layer, 11
X.25, 367, 372-374
Data Network Identification Codes (DNIC), 368
Data VCCs (LANE), 89
Data-Link Switching. *See* **DLSw**
databases
link-state (OSPF), 230-232
neighbor (OSPF), 230
Datagram Delivery Protocol. *See* **DDP**
datagram mode (NetBIOS), 330
datagrams
headers, 313, 317
packets, 313, 317
DDP (Datagram Delivery Protocol), 309, 312-313, 317
DDR (Dial-on-Demand Routing), ISDN
configuration, 349-350
Dial Backup, 352-354
dialer in-band command, 352
dialer map command, 351, 355-356
dialer-string command, 351
interesting traffic, 350-351
ip unnumbered command, 351
SPIDs, 349
switch type, 349
DE (Discard Eligible) bit, frame relay, 404
debug dialer command (ISDN example), 358-359
debug ip igrp command (IGRP), 216
debug ip ospf command, 239
debug isdn q921 command, 343-344
debug isdn q931 command, 343-345

debug ppp authentication command, 346, 356-357

debugging (OSPF), 239

DEC (Digital Equipment Corporation), 326. *See also* **DECnet**

DEC LAT (Digital Equipment Corporation Local Area Transport), 124

DEC MOP (Digital Equipment Corporation Maintenance Operation Protocol), 124

decimal values
bits, 26
bytes, 26
converting, 26-27

DECnet, 326
addresses, 327
Cisco/DECnet router interoperability, 328
configuration, 328-330
cost, 328-329
DECnet Phase IV, 326
DECnet/OSI, 326-327
DNA, 326
DRP, 327
interarea routers, 328-330
intra-area routers, 328-330

DECnet Routing Protocol (DRP), 327

default routes
configuration, 186-188
uses, 187

default-metric command, 255, 263

defaults
administrative distances, 189
encapsulation types, 292

deleting
Access Lists, 29
routes, timers (RIP), 198

dense mode, 275

DES (Data Encryption Standard), 40

description command, 401

Designated Router (DR) election, 231-232

detecting collisions
collision detection, 61
Frame Check Sequence (FCS), 61
random backoff, 61
troubleshooting, 65

determining network/broadcast addresses (IP addresses), 156-158

deterministic media access
FDDI, 72
Token-Ring, 16, 72

DHCP (Dynamic Host Configuration Protocol), 168-169

dhcp-proxy-client command, 346

Dial Backup (DDR), 352
basic, 353
dialer load-threshold command, 354
floating static routes, 353-354

Dial-on-Demand Routing. *See* **DDR**

dialer in-band command (DDR), 352

dialer load-threshold command, 354

dialer map command (DDR), 351, 355-356

dialer-group command, 350

dialer-list command, 350-351

dialer-string command (DDR), 351

Diffie-Hellman algorithm, 40

Diffusing Update Algorithm (DUAL), 183, 217-218

Digital Equipment Corporation (DEC), 326. *See also* **DECnet**

Digital Equipment Corporation Local Area Transport (DEC LAT), 124

Digital Equipment Corporation Maintenance Operation Protocol (DEC MOP), 124

Digital Network Architecture (DNA), 326

digital/voice signal conversion (codecs), 41

Dijkstra algorithm, 228, 232

Disable mode (STP), 109

Discard Eligible (DE) bit, frame relay, 404

distance command, selecting routes, 273-274

Distance Vector Multicast Routing Protocol. *See* **DVMRP**

Distance Vector protocols (RTMP), 318

distance-vector routing protocols, 298

Distant Vector protocols, 183

distribute lists, 33. *See also* **Access Lists**
distribute-list in command, 268-269
distribute-list out command, 269-270

Distributed Queue Dual Bus (DQDB) architecture, 16

Distribution level (networks), 48

DLCI (Data Link Connection Identifier) fields (PVCs), 395-396, 402

DLSw (Data-Link Switching), 139, 331
advantages, 139
circuits, 139-140
command output examples, 142
configuration, 141-142
NetBIOS, 331
peer connections, 139-140
peers, 139
process, 140-141
SSP, 139

DNA (Digital Network Architecture), 326

DNIC (Data Network Identification Codes), 368

DNS (Domain Name Service), 165-166
iterative queries, 166
NBP comparison, 315

recursive queries, 165
servers, 166
documentation (Cisco Web site), 481
Domain Name Service. *See* **DNS**
Domain Specific Part (DSP), NSAPA, 418
domains (VTP), 114
dotted-decimal format
IP addresses, 154
AppleTalk addresses, 310
downstream neighbors (Token-Ring), 73
DQDB (Distributed Queue Dual Bus) architecture, 16
DR (Designated Router) election, 231-232
DRP (DECnet Routing Protocol), 327
DSP (Domain Specific Part), NSAPA, 418
DUAL (Diffusing Update Algorithm), 183, 217-218
dual-attachment stations (DAS), FDDI, 77
DVMRP (Distance Vector Multicast Routing Protocol), 278-279
MBONE project, 278-279
mrouted program, 278
Dynamic Host Configuration Protocol (DHCP), 168-169

E

E.164 (ATM addresses), 417
early release (Token-Ring), 73
EBGP (Exterior Border Gateway Protocol), 252-253
EBGP multihop (BGP), 247
EEPROM (electronic erasable programmable read-only memory), routers, 42
EIGRP (Enhanced IGRP), 210, 319
adjacency process, 220
advantages, 217
AppleTalk, 219
bandwidth, 220

configuration, 221-222
DUAL, 183, 217-218
IP, 219
IPX, 219
IPX EIGRP, 295
metrics, 217
multiple networking protocols, 217-219
neighbor discovery/recovery, 217
passive/active router feature, 218
redistribution metric issues, 263
reliable transport protocol, 218
route convergence, 220
route summarization, 219
VLSM, 219
ELANs (Emulated LANs), 86
ELAP (Ethernet Link Access Protocol), 309
electing
BDRs (OSPF), 231-232
DRs (OSPF), 231-232
enable passwords (routers), 46
enabling
policy routing, 271-272
routing (X.25), 371
encapsulation. *See* **tunneling**
encapsulation types, 291-292
encryption, 40
Enhanced IGRP. *See* **EIGRP**
errors
control (X.25), 374-375
correction (frame relay), 395
checking
checksums, 19
frame relay, 395
X.25, 366
handling, packet-level (X.25), 374
establishing
connections (TCP), 163
encapsulation map (X.25), 380
EtherChannel, 113
Ethernet, 58
10BASE-2, 59
10BASE-5, 59
10BASE-T, 59
100BASE-FX, 59
100BASE-T, 59

cabling, 15
collisions, 61, 65
CSMA/CD, 14-15, 58-60
carrier sense, 60
multiple access, 60
troubleshooting, 65
encapsulation types (IPX), 291-292
full-duplex operation, 60-61
Gigabit, 64-65
half-duplex operation, 60-61
history, 58
IEEE 802.3, 58
comparison, 14-15
CRC, 63
CSMA/CD, 14-15
Ethernet Version II comparison, 63-64
LLC, 58
MAC frame format, 62-63
MTU, 63
OSI Reference Model, 58
PDU, 63
SAP, 63
speeds, 58-59
Start of Frame (SOF), 62
STP, 58
interfaces, 59
shared media, 60
Token-Ring MAC address conversion, 136-137
transparent bridges, 106
Version II, 58
IEEE 802.3 comparison, 63-64
SNAP, 64
Ethernet Link Access Protocol (ELAP), 309
exam
Access List questions, 27
CCIE Certification exam registration site, 476, 479
CCIE Certification process, 475
Exam Blueprint (Cisco Web site), 3, 477
lab exam
format, 478
lab exam practice facilities list (Cisco Web site), 479

locations, 478
preparation, 479
registering, 478-479
scheduling, 478-479
practice tests
Chapter 1, 22-23
Chapter 2, 51-53
Chapter 3, 67-70
Chapter 4, 81-84
Chapter 5, 99-101
Chapter 6, 119-121
Chapter 7, 144-147
Chapter 8, 173-177
Chapter 9, 191-194
Chapter 10, 206-208
Chapter 11, 224-226
Chapter 12, 241-244
Chapter 13, 258-260
Chapter 14, 284-286
Chapter 15, 303-305
Chapter 16, 321-323
Chapter 17, 332-334
Chapter 18, 361-362
Chapter 19, 388-392
Chapter 20, 410-412
Chapter 21, 425-427
Test Pro software, 483-484
written exam
cost, 476
preparation, 476-477
registering, 476
results, 476
scheduling, 476
testing tips, 476-477
Excess Burst Size (frame relay), 403
expiration times (RIP), 198
extended networks (AppleTalk), 310
extensions (RIPv2), 200
Exterior Border Gateway Protocol (EBGP), 252-253
exterior routes (IGRP), 214

F

Fast EtherChannel, 113
FCS (Frame Check Sequence), 61, 373

FDDI (Fiber Distributed Data Interface), 72
address-recognized indicator bits, 80
deterministic media access, 72
encapsulation types, 292
fault management
counterrotating rings, 78-79
optical bypass switches, 79
frame formats, 79-80
frame-copied indicator bits, 80
history, 76
Media Access Control, 77
Physical Layer Medium (PMD), 77
Physical Layer Protocol (PHY), 77
priorities, 79
rings, 77
specifications, 76-77
wrapping, 16
FDDITalk Link Access Protocol (FLAP), 309
FECN (Forward Explicit Congestion Notification), frame relay, 404
Fiber Distributed Data Interface. See FDDI
fields
boot (configuration registers), 43-44
DLCI (PVCs), 395-396, 402
frame formats
FDDI, 79-80
Token-Ring, 73-75
frame status (Token-Ring), 73
Generic Flow Control (ATM cell headers), 416
IP headers, 152-154
LAPB
address, 372
control, 373
data, 373
FCS, 373
flag, 372
priority (Token-Ring), 76
reservation (Token-Ring), 76

RIFs, 129
building, 131-132
Ring Information Indicators (RIIs), 129
route descriptor field, 130
routing control field, 130
RIPv1 packets, 199-200
RIPv2 packets, 200-201
SAP, 15
TCP headers, 162
UDP headers, 164
filtering
interesting traffic (DDR), 350-351
routing/switching comparison, 13
transparent bridges, 106
filters. See also Access Lists
BGP
filter by community example, 249-250
filter by path example, 249
filter by route example, 248
cable range filters, 33
network filters, 32
NLSP, 32
NPP filters, 33
range filters, 33
SAP, 32, 301
zone filters, 33
firewalls
PIX, 39
proxy, 39
fixing errors (frame relay), 395
flag fields (LAPB), 372
FLAP (FDDITalk Link Access Protocol), 309
flapping
interfaces, Holddown Timer (routers), 182
routes, dampening (BGP), 256
flash memory (routers), 42
floating static routes (Dial Backup), 353-354
flow control (protocols), 18, 376-377
flush timer (RIP), 198
format
ATM cell headers, 416
command conventions, 4-5

frames
  FDDI, 79-80
  IPX headers, 290
  NetBIOS, 331
  PPP, 347-348
  Token-Ring, 73-75
  lab exam (CCIE
    Certification), 478
**Forward Explicit Congestion
  Notification (FECN), frame
  relay, 404**
**forwarding transparent
  bridges, 106**
Forwarding mode (STP), 109
**Frame Check Sequence (FCS),
  61, 373**
frame formats
  FDDI, 79-80
  IPX headers, 290
  NetBIOS, 331
  PPP, 347-348
  Token-Ring, 73-75
frame relay, 394
  error checking, 395
  error correction, 395
  frame-relay custom-queue-list
    command, 407
  frame-relay map commands,
    400
  frame-relay priority-group
    command, 407
  frame-relay traffic-rate com-
    mand, 407
  Inverse ARP, 399-400
  LAPF, 395
  LMI, 396-398
    autosense, 397
    *interface configuration,
      397-398*
    message types, 397
    messages, 396
  NNIs, 394
  PVCs, 395
    DLCI fields, 395-396, 402
    *show frame-relay pvc com-
      mand, 398*
  show frame-relay pvc com-
    mand, 407

subinterfaces, 403
  advantages, 401
  creating, 401-402
  description command, 401
  example, 402
  multipoint, 401
  point-to-point, 401
traffic
  *Cisco traffic-shaping configu-
    ration, 406-407*
  *Cisco traffic-shaping options,
    405*
  *Cisco traffic-shaping steps,
    405*
  congestion causes, 403
  *congestion notification meth-
    ods, 404*
  parameters, 403-404
  traffic-shaping example, 404
  UNIs, 394
  X.25 comparison, 394
**frame relay custom-queue-list
  command, 407**
**frame status fields (Token-
  Ring), 73**
frame-copied indicator bits
  FDDI, 80
  Token-Ring, 75
**frame-relay interface-dlci com-
  mand, 402**
**frame-relay map commands,
  400**
**frame-relay priority-group
  command, 407**
**frame-relay traffic-rate com-
  mand, 407**
frames
  FDDI, 79-80
  IPX headers, 290
  LAPB, 372-373
  NetBIOS, 331
  PPP, 347-348
  Token-Ring
    frame formats, 73-75
    frame status fields, 73
    information frames, 73
    RIIs, 129
full-duplex operation, 60-61
**function groups (ISDN),
  340-341**

**functional addresses (MAC
  addresses), 60**
**functions (routing protocols),
  180**

G-H

**garbage collection timer
  (RIP), 198**
**GBIC (Gigabit Ethernet
  Interface Carrier), 65**
**Generic Flow Control field
  (ATM cell headers), 416**
***Get Cisco Certified and Get
  Ahead*, 482**
**Get Nearest Server requests,
  293**
**GFC (Generic Flow Control)
  field (ATM cell headers), 416**
Gigabit Ethernet, 64-65
  GBIC, 65
  UTP, 64
**Gigabit Media Independent
  Interface (GMII), 59**
global address space, 169-171
**group addresses (MAC
  addresses), 60**

H.323, 41
half-duplex operation, 60-61
**handling packet-level errors
  (X.25), 374**
**handshakes (protocols), 17,
  163**
**HDLC (High-Level Data Link
  Control), 342-345**
**Header Error Check (HEC),
  ATM cell header, 416**
headers
  ATM cell headers, 416
  datagrams, 313, 317
  IP
    fields, 152-154
    size, 152
  IPX frames, 290
  TCP, 161-162
  UDP, 164
hello packets (OSPF), 231
hello protocol (OSPF), 231

help. *See also* problems; troubleshooting
- Advanced IP Routing with Cisco Networks, 482
- Building CISCO Remote Access Networks, 482
- CCIE Fundamentals: Network Design and Case Studies, 481
- CCIE Fundamentals: Network Design and Case Studies, Second Edition, 481
- CCIE Professional Development: Advanced IP Network Design, 482
- CCIE Professional Development: Cisco LAN Switching, 481
- CCIE Professional Development: Routing TCP/IP, 481
- Cisco Certification: Bridges, Routers, and Switches for CCIEs, 481
- Cisco IOS 12.0 Configuration Fundamentals, 481
- Cisco Web site, 481
- Cisco: A Beginner's Guide, 482
- Exam Blueprint (Cisco Web site), 3, 477
- exam preparation tips, 477
- exam taking tips, 477
- Get Cisco Certified and Get Ahead, 482
- Internetworking Technologies Handbook, Second Edition, 481
- lab exam practice facilities list (Cisco Web site), 479
- lab exam preparation tips, 479
- practice tests
  - Chapter 1, 22-23
  - Chapter 2, 51-53
  - Chapter 3, 67-70
  - Chapter 4, 81-84
  - Chapter 5, 99-101
  - Chapter 6, 119-121
  - Chapter 7, 144-147
  - Chapter 8, 173-177
  - Chapter 9, 191-194
  - Chapter 10, 206-208
  - Chapter 11, 224-226
  - Chapter 12, 241-244
  - Chapter 13, 258-260
  - Chapter 14, 284-286
  - Chapter 15, 303-305
  - Chapter 16, 321-323
  - Chapter 17, 332-334
  - Chapter 18, 361-362
  - Chapter 19, 388-392
  - Chapter 20, 410-412
  - Chapter 21, 425-427
  - Test Pro software, 483-484
- RFCs, 482
- written exam preparation tips, 476
- written exam taking tips, 476

hex values
- bits, 26
- bytes, 26
- configuration registers (routers), 43
  - bit 6, 44
  - boot fields, 43-44
- converting, 26-27
- hex character binary values table, 26-27

High-Level Data Link Control (HDLC), 342-345

history
- Ethernet, 58
- FDDI, 76
- RIP, 196

holddown timer (RIP), 198

Holddown Timer (routers), 182

holddowns (IGRP), 211

home pages. *See* **sites**

hops
- BGP
  - BGP next hop, 246
  - EBGP multihop, 247
- Count to Infinity (routers), 182
- hop counts
  - IPX, 298
  - OSPF, 228-229
  - RIP, 197
- next hop field (RIPv2), 201

HSRP (Hot Standby Routing Protocol), 167
- Active routers, 167
- configuration, 167-168

I

I/G (Individual/Group) Address Bit, 60

IBGP (Interior Border Gateway Protocol), 252

IBM Token-Ring specification, 72

ICMP (Internet Control Message Protocol), 166
- extended IP Access Lists, 31
- Network layer (OSI model), 166
- ping command, 166-167

identifying
- routes
  - IPX, 297-299
  - OSPF, 232
- servers (IPX), 299

IDN (International Data Number), 368

IDP (Initial Domain Part), NSAPA, 418

IEEE (Institute of Electrical and Electronics Engineers), 58
- 802.2
  - LLC, 11, 15
  - MAC layer, 11
  - SAP fields, 15
- 802.3, 58
  - CRC, 63
  - CSMA/CD, 14-15
  - Ethernet comparison, 14-15
  - Ethernet Version II comparison, 63-64
  - LLC, 58
  - MAC frame format, 62-63
  - MTU, 63
  - OSI Reference Model, 58
  - PDU, 63
  - SAP, 63
  - speeds, 58-59
  - Start of Frame (SOF), 62
  - STP, 58
- 802.3z, 64-65
  - GBIC, 65
  - UTP, 64
- 802.5. *See* Token-Ring
- 802.6, 16

IGMP
Internet Group Management Protocol, 116-117, 280
IGP (Interior Gateway Protocol), 228
IGRP (Interior Gateway Routing Protocol), 210
AS numbers, 210, 216
configuration, 216
holddowns, 211
metrics, 210-212
formula, 212-213
show interface command, 213
monitoring, 214-216
multipath routing, 211
poison reverse updates, 211
redistribution metric issues, 263
route types, 214
route updates, 213-214
split-horizons, 211
stability features, 211
IISP (Interim-Interswitch Signaling Protocol), 419
implementing X.25 routing, 369
implicit congestion notification (frame relay), 404
implicit deny feature (routers), 29
Individual/Group (I/G) Address Bit, 60
information frames
LAPB, 373
Token-Ring, 73
Initial Domain Part (IDP), NSAPA, 418
installing Test Pro software, 484
Institute of Electrical and Electronics Engineers. *See* **IEEE**
Integrated Routing and Bridging. *See* **IRB**
Integrated Service Digital Network. *See* **ISDN**
interarea routers (DECnet), 328-330

interface command (IGMP), 280
interfaces
CRB, 125
Ethernet, 59
flapping, Holddown Timer (routers), 182
IRB, Bridge Virtual Interface (BVI), 126-127
LocalTalk, 309
loopback, 247
LUNI (LAN Emulation User-to-Network Interface), 87
MTU, 19
NNI, 415
NNIs, 394
passive, 268
PNNI, 415-416
serial, 292
speed
LAN interfaces, 19-20
Physical layer (OSI model), 19
WAN interfaces, 20
subinterfaces (frame relay), 403
advantages, 401
creating, 401-402
description command, 401
example, 402
multipoint, 401
point-to-point, 401
UNIs, 394, 414
Interim-Interswitch Signaling Protocol (IISP), 419
Interior Border Gateway Protocol (IBGP), 252
Interior Gateway Protocol (IGP), 228
Interior Gateway Routing Protocol. *See* **IGRP**
interior routes (IGRP), 214
Internal Routers (OSPF), 234
International Standards Organization (ISO), 10
Internet Control Message Protocol. *See* **ICMP**
Internet Group Management Protocol (IGMP), 116-117, 280
Internet Packet Exchange. *See* **IPX**

Internet Protocol. *See* **IP**
Internetworking Operating System. *See* **IOS**
Internetworking Technologies Handbook, Second Edition, 481
intra-area routers (DECnet), 328-330
invalid timer (RIP), 198
Inverse ARP, 399-400
IOS (Internetworking Operating System), 42
booting routers, 42
copying (TFTP servers), 44-45
IP (Internet Protocol), 152
addresses
ARP, 158-160
classes, 154-155
determining network/broadcast addresses, 156-158
DHCP, 168-169
DNS, 165-166
dotted-decimal format, 154
frame-relay map commands, 400
global address space, 169-171
Inverse ARP, 399-400
IP address pooling (PPP), 346
masks, 156-158
NAT, 169-171
private address space, 155, 169-171
public address space, 155
reserved, 155
router IDs, 231
subinterfaces, 401-403
subnetting, 156
VLSM, 156
wildcard masks, 30
as connectionless protocol, 152
EIGRP, 219
headers
fields, 152-154
size, 152
IP Access Lists
extended, 30-31
standard, 29-30
Network layer (OSI model), 152

ip address-pool command, 346

ip address-pool local command, 346

ip unnumbered command (DDR), 351

IPX (Internet Packet Exchange), 290

Access Lists, 300
  extended, 300-301
  SAP filters, 301
  standard, 300

addresses, 290-291

command-line keywords, 294

configuration
  example, 295-297
  steps, 293-294

EIGRP, 219

encapsulation types, 291-292
  defaults, 292
  Ethernet, 291
  FDDI, 292
  serial interfaces, 292
  Token-Ring, 292

headers (frames), 290

hop counts, 298

identifying routes, 297-299

IPX Access Lists
  extended, 32
  NLSP filters, 32
  SAP filters, 32
  standard, 31

ipx delay command, 298

ipx maximum-paths # command, 298

ipxwan, 294

routing, 294-295
  IPX EIGRP, 295
  IPX NLSP, 295
  IPX RIP, 294

show ipx route command, 297-298

show ipx server command, 299

tick counts, 298

ipx delay command, 298

IPX EIGRP routing, 295

ipx maximum-paths # command, 298

IPX NLSP routing, 295

IPX RIP routing, 294

ipxwan, 294

IRB (Integrated Routing and Bridging), 126

Bridge Virtual Interface (BVI), 126-127

configuration, 127

nonroutable protocols, 126

ISDN (Integrated Service Digital Network), 340

configuration, 354-355

connections
  BRI, 340
  checking, 343
  PRI, 340
  PSTN, 340

DDR
  configuration, 349-350
  Dial Backup, 352-354
  dialer in-band command, 352
  dialer map command, 351, 355-356
  dialer-string command, 351
  interesting traffic, 350-351
  ip unnumbered command, 351
  SPIDs, 349
  switch type, 349

debug dialer command, 358-359

debug isdn q921 command, 343-344

debug isdn q931 command, 343-345

function groups, 340-341

HDLC, 342-345

LAPD, 342-345

PPP, 345
  autodetect encapsulation ppp command, 346
  callback, 347, 352
  CHAP, 346, 355-357
  data compression, 346
  debug ppp authentication command, 346, 356-357
  encapsulation example, 355-356
  features, 345-347
  frames, 347-348

IP address pooling, 346
  LCP, 348
  LQM, 346
  NCP, 348
  PAP, 345
  ppp authentication chap command, 346
  ppp authentication pap command, 346
  PPP Multilink, 346
  reliable link, 347
  VPDNs, 347

reference points, 341

show dialer command examples, 357-358

show isdn status command, 343-344

ISO (International Standards Organization), 10

iterative queries (DNS), 166

ITU-T (International Telecommunication Union-Telecommunication Standardization Sector), 366

J-L

keys, 40

keywords, IPX command-line keywords, 294

L2F (Level 2 Forwarding) protocol, 347

lab exam (CCIE Certification)
format, 478

lab exam practice facilities list (Cisco Web site), 479

locations, 478

preparation, 479

registering, 478-479

scheduling, 478-479

LAN Emulation. *See* **LANE**

LAN Emulation Client. *See* **LEC**

LAN Emulation Configuration Server. *See* **LECS**

LAN Emulation Server. *See* **LES**

LAN Emulation User-to-Network Interface (LUNI), 87

LANE (LAN Emulation), 86
BUS (Broadcast and Unknown Server), 88, 94
ELANs, 86
LEC (LAN Emulation Client), 87, 94
LEC communication, 92-93
LEC setup, 90-91
LECS (LAN Emulation Configuration Server), 87, 94-95
LES (LAN Emulation Server), 88, 94
LES NSAP address configuration, 95
LUNI, 87
SSRP, 95-97
supported networks, 86
VCCs (Virtual Circuit Connections), 88-89
LANs (local area networks), 58. *See also* **Ethernet**
ELANs, 86
interface speeds, 19-20
LAN switching, 106-107
LANE. *See* LANE
VLANs
characteristics, 111
trunks, 111-112
VTP, 114-116
LAP (Link Access Protocol), 309
LAPB (Link Access Procedure Balanced), 372-374
frames, 372
address field, 372
control field, 373
data field, 373
FCS, 373
flag field, 372
information, 373
supervisory, 373
unnumbered, 373
X.25 layers, 372-374
LAPD (Link Access Procedure D), 342-345
LAPF (Link Access Protocol for Frame bearer services), 395

LAT (local-area transport), 383
layers
ATM, 416-417
OSI model, 10-12
Application, 12, 310
Data Link, 10, 309
Network, 11, 152, 166, 309
Physical, 10, 19, 309
Presentation, 12, 310
Session, 12, 310
Transport, 11, 160, 163, 309
X.25, 367, 372-374
LCP (Link Control Layer Protocol), 348
learning (transparent bridges), 106
Learning mode (STP), 109
LEC (LAN Emulation Client), 87
configuration, 94
LEC communication, 92-93
LEC setup, 90-91
LEC communication (LANE), 92-93
LEC setup (LANE), 90-91
LECS (LAN Emulation Configuration Server), 87
configuration, 94-95
SSRP, 95-97
LES (LAN Emulation Server), 88
configuration, 94
SSRP, 95-97
LES NSAP address configuration (LANE), 95
level 1 routers (DECnet), 328-330
Level 2 Forwarding (L2F) protocol, 347
level 2 routers (DECnet), 328-330
levels (networks), 48
line passwords (routers), 45
Link Access Procedure Balanced. *See* **LAPB**
Link Access Procedure D (LAPD), 342-345
Link Access Protocol (LAP), 309

Link Access Protocol for Frame bearer services (LAPF), 395
Link Control Layer Protocol (LCP), 348
Link Management Interface protocol. *See* **LMI protocol**
Link Quality Monitoring (LQM), 346
link speeds
LAN interfaces, 19-20
Physical layer (OSI model), 19
WAN interfaces, 20
Link State Advertisements (LSAs), 232, 235
Link State protocols, 183
Link State Updates (LSUs), 232
link-state databases (OSPF), 230-232
links, virtual (OSPF), 236-239
Listening mode (STP), 109
lists
Access Lists, 27
access-class, 34
AppleTalk, 32-33
Cisco Access List numbers, 28
commands, 28-29
configuring, 28-29
deleting, 29
Distribute Lists, 33
exam questions, 27
implicit deny feature, 29
IP extended, 30-31
IP standard, 29-30
IPX, 300
IPX extended, 32, 300-301
IPX standard, 31, 300
NLSP filters, 32
SAP filters, 32, 301
boot order (routers), 44-45
distribute, 33
distribute-list in command, 268-269
distribute-list out command, 269-270
lab exam practice facilities list (Cisco Web site), 479
method (AAA), 38

priority (Priority Queuing), 34
queue (Custom queuing), 35
LLAP (LocalTalk Link Access Protocol), 309
LLC (Logical Link Control), 15
IEEE 802.3 standard, 58
OSI model, 11
LMI (Link Management Interface) protocol, 396-398
autosense, 397
frame relay interface configuration, 397-398
message types, 397
messages, 396
load balancing, 37
loading router configuration, 45
local area networks. *See* LANs
local X.25 switching, 369
local-area transport (LAT), 383
LocalTalk, 309
LocalTalk Link Access Protocol (LLAP), 309
locations, lab exam (CCIE Certification)
lab exam practice facilities list (Cicso Web site), 479
lab exam testing centers, 478
Logical Link Control. *See* LLC
logical ring, 72. *See also* Token-Ring
loopback interfaces, 247
loops
broadcast storms, 108
preventing, 180-181
Poison Reverse, 181-182
STP, 107-111
reverse route (RIP), 198
routing, 211
LQM (Link Quality Monitoring), 346
LSAs (Link State Advertisements), 232, 235
LSUs (Link State Updates), 232
LUNI (LAN Emulation User-to-Network Interface), 87

M

MAC (Media Access Control), FDDI, 77
MAC (Media Access Control) layer, 59-60
IEEE 802.3 MAC frame format, 62-63
MAC addresses
ARP, 158-160
broadcast addresses, 60
Ethernet/Token-Ring MAC address conversion, 136-137
functional addresses, 60
I/G Address Bit, 60
multicast bits, 128
OUIs, 60
U/L Address Bit, 60
unicast traffic, 60
OSI model, 11
maintenance, routes (OSPF), 233
Management Information Base (MIB), 47
MANs (Metropolitan Area Networks), 16
mapping (X.25), 379, 386-387
maps, frame-relay map command, 400
masks
IP addresses, 156-158
determining network/broadcast addresses, 156-158
subnetting, 156
VLSM, 156
subnet mask field (RIPv2), 201
VLSM
EIGRP, 219
OSPF, 230
wildcard, 30
Maximum Transmission Unit (MTU), 19, 63
MBONE (Multicast Backbone) project, 278-279
MED (Multi-Exit Discriminator), BGP, 255
Media Access Control (MAC), FDDI, 77

Media Access Control layer. *See* MAC layer
Media Independent Interface (MII), 59
memory
flash (routers), 42
NVRAM (routers), 42-43
OSPF requirements, 230
RAM (routers), 42-43
ROM (routers), 42
messages
LMI, 396-397
multicasts, 116
CGMP, 117
IGMP, 116-117
request
RIP, 197
response (RIP), 197
source-quench, 377
VTP, 115-116
method lists (AAA), 38
metrics
DECnet, 328-329
EIGRP, 217
IGRP, 210-212
formula, 212-213
show interface command, 213
OSPF, 228-229
RIP, 196-197
route redistribution issues, 262-264
routing protocols, 183
Metropolitan Area Networks (MANs), 16
MIB (Management Information Base), 47
MII (Media Independent Interface), 59
modes (NetBIOS), 330
monitoring
IGRP, 214-216
Token-Ring, 75
mrouted program, 278
MTU (Maximum Transmission Unit), 19, 63
Multi-Exit Discriminator (MED), BGP, 255
Multicast Backbone (MBONE) project, 278-279

multicast bits (MAC addresses), 128
multicast traffic
  CGMP, 281
  DVMRP, 278-279
    MBONE project, 278-279
    mrouted program, 278
  IGMP, 116, 280
    CGMP, 117
    IGMP snooping, 116
  PIM, 275
    dense mode, 275
    sparse mode, 275-277
    sparse-dense mode, 277-278
multimedia
  H.323 protocol, 41
  RTP, 42
multipath routing (IGRP), 211
multiple access (CSMA/CD), 60
multipoint subinterfaces (frame relay), 401

N

Name Binding Protocol. *See* NBP
names
  DNS, 165-166
    authoritative servers, 166
    iterative queries, 166
    NBP comparison, 315
    nonauthoritative servers, 166
    recursive queries, 165
  NBP, 309, 315
  zones, 312
NAT (Network Address Translation), 169-171
NAUN (nearest upstream neighbor), 75
NBP (Name Binding Protocol), 33, 309, 315
  DNS comparison, 315
  filters, 33
  NVEs, 315
NCP (Network Control Layer Protocol), 348
nearest upstream neighbor (NAUN), 75

neighbor send-community command, 249
neighbors. *See also* peers
  EIGRP, 217, 220
  OSPF, 230-231
NetBEUI (NetBIOS Extended User Interface), 331
NetBIOS (Network Basic Input/Output System), 124, 330-331
  bridging, 331
  datagram mode, 330
  DLSw, 331
  frames, 331
  NetBEUI, 331
  session mode, 330
NetWare. *See* Novell NetWare
NetWare Link Services Protocol. *See* NLSP
Network Address Translation (NAT), 169
Network Basic Input/Output System. *See* NetBIOS
network filters, 32
Network layer (OSI model), 11
  AppleTalk, 309
  ICMP, 166
  IP, 152
Network Monitoring Stations (NMS), 47
Network Operating Systems (NOSs), 290. *See also specific NOSs*
Network Service Access Point address (NSAPA), 417
Network Visible Entities (NVEs), 315
Network-to-Network Interfaces (NNIs), 394, 415
networks, 48. *See also specific network types*
next hop field (RIPv2), 201
NLSP (NetWare Link Services Protocol), 32, 295
  IPX Access Lists, 32
  IPX NLSP, 295
NMS (Network Monitoring Stations), 47
NNIs (Network-to-Network Interfaces), 394, 415

no auto-summary command, 202, 219
nodes
  transactions, 314
  zones, 312
noncanonical order, 137
nonextended networks (AppleTalk), 310
nonroutable protocols, 124
  CRB, 125
  IRB, 126
NOSs (Network Operating Systems), 290. *See also specific NOSs*
not-so-stubby areas (NSSAs), 234
Novell NetWare
  Get Nearest Server requests, 293
  IPX, 290
    Access Lists, 300-302
    addresses, 290-291
    command-line keywords, 294
    configuration example, 295-297
    configuration steps, 293-294
    encapsulation types, 291-292
    frames, 290
    hop counts, 298
    identifying routes, 297-299
    identifying servers, 299
    ipx delay command, 298
    ipx maximum-paths # command, 298
    ipxwan, 294
    routing, 294-295
    show ipx route command, 297-298
    show ipx server command, 299
    tick counts, 298
  NLSP, 32, 295
    IPX Access Lists, 32
    IPX NLSP, 295
  SAP, 293
NSAPA (Network Service Access Point address), 417-418
NSSAs (not-so-stubby areas), 234

NTN (National Terminal Number), 368
numbers, AS (autonomous system), 210, 216
NVEs (Network Visible Entities), 315
NVRAM (routers), 42-43

O

Open Shortest Path First. *See* OSPF
open standards (OSPF), 228
Open System Interconnect (OSI), 367
Open Systems Interconnect Reference Model. *See* OSI Reference Model
operating systems. *See* OSs
optical bypass switches (FDDI), 79
Organizational Unique Identifiers (OUIs), 60
OSI (Open System Interconnect), 367
OSI (Open Systems Interconnect) Reference Model, 10, 58
  DECnet/OSI, 326-327
  IEEE 802.3, 58
  layers, 10, 12
    Application, 12, 310
    Data Link, 10, 309
    Network, 11, 152, 166, 309
    Physical, 10, 19, 309
    Presentation, 12, 310
    Session, 12, 310
    Transport, 11, 160, 163, 309
  protocol map, 12-13
  routing/switching comparison, 13
OSPF (Open Shortest Path First), 228
  ABRs, 234
  adjacencies, 231
  areas, 230, 233-234
    backbone, 233-234
    NSSA, 234
    stub, 234, 237-238
    totally stubby, 234

ASBRs, 234
authentication, 230
Backbone Routers, 234
bandwidth conservation, 229
BDR election, 231-232
configuration
  basic, 236-237
  stub area, 237-238
  virtual link, 238-239
convergence, 229
cost, 228-229
CPUs, 230
debug ip ospf command, 239
debugging, 239
DR election, 231-232
features, 228
hello packets, 231
hello protocol, 231
hop counts, 228-229
identifying routes, 232
Internal Routers, 234
link-state databases, 230-232
LSAs, 232, 235
LSUs, 232
memory requirements, 230
neighbor databases, 230
open standard, 228
redistribution metric issues, 263
route maintenance, 233
router IDs, 231
router priority, 231
routing tables, 230
scalability, 228, 233
selecting routes, 232
show ip ospf database command, 239
show ip ospf neighbor detail command, 239
SPF algorithm, 228, 232
summarization, 265
troubleshooting, 239
virtual links, 236-239
VLSM support, 230
OSs (operating systems)
  IOS
    booting routers, 42
    copying to/from TFTP servers, 44-45
  NOSs, 290
OUIs (Organizational Unique Identifiers), 60

P

Packet-Layer Protocol (PLP), 381
packet-switched network layer (X.25), 367
packets
  AARP, 314
  checksums, 19
  datagrams, 313, 317
  hello (OSPF), 231
  load balancing, 37
  RIPv1, 199-200
  RIPv2, 200-202
    authentication, 200-202
    extensions, 200
    next hop field, 201
    route tags, 201
    subnet mask field, 201
  switching (X.25), 366-367
PAP
  Password Authentication Protocol, 345
  PPP, 345
  Printing Access Protocol, 310, 316
  Session Listening Sockets (SLSs), 316
parameters, traffic, 403-404
passive interfaces, 268
passive-interface command, 268
Password Authentication Protocol. *See* PAP
passwords. *See also* security
  CHAP
    debug ppp authentication command, 356-357
    PPP, 346, 355-356
  community strings, 47
  PAP, 345
  routers
    configuring, 45-46
    enable, 46
    line, 45
    recovering, 44
path costs, 108
Payload Type (PT), ATM cell header, 416
PDNs (Public Data Networks), 368

PDU (Protocol Data Unit), 63
peers. *See also* **neighbors**
  BGP
    defined, 250
    neighbor definition, 254
    validating peer connections,
    254
  DLSw, 139-140
Permanent Virtual Circuits.
  See **PVCs**
Phase 1 networks (AppleTalk),
310
Phase 2 networks (AppleTalk),
310
Physical layer (OSI model), 10
  AppleTalk, 309
  interface speeds, 19
physical layer (X.25), 367
Physical Layer Medium
(PMD), FDDI, 77
Physical Layer Protocol
(PHY), FDDI, 77
physical-layer protocol (X.25),
377-378
physical star, 72. *See also*
Token-Ring
PIM (Protocol Independent
Multicast), 275
  dense mode, 275
  sparse mode, 275-277
  sparse-dense mode, 277-278
  Auto-RP feature, 277
  RP mapping agents, 277-278
ping command (ICMP),
166-167
PIX, 39
PLP (Packet-Layer Protocol),
381
PMD (Physical Layer
Medium), FDDI, 77
PMD (Physical Layer
Protocol), PHY, 77
PNNI (Public or Private
Network-to-Network inter-
face), 415-416
Point-to-Point Protocol. *See*
PPP
point-to-point subinterfaces
(frame relay), 401

Poison Reverse
  poison reverse updates
    (IGRP), 211
  routers, 181-182
  split horizon with poison
    reverse (RIP), 198
policy routing, 270-272
  enabling, 271-272
  example, 271-272
ports
  EtherChannel port modes, 113
  root, 108
  STP port modes, 109-111
  TCP, 164-165
  trunks (VLANs), 111-112
  UDP, 164-165
PPP (Point-to-Point
Protocol), 345
  autodetect encapsulation ppp
    command, 346
  callback, 347, 352
  CHAP, 346, 355-357
  data compression, 346
  debug ppp authentication
    command, 346, 356-357
  encapsulation example,
    355-356
  features, 345-347
  frames, 347-348
  IP address pooling, 346
  ISDN, 345
  LCP, 348
  LQM, 346
  NCP, 348
  PAP, 345
  ppp authentication chap com-
    mand, 346
  ppp authentication pap com-
    mand, 346
  PPP Multilink, 346
  ppp multilink command, 346
  ppp quality 70 command, 346
  ppp reliable-link command,
    347
  reliable link, 347
  VPDNs, 347
practice tests. *See also* **help**
  Chapter 1, 22-23
  Chapter 2, 51-53

  Chapter 3, 67-70
  Chapter 4, 81-84
  Chapter 5, 99-101
  Chapter 6, 119-121
  Chapter 7, 144-147
  Chapter 8, 173-177
  Chapter 9, 191-194
  Chapter 10, 206-208
  Chapter 11, 224-226
  Chapter 12, 241-244
  Chapter 13, 258-260
  Chapter 14, 284-286
  Chapter 15, 303-305
  Chapter 16, 321-323
  Chapter 17, 332-334
  Chapter 18, 361-362
  Chapter 19, 388-392
  Chapter 20, 410-412
  Chapter 21, 425-427
  lab exam practice facilities list
    (Cisco Web site), 479
  Test Pro software
    installation, 484
    starting, 484
    system requirements, 484
    test types, 483
preparation
  CCIE Certification exams
    lab exam, 479
    written exam, 476-477
Presentation layer (OSI
model), 12, 310
preventing loops, 180-181
  Poison Reverse, 181-182
  Split Horizon, 180, 318
  STP, 107-111
Primary Rate Interface (PRI),
340
primary rings (FDDI), 77
Printing Access Protocol. *See*
PAP
priorities
  FDDI, 79
  router priority (OSPF), 231
  Token-Ring, 76
priority fields (Token-Ring),
76
priority lists (Priority queu-
ing), 34

Priority queuing, 34-36
  commands, 35
  priority lists, 34
**private address space, 155,
169, 171**
private keys, 40
problems. *See also* **help; troubleshooting**
  FDDI fault management
    counterrotating rings, 78-79
    optical bypass switches, 79
  Token-Ring fault manage-
    ment, 75
processes (Token-Ring), 73
processors. *See* **CPUs**
Protocol Data Unit (PDU), 63
**Protocol Independent
Multicast.** *See* **PIM**
protocols, 17
  AAA, 38
  ACKs, 18
  AppleTalk
    AARP, 309, 313-314
    Access Lists, 32-33
    addresses, 310-312
    ADSP, 310, 316
    AEP, 309, 314
    AFP, 310, 316
    *Application layer (OSI model),
     310*
    ASP, 310, 316
    ATP, 309, 314-315
    AURP, 309, 318-319
    cable ranges, 310
    configuring routing, 319
    *Data Link layer (OSI model),
     309*
    DDP, 309, 312-313, 317
    EIGRP, 219, 319
    ELAP, 309
    FLAP, 309
    LAP, 309
    LLAP, 309
    LocalTalk, 309
    NBP, 309, 315
    *Network layer (OSI model),
     309*
    PAP, 310, 316
    Phase 1, 310

    Phase 2, 310
    *Physical layer (OSI model),
     309*
    *Presentation layer (OSI
     model), 310*
    routing, 317
    RTMP, 309, 318
    seed routers, 317
    *Session layer (OSI model),
     310*
    sockets, 311
    TLAP, 309
    *Transport layer (OSI model),
     309*
    tunneling, 318-319
    ZIP, 310-312, 315-316
  AppleTalk protocol suite, 308
  ARP, 158-160
    Inverse ARP, 399-400
    proxy ARP, 159
  ATM, 414
    addresses, 417-418
    cell header format, 416
    IISP, 419
    layers, 416-417
    NNI, 415
    PNNI, 415-416
    PVCs, 414, 420-422
    QoS, 419-420
    signaling, 418
    SSCOP, 418-419
    SVCs, 414, 422-423
    UNI, 414
  BGP, 246
    autonomous system, 254
    backdoor command, 255
    BGP next hop, 246
    CIDR, 253-254
    communities, 256
    confederations, 256
    EBGP, 252-253
    EBGP multihop, 247
    *filter by community example,
     249-250*
    filter by path example, 249
    filter by route example, 248
    filters, 248
    IBGP, 252
    loopback addressing, 247

    MED, 255
    neighbor definition, 254
    overlapping protocols, 247
    peers, 250
    redistribution, 247, 255
    *redistribution metric issues,
     263*
    route flap dampening, 256
    route maps, 247, 255
    route reflectors, 257
    route selection process, 250-252
    TCP, 246
    *validating peer connections,
     254*
  CDP, 46-47
  CGMP, 281
  CHAP, 346, 355-356
  Cisco Connection Online Web
    site, 36
  connection-oriented, 17
  connectionless, 17
  DEC LAT, 124
  DEC MOP, 124
  DECnet, 326
    addresses, 327
    *Cisco/DECnet router interop-
     erability, 328*
    configuration, 328-330
    cost, 328-329
    DECnet Phase IV, 326
    DECnet/OSI, 326-327
    DNA, 326
    DRP, 327
    interarea routers, 328-330
    intra-area routers, 328-330
  DHCP, 168-169
  distance-vector routing proto-
    cols, 298
  DVMRP, 278-279
    MBONE project, 278-279
    mrouted program, 278
  EIGRP, 210, 319
    adjacency process, 220
    advantages, 217
    AppleTalk, 219
    bandwidth, 220
    configuration, 221-222
    DUAL, 183, 217-218
    IP, 219
    IPX, 219

IPX EIGRP, 295
  metrics, 217
  multiple networking protocols,
    217-219
  neighbor discovery/recovery, 217
  passive/active router feature,
    218
  redistribution metric issues, 263
  reliable transport protocol, 218
  route convergence, 220
  route summarization, 219
  VLSM, 219
error checking, 19
flow control, 18
frame relay, 394
  Cisco traffic-shaping configu-
    ration, 406-407
  Cisco traffic-shaping options,
    405
  Cisco traffic-shaping steps, 405
  error checking, 395
  error correction, 395
  frame-relay custom-queue-list
    command, 407
  frame-relay map commands,
    400
  frame-relay priority-group
    command, 407
  frame-relay traffic-rate com-
    mand, 407
  Inverse ARP, 399-400
  LAPF, 395
  LMI, 396-398
  NNIs, 394
  PVCs, 395-398, 402
  show frame-relay pvc com-
    mand, 407
  subinterfaces, 401-403
  traffic congestion causes, 403
  traffic congestion notification
    methods, 404
  traffic parameters, 403-404
  traffic-shaping example, 404
  UNIs, 394
  X.25 comparison, 394
H.323, 41
handshakes, 17
HDLC (ISDN), 342-345

HSRP, 167
  Active routers, 167
  configuration, 167-168
ICMP
  extended IP Access Lists, 31
  Network layer (OSI model),
    166
  ping command, 166-167
IGMP, 280
IGP, 228
IGRP, 210
  AS numbers, 210, 216
  configuration, 216
  holddowns, 211
  metrics, 210-213
  monitoring, 214-216
  multipath routing, 211
  poison reverse updates, 211
  redistribution metric issues,
    263
  route types, 214
  route updates, 213-214
  split-horizons, 211
  stability features, 211
IP
  addresses, 154-160, 168-171,
    231
  as connectionless protocol, 152
  EIGRP, 219
  headers, 152-154
  masks, 156-158
  Network layer (OSI model),
    152
IPX, 290
  Access Lists, 300-302
  addresses, 290-291
  command-line keywords, 294
  configuration example,
    295-297
  configuration steps, 293-294
  EIGRP, 219
  encapsulation types, 291-292
  frames, 290
  hop counts, 298
  identifying routes, 297-299
  identifying servers, 299
  ipx delay command, 298
  ipx maximum-paths # com-
    mand, 298

ipxwan, 294
  routing, 294-295
  show ipx route command,
    297-298
  show ipx server command,
    299
  tick counts, 298
ITU-T, 366
L2F (VPDNs), 347
LANE, 86
  BUS (Broadcast and
    Unknown Server), 88, 94
  ELANs, 86
  LEC (LAN Emulation
    Client), 87, 94
  LEC communication, 92-93
  LEC setup, 90-91
  LECS (LAN Emulation
    Configuration Server), 87,
    94-95
  LES (LAN Emulation Server),
    88, 94
  LES NSAP address configura-
    tion, 95
  LUNI (LAN Emulation User-
    to-Network Interface), 87
  SSRP, 95-97
  supported networks, 86
  VCCs (Virtual Circuit
    Connections), 88-89
LAPD (ISDN), 342-345
LAPF, 395
LCP, 348
LMI, 396-398
  autosense, 397
  frame relay interface configu-
    ration, 397-398
  message types, 397
  messages, 396
NCP, 348
NetBIOS, 124, 330-331
  bridging, 331
  datagram mode, 330
  DLSw, 331
  frames, 331
  NetBEUI, 331
  session mode, 330
NLSP
  IPX Access Lists, 32
  IPX NLSP, 295

nonroutable, 124
  CRB, 125
  IRB, 126
OSI model, protocol map, 12-13
OSPF, 228
  ABRs, 234
  adjacencies, 231
  areas, 230, 233-234
  ASBRs, 234
  authentication, 230
  Backbone Routers, 234
  bandwidth conservation, 229
  basic configuration, 236-237
  BDR election, 231-232
  convergence, 229
  cost, 228-229
  CPUs, 230
  debug ip ospf command, 239
  debugging, 239
  DR election, 231-232
  features, 228
  hello packets, 231
  hello protocol, 231
  hop counts, 228-229
  identifying routes, 232
  Internal Routers, 234
  link-state databases, 230-232
  LSAs, 232, 235
  LSUs, 232
  memory requirements, 230
  neighbor databases, 230
  open standard, 228
  redistribution metric issues, 263
  route maintenance, 233
  router IDs, 231
  router priority, 231
  routing tables, 230
  scalability, 228, 233
  selecting routes, 232
  show ip ospf database command, 239
  show ip ospf neighbor detail command, 239
  SPF algorithm, 228, 232
  stub area configuration, 237-238
  summarization, 265
  troubleshooting, 239
  virtual link configuration, 238-239
  virtual links, 236-239
  VLSM support, 230
PAP, 345
Physical Layer Protocol (PHY), FDDI, 77
PIM, 275
  dense mode, 275
  sparse mode, 275-277
  sparse-dense mode, 277-278
PLP, 381
PPP
  autodetect encapsulation ppp command, 346
  callback, 347, 352
  CHAP, 346, 355-357
  data compression, 346
  debug ppp authentication command, 346, 356-357
  encapsulation example, 355-356
  features, 345-347
  frames, 347-348
  IP address pooling, 346
  ISDN, 345
  LCP, 348
  LQM, 346
  NCP, 348
  PAP, 345
  ppp authentication chap command, 346
  ppp authentication pap command, 346
  PPP Multilink, 346
  ppp multilink command, 346
  ppp quality 70 command, 346
  ppp reliable-link command, 347
  reliable link, 347
  VPDNs, 347
RADIUS, 38-39
reliable, 17
RIP
  garbage collection timer, 198
  history, 196
  holddown timer, 198
  hop count, 197
  IPX RIP, 294
  limitations, 196
  metrics, 196-197
  redistribution metric issues, 263
  request messages, 197
  response messages, 197
  reverse route, 198
  RIPv1, 199-200
  RIPv1 configuration, 202-203
  RIPv2, 200-202
  RIPv2 configuration, 203-205
  split horizon with poisoned reverse, 198
  timeout, 198
  update synchronization, 197
  updates, 197-198
routing
  classful, 184
  classless, 184
  Count to Infinity, 182
  Distance Vector, 318
  Distant Vector, 183
  functions, 180
  Holddown Timer, 182
  Link State, 183
  loop prevention, 180-181
  metrics, 183
  Poison Reverse, 181-182
  selecting routes, 184
  Split Horizon, 180, 318
  Timed Update, 182
  Triggered Update, 182
RSVP, 36
RTP, 42
SAP, 293
  common SAP types, 293
  IPX Access Lists, 32, 301
sliding window flow control, 376
SNAP, 64
SNMP, 47-48
SS7, 41-42
SSP, 139
STP, 107-108
  Bridge Protocol Data Units (BPDUs), 108-109
  port modes, 109-111
  types, 108
TACACS, 38

TCP, 160
  BGP, 246
  connection-oriented, 160
  establishing connections, 163
  extended IP Access Lists, 31
  features, 160-161
  headers, 161-162
  ports, 164-165
  Transport layer (OSI model), 160
TFTP, 44-45
tunneling, 13-14
UDP, 163
  as connectionless protocol, 163
  extended IP Access Lists, 31
  headers, 164
  ports, 164-165
  Transport layer (OSI model), 163
unreliable, 17
VTP, 114
  configuration, 116
  domains, 114
  messages, 115-116
  routers, 114
  VTP mode types, 114-115
  VTP Pruning, 115
windowing, 18
X.25, 367
  addressing, 368
  configuring example, 386-387
  encapsulation map, 380
  encapsulating, 369
  error checking, 366
  error control, 374-375
  flow control, 376-377
  frame relay comparison, 394
  layers, 367, 372-374
  local switching, 369
  mapping, 379
  packet switching, 366-367
  Physical-layer, 377-378
  PLP, 381
  protocol translation, 383-386
  PVC, 380-382
  route tables, 371
  routing, 369-371
  signaling, 377-378
  sliding window control protocol, 376

  source-quench messages, 377
  SVC, 380-382
  TCP/IP (XOT), 370
  translating, 383
  virtual interface templates, 385
  windowing, 376-377
  X.121, 368
proxy ARP, 159
proxy firewalls, 39
Pruning, VTP, 115
PSN subfield (DNIC), 368
PSTN (Public Switched Telephone Network), 340
PT (Payload Type), ATM cell header, 416
public address space, 155
Public Data Networks (PDNs), 368
public keys, 40
Public or Private Network-to-Network interface (PNNI), 415-416
PVCs (Permanent Virtual Circuits), 380-382, 395, 414
  configuration example, 420-422
  defined, 414
  DLCI fields, 395-396, 402
  show frame-relay pvc command, 398

Q-R

QoS (Quality of Service), 419-420
queries (DNS)
  iterative, 166
  recursive, 165
queue lists (Custom queuing), 35
queuing
  Custom, 35-36
    commands, 35-36
    queue lists, 35
  Priority, 34-36
    commands, 35
    priority lists, 34
    Weighted Fair, 34-36

RADIUS (Remote Authentication Dial-In User Services), 38-39
RAM (random access memory), 42-43
random backoff, 61
range filters, 33
read-only memory (ROM), 42
Real-Time Transport Protocol (RTP), 42
real-time video, X.25 packet switching, 366
receiving results of written exam (CCIE Certification), 476
records (SDRs), 280
recovering
  errors (X.25), 374-375
  passwords (routers), 44
recursive queries (DNS), 165
redistribute command, 263
redistribute metric command, 263
redistribute route-map command, 263-264
redistribute static command, 263
redistribution (routes), 262
  BGP, 247, 255
  commands, 263-264
  defined, 262
  implementation cases, 262
  metric issues, 262-264
  route tagging, 266-267
    setting tags, 266-267
    tagging schemes, 266
  summarization, 264-266
reference points (ISDN), 341
registering for CCIE Certification exams
  lab exam, 478-479
  phone number, 476, 479
  Web site, 476, 479
  written exam, 476
reliable link (PPP), 347
reliable protocols, 17
reliable transport protocol (EIGRP), 218

Remote Authentication Dial-In User Services (RADIUS), 38-39
Remote Source-Route Bridging (RSRB), 134-135
reports, traps (NMS), 47
request messages (RIP), 197
request/response pairs (TACACS), 38
requests, Get Nearest Server (Novell NetWare), 293
reservation fields (Token-Ring), 76
Resource Reservation Protocol (RSVP), 36
response messages (RIP), 197
restrictions. *See* **Access Lists**
results, CCIE Certification exams, 476
reverse route (RIP), 198
RFCs Web site, 482
RIFs (Route Information Fields), 129
  building, 131-132
  Ring Information Indicators (RIIs), 129
  route descriptor fields, 130
  routing control fields, 130
RIIs (Ring Information Indicators), 129
rings
  counterrotating (FDDI), 78-79
  dual-attachment stations (DAS), FDDI, 77
  primary (FDDI), 77
  secondary (FDDI), 77
  single-attachment stations (SAS), FDDI, 77
RIP (Routing Information Protocol), 196
  history, 196
  hop counts, 197
  IPX RIP, 294
  limitations, 196
  metrics, 196-197
  redistribution metric issues, 263
  reverse route, 198

RIPv1, 199-200
  configuration, 202-203
  packets, 199-200
RIPv2
  authentication, 200-202
  configuration, 203-205
  extensions, 200
  no auto-summary command, 202
  packets, 200-202
  route tags, 201
  subnet mask field, 201
  version command, 202
split horizon with poisoned reverse, 198
timers, 198
update synchronization, 197
updates, 197
  request messages, 197
  response messages, 197
  triggered, 198
RIPv2, next hop field, 201
ROM (read-only memory), 42
root bridges, 108
root ports, 108
route descriptor fields (RIFs), 130
Route Information Fields. *See* **RIFs**
route maps (BGP), 247, 255
route reflectors (BGP), 257
route tables (X.25), 371
route tags (RIPv2), 201
route-map setcommunity command, 249
router IDs (OSPF), 231
Router Table Maintenance Protocol (RTMP), 309, 318
routers. *See also* **routing; bridging**
  Active, 167
  administrative distances
    default, 189
    selecting routes, 189-190
  AppleTalk seed routers, 317
  booting
    boot order lists, 44-45
    IOS, 42
    ROM, 42

CDP, 46-47
components, 42
configuration
  copying to/from TFTP servers, 45
  loading, 45
  NVRAM, 43
  RAM, 43
configuration register, 43
  bit 6, 44
  boot fields, 43-44
CPUs, 43
DECnet
  Cisco/DECnet router interoperability, 328
  configuration, 328-330
  interarea, 328-330
  intra-area, 328-330
default routes
  configuration, 186-188
  uses, 187
dense mode, 275
EtherChannel, 113
implicit deny feature, 29
information required for route selection, 196
load balancing, 37
multicasts, 116
  CGMP, 117
  IGMP, 116-117
OSPF
  ABRs, 234
  ASBRs, 234
  Backbone Routers, 234
  BDR election, 231-232
  DR election, 231-232
  Internal Routers, 234
  LSAs, 232, 235
  LSUs, 232
  router IDs, 231
  router priority, 231
passwords
  configuring, 45-46
  enable, 46
  line, 45
  recovering, 44
peers (DLSw), 139-140
sparse mode, 275-277

sparse-dense mode, 277-278
  Auto-RP feature, 277
  RP mapping agents, 277-278
static routes, 185-186
successors, 218
transparent bridges, 107
VTP, 114
wildcard masks, 30

routes
convergence (EIGRP), 220
deleting, timers (RIP), 198
distribute lists, 268-270
  distribute-list in command,
  268-269
  distribute-list out command,
  269-270
exterior (IGRP), 214
flapping, dampening (BGP),
  256
floating static routes (Dial
  Backup), 353-354
identifying
  IPX, 297-299
  OSPF, 232
interior (IGRP), 214
maintenance (OSPF), 233
passive interfaces, 268
redistribution
  defined, 262
  implementation cases, 262
  metric commands, 263-264
  metric issues, 262-264
  route tagging, 266-267
reverse route (RIP), 198
selecting
  administrative distances,
  189-190
  BGP, 250-252
  distance command, 273-274
  information required by
  routers, 196
  OSPF, 232
  routing protocols, 184
  rules, 273
setting tags, 266-267
summarization (EIGRP), 219
system (IGRP), 214
tagging schemes, 264-266
updates (IGRP), 213-214

routing. *See also* **bridging;**
  routers
AppleTalk, 317
  AURP, 318-319
  configuring, 319
  EIGRP, 319
  routing tables, 317
  RTMP, 318
bridging comparison, 124
CRB, 124
  configuration, 125-126
  interfaces, 125
  nonroutable protocols, 125
DDR
  configuration, 349-350
  Dial Backup, 352-354
  dialer in-band command, 352
  dialer map command, 351,
  355-356
  dialer-string command, 351
  interesting traffic, 350-351
  ip unnumbered command,
  351
  SPIDs, 349
  switch type, 349
distance-vector routing protocols, 298
Distribute Lists, 33
HSRP, 167
  Active routers, 167
  configuration, 167-168
IPX, 294-295
  IPX EIGRP, 295
  IPX NLSP, 295
  IPX RIP, 294
IRB, 126
  Bridge Virtual Interface
  (BVI), 126-127
  configuration, 127
  nonroutable protocols, 126
multipath (IGRP), 211
policy, 270-272
  enabling, 271-272
  example, 271-272
protocols
  classful, 184
  classless, 184
  Count to Infinity, 182

  Distance Vector, 183, 318
  functions, 180
  Holddown Timer, 182
  hybrid, 183
  Link State, 183
  loop prevention, 180-181
  metrics, 183
  Poison Reverse, 181-182
  selecting routes, 184
  Split Horizon, 180, 318
  Timed Update, 182
  Triggered Update, 182
RSRB, 134-135
SR/TLB, 134
  advantages, 136
  configuration, 137-138
  drawbacks, 136
  transparent bridges, 137
SRB, 127
  configuration, 132-134
  process, 128-129
  RIFs, 129-132
  size limitations, 128
SRT, 134-136
switching comparison, 13
tuples, 318
X.25, 369-371
routing control fields (RIFs),
  130
Routing Information Protocol.
  See RIP
routing loops, 211
routing tables (OSPF), 230
RP mapping agents (sparse-
  dense mode), 277-278
RSRB (Remote Source-Route
  Bridging), 134-135
RSVP (Resource Reservation
  Protocol), 36
RTMP (Router Table
  Maintenance Protocol), 309,
  318
RTP (Real-Time Transport
  Protocol), 42
running X.25 Over TCP/IP
  (XOT), 370

S

SAP
Service Access Point, 63
Service Advertising Protocol,
32
common SAP types, 293
IPX Access Lists, 32, 301
**SAP (Service Access Point)
fields, 15**
**SAS (single-attachment sta-
tions), FDDI, 77**
scalability (OSPF), 228, 233
**scheduling CCIE Certification
exams**
lab exam, 478-479
written exam, 476
schemes, tagging, 266
**SDRs (session directory proto-
col records), 280**
secondary rings (FDDI), 77
security. *See also* **passwords**
AAA, 37-38
encryption, 40
firewalls, 39
RADIUS, 38-39
TACACS, 38
selecting
routes
*administrative distances,
189-190*
BGP, 250-252
distance command, 273-274
*information required by
routers, 196*
OSPF, 232
routing protocols, 184
rules, 273
switches, ISDN DDR configuration, 349
self-tests. *See* **practice tests**
**serial interfaces (encapsulation
types), IPX, 292**
servers
BUS (Broadcast and Unknown
Server), 88, 94
DNS, 166
Get Nearest Server requests,
293

identifying, IPX, 299
LECS (LAN Emulation
Configuration Server), 87
configuration, 94-95
SSRP, 95-97
LES (LAN Emulation Server),
88
configuration, 94
SSRP, 95-97
NMS, 47
SAP, 293
TFTP
*copying configuration files
(routers), 45*
copying IOS, 44-45
Service Access Point. *See* **SAP**
**Service Access Point (SAP)
fields, 15**
Service Advertising Protocol.
See **SAP**
**Service Profile Identifiers
(SPIDs), 349**
**Service Specific Convergence
Protocol (SSCOP), 418-419**
**session directory protocol
records (SDRs), 280**
**Session layer (OSI model), 12,
310**
**Session Listening Sockets
(SLSs), PAP, 316**
session mode (NetBIOS), 330
**set metric command, 255,
263-264**
shared media, 60
**shortest path first (SPF) algo-
rithm, 228, 232**
show dialer command, 357-358
**show frame-relay pvc com-
mand, 398, 407**
**show interface command, 213,
396**
show ip bgp command, 253
**show ip bgp neighbor com-
mand, 254**
show ip eigrp command, 220
**show ip interfaces command,
215**
**show ip ospf database com-
mand, 239**

**show ip ospf neighbor detail
command, 239**
**show ip protocol command,
214-215**
**show ip route igrp command,
214**
show ip sdr command, 280
**show ipx route command,
297-298**
**show ipx server command,
299**
**show isdn status command,
343-344**
signaling
ATM, 418
IISP, 419
SSCOP, 418-419
X.25, 377-378
**Signaling System 7 (SS7),
41-42**
**Simple Network Management
Protocol (SNMP), 47-48**
**Simple Server Replication
Protocol (SSRP), 95-97**
**single-attachment stations
(SAS), FDDI, 77**
sites
CCIE Certification exam registration, 476, 479
Cisco
*CCIE Certification home
page, 475, 481*
CCIE program overview, 475
CCIE program updates, 475
certification information, 2
*documentation home page,
481*
Exam Blueprint, 3, 477
*lab exam practice facilities list,
479*
*lab exam preparation infor-
mation, 479*
Cisco Connection Online, 36
RFCs, 482
size
IP headers, 152
SRB size limitations, 128
**sliding window flow control
protocol, 376**

SLSs (Session Listening Sockets), PAP, 316

SMDS (Switched Multi-Megabit Data Service), 16

SNA (Systems Network Architecture), 124

SNAP (Subnet Access Protocol), 64

SNMP (Simple Network Management Protocol), 47-48

snooping, IGMP, 116

sockets
  addresses (AppleTalk), 311
  Session Listening Sockets (SLSs), PAP, 316

SOF (Start of Frame), 62

software, Test Pro
  installation, 484
  starting, 484
  system requirements, 484
  test types, 483

source-quench messages, 377

Source-Route Bridging. *See* SRB

Source-Route Translational Bridging. *See* SR/TLB

Source-Route Transparent Bridging (SRT), 134-136

Spanning Tree Protocol. *See* STP

sparse mode, 275-277

sparse-dense mode, 277-278
  Auto-RP feature, 277
  RP mapping agents, 277-278

specifications (FDDI), 76-77

speed
  IEEE 802.3, 58-59
  interfaces
    LAN interfaces, 19-20
    Physical layer (OSI model), 19
    WAN interfaces, 20
  OSPF, 229

SPF algorithm (shortest path first), 228, 232

SPIDs (Service Profile Identifiers), 349

Split Horizon
  IGRP, 211
  routers, 180, 318
  split horizon with poison reverse (RIP), 198

SR/TLB (Source-Route Translational Bridging), 134
  advantages, 136
  configuration, 137-138
  drawbacks, 136
  transparent bridges, 137

SRB (Source-Route Bridging), 127
  configuration
    multiport SRB, 133-134
    pure SRB, 132
  process, 128-129
  RIFs, 129
    building, 131-132
    Ring Information Indicators (RIIs), 129
    route descriptor fields, 130
    routing control fields, 130
  RSRB, 134-135
  size limitations, 128
  SR/TLB, 134
    advantages, 136
    configuration, 137-138
    drawbacks, 136
    transparent bridges, 137
  SRT, 134-136

SRT (Source-Route Transparent Bridging), 134-136

SS7 (Signaling System 7), 41-42

SSCOP (Service Specific Convergence Protocol), 418-419

SSP (Switch-to-Switch Protocol), 139

SSRP (Simple Server Replication Protocol), 95-97

standards, open (OSPF), 228

Start of Frame (SOF), 62

starting Test Pro software, 484

static routes, configuration, 185-186

STP (Spanning Tree Protocol), 58, 107-108
  Bridge Protocol Data Units (BPDUs), 108-109
  IEEE 802.3, 58
  port modes, 109, 111
  types, 108

stream ciphers, 40

stub areas (OSPF)
  configuration, 237-238
  defined, 234

subfields (DNIC), 368

subinterfaces (frame relay), 403
  advantages, 401
  creating, 401-402
  description command, 401
  example, 402
  multipoint, 401
  point-to-point, 401

Subnet Access Protocol (SNAP), 64

subnet mask field (RIPv2), 201

subnet masks. *See* masks

subnetting, 156

Subset Advertisements (VTP), 115

successors, 218

summarizing
  route redistribution, 264-266
  routes (EIGRP), 219

Summary Advertisements (VTP), 115

supervisory frame (LAPB), 373

SVCs (Switched Virtual Circuits), 380-382, 414
  configuration example, 422-423
  defined, 414

switch ports. *See* ports

Switch-to-Switch Protocol (SSP), 139

Switched Multi-Megabit Data Service (SMDS), 16

Switched Virtual Circuits. *See* SVCs

switches. *See also* **transparent bridges**
CDP, 46-47
EtherChannel, 113
ISDN, 349
multicasts, 116
CGMP, 117
IGMP, 116-117
optical bypass switches (FDDI), 79
VTP mode types, 114-115
switching
DLSw, 139
advantages, 139
circuits, 139-140
command output examples, 142
configuration, 141-142
NetBIOS, 331
peer connections, 139-140
peers, 139
process, 140-141
SSP, 139
LAN, transparent bridges, 106-107
packets (X.25), 366-367
routing comparison, 13
synchronous traffic (FDDI), 79
system routes (IGRP), 214
Systems Network Architecture (SNA), 124

T

tables
link-state databases (OSPF), 230-232
neighbor databases (OSPF), 230
routing
AppleTalk, 317
OSPF, 230
TACACS (Terminal Access Controller Access Control System), 38
tagging routes
route redistribution, 266-267
setting tags, 266-267
tagging schemes, 266

taking CCIE Certification exams
lab exam, 478
written exam, 476-477
TCN (Topology Change Notification) BPDUs, 109
TCP (Transmission Control Protocol), 160
BGP, 246
connection-oriented, 160
connections, establishing, 163
extended IP Access Lists, 31
features, 160-161
headers, 161-162
ports, 164-165
Transport layer (OSI model), 160
TCP/IP (X.25), 370
telecommunications, SS7, 41-42
telnet, Access Lists, 34
templates, virtual interface, 385
Terminal Access Controller Access Control System (TACACS), 38
termination (connections), 19
Test Pro software
installation, 484
starting, 484
system requirements, 484
test types, 483
tests. *See* **exam; practice tests**
TFTP servers
copying configuration files (routers), 45
copying IOS, 44-45
throughput, windowing (protocols), 18
tick counts (IPX), 298
TIDs (transaction identifiers), 314
Timed Update (routers), 182
timeout (RIP), 198
timers (RIP), 198
TLAP (TokenTalk Link Access Protocol), 309

Token-Ring, 15-16, 72
active monitors, 75
address-recognized indicator bits, 75
auto reconfiguration, 75
beaconing, 75
cost, 16
deterministic media access, 16, 72
downstream neighbors, 73
early release, 73
Ethernet MAC address conversion, 136-137
fault management, 75
frame formats, 73-75
frame status fields, 73
frame-copied indicator bits, 75
frames (RIIs), 129
IBM, 72
IEEE 802.5, 72
information frame, 73
logical ring, 72
NAUN, 75
physical star, 72
priorities, 76
process, 73
SRB, 127
configuration, 132-134
process, 128-129
RIFs, 129-132
size limitations, 128
tokens, 73
TokenTalk Link Access Protocol (TLAP), 309
topological databases, 230-232
Topology Change Notification (TCN) BPDUs, 109
totally stubby areas (OSPF), 234
trace command (IGRP), 216
traffic
Access Lists. *See* Access Lists
asynchronous (FDDI), 79
compressing, 36
frame relay
Cisco traffic-shaping configuration, 406-407
Cisco traffic-shaping options, 405

Cisco traffic-shaping steps, 405
congestion causes, 403
congestion notification methods, 404
parameters, 403-404
traffic-shaping example, 404
interesting (DDR), 350-351
multicast
CGMP, 281
DVMRP, 278-279
IGMP, 280
PIM, 275, 277-278
synchronous (FDDI), 79
unicast, 60
transaction identifiers (TIDs), 314
transactions, 314
translating protocols (X.25), 383-386
Transmission Control Protocol. *See* **TCP**
transparent bridges, 106. *See also* **switches**
configuration, 107
Ethernet, 106
filtering, 106
forwarding, 106
learning, 106
routers, 107
SR/TLB, 137
SRT, 134-136
Transport layer (OSI model), 11
AppleTalk, 309
TCP, 160
UDP, 163
traps (NMS), 47
Triggered Update (routers), 182
triggered updates, 198
Triple DES, 40
troubleshooting. *See also* **help; problems**
CSMA/CD, 65
OSPF, 239
trunks (VLANs), 111-112

tunneling
AppleTalk, AURP, 318-319
autodetect encapsulation ppp command, 346
PPP encapsulation example, 355-356
protocols, 13-14
X.25, 369
tuples (routing), 318
two-step translation (X.25), 385

U

U/L Address Bit (Universally or Locally Administered Address Bit), 60
UDP (User Datagram Protocol), 163
as connectionless protocol, 163
extended IP Access Lists, 31
headers, 164
ports, 164-165
Transport layer (OSI model), 163
unicast traffic, 60
UNIs (User-to-Network Interfaces), 394, 414
unnumbered frame (LAPB), 373
unreliable protocols. *See* **connectionless protocols**
Unshielded Twisted Pair (UTP), 64
update synchronization (RIP), 197
updates
CCIE program updates (Cisco Web site), 475
RIP, 197
request messages, 197
response messages, 197
triggered, 198
routes (IGRP), 213-214
Timed Update (routers), 182
Triggered Update (routers), 182

User Datagram Protocol. *See* **UDP**
User-to-Network Interfaces (UNIs), 394, 414
UTP (Unshielded Twisted Pair), 64

V

validating peer connections (BGP), 254
Variable Length Subnet Mask. *See* **VLSM**
VCCs (Virtual Circuit Connections), 88-89
VCI (Virtual Channel Identifier), ATM cell headers, 416
version command (RIPv2), 202
Version II (Ethernet), 58
IEEE 802.3 comparison, 63-64
SNAP, 64
video, streaming (X.25 packet switching), 366
Virtual Channel Identifier (VCI), ATM cell header, 416
virtual circuits, 380-382
PVCs, 380-382
configuration example, 420-422
defined, 414
SVCs, 380-382
configuration example, 422-423
defined, 414
virtual interface templates, 385
Virtual LANs. *See* **VLANs**
virtual links (OSPF)
configuration, 238-239
defined, 236
Virtual Path Identifier (VPI), ATM cell header, 416
Virtual Private Dial-up Networks (VPDNs), 347
virtual rings (SRB), 133-134
VLAN Trunk Protocol. *See* **VTP**

VLANs (Virtual LANs)
characteristics, 111
trunks, 111-112
VTP, 114
  configuration, 116
  domains, 114
  messages, 115-116
  routers, 114
  VTP mode types, 114-115
  VTP Pruning, 115
**VLSM (Variable Length
Subnet Mask), 156**
EIGRP, 219
OSPF, 230
**voice/digital signal conversion
(codecs), 41**
**VPDNs (Virtual Private Dial-
up Networks), 347**
**VPI (Virtual Path Identifier),
ATM cell header, 416**
**VTP (VLAN Trunk Protocol),
114**
configuration, 116
domains, 114
messages, 115-116
routers, 114
VTP mode types, 114-115
VTP Pruning, 115
VTP Join Message (VTP), 115

W

**WANs (wide area networks),
20, 294**
frame relay, 394
  *Cisco traffic-shaping configu-
ration, 406-407*
  *Cisco traffic-shaping options,
405*
  *Cisco traffic-shaping steps,
405*
  error checking, 395
  error correction, 395
  *frame-relay custom-queue-list
command, 407*

*frame-relay map commands,
400*
*frame-relay priority-group
command, 407*
*frame-relay traffic-rate com-
mand, 407*
Inverse ARP, 399-400
LAPF, 395
LMI, 396-398
NNIs, 394
PVCs, 395-398, 402
*show frame-relay pvc com-
mand, 407*
subinterfaces, 401-403
traffic congestion causes, 403
*traffic congestion notification
methods, 404*
traffic parameters, 403-404
traffic-shaping example, 404
UNIs, 394
X.25 comparison, 394
interface speeds, 20
ipxwan, 294
Web sites. *See* **sites**
Weighted Fair queuing, 34-36
wide area networks. *See* **WANs**
wildcard masks, 30
**windowing (protocols), 18,
376-377**
wrapping (FDDI), 16
**written exam (CCIE
Certification)**
cost, 476
preparation, 476-477
registering, 476
results, 476
scheduling, 476
testing tips, 476-477

X-Z

X.25
addressing, 368
configuring example, 386-387
encapsulating (XOT), 369

encapsulation map, 380
error checking, 366
error control, 374-375
flow control, 376-377
frame relay comparison, 394
layers
  data link, 367, 372-374
  packet-switched network, 367
  physical, 367
local switching, 369
mapping, 379
packet switching, 366-367
physical-layer (X.25), 377-378
PLP, 381
protocol translation, 383-386
  commands, 386
  one-step, 384
  two-step, 385
PVC, 380-382
route tables, 371
routing, 369-371
signaling, 377-378
sliding window control protocol, 376
source-quench messages, 377
SVC, 380-382
TCP/IP (XOT), running over,
370
translating, 383
virtual interface templates, 385
windowing, 376-377
X.121, addressing X.25, 368
XOT, 369-370

**ZIP (Zone Information
Protocol), 310, 315-316**
ZITs, 315
zones, assigning, 312
**ZITs (Zone Information
Tables), 315**
zone filters, 33
zones, 312

Baer Wolf Inc.

Baer Wolf, Inc delivers targeted training solutions for businesses that specifically address your unique training needs. The most popular Baer Wolf, Inc's services for the IT and skills development markets include: programming, networking, IT management and the development of programming and networking course content like you see in this Cisco Certified Internetwork Expert (CCIE) book.

Baer Wolf works with you to develop a training program uniquely suited to your situation and circumstances. With Baer Wolf, training is delivered to you when you need it, where you need it, and in a format that best matches your desired learning style. Our customized approach to training solutions includes helping you assess your training goals, determining the existing skills of those who need training, and delivering the training to you in the method you want, including in a classroom, mentoring, in a lab/workshop, on-line, as self-study materials, or a combination of these methods.

Baer Wolf's long list of satisfied clients include: Andersen Consulting, Boeing, Born Information Services Group, Gateway 2000, Lutheran Brotherhood, Macmillan Computer Publishing USA, Mayo Medical Center, MCC Behavioral Care, and US West Communications, Inc. We look forward to adding your company to this list. **Contact us today at www.baerwolf.com.**

NetworkCare
The knowledge behind the network

Lucent Technologies NetworkCare℠ is a global provider of network consulting and software solutions for the full lifecycle of a network, including planning and design, implementation, and operations. Lucent NetworkCare maintains expertise in the most complex network technologies and multi-vendor environments and offers industry-leading software solutions for managing and optimizing application-ready networks.

An approach to helping customers stay ahead of network problems is at the heart of the Lucent NetworkCare Network Engagement Methodology (NEM) – a collaborative knowledge management tool that helps assure quality, consistency, and best practices in every Lucent NetworkCare network consulting engagement.

At the root of NEM is the Lucent NetworkCare Network Lifecycle Methodolgy (NLM) - the basis for providing quality solutions to Lucent clients. NLM provides the engineers with a framework for applying their technology expertise during the various stages of the network lifecycle to assure maximum client benefits.

This book was written through a collaborative effort with Baer Wolf, Inc. and over a dozen Lucent NetworkCare engineers and consultants who are subject matter experts averaging more than 10 years networking experience and/or are Cisco Certified Internetwork Experts (CCIE), Cisco Certified Network Professionals (CCNP), Cisco Certified Networking Associates (CCNA), and/or Cisco Certified Design Associates (CCDA).

Lucent NetworkCare is the world's leading network consulting and solutions provider. Over 75% of the Fortune 500 rely on us to design, manage, and evolve their complex multi-vendor networks. Our integrated portfolio of data and voice network services cannot be matched.

For employment opportunities at Lucent NetworkCare, visit our website at www.lucent-networkcare.com/careers

www.baerwolf.com   www.mcp.com   www.keystonetraining.com   www.lucent-networkcare.com

Other Related Titles

Practical Networking
Frank Derfler
ISBN: 0-7897-2252-6
$29.99 US
$44.95 CAN

Read This Before Opening the Software